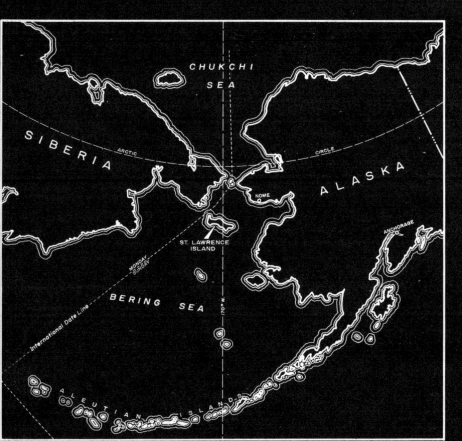

*Studies in Anthropology, No. 8*

# Eskimo Boyhood

# Eskimo Boyhood

*An Autobiography in Psychosocial Perspective*

Charles C. Hughes

The University Press of Kentucky

Publication of this book was assisted by
the American Council of Learned Societies
under a grant from the Andrew W. Mellon Foundation.

Illustrated by Dirk Gringhuis

ISBN: 0-8131-1301-6

Library of Congress Catalog Card Number: 73-80465

A statewide cooperative scholarly publishing agency
serving Berea College, Centre College of Kentucky,
Eastern Kentucky University, Georgetown College,
Kentucky Historical Society, Kentucky State University,
Morehead State University, Murray State University,
Northern Kentucky State College, Transylvania University,
University of Kentucky, University of Louisville, and
Western Kentucky University.

*Editorial and Sales Offices:* Lexington, Kentucky 40506

*For Leslie, John, and Calisse*

# Contents

# Acknowledgments

First, of course, to the
person here called Nathan, for
sharing the story of his life.
And my thanks to Dr. Seymour Parker,
Dr. C. L. Winder, Dr. Albert H.
Rabin, and Dr. Cyril Worby for
helpful comments on portions of the
analysis and to Dr. Margaret Lantis
for her continued encouragement
to publish the life story.

# Part One

# Place, Time, and Person

"When we got close, those who had been at home were coming down the hill to the beach. I saw my cousins running and rolling down like I did when the boat came in from hunting. I jumped out of the boat, feeling very proud. I had lots to tell my folks while we unloaded the boat. My uncle said that now he would have one more crew member, because I had not been afraid—not even a little bit. I felt a little funny, and I was glad he hadn't seen my fright. That meant I was a real man and a real hunter from then on." The young Eskimo man who with these words tells of his first hunting trip in a skin boat had been but six years old at the time. Six years old; but for him the beginning of manhood, because hunting was the life of the Eskimo man.

Later, many times, coming back with seal carcasses or walrus flesh in the boat, he was to relive the excitement and sense of mastery of that first trip. But just as often he was to experience another lesson as well—the other coinage of a mature self-reliance—when he returned with nothing for his day's work, tired, numbed from cold, and edgy with the disappointments so common in the life of an Eskimo hunter: perhaps a sea barren of animals, perhaps the erring of rifle shot, the sudden movements of ice floes shielding a carcass from the harpoon throw, or the capricious closing in of weather that changed the world to wind and snow. Throughout life, as backdrop to the affairs of men, he was always to contest with an unrelenting nature that threatened not only his survival but also his sense of well-being and hope for fulfillment.

The purpose of this book is to portray the first steps taken into that life by a young Eskimo, Nathan Kakianak,* who lived it and who here recounts it. With only slight editorial changes, the portrayal is principally in the form of an autobiography written by a young man in his early twenties, who tells of his life up to the middle years of his youth. The life story was written (in English) at my request and mostly

* This and all other personal names used are fictitious.

under conditions conducive to recalling nostalgic personal memories, for much of the first part was set down while he was hospitalized with an advanced case of tuberculosis. The autobiography is presented almost in its entirety; only a few sections have been deleted to shorten the document and minor editorial revisions and grammatical alterations made for easier reading. It is important, however, to reaffirm the essential authenticity of the phraseology and vocabulary used, for Nathan had only a fourth-grade education, and that obtained very sporadically.

How accurate is his detailed recollection of events and conversations? I do not know for certain, but for one thing, ethnographers working with the Eskimos (and many other hunting peoples) have often commented on their unusual capabilities for remembering minute detail. My position regarding the following document is that for the purposes intended here, the matter of minute accuracy of detail (such as specific conversations) is of relative unimportance, since my interests are not so much in the exact way Nathan says something, but rather more in what events and associations of events he brings forth. In any case, it can be asserted on the basis of outsider's studies of this group that whether or not all the situations and events mentioned in the autobiography actually took place as described, they are at least common enough types of events in the cultural life of these people that they *could* have taken place in his life (e.g., see Hughes, 1960).

However that may be, the life recounted here—indeed, *any* life—can teach something about other lives as well; and following the life history I attempt to indicate some of the ways in which this life exemplifies more widespread human personality processes in the midst of highly unique cultural, social, and geographic conditions. Such an attempt is, of course, a venture into controversy; for viewed in a behavioral science framework an autobiographical document is suspect from several points of view. First is its representativeness or "typicality" for a wider range of subjects—whether in terms of age, sex, socioeconomic conditions, or sheer involvement in particular historical events—even beyond the fact that the

4

single document is only one case from a larger population of instances.* Then, too, is its validity—how accurately and honestly does the subject reveal himself to the anonymous reader? How much does he distort, suppress, expand, and exaggerate? To what extent does selective recall influence the character of the chain of associations and memories which constitute the structure of the recollected life?†

To such questions I have no final answers, only the judgment that in view of all available evidence what follows is not the record of a highly deviant life career in this society. But such questions as those above, even if they cannot be fully answered, do raise further issues on which it is necessary to comment: why this life history? What is its presentation intended to accomplish? Why this single case?

In my view there are several reasons to publish it simply as it is. For one thing, it is a statement that absorbingly conveys much of the "inner meaning" of another culture, another way of life, and the personal quandaries and struggles of a growing boy to establish himself in that life. As such, the document makes perhaps a useful contribution to the "study of lives," comparatively an underdeveloped area in the behavioral sciences, skilled though these sciences be in the analysis of fragments of behavior abstracted from the evolving dynamic and creative structures which are "personalities." Personal documents, if they serve no other purpose, provide a check on theoretical assumptions that would make man an automaton, a passive actualizer of a comprehensive sociocultural programming (see Wrong, 1961). Paradoxically, while underscoring on the one hand the enormous molding influence of cultural circumstances, personal documents at the same time provide cogent evidence for man's ability to have

---

* In this connection, however, it may be noted that for some purposes use of the well-documented single case can be of considerable value in establishing statistical relationships among phenomena; e.g., Chassan, 1960, 1962.

† Considerations of these questions have been fairly extensively explored in the behavioral science literature and it is not necessary to recall all such discussions at this point. Among the reviews pertaining to the use of life history materials is Kluckhohn's anthropologically oriented monograph of a generation ago (1945) and, with more general reference, Langness (1965), Block (1971), and Mandelbaum (1973).

some influence in constructing his destiny, in shaping his "inevitabilities."

But no human life is so unlike all others that at some levels of analysis there cannot be found attributes in which it resembles others. The uniqueness of any event—or, indeed, of any life—can therefore be turned to double account: on the one hand, toward a focus on what separates it from all other occurrences, the idiographic approach, in a manner resembling the artistic and humanistic strategy; and, on the other, toward those features which, when made explicit, render it a member of a class or classes of phenomena, in the ethos of a scientific, or "nomothetic," approach to understanding. My investment in the following autobiography is rooted in both interests, and in Part Three I attempt to outline some aspects of the class-relevant features of this life and its transactions over time with its environment.

Toward that end, then, the salient aspects of that specific context—physical, sociocultural, and historical—must be established, the time, place, and circumstances in which this life occurred; for they relate not only to an understanding of the particular episodes and activities of Nathan, the person, but also to a broader understanding of what the socialization process can imply for personality structure in a so-called simpler or preindustrial society as contrasted to the complex socioeconomic context of the life course in other social settings. Here, for example, the "Who am I?" and "Where am I going?" questions of adolescent life structure found elsewhere in the United States do not (or, rather, did not) exist.

The years covered by the events recounted here were portentous beyond this boy's knowing, for it was during that time—the 1930s and 1940s—that his inherited cultural world began to be critically undercut by influences from the outside industrialized world. Those influences took many forms, among which were the coming of more white people to live in the village, the appearance of new economic opportunities (including regular jobs), the reality of war, demands for schooling and training in new skills, and pressures toward change in religion. Such events are recounted as seen through a young boy's eyes and are but examples of the changed milieu in which he, by contrast with his father, now had to conduct his life and evolve his own pattern of dealing with conflicts, dilemmas, and opportunities for personal growth and satisfactions as these were structured by the cultural and social systems of his immediate world, the village in which he lived.

This life history is, then, at one and the same time a story not only of the evolving personality structure of one person; it is also a partial statement of major trends in sociocultural change in a very small and isolated corner of the world. As with any life, the main themes of the story have therefore to do first of all with the many types of social relations, sentiments, ideas, and values endorsed by his parents and their peers as proper and worthy of emulation. In this instance, however, given the context of change, such themes also are concerned with the confrontation between this young boy and a new set of norms and orientations in life which at many points are sharply in conflict with those of his parents. The life story that follows is consequently one of a person transacting the business of living with an increasingly complex social and symbolic world, a world for which his own society and its cultural framework, ingenious and straightforward though it had been for thousands of years in devising answers to life's demands, could offer little direct help. For the answers it gave, the solutions and techniques which it, Eskimo culture, provided were answers to questions based upon Eskimo cultural premises and orientations: how best to pursue and kill seals and other animals, how best to train the body and mind for the hard life of the hunter, how to act toward other people no matter what one's real feelings about them, how to rationalize early and meaningless death. But now, and not reflected in the statement from his early life which opened this chapter, rather different questions were being raised; for example, not how to hunt, but whether to hunt? Not how to train the body, but for what? The answers corresponding to these new questions were at best equivocal and sometimes contradictory, only vaguely outlined in the mix of new standards and values for behavior coming from the mainland.

Another feature of the perceived mainland culture was also

to have disturbing effects on the stability of traditional Eskimo ways—its general and persuasive aura of excellence. For (as seen through Eskimo eyes) on the mainland there was little sickness and few children died in infancy, jobs paying good salaries were plentiful, education—the key to wealth—existed for all children, and the houses, clothing, food, tools, and other material resources of the mainland were more desirable than those of the Eskimos.

Such a process of cultural confrontation did not operate simply as a background for behavior. Though not always posed directly in so stark a form as this, such beliefs insinuated themselves as behavioral issues into the contrapuntal interplay of daily events, often leading to inevitable comparisons between the two ways of life. And, with a heavy load of sickness and death, with an always present threat of famine, with a feeling of cultural inferiority in the face of the world of machines, numbers, and written words confronting them, for many people (especially the young) Eskimo culture often came out second-best in any comparison.

But is was not a complete acceptance of the outside world nor a total rejection of traditional Eskimo culture—perhaps it would have been easier had it been so simple. For there remained, and still remains, pride in many aspects of St. Lawrence Eskimo culture history transmitted to the young; a pride, for example, in the ethos of self-reliance, the facing of challenge, the image of lone man against nature. After all, Eskimo culture has a long history in these surroundings. The tradition into which the person of this story was born traces its antecedents for many centuries in the region of the North Bering Sea between Alaska and Siberia. Providing a link across several thousand years, some of its beginnings can still be seen near the modern village in the form of carved ivory harpoon heads, points and blades, and house stones in the debris of talus slopes at the base of the mountain that stands as the boldest landmark on the northernmost tip of the island, St. Lawrence, where the subject of this story lived in the village of Gambell (see endpaper maps).

St. Lawrence Island, the largest in the Bering Sea, lies only thirty-eight miles from the Siberian shore and some hundred or so miles from Alaska. About a hundred miles long by some twenty to thirty miles wide, it is a good example of the barren Arctic tundra found in many places in the north—treeless, in some spots swampy, in other places mountainous, with ancient rock outcroppings scraped clean by glacial action, here and there colored with bright lichen growth. It is also similar to other Arctic areas in its weather, although in some respects more severe than inland regions. For eight months of the year the ice pack makes travel by ship impossible, and the high winds that sweep across the tundra or in from the sea pile the snowfall, somewhat moderate by inland Arctic standards, into huge drifts in the village. At times the winds blow at gale velocities of sixty to seventy miles an hour for several days, sometimes then to be replaced by dense fog. According to Weather Bureau data on the average there are only thirty-two days of sunshine in the year.*

For the St. Lawrence Island Eskimos over many hundreds of years food came primarily from seals, walruses, and whales, with supplementary supplies obtained from birds (flesh and eggs), fish, seaweeds, and plants. The technology employed in the hunt was a "stone age" one, i.e., based on nonmetal cutting tools (such as slate edges for the ivory harpoon heads), with metal implements becoming readily available only in the nineteenth century, although before then an occasional bit of usable metal reached them by trade from their close cultural relatives on the Siberian shore.

Sustained contact with non-Eskimo outsiders has occurred since the latter part of the nineteenth century. Visited by several European explorers prior to that time (e.g., Bering, Kotzebue, Captain Cook), the island was not permanently inhabited by outsiders until the 1890s. After 1848 American and other commercial whalers had begun stopping for barter on their seasonal voyages into the North Bering Sea, the Chuckchee Sea, and the Beaufort Sea in pursuit of the Bowhead and other whales, and it is reported that a few of these whalers occasionally wintered on St. Lawrence Island follow-

---

* For a fuller description of the environment and the people of St. Lawrence Island, see my book *An Eskimo Village in the Modern World* (Ithaca: Cornell University Press, 1960).

ing the freeze-up in October. Sometimes Eskimos from the region worked as members of whaling crews for the summer season, including some from St. Lawrence Island.

Sustained interest of the United States government in the island and its people was aroused in 1879, partially as a result of certain activities of such whalers. In the winter of 1879 and spring of 1880, over 1,000 of the 1,500 people inhabiting the island died from starvation and sickness, according to some accounts, brought about by the trading of large quantities of hard liquor to the Eskimos at the beginning of the critical fall hunting season. The story has it that as a result of a prolonged debauch hunters lost their chance to lay in a supply of walrus meat from herds migrating southward for the winter, and famine set in. Rumors of the catastrophe reached the Alaskan mainland, and the United States Revenue Cutter *Corwin* was dispatched to investigate. One member of the shipboard party was E. W. Nelson, who later compiled the first comprehensive ethnography of the Bering Sea area. Another was the famous naturalist John Muir, who poignantly described the evidences of tragedy he found:

A few miles farther on we anchored before a larger village, situated about halfway between the east and west ends of the island, which I visited in company of Mr. Nelson, the Captain, and the Surgeon. We found twelve desolate huts close to the beach with about two hundred skeletons in them or strewn about on the rocks and rubbish heaps within a few yards of the doors. The scene was indescribably ghastly and desolate, though laid in a country purified by frost as by fire. Gulls, plovers, and ducks were swimming and flying about in happy life, the pure salt sea was dashing white against the shore, the blooming tundra swept back to the snowclad volcanoes, and the wide azure sky bent kindly over all—nature intensely fresh and sweet, the village lying in the foulest and most glaring death. The shrunken bodies, with rotting furs on them, or white, bleaching skeletons, picked bare by the crows, were lying mixed with the kitchen-midden rubbish where they had been cast out by surviving relatives while they yet had strength to carry them. (Muir, 1917, pp. 108-9)

The population of the island never recovered from this traumatic event; there were, in fact, only some 600 Eskimo inhabitants on the island during the middle 1950s, as compared to the 1,500 in 1878.

Following Muir's visit, scattered contacts occurred between the St. Lawrence Islanders and outside commercial and governmental vessels for the next decade. Finally, in 1894, the Presbyterian Church established a mission station in the principal village of the island, located on the northwestern tip and then known by its Eskimo name, "Sivuokakh." The first missionary-teacher, the Reverend V. C. Gambell, was drowned three years later when he and his family were returning to the island after home leave, and the village was renamed in their honor.

Other missionaries followed. During the time of Dr. E. O. Campbell (in the first decade of this century) reindeer were introduced onto the island and a village store organized. Arctic fox-trapping became important and continued to be so during the years of World War I and the 1920s. The first outboard motor for the hunting boats was acquired in 1916 and its subsequent importance was presaged in the report of the American school teacher at the time: "Evinrude demonstration given on the lake. Worked fine. Everyone much interested. Had a walrus chase with it on the ocean. Got two walruses and brought them in, with the Evinrude working like a charm."

The 1920s was a period of prosperity, for foxes were plentiful and the market for their pelts extremely lucrative. But this economic affluence began to decline in the decade of the 1930s, and the St. Lawrence Islanders had to return to primary dependence upon hunting for their food and meager sale of fox furs or ivory carving for cash income. The money received went to provide the tools for carrying out basically Eskimo subsistence activities, such as guns and gasoline, and only a few "luxuries" like food and clothing. During the 1930s the character of the population also was little changed from earlier decades, there being few white people in the village. School teacher, missionary, and nurse (with families, if any)—these were the principal contacts the St. Lawrence Islanders had with people from the mainland.

World War II changed all this. A small detachment of

American soldiers was stationed in the village, some Eskimo young men served in the armed forces, more economic opportunities stimulated by the mainland white culture became apparent, and the possibility of actual warfare and violence loomed before the village (an incident described in the life story). But it was not until the middle years of World War II that major inroads into the traditional culture began. Then were established a government weather station consisting of several houses for white families; an aircraft landing strip; an air force station and later an army site, built just a couple of miles from the village. Other construction work on the island similarly provided jobs and easy access to outside goods, and there was greater contact with the mainland through hospitalization and schooling.

These several developments had their multiple effects on traditional Eskimo culture, in many instances providing vivid dramatizations of an alternative way of life, of different means of coping with life's problems and, indeed, different and equally legitimate goals in life. Something of the manner in which this complex of psychosocial forces worked to effect changes in Eskimo culture is suggested in Hughes's book (1960).

But even in the mid-1950s the cultural reality that was beginning to show signs of shift in orientational sentiments and behavioral patterns was still to be characterized as largely "Eskimo"; for, although many material goods from the outside world had been adopted, the social system remained solidly traditional in its patterning. That is to say, St. Lawrence Island social culture was characterized by the existence of patrilineal clans or lineages, which was not true of most of the Eskimo groups about which the bulk of ethnographic literature has been written. For any individual, the clan unit was his primary social affiliation, for from this came his sense of identity, both in this world and the next (one of the most important of a person's several souls—his "name soul"—was considered immortal, reincarnatable). Also from his clan came many of his playmates as a child, his set of companions on the hunt, his main line of defense in disputes, quarrels, and violence, and frequently his closest neighbors.

For a male these patrilineal kin bonds were of enduring importance, particularly the close tie to his male parallel cousins, children of his father's brothers. Since descent was patrilineal, both parties to the relationship belonged to the same clan group. But beyond this, within a more restricted sphere, there was an intimacy of relation, a sustained loyalty and mutual helpfulness akin to the bond found between brothers. So close was this tie supposed to be, and so close was it often in fact, that the primary kinship term for "brother" was used interchangeably with the more specific term designating "father's brother's son" in referring to the relationship. As seen in the life history, such a relationship with his father's brother's children figures importantly in Nathan's early life, for the young boy's primary supportive social world is built upon it and only hesitantly does he move outside it.

Adherence to the cultural structuring of kin ties within the nuclear family is also clearly seen in the following document. Sons develop an extremely strong bond to their fathers, a bond composed of awe, fear, respect, dutiful obedience, love, and affection. The father is the primary tutor in the arts and skills of life, the most important disciplinarian, authority, and judge. At the same time, except for the higher status given the oldest brother, the father is in a sense interchangeable with his own brothers and it is toward a class of kinsmen that the son feels such profound sentiments. This flexibility in such emotional attachment is vividly seen in Nathan's story, when at one point he lives with his father's older brother and in doing so suffers no loss of identity or sense of estrangement. Such interchangeability of parental figures, indeed, far from appearing to have detrimental effects on the growing infant and child, would seem instead to provide multiple sources of security and serve as a buffer against the trauma (and strong likelihood) of loss of the father by death.

Relations with siblings are also culturally constituted along lines of strong affection but restraint in overt behavior, especially with regard to any expression of hostility, aggression, or selfish action. The major differences between brother-brother and brother-sister relations lie in the greater degree of aloofness and inhibition against disclosure of personal

13

intimacies expected between brothers and sisters as they grow into childhood and beyond.

Between mothers and their children—real or adopted (and cases of adoption were numerous)—relations are warm and affectionate. It is the same between grandparents and grandchildren, again both in a restricted and in a diffuse sense; for the St. Lawrence Island Eskimo terms for "grandfather" (*apa*) and "grandmother" (*ningyouei*) are widely applied both as general honorific titles and as literal references to older persons in the village. Under some conditions these bonds of affection are doubly strengthened (and, perhaps, a bit compromised by the structural aspects of the relationships involved), for it also often happens that an older couple whose children have left the house upon marriage will adopt one or more of their grandchildren to come and live as offspring and assume a son's or daughter's role in the household.

Such, then, is a brief statement of the main features of the "average expectable environment" of importance as background in understanding many of the interpersonal relations recounted in the following life history. Ethnographic details and extended discussion of the sociocultural dynamics of the village have necessarily been omitted (see Hughes, 1958, 1960, in press); but where appropriate, explanatory notes summarize the social and cultural patterns relevant to understanding the behavioral event or incidents in question.

The "average expectable environment" is, of course, a statistical abstraction, useful in giving a general sense of approximation regarding the way in which a given society structures its interpersonal relations by contrast with that of other groups, but not a good predictor of minute behavioral activity. As such, it forms part of the cultural context in which specific lives are lived and according to which they vary in concrete detail. Such a cultural programming provides, then, a series of mostly implicit values, beliefs, and frames for evaluation of behavior, behavior of oneself as well as that of other people.

But always operating within such frames is the concrete person and the concrete set of experiences—as Edward Sapir so often insisted in his writings on the study of "cultures" and

the person—and it is out of the primary situations and experiences, with all their tensions and implications for change
in behavior, that both the cultural norm is born and the
personality pattern forged. Sapir says, for example, "A personality is carved out by the subtle interaction of those
systems of ideas which are characteristic of the culture as a
whole, as well as of those systems of ideas which get established for the individual through more special types of
participation, with the physical and psychological needs of
the individual organism, which cannot take over any of the
cultural material that is offered in its original form but works
it over more or less completely, so that it integrates with those
needs" (1951, pp. 518-19). And in another place, continuing
on the theme of the dynamic relation between a "personality"
and a cultural context, he notes:

The so-called culture of a group of human beings, as it is ordinarily
treated by the cultural anthropologist, is essentially a systematic list
of all the socially inherited patterns of behavior which may be
illustrated in the actual behavior of all or most of the individuals
of the group. The true locus, however, of these processes which,
when abstracted into a totality, constitute culture is not in a
theoretical community of human beings known as society, for the
term "society" is itself a cultural construct which is employed by
individuals who stand in significant relations to each other in order
to help them in the interpretation of certain aspects of their
behavior. The true locus of culture is in the interactions of specific
individuals and, on the subjective side, in the world of meanings
which each one of these individuals may unconsciously abstract
for himself from his participation in these interactions. (Sapir,
1951, p. 515)

What, then, of the concrete person who here serves as a
point of entry into understanding the interpenetration of
culture and personality? What are some of the specific features
of Nathan's life and circumstances—his village, his family and
their story, his particular appearance and behavior?

Nathan's family was among the poorer families in the village,
with little money and few means of getting it. It was poor,
too, in another sense that mattered greatly in the Eskimo
scheme of things: there were few adult male relatives to

constitute a clan group, strong hunters who would form the nucleus of a boat crew. And without a crew (and without men trapping in order to buy the necessary gasoline and ammunition), a family was destined to remain poor by Eskimo standards; for the man of the house might well have to work as a mere member in the crew of another family from another clan—in effect, a social and economic outsider, a "hired hand." He received his due portion from the successes of the hunt, but his relationship to the social and economic means of production was a tenuous and fragile one, not undergirded by the more durable bonds of kinship. The economic importance of a family having enough adult or near-adult male members to form a boat crew and the social and psychological significance of those male kin for any given person is well brought out in the autobiography. The long-term efforts of Nathan's father and uncle to get and maintain a boat—and their high hopes built on the assumption that Nathan's uncles, brothers, and cousins would live to man the boat—form a poignant theme in his early life.

The house in which Nathan lived at the time of writing this autobiography was similar in general construction to most others in the community, although smaller than many (having not much more than one hundred square feet for the living area). It was, in fact, the same house that Nathan describes in the story—a lumber structure, placed near the outer edge of the community. Since the early years of the twentieth century, the custom of building houses from imported lumber rather than indigenous materials had taken hold, and at the time of the study, none of the older houses remained (such as that described by Nathan, the *mongtighapek*, a driftwood frame house covered with walrus hide and insulated with moss). Nathan's house was located almost at the end of a "street," the village being laid out in approximately three rows of houses, most of them with the main entrance facing the sea. The "central business district" (as the geographers would say) consisted of the modern schoolhouse and teachers' apartments, the native cooperative store, the church building (containing also the missionary's living quarters), and the house occupied by the (then) Territorial health department nurse. Also in this central "plaza" was a community hall, occasionally used in the summer for social and recreational gatherings, such as movies.

Stretching out on both sides from this cluster of buildings were the houses, about sixty in all, and so arranged that clansmen tended to live near each other as neighbors. Some houses were occupied by only a nuclear family—man, wife, and children. In others, grandparents or unmarried siblings of the householder also lived, the principal determining feature being availability of space in view of growth in family size.

At the time of my field research, the subject of this life story, Nathan Kakianak, was a young man of average height and appearance compared to his fellows. Although not of a robust build, he nonetheless participated fully in hunting and other strenuous activities required of men, such as fox trapping. Certainly there was no obvious sign early in the year of the overall weakening effects of the tuberculosis he had even then, which was to send him to his sick bed and result in his hospitalization on the mainland with an uncertain prognosis during the year this autobiography was begun.

But during the first several months I knew him, he was as active as any other young man in the village—hunting for ducks along the shore, dog teaming to his traps, going out with a boat crew during the winter search for walruses, seals, and polar bears. In fact, it was he who put the first bullet into the only polar bear killed that winter, something he was very proud of—and with good reason, for it won him the praise and compliments of all other hunters.

Despite such successes, however, one had the impression that Nathan was not quite comfortable fitting into the mold of the typical young Eskimo male, and that he was a bit on the edge of his peer society, reserved and cautious. It is difficult to say with certainty how much of this might be due to factors of kinship—such as his belonging to a very small and not very powerful kin group—and how much due to other factors more deeply rooted in his particular life experience. Perhaps some of it may be due to the impact of his earliest years, when his family chose to live mainly in an isolated hunting camp rather than the village, which was somewhat unusual at the time. But to judge from the life story, shyness and a lack of self-confidence seem always to have been a distinct mark of his personality.

Whatever the case, his observed interpersonal manner can be described as outgoing, congenial, and engaging without being effusive. Such a characterization does not make Nathan very different from most young Eskimo males of his time, although some were more outspoken and interpersonally aggressive. From the point of view of an outsider, however, another aspect of his personality would appear unusual: his intellectual curiosity and interest in a wide range of subjects. He spoke about events and ideas in a clear and easy manner, enjoyed talking about the outside world, was trying to learn to play the piano, borrowed and read books from me as well as the school and church libraries. He was, in short, perhaps more catholic in his orientation to the mainland world than many others of his age set, for he included not just mainland technology but also many features of its ideational and moral culture as well.

Clearly this is not the place to attempt a rounded analysis of Nathan's personality; that would best be done at a level of consideration which probed more deeply into the data presented in the life story given here, as well as with additional data. It may be helpful, however, to comment briefly upon a theme in Nathan's life that is quite evident in these data and appears to have important structural implications for his personality generally. This theme, one to which a great deal of attention is being paid in personality and developmental psychology, is the pervasiveness of coping behavior and the striving for competence as a prime motivational element in personality functioning (as one example of theoretical statements in this area, see the several publications of Robert W. White listed in the bibliography).

Nathan feels the need to prove himself competent and effective in everything he does—whether the behavioral arena be that of helping his father with household tasks, learning the skills of the hunt, receiving the respect and gratitude of his mother when bringing home birds or an animal for the family's meal, mastering tasks of the mind in the schoolroom, getting praise for a good ivory carving, repairing a broken boat motor or other piece of equipment, or—an equally critical arena for public demonstration of competence or ineffectiveness—coming out best in a competition with his peers. In the latter respect, Nathan seems to have been continually stressed and anxious about buffets to his self-esteem in those semi-serious joustings of childhood. All the more pleasure, then, when he would hold his own or even come out "one up" from a situation of threat and public embarrassment, as when his friends would praise him or support him against the teasing and degradation of others.

In any case, let us turn to the story of Nathan's life, keeping in mind what appears to be a salient theme in this personality: constant concern with his coping abilities and his overall effectiveness as a person. White commented in one passage from the literature referred to above, "The ideal thing would be to know the whole history of explorations in efficacy and of the sense of competence which is produced by the outcome of these explorations" (1963a). Although these data will necessarily fall short of that ideal, they may help point the way toward a fuller understanding of the essential dynamics of a human life.

# Part Two

# The Life

# 1. At Camp

I don't know how to begin, but I was born at camp in a big old-fashioned Eskimo hut, called a *mongtighapek,* and I lived in it for the first few years of my life.

My grandparents and my aunt* were living with us in the old house. We lived in this house only at winter time. In summer time we moved to a new house, which my father and his brothers bought and built. We took off the roof [walrus hide] from the old house, and put it away for summer. In the summer we and my uncle's† family lived in one house, we in the lower room and my uncle in the upper room.

David‡ and I played together nice. Sometimes we would fight and then play again on the same day. When it was rainy we played indoors, sometimes in his room and sometimes in our room. On other days I would go with my father when he went to hunt for seals or birds. Sometimes David came along, or else I would go with him and his father, but we didn't do any shooting because the gun was too big and heavy for us. Watching our fathers was great fun anyway.

How I wanted to go with the men when they went hunting in the boat! My father said he would let me go with him later, when I was old enough, because it was too dangerous. Everytime they were going hunting in the boat I went to my father and said: "I'm a man now; aren't I old enough?"

My father would answer, "Well, be a good boy and wait a little while longer. Help your mother or aunt with their work."

Then I would help them get ready and watch them go, and turn around and go home with a big lump in my throat. I cried a little sometimes, and after that I felt better. And I

* Nathan's father's parents and his father's unmarried sister.
† Nathan's father's brother, Akoak.
‡ Nathan's cousin—his father's brother's son and therefore, in the St. Lawrence Island Eskimo kinship system, the most important type of relative among all his age-mates (see p. 13). The pseudonym "David" is used in place of Nathan's cousin's English name; in all cases pseudonyms are used, both for English and Eskimo personal names. The life story opens when Nathan is living in a small familistic settlement on the other side of the island, about forty miles from Gambell.

went with my mother or aunt to gather berries, greens, roots, or other plants. Or helped them with work at home such as getting wood for fire, getting water, or chopping fire wood.

I found lots of time for playing, too. I would play by myself or with my sister or with my cousins. When we all played together, it was fun. We played some games such as hide-and-seek, or other games which are probably unknown to the children now. When we heard or saw the boat coming, we all rushed to the beach to see what they were bringing home, and to help them.

Early in the fall, the winter or "Eskimo" house was fixed and made ready for winter. Almost everybody helped in the work. It was the time when my oldest uncle, Nagotak, returned from fishing camp in the big lagoon east of Southwest Cape. It was a good season for seal hunting. I went with my father whenever he went to watch for seals to come up in the water. All I could do was watch for seals and tell my father; of course he did all the shooting. I wished I could shoot at least once, to try it, but my father told me I was too small and the rifle would kick me hard. And my granma often told me to be a good boy and obey my father and do as he said. Sometimes when my father got a seal soon after we got to the shore where we hunted for seals, he would take it home while I waited for him in the same place. He told me never to touch his rifle and not to go too near the edge of the rocks—I might fall into the water. Well, I did as he said, but sometimes when I saw a seal coming to breathe I was tempted to grab the rifle, but I kept the words of my granma and tried my best to be a good boy. Another thing that made me obey was that she told me being good would make me grow faster and become a man soon. The gooder I was, the faster I would grow. And she said that bad boys grow slow and never become men if they are real bad. Besides, they would not be good hunters even if they grew to be men. I wanted to be a good hunter when I grew up.

One morning I was up early because I was going with my father to hunt for seal. Everytime we got home with a seal, or even without one, my granma told me that I was growing and would be a man soon. That made me feel proud. Well, the morning was a bright and good one—the ground covered with snow and a little north wind: perfect for hunting. When we got to the spot we chose for hunting [some breast-works along the shore used as blinds], the water was smooth and the little waves made a noise.

We were by ourselves. My uncles were at home that morning and nobody else was hunting near. Soon my father shot a seal and took it home like the other times. He told me not to touch the rifle or to go near the water. It was dangerous then because the rocks were covered with ice, making them very slippery. A while after when he had gone, a seal came up and went down again and came up again, every time coming closer. Oh! what a temptation when it went down! I stood up and looked around. Nobody was within sight. I sat down and took the rifle. It was a bit too heavy and the stock was too long, and I could barely reach the trigger.

I was glad that my older cousin had told me how to sight a rifle, but I hadn't shot any before. Then the seal came up. I had it in my rifle sights, then pulled the trigger. Bang! and Ouch! Boy, it really kicked, and hard, too! I thought my father and cousins had meant only to scare me. But, look, I got the seal—if I wasn't dreaming. It was too good to be true, yet it was true. And suddenly I remembered what my father had said. I was a bad boy—or maybe a hunter. I couldn't worry too much about being a good boy now; I must try to get the dead seal with the seal hook, like my father would do, before the current carried it away—or I would have no seal to take home.

I started to stand up with the seal hook in my hand. At the same time I heard somebody say, "Don't try it, I'll get it." I looked around and saw my uncle coming. He got the seal. It was a small one. He tied a rope to it and I drew it home. Boy! I felt proud when my uncle praised me.

I gave my seal to Aiyaksaq because he was an old person, and we were supposed to give them the first animals we killed.

From that time on my father let me use a small rifle, .22 long. I wasn't too good at shooting, but I got something once in a while. But I wasn't allowed to go hunting by myself. My father began to teach me how to handle hunting equipment, especially firearms—how to use them safely. I learned how to use my shells carefully, too. If I shot anything we could not use, that was wasting a bullet.

The same year I learned how to trap foxes. My father showed me how and where to set my traps. I didn't catch any foxes that season. They would step in my trap but would get away, and most of the bait would have been eaten. Maybe I didn't set my trap quite properly, or was just unlucky. But I didn't pay too much attention to my traps, because I still wanted to play and help around the house. But I did check my traps once in a while. I would return from checking them either interested or disappointed, but I would forget my disappointment when my father came home with a fox or two.

I didn't help much in skinning them, but I liked to take the skin off the stretcher when it was dry, and clean it. I liked to help in fixing the fox skins, because my father would bring some good things from the store in trade for the fox skins. It was a happy time when my father or his brothers returned from a trip to Gambell. I and my cousins got together and shared the good things. Our mothers gave us our share of things, some to my cousins to take home. Sometimes my mother and my aunt took some tea and other things to the other family, because the other family did the same thing when one of my uncles or Aiyaksaq went to trade fox furs at Gambell or Savoonga.

We, I and my cousins, liked to go to Aiyaksaq's house and help with the work around the house, or play there. When we had been good or helpful he would reward us with some good thing to eat or to play with. The reward was sometimes a bunch of dried fruit or some pilot bread, candy, or even specially fixed greens. Or if it was to play with, it would be some kind of whistle made with a piece of wood or baleen, or a wooden boat, or some American toys.

When a storm came we the children stayed in our home or went to one of the cousin's home and played all sorts of games, or played with anything. When the storm lasted a long time, we got tired of playing indoors. We wanted to go outdoors and play or work.

28

We slid down the hillside in winter. I used my little sled made by Edward Aiyaksaq; but I would slide down on anything—a piece of baleen, old pan, shovel, or even the seat of my sealskin pants was good enough for hard snow.

When I first knew Christmas I was about three. It didn't mean anything else to me than receiving good things, and it came once a year, and you can guess it was a happy time. I wished that it came more than once a year. David Akoak and I often shared the toys that we got at Christmas, and our sisters shared theirs. What a good time we had for a while! Sometime after this they showed me where the Christmas is on the calender, as I was learning to use the calendar. When I wanted some toys, candy, and popcorn I counted the months or days before Christmas and if it was far away it made me cry and wish the days would go faster. But I would then forget about it when some excitement happened. When I remembered Christmas again I counted the days again. Boy! It was only a few days away. And my father and my older cousins or one of the uncles would get ready to make a trip to the village. If the weather became stormy a few days before, it made me sad again. And when it was good my father and his brothers brought a box of good things for each family, besides the box from the Mission, things they got by trading fox furs from the store. I believe it's the happiest time of every year, even now. It brings me happiness one way or the other.

When I was about five years old we all had bad luck. Not much hunting and lots of bad weather. Not much game and during the long winter storms we ran out of fuel (seal oil), food, and almost everything. The seal oil lamps were our only light and heat. So we had to live in a dark, cold room. My father made a stove out of a five-gallon gasoline can. What sad days we spent—no playing in or out-of-doors, because of darkness indoors and storm outdoors, and a wild one, too. Some of our dogs starved to death. Only a few thin ones were left.

At last the storm cleared up and the wind died down. We were happy to be playing outdoors. The sun shone once more, making the snow sparkle brightly. What a happy day!

29

In the evening of the cleared-up day some men arrived from Gambell with their sleds loaded with food, kerosene, and dog food. They brought more happiness—but I was afraid of the strange men. I hadn't seen them before, and some of them were staying in our house. I stayed in one corner most of the time. They had come to help us, but I was too shy. They were the councils of the village [i.e., members of the village council]. They had heard about our hard time, and they organized and bought things at the store and brought them to us. After they had gone I asked my parents who these men were. And I learned they were the councils. I thought they were very good men and I found out for the first time what "councils" were.

That winter of my fifth year was not a very good one. We were short of food and out of fuel oil and seal oil. We got some help from the village, but that was not enough, and we had to go to Gambell. I was going to see the village for the first time. I hadn't any idea what the village looked like. I was a little afraid to go, but I knew I couldn't be left behind. I must go, too, but somehow I was anxious about seeing the village. I wondered what it would look like, how long the way would be.

My mother and my aunt and everybody began to get ready for the trip. The women made new clothing and the men got the other things they would need during the trip and while in the village. I was glad to have the new clothing. I didn't want to be seen in my old ones in the village. My old sealskin pants had no more fur on the knees and my boots were dirty and out of shape and my parka was worn too. I thought I looked like a mess in them.

The men got some dog teams from the village. I forget how many came to help and who they were. But enough teams from the village took all the family in from our camp, including Aiyaksaq and my father's two brothers, Akoak and Nagotak. My father and one man made a shelter of canvas on one of the sleds. Myself and my little sister, Ruth, rode in that shelter. I wanted to ride on another sled without a canvas, but they wouldn't let me.

The way seemed long and I played with Ruth, who is dead

a long time now. I had taken a toy. I wanted to take more toys, and my little sled, but they told me we had to take as little as possible. I liked to look out, but my father had closed the opening tightly, so the wind wouldn't get in.

After some time and some miles the dog teams stopped and Dad opened the door and let me out. We were stopping for lunch. I looked around. We had stopped among some mountains. There were here and there small ones and high ones. Toward the north was a plain all covered with snow. The ground everywhere was all white. There was a small mountain a long way off. They pointed to it and said it was Gambell hill. We were only halfway.

We had some frozen boiled meat, bread that was frozen, and some hot tea from thermos bottles. How good that tasted, when I was cold from eating frozen meat!

We started again after the lunch. After what I thought was a long time, the driver told us we were getting near the village. A little shiver ran up and down my spine. I felt the strange chill. I wished we didn't have to come to the village. I didn't want to be among the strange people and houses. I was afraid, but I didn't say so. I thought that was sissy. To be afraid is strictly for girls and women.

When we got there they opened the door and I got out and looked. There were lots of houses—more than I thought about, and lot of people, too. A tall young woman carried me to the nearest house and took me right into it. That was her home. It was nice in the home. There were seal oil lamps like ours back home, and other members of the family. There were two men, very young fellows, and herself, and no children. The woman that took me in told me the names of the other members of the family. The older looking man was Igalok. The younger one was Ted Apazu. And she was Jane Igalok. Then she served me some hot tea with crackers, but I didn't drink much—a sip or two of tea and a bite of cracker. And I didn't say much when they asked me something. I said "yes," "no," or "I don't know"—in almost a whisper. Then my father and my mother came in, along with Akoak's family. Igalok said that both families might stay in his big house. So we stayed with them.

31

David Akoak and I played mostly inside. When it was time to play out-of-doors, we stayed close around the house, and when any strange person came, we went right in the house and watched through the door until they passed by, or hid behind the door or something until the person went into the inner room.

One day our parents took us to the church service. My! Lots of people were going there, too. There were lots of little boys and girls our own age. Some of them smiled at me and I smiled back at them but I held real tight to my father. I was afraid of the old people. But after not too long, I started to answer some of the boys and girls. I hadn't seen any service before like this one. How good the organ sounded when the white woman played on it, and the hymns the people sang. Some of them I knew.

I was surprised by a white man who was leading the service. He talked in our talk. When we got out of the church I asked my father "Do white man talk in our talk?"

He laughed and said that the only white man there was only a white woman in the service who played the organ. The one I thought was a white man was Kogoyak, the elder of the church at that time. After a week, they let me go to the Sunday School, and after I got a few friends in the Sunday School and got acquainted I was not afraid so much as before.

After a few weeks I began to get homesick. I thought of the old house at our camp. I thought of the fun I used to have at home, even if I did have a few friends to play with now.

When the spring hunting started, my father and uncle, Akoak, talked of going back to camp, since it would not be too hard, because we could get some seals and young and old mukluks then. That sounded real good to me, because some nights I stayed up until late thinking about good old home, and that even made me cry sometimes at night. A few days later we packed up and again some people helped us to get back to our camp. Before we left, my new friends gave me some presents—toys and nice clothing. One man gave me a box of .22 shells when I told him I could shoot seals, and birds. Another man gave me some tools to be my own, so I could learn how to carve ivory. I had lots of things to take home, including a little wooden pistol Robert Sakigak* made for me for sweeping his work bench and floor for a few days.

The way back home didn't seem as long as when we came. I rode one of the teams without a canvas shelter because it wasn't too cold then—maybe some time in the last part of April. So I watched all the way; in some places the ground was bare and on mountain tops the wind had blown away the snow and the sun melted it. It was a very happy trip for me—the dog teams went in line and sometimes side by side, sometimes fast, and sometimes slow. The dog teams stopped about halfway, among the mountains, for a lunch of bread and tea. After lunch we went on again on our way. After some time of riding, the snow over which we rode was very smooth. The sun became warm. I got drowsy and then slept.

I might have slept for quite a while, because when the rough places in the snow woke me up, I saw our old home a little way ahead. Boy! That was a joy after being away from home! When we got there some of the snow had melted and the old house we lived in was moldy and smelled of lot of damp air, and had to be cleaned. The women did a fast clean-up, because some of the dog teams wanted to turn back after a dinner. But some of them stayed overnight.

Before I had some fun looking around, I helped the men with their dogs—unharnessing and feeding thm. After a bite to eat I ran here and there. Got on top of a little hill, looking this way and that way. The ice was still around the shore, but the water was near. The little birds were singing on tops of the old poles that had been meat racks. Quite a happy day it was. I thought there was no place like our camp.

* Nathan's mother's brother, who in this predominantly patrilineal society plays a secondary role in Nathan's life.

# 2. A Child's View of School

After my sixth birthday my father began to let me go with them when they went hunting in the boat. One morning it was very calm and the weather was very good. The water was smooth. My father and his brother were going to hunt for sea lions by boat. Like other times, I was going to help them get ready; but I didn't expect to go, because I knew what my father would say if I asked to go. He would say, "Wait a little longer until you are old enough." But this time he looked at me and said, "Aren't you getting ready? Are you not coming with me?"

"Oh, yes, I'm going," I said, almost shouting. I ran to get my hunting clothing, and I put it on as fast as I could, and didn't eat much of my breakfast. I was too excited to eat or drink. I wanted to take my rifle with me, but my father wouldn't let me take it. He said I might handle it carelessly and shoot somebody. So I went without it.

I saw lots of birds—more birds than I had seen at home, and I wished I had my rifle with me to shoot some. But I had to behave, or no boat hunting for me. My cousin, Kenneth Nagotak,* ran the motor. I thought that was fun and thought "that's what I'll do when I grow up."

We were going to paddle to the high cliffs. The birds were aroused by the noise of our motor, and were screaming, flying here and there. They darkened the sky. Boy! I thought there were lots of them! There were murres, puffins, sea gulls, cormorants, and kittiwakes. The cliffs sure were alive with birds. My father was in the bow; he shot down a bird or two once in a while. Kenneth and Dad reached over the side of the boat and grabbed the dead birds. When Dad missed, Kenneth or Akoak did the grabbing. I would have liked to, but one of them said, "No, no." They didn't want me to get my sleeves wet. Thought I might get cold.

Soon we got in sight of two little islands, or two rocks sticking out of the water. Kenneth pointed to them and said they are full of sea lions. That was our destination, because

---

* Another of Nathan's patrilineal parallel cousins—a son of his father's eldest brother, Nagotak.

37

we were after sea lions. Sure enough, when we got closer I saw some brown, almost ugly, mammals. All of them were asleep. There was a good herd of them. They looked more like brown burlap bags to me. On one side of the island there were not very many of them, and the men chose that place to get on the island. Kenneth throttled the motor very low and then cut it off. They paddled to the side of the sloping side of the rock, making as little noise as possible. They didn't want to waken the herd, because they could look for small ones better that way, and shoot better, too.

My father and Akoak climbed to the island with their rifles swiftly, so they could look over and shoot better. I began to be afraid a little; some kind of a chill ran up and down my back. I worried that some of the sea lions might jump into our boat or push Akoak or my father over the edge of the rock. They disappeared to the other side of the rock. I felt my heart pounding like a sledge hammer in my chest. I was shivering even though the sun was shining and the water was smooth as glass.

Roaring rifles broke the stillness suddenly. The little island was alive with roaring and splashing, and the water around us was full of sea lions breaking the surface with their huge brown heads with their mouths wide open. Every lion seemed to be facing to me. Oh my! I was really frightened. Almost enough to make me jump out of my skin! But when I came to myself again, I was very much ashamed, and looked at Kenneth and Akoak. They didn't even seem to notice my fear. Because being afraid is strictly for women and babies— not a bit for a man or hunter-to-be.

I wondered what I would do if I had had my gun with me, because some of the sea lions got quite close to us. Then one of the shooters appeared over the island and told us to go to the other side. They had shot two small ones and one big one. They tied the boat to the rocks and Kenneth and Akoak got on them to butcher the big bull. But I stayed in the boat and I watched the big herd of lions swimming in the water. Some of them climbed back to the other island close by. Others kept on swimming, and playing in the water, because they were not too excited then, not roaring all of the time. But to my real joy, none of them tried to attack us.

Their odor was very strong; it made me a little sick in the stomach, made me not sure of eating some of the meat. Yet I like the calves' meat. I was not sure then that I would like some. After the meat was loaded into the boat, we started for home. I had become a little hungry by now.

About three hours later we got within sight of home. When we got close enough, those who had been at home were coming down the hill to the beach. I saw my cousins running and rolling down like I did when the boat was coming in from hunting. I jumped out of the boat, feeling very proud. I had lots to tell my folks while we unloaded the boat. Akoak said that he would have one more man for the boat, because he said I had not been afraid—not a little bit. I felt a little funny, but I was glad he hadn't seen my fright. That meant I was a man and a real hunter from then on.

But after that I was not always much of a man. Sometimes when I got hurt or something had happened to me, I would open my big mouth and cry. But worst of all, I was bad because I fought with my sister and cousin once in a while. It was hard for me to be good and be a man.

When I was about six or seven years old, my heart was broken badly for the first time. It was when my loved grandmother died. I was broken-hearted when my grandfather passed away some years before my grandmother died, but I was very small and I felt not so bad. I thought my life would not be without her. I thought nothing would ever separate me from her, or that she would ever pass away. She got sick once in a while like me, but she often got well. Now she was sick and it took a longer time to get well than she used to. She seemed to be getting weaker and more ill. I began to worry, and fear was forcing its way into my mind. But I kept on telling myself that "She will get well; she must not die; she must not. That is more than I can bear."

But one night I realized all this was no use; my beloved granma was going home, leaving us behind. After that I was broken-hearted for quite a while. I was too broken-hearted to eat much or sleep much. Many times I made my father and aunts weep because I mourned too much. Many times

I wept when I found her belongings and things she made for me, or when her name was mentioned. When my heart was better and my sorrow got soothed a little, I got better and well. I got a little happier when my little brother grew big enough to play with. His name was Douglas, born a year before. But I didn't forget it at all, and I think I never will forget.

Another thing I wanted to have was to learn how to read and write. But I had to have some school to learn these things, and there was no school of any kind in our camp. We would have to get our schooling in the village, and I wasn't sure I wanted to be in the village. I was used to camp life. I didn't want to be with so many strange people, even my own age. Besides I didn't know what the school was like. I didn't know if I would like it in school. But if I wanted to learn, I must have some schooling. And my parents wanted me to learn, too, because they knew themselves it's real hard if we don't learn these three: reading, writing, and speaking English. Our parents said we (the children in the camp) must have some school somehow. And the school teachers wanted us to have some too. They sent us old books and some school material, but without a teacher they were useless. To us the books were nothing much more than to look at the pictures in them; and the pencils and papers were nothing but to draw pictures with. But some of our parents had been in school a little bit. It was too bad, but they had lost what little they had learned, because they didn't have much time for reading and writing, or they weren't too interested in that. But they gave us what they had learned—such as how to say and write the numbers and alphabet. And they did something for me by that—at least they got me started and increased my interest in learning.

My uncles and Dad decided to go to the village after trapping season closed in March every year, and come back to the camp before the snow melted. So we could have school that way. Maybe the same year my granma died I went to school for the first time. I made up my mind to go to school just because I wanted to learn and be like the other learned people. At the time we stayed with George Danagik. George had been in our camp staying with us some times when he trapped, so I was used to him and liked him very much. Barbara and Frances Danagik were little girls, and too small to go to school. But they were very good playmates, and I learned to like Louise, George's mother, because she was very good to us. And I didn't like any bad thing to happen to her.

I'm not sure how old I was then—maybe six or seven years old—when it was my first school day. On the first Monday we got to Gambell the school was in the mission building that morning. I was getting ready for school. I got up as early as I could, and put on my best clothing. I went out to wait for the bell to ring. At last the bell rang, and I ran into the school. I went in with other children. In the room there tables and chairs that were homemade. The other children sat around the tables. But I had no place to sit. One of the boys asked me to sit with him, and I did.

Everybody was looking at me and some were asking me questions. My face got hot and I felt funny. I answered a few of them in a whisper. Everything seemed to be strange. Just then the teacher came into the room. She was a tall thin woman with glasses. She looked at me in a surprised way and said "Hello" to me and that was all I said to her. She talked to me but I couldn't answer her. I just looked at her and tried to smile. I couldn't understand a thing she said. Then she went into the other room and came back with a girl and the girl asked me a few things, such as where I came from, how old I was, and what my name was. Then the teacher called her husband from the other room. A tall, queer-looking man came in and she told him about me and he shook hands with me. They told me they were Mr. and Mrs. Riley. They gave me a seat right beside the boy who asked me to sit with him. I was glad for that. She brought me pencils, papers, and a book to study. I didn't know what to do with them at first. I saw they were too hard for me.

A few days later some boys got tough on me and I had a few fights already. Some bigger boys were too tough and made me cry. Some were good, though, like the girl next to me; and the others pushed me close to her and called us "Mr. and Mrs." I didn't like that.

The school was too much for me. There were things too hard to learn, and I had to stay inside long hours. I especially didn't like that on nice days. I wasn't used to that. After maybe two weeks I refused to go to school. The other children came for me, but I wouldn't go. The teacher sent for me. I still wouldn't go; I was too stubborn for them. But my parents thought of a plan to make me go to school, and they did a good job on me. It was a good idea—they told me that the teacher was going to have Louise (George Danagik's mother) nailed to the door of the school house for punishment for my not going to school, and she would be taking my place, for otherwise I was the one to be nailed. I liked her as my own grandmother, and I didn't want that to happen to her. I wouldn't let them do that to her on account of me. I promised to go to school the next day, and I did keep my promise. The teacher fixed the big bullies. Later I got used to school and liked it a little better. I learned a few things. I'm always glad now that I have been in school at least that much, and I'm glad that my parents thought of such a good idea to make me go back to school.

I had to get out of school in less than a month, because we had to go back to camp before the snow was too soft for dog teams. I had my school like that for a few years—a month or less in a year.

Akoak and his family stayed most of the time in the village, so his children could have better schooling, and he built his house in the village. And Aiyaksaq and his family moved to the village to build their home, too. So I was kind of lonesome when we got back to the camp, but I got used to it because Nagotak's family was there. Besides, Ann, my sister, played with me; and my younger brother was old enough to play with when I felt like doing that. A year or two before, my younger sister had passed away, and I missed her a lot. And often I think of her now.

Between my age of eight and nine we quit using our old house, I think because of too much work to take care of it. There were far too few of use to get it ready for winter and clean it up for summer and put away the grass insulation, the walrus hides for the roof, and leather ropes. Besides, it was too old and out of repair. And not warm enough in winter. But we used it for storage for quite a while, and when it got too old for storage, it was a good shelter for our dogs. We now live in the place where Akoak used to live in camp. We have lived in it since then.

But once I got a whole year of school, one time when we stayed at Gambell all year round because my brother needed school, too. We stayed most of the time in the village on account of danger from the war.

# 3. The New House

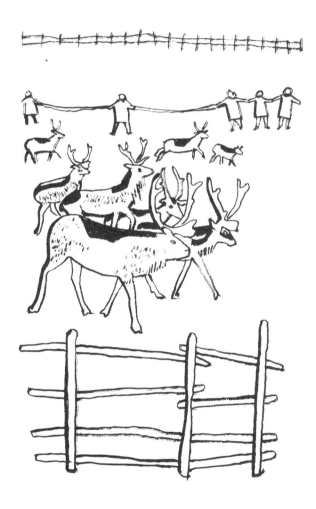

It was around my ninth year that we spent the whole year at Gambell. The same summer my second brother was born, Martin. He added more joy to my life. It was very good for me to have one more brother to play with and take care of. He seemed more dear to me because he was the youngest brother I had. In that year we were living with Akoak's family. We even played, worked, and went to school together. But I was not completely happy, because I missed something very much—hunting, good hunting. I had learned to like it very much.

My father went hunting in Kazighia's boat. David and I helped our fathers when they came in from hunting. We harnessed the dogs while our fathers changed their clothes and then rode back with them to get the meat. That was fun. But we still didn't go out with them. Sometimes we helped the hunters with the boat when they started out in the morning, and watched them out on the blue sea. That made me feel unhappy, but it was nobody's fault. My father was willing to take me with him, and his captain would like me in his boat. But now I had to go to school. I needed it more than hunting. I would have more time for hunting than for school in the future.

From the beach I went to join the other schoolmates playing around the school house. I liked the school much better by now, but still didn't care too much for it. I always had more fun in hunting. I was glad when school was out, but I still didn't have much hunting in Gambell. The hunting places were too far, and hunting was not as good as at our camp.

During the time Daniel Kazighia and I became good friends and he often came over to us. So David and I had lots of fun with him. I went to his place once in a while and stayed there all day.

That same summer there was going to be a reindeer slaughter at the place near Savoonga, and Kazighia and his folks were going. My Dad was going, too, with Kazighia. Oh! How I wished I could go, but I didn't know if my Dad would like me with him. I was afraid to ask him. If he said "no," I would be very much disappointed. I made up my mind at last and I asked him if he might let me go with him. He was packing. He looked up at me from what he was doing. My heart beat faster and my face got warm. He thought for a moment and asked me, "Do you really want to go? Are you sure you'll not get homesick?"

I said, "I sure want to go, and I will not be a bit homesick."

Then he said, "I'm not sure if Kazighia would be willing to take you along, but come, let's go ask him."

We walked fast to Kazighia's house. We met him at the door; he was just coming out. I was praying in my heart all along. My Dad asked him if he would mind taking me with them. He said to my father that it's up to him and me. Then Kazighia looked at me, grinning, and said, "But I think Nathan doesn't want to come along."

I told him, "I *do* want to come along."

He laughed in a jolly way and then said, "Hurry up and get your things."

I turned around and ran as fast as I could, half laughing and half crying. I was so happy I couldn't run fast enough. I packed my things in a big hurry.

We carried our things on our backs to the north shore. Some other people were getting ready for the camp, too. Some of them were already loading their camping bags into their boats. When Daniel knew that I was going too, he was glad. We were going to be happy at the round-up. We happily helped with the things and the boat. On the way we sat together in the boat and talked about what we would do at the camp, and how fun it was going to be. He told me his uncle, Sukak, and his family were at the camp already. I hadn't been in any reindeer camp before, so I didn't know much about it. But I knew I was going to have lots of fun.

A little wind was blowing and it was quite cold. The breeze was chilly, but from a good direction. We were going close to the shore. Daniel and I watched over the boat curtain ( a canvas shelter against spray and waves). We saw some ducks and geese along the shore. Victor boiled some tea. Some cooked meat and fruits were passed around the boat. They tasted good, because I was cold and hungry. When the tea was ready some cups of steaming hot tea with crackers were passed around. It was a most welcome thing on a chilly day. It warmed me a little, but I was tired. I looked over the curtains and saw a bunch of sea gulls feeding on the shore, and I showed it to Victor. He got out his binoculars and looked and said, "Dead walrus." The boat was turned toward it then so we could see if it still had the tusks on.

When the boat hit the shore, Koyogak got out to see the walrus. He walked around it and called for a paddle. They handed one to him, and he dug at one end of the dead walrus. Sure enough, there were the tusks buried under gravel, and big ones too. He took them off with the ax. We were on our way again. Other boats had passed by the walrus without seeing it. I think we were the lucky ones of all the boats.

After some time we got to the reindeer camp. As soon as we hit the shore some people helped us unload our things onto the beach. There were some tents here and there. Sukak asked Kazighia to set up a tent just at the back of his tent. Sukak's sons helped us with the tent and our gear, so everything was done in a short time. The women were busy with the supper while we set up the tent and were caring for our things; so it was ready just as we got everything in place. We ate in Sukak's tent. It was crowded, because there were quite a few of us, but the supper was good after a hard day.

After supper, just before darkness, Victor, Daniel, and I got firewood. We each got an armload and got back after dark. We dropped the wood at the front of the tent. Victor chopped some of it, and Daniel and I took the sticks into the tent. The camp stove was burning high, and we had a kerosene lantern for light. The girls had spread our deerskin mats over the walrus hide floor of the tent, so we went right to bed, tired and sleepy. In no time we were fast asleep.

It was a very good time for me at the camp. Most of the place was sandy, with some grass and rocks at other places. I found a few playmates among Savoonga children, but most of the time I stayed with Daniel and his cousins. We got firewood and water every day.

We heard that the herd of reindeer was still far away from the camp, and it would take the herders a long time to round it up to bring it into the corral. So Kazighia, Sukak, his little girl, Anna, and his boy, Stanley, I and my Dad, all of us walked to Savoonga to visit and to buy some grub and other needed things. We went through a rocky lava and along some beach covered with gravel and sand, and on the wet and muddy tundra following the trail all the way. Stanley and his little sister told me all about themselves as we walked along, and it was a nice day. We talked so much that we lagged behind and one of the men had to call us, "Come on, let's go." At that we walked on again, and ran to catch up with the rest. Sukak had to carry little Anna at some places that were too rough, and in muddy places. But we were so happy that the way seemed short.

We got to the village sometime in the afternoon. After we washed up and ate, my Dad and I visited around with our relatives, like Ethel Awigiyak, and my Dad's in-laws. We all stayed in Sukak's house that night. Stanley and I were up very early the next morning before the rest of the others in the house. We just washed and went out-of-doors to play. Stanley took his air rifle and we went to the beach and shot at some small birds washing in the shallow water, and did all sorts of playing. And then we lay down on the warm sand in the sunshine, and told each other what we had done before. Suddenly we heard somebody calling us. When we looked up there was Stanley's older sister. She kind of scolded us for being absent without notice. She said, "We all have been looking for you. Come home right away, and have some breakfast. I'll look around for Kakianak° and Sukak and let them know I've found you both."

We got back to the house and had some breakfast. While we were eating my Dad came in and said, "Kazighia is waiting for us at the store. He wants you to get the things you'll need at the camp."

I went with my Dad to the store and Kazighia was there. He had brought those tusks from the dead walrus we had found on our way from Gambell. He was trading them for the things he liked. He turned to us and said, "I have taken

° Nathan's father.

50

my share and saved you the other half." I got a few pairs of gloves and socks, and some candy. My Dad got a box of other things, and some of my relatives bought me many other good things. We all returned to the camp with some others in a skin boat the same day. I was sort of glad to get back to the camp, because I always liked camping.

On the next day it was a very nice day, the water smooth and the sun shining. I went to the sandy beach and lay down on the warm sand. Oh! I was happy, and other children came and we all talked and played in the sand and made igloos of wet sand.

While I was playing, Dad called me and told me to put on my boots. We were going to the cliffs after young cormorants. Like the other hunting times, we had to get a big fill before we went out for the long day. And even if it is a warm day, we had to take our parkies and other clothes. I had learned this before and was willing to take some warm clothing with me. There was Kazighia, Sukak, Ronald, Daniel, Igalok, Penina and his boy Amos, me, and my Dad in the boat. We went to the cliffs somewhere between Camp Collier and the reindeer camp where there were many cormorants and other sea birds. The boat was pulled up on the rocky beach. Dad and Kazighia walked off to the other places with a long rope and the other things they would need to climb the high cliff and get some of the young cormorants. Ronald, Daniel, Amos, and I stayed around the boat. The men wanted us to stay together and close to the boat, because it was dangerous for us. There was Penina and Igalok to look after us, while the other men spread out, two by two, with .22 long rifles and shotguns.

We watched the other men shoot down some birds close by. Penina got his rifle, and he shot a few of the birds that were above us. Again, I wished to have my rifle, but that was at home. My Dad had told me not to handle any firearms, for fear I might hurt or even kill somebody. So we threw rocks as the birds flew by. But Penina was a very good old man, and he said he would let us each shoot one time. Luckily I downed a bird, and he let me shoot a few more times. Boy! He had a very nice rifle, too. I longed to have one like that. I was very proud when he and the others praised me for good shooting.

Penina let us look around a little, too. The cliffs were not as high as those near Southwest Cape and there were not as many birds. As we were looking around we shared what we had in our pockets. I passed around some dried fruit and some candy that my Dad had given me that morning. The others had some pilot bread and other things.

At some places the rocks were covered with slick green stuff and were slippery. Once I slipped and fell hard and hurt my leg. I opened my big mouth and cried. Another man picked me up and looked at my leg. When they found out it was not badly hurt, they teased me, and I felt ashamed and sort of mad and stopped crying.

Later the men were coming back carrying the birds they had gotten, and some more men were with them. While they were still far off we prepared the lunch and lighted the primus stove with a big pot of coffee on it. The other men were the boys who were going after the reindeer. Kenneth Nagotak, my older cousin, was with them. Nagotak and his family had been at Southwest Cape; the herder boys came through there, so Kenneth had joined them. But they said there were no reindeer that way. Other herder boys had gone to other places, and they had not returned yet.

We had our lunch and loaded everything into the boat and were on our way to the camp. I was very glad to see Kenneth. The boat was loaded until there was not a bit of room for another person. When we got back to the camp, the birds were divided, the other things were taken care of, and I was tired and sleepy.

The next few days were full of fun and I thought that was my happiest time, walking around all over the camp with other boys and girls wading in the stream with bare feet, and eating berries at some places. I was so happy that sometimes I forgot what my Dad told me not to do. But I was scolded well when I had done some mischief or some other bad things.

Almost every day some people climbed to the height and looked all around with binoculars. So not long afterwards, somebody saw the boys with the big herd of reindeer. The boys who had been at the camp went out to meet them at once, to help them with the herd of reindeer. Other men got the corral ready that evening. All the children were kept in the tents so they wouldn't get in the way, or make any trouble. We all wanted to go out and see how the herd was driven into the corral, but they wouldn't let us; because if one little thing went wrong, it would cause lots of trouble, or else frighten the whole herd away. So we stayed put and slept. The next morning we had reindeer fat to butter our bread. My! That tasted very good.

We all had a job to do then. Daniel and Ronald worked with the older group, and I and Stanley worked together in another. Very soon I found a working mate named Huston. We had fun while working, and later I found out he was closely related to me. He was my mother's nephew. Our job was carrying away the deer stomach, and the other unneeded things. It was messy work, but we were earning some reindeer meat, or skin—the best and warmest fur for winter clothing. So we worked on and watched the herd in the corral run around and around, sometimes eating grass, the big ones and the little calves, brown ones and white ones, some brown and white.

Some men and the women and big girls skinned the deers and calves. Some big boys did the harder work—like catching the deers to be slaughtered, and roping some. Other men did the slaughtering. They were spattered with blood. Oh! It was an awful sight to see the old deers and young being killed by cutting the throat with knives and stepping on the chest. I felt very sorry for them. At first they kicked and struggled, and then died. So I kept away from the slaughtering places. My Dad worked on skinning, and Kazighia was the time keeper. I was glad they were not killers. At noon the cowbell was rung and we were off for lunch to our tent, a hot lunch of reindeer meat, or young birds. Boy! It tasted good.

Even though I was happy at times and was having a good time, I was getting a little sad everyday. Long before, I had started to get homesick. I began to think of my mother, sisters, and brothers, even David Akoak. Earlier, we had played games on rainy days, and other children would come over to our tent to play or do something else. But now we worked every day at the corral. It was rainy on some of these working days, so I caught cold while working. I got sick. I stayed in the little tent where Kazighia worked. He was keeping a record of the workers and time, so the little tent was his office. I lay on the planks, and he made some coffee for us. My homesickness became worse. That was the first time I had been away from my folks, too. The camp that had been so full of fun and happiness became dull, and the days dragged on slowly. A little bit of teasing would make me cry even if the people didn't mean to do so. The rain lasted a long time—or it seemed to. The wind was blowing wildly, with big waves on the beach. Oh! What a sadness I had.

But my cold got better and the men weren't working much at the corral, because of the bad weather. At last at the end of more than a week or so the weather let up a little. We started working again, so I felt a little better when I would work again—but I still was homesick. The wind was dying down every day, and it was only foggy, with no more rain. The work was almost done now. Only a little herd of reindeer were in the corral.

At last all of the work was done. The carcasses and skins were given out to all the people, as much as they each had earned by their work. I'd earned three reindeer calf skins and one calf carcass, and half a big one. My Dad earned more than that.*

The next day the weather was good, and the camp was busy packing to go home. Tents were taken down. But one thing was not very good with us. Kazighia wanted to make a trip to Savoonga first, before we went back to Gambell. Some stayed at the camp to pack and get ready to leave, while the rest of us, including me and Dad, loaded some of our meat and skin, to give to the old people in Savoonga, as we always do—some of the first things I got must be given away to the old people. Some of Sukak's family and their stuff went home

---

* The history of the reindeer herd on St. Lawrence Island, the manner of ownership, the methods of payment for work in the herding and slaughter, and its decimation are discussed in Hughes (1960).

in our boat. I liked the trip all right, and the visiting among our relatives, but I felt more like going home.

On the next day we were on our way home at last, very early. I hadn't slept a wink during the night, because I couldn't, and the night seemed to be long. I was too anxious to go home and was thinking, "What if the wind blows again?" When we got back to the camp from Savoonga, almost everything was ready to load into the boat, except the tent and other things needed on the way. We had a hasty meal and loaded everything into the boat. There was so much of a load that there was hardly room for us.

The boat seemed to go awfully slow. To save time, we were not following the shoreline this time and the sea was very calm. But still the Gambell mountain didn't seem to come any closer. One good thing, since I hadn't slept the night before, after lunch I fell asleep. I had been sleeping most of the way when I was awakened by the rocking of the boat. I was cold and my teeth chattered and I shivered. I looked around and saw that we were almost at the point of the mountain. It was rough at that particular place, like it always was. It was getting dark. The cold breeze was blowing. But I felt some happiness coming on. A little light came into our sight ahead, on the north beach. Daniel and I cheered for joy, and Victor signaled with the flashlight, so they would know we were coming. When we got to the north shore, the waves were big—or they looked big in the dark—and we hit the gravel. I helped with the things and could hardly wait to see my folks.

The boat was put on the rack, and our things put on the sled, which was pulled by the tractor. The first stop was at front of Kazighia's house, and then at Kogoyak's; last of all at Akoak's, the place where we lived. Everybody was asleep. Dad woke Mom, and she came out to help us bring in our meat and bags. My brothers were asleep—Douglas and Martin. They looked taller now. I was tired and cold and hungry, but very happy. Oh! it was nice to be with my folks, and home again.

Mom showed us what she got from the *Trader* (a little boat). There was a pretty new sweater, socks, a pair of canvas shoes for me, and all kinds of good things to eat. But best of all, she pulled out a slick new air gun for me. Boy! That looked swell, and I'd wanted one for so long a time. And Ann (my sister) had got some berries for me. I was too tired to see everything.

Soon I was in bed, and sleeping soundly. The next morning my brothers and David were surprised to see me and Dad. David, too, showed me what he had got while I was gone. We told each other what we had done. Both of us were proud of our story. Best of all, we each had air guns now; we wouldn't have to share his. We had a target shooting, and he shot better, because I had to learn how to shoot mine. He had had his for a long time.

After we returned to Gambell from camp in that same year that I was nine, the school teacher and the health nurse talked to my parents and Akoak. They said that we were too crowded in Akoak's house and that it was not too good for our health because we were both big families. But how could we find a home? We were poor and couldn't buy a house or the lumber to build one. The school teacher was willing to help us. He said he would ask the owner of the tiny house where we live, and said he would let us know what he found out. After a few weeks we got a card from the owner of the house. He was willing to let us use and care for it for five years and after that he would tell us what he wished to do with it. That was very good news for me, because I always wanted to live in a home of our very own. It was all right for our parents too, but in another way not very good, because in our ways brothers are supposed to live together, help each other and share everything they have and get, and teach their children to do the same. We had been doing that. But as long as the ways and things are changing we'll have to live by the new ways.

We found the house was very much out of shape and needed lots of repair and cleaning. Napartuk and his boys had been using it as a dog house, so it was almost half full of dog mess, with no doors or windows that were not broken and no shingles on the roof, and everything out of shape, not a bit good for living in it. But it was the only house we could have. First we tried to clean it. Raymond Napartuk helped us with the cleaning, because they had gotten it in that condition. We started gathering the dog mess with shovels and hauled it away in wheelbarrows. Then we scrubbed. I did my part by getting water for the scrubbing. Mom and Dad did the scrubbing. It was very hard work bringing the two buckets of water with a yoke, but I kept on. I wanted to be in my own home. David liked it too, but he said he would always visit me when he came around, and so he did. He liked to help, too, but he had things to do for his own parents.

We gathered whatever we could get from the store, and some people helped us with a few pieces of boards and nails or other things like that. But mostly it was scrap material. That was by far not enough, but it was good enough for us. Napartuk lent his tools for us to use until we got through with the house. We moved into it much before it was finished— as soon as it was clean enough and the windows were fixed; and we nailed a piece of roof paper over the door opening because the door was not fixed yet.

We had a little party. It was our way of house warming when we moved in—by calling in few of the neighbors and eating what my mom had prepared, and the neighbors brought in food. At the same time we were beginning to be Christian, so my father invited one of the church elders and had him read some scripture, and we had prayers before we ate our dinner. We all had a good time, but David and I were the happiest of all, I think. We called the poor little house our home from that time on.

Mom and I gathered some moss and filled bags with it for use as insulation to make our house warm. Sometimes I took care of my brothers, Douglas and Martin, while Ann got water or cooked a meal for us. Sometimes I helped my father. Still it was out of repair, because we didn't have enough to repair it with, but we liked it, as long as it was something to live in. Some people came to see how we were doing. Some laughed at us, but some others were glad we had a home to live in.

Bessie, my aunt,* was still living with us. She stayed with

* Nathan's father's unmarried sister.

57

Akoak until our home was ready and then she moved in, too. She often went to gather sea plants or sea weeds. I always would go along with her, or sometimes my sister, Ann, or David or his sister would come with us. We gathered all we could find and shared them when we got home. The sea plants were always good, especially when we got short of fresh food at summer time. We could use many kinds of sea plants. At other times I went with her when she would go to gather some greens on the mountain. Sometimes I helped her gather the greens and other times I just walked around to look at a place that was new to me, or to hunt for auklet eggs, or just play with other boys who had come with their mothers or big sisters. We boys came along with the women mostly to help them take back what they had gathered. We usually made a fire of twigs if there were any around, and made some tea or coffee. When the tea or coffee was ready we called the women to have a lunch. Then everybody would sit around the fire and spread their lunch on papers or flour sacks. Oh! That all was lots of fun.

In September of that same summer of my ninth year Bessie, my aunt, and her friend Betty Seuak were planning to go to the beach at the other side of the mountain for some sea plants—mostly for one kind, the kind that we call Oopa, which we like best. I asked them if I could come along with them, and they let me.

It was the first time I ever saw the place. It was about a mile east of Annatuk's camp, and was the longest walk I had ever had. We each carried a walrus hide bag on our back on the way to the place where we were going. It was very new to me, and I like seeing a place that I hadn't seen before. It was new to my aunt too, but Betty knew the way very well. She led us all the way. She told us the names of the places and about the other times she had gone to that place.

Most of the way was wet tundra, and muddy in some places. We got to the place while it was still morning. The beach was piled up with sea weeds and plants of all kinds. And it was low tide—just the time for gathering sea plants. We filled our bags full before noon. I'd been eating, even though they had told me not to eat, saying that I might get very thirsty because it is not good to walk with a heavy load. Betty showed us how to put some kind of sea weeds over the mouth of our bags and lace it up tight.

After resting a while we started to walk home. My bag was not too heavy at first, and I didn't have any trouble to keep up with the women. But after an hour or so my load was getting heavier. I didn't like the tundra. More and more they seemed to walk a little too fast now. I knew now that they had told me not to eat those plants for my own good. I got very thirsty. There was lots and lots of water, but it was too muddy to drink. My throat and mouth were as dry as a powder horn. My shoulders were sore from the strap of the bag; it seemed to eat in deeper at every step.

I was glad when we came to a large flat rock. The women stopped and sat on the rock. I threw myself on the rock. Betty told us to put our bags upside down, and when we did, some water ran out of the bags. It was a good thing for the extra weight to be removed that way. I looked at the women to see if they were tired, too. They were a bit sweating, but I thought I was more tired than they. My bag was smaller than theirs, but it was heavy for me now. Before I could rest my sore, tired shoulders, we were on our way. I felt a little better after the rest, but not for long. When we got to the dry ground it was at least better, for we were out of the muddy tundra.

Our next rest was at the other end of the lake. As soon as I got my bag off I asked to take a drink of water. Bessie said, "Yes, but take just a little." I got down on my stomach and drank. Best tasting water I ever had. But I took only a little, as Bessie said. They drank some tea. I felt a little cooler after a short rest, and then we were on our way again. After one more rest we made it to the village.

A short way from the village my sister, Ann, came running to meet us. She took my bag and told me that I had missed the first day of school, showing me the papers she had written at school. She said they had had lots of fun and the teacher had passed out some candy and cookies and other good things. She had saved some for me. I was sorry I had missed the first day of school, because I hadn't attended the first day of school in all my life. But I had had fun enough that day, anyway, and was tired, too.

From that time on I and my sister kept on going to school. I wanted to get something out of school. In the last part of October of that same year my Dad was preparing to go back to Southwest Cape, but this time I and Ann and Aunt Bessie were to stay at Gambell in our tiny little house. My teacher had been talking to my Dad and me to ask if I would stay for school until at least after Christmas. I liked to do that and my Dad agreed. Dad, Mom, and my brothers left the last part of the month. Kazighia and Otto Kogoyak went along with them as his helpers.

After they had left, the house was very empty and too quiet. I felt left behind for a while, but not for long. Bessie, my aunt, was engaged to Louis Kogoyak by then, so I'd come to know Herbert and Joanna Kogoyak besides. Herbert was my classmate. My classmates told me about the coming Thanksgiving day and Christmas. Best of all, they told me about some toys and other good things we would get on Christmas from the Junior Red Cross. There would be a package for me if I stayed long enough for Christmas. So I was eager to be present at the Holidays. I was happy in school, but I wasn't too happy when the older guys were bullying around with us, and when it was a hard time in spelling and math. Even though I missed my brothers, I had fun with the other boys and girls my age—without the bother from little ones to take care of. Almost every day there was a group of us in my home. I invited a few for lunch quite often.

On Saturdays I often spent the day working, getting ice from the lake for water, almost enough for a week, or shoveling the snow around our house. On some Saturdays all of us walked along the beach looking for sea weeds and plants. My Dad made trips quite often from the camp for supplies and other things. Every time he asked me if I would like to go back with him. I still wanted to stay for Christmas. Every time after he left I wished a little bit that I might go with him, but I didn't say so. I liked it very much in school and at home now. School was more fun now, because we had a party at Halloween which I thought was big fun. I hadn't been at any kind of party before, so the first one I went to was the best I could have, and the happiest too.

Then came Thanksgiving, my very first holiday, I think. We had a party at school for that. We had some games and the school room was decorated with turkeys, Indians, and pictures of Pilgrims. I didn't understand very much what it was for, but I had a good time. Then came the Thanksgiving service at the church. To me it was like the other service, except there was more than one speaker. I was a little disappointed. I thought I was going to see lots of new things. But one more excitement was coming on anyway—the Thanksgiving dinner. One of the speakers had announced it was to be that evening and that we were to bring our own cups and spoons. Right after the service I and my sister shined the cups and spoons. While we were doing that, my Dad arrived from the camp. I was very glad he came in time for the dinner. I was glad because I could send something for Mom and my brothers. Bessie was to get some food, because she had been cooking with the other women. My Dad had brought some fresh meat and fox furs to trade at the store.

Now for the dinner. The bell rang and we were in the school. Desks and chairs had been cleared and we sat on the floor in rows. I and Dad sat with the other men and boys. When everybody was seated Seuak said a few words concerning the dinner at the same time as the girls were passing around some paper plates and forks. The people were murmuring and making too much noise, and it was too warm in the room. I was glad we had sat near a window that was open. Some fresh air coming through the window smelled and felt very good. Soon the dinner was served. There was some bread, reindeer meat, and doughnuts and fruit. I didn't feel like eating, because it was too crowded and the people looked at me too much. I ate a little and Ann saved my dinner and what we had left, and later I ate my dinner at home. But somehow it was new and full of fun. There was a movie later that evening too. I liked that part of the holiday best.

It seemed to be just a little while after Thanksgiving when

December came. On the very first day back in school after Thanksgiving something new happened. We didn't work on regular school work. We talked about the Christmas program. Our teacher told us of her plans for the program, and it all sounded very interesting to me and very new. She gave us each something to memorize. Mine was not a very long one, but I also had a verse or two to learn at the Sunday School to be said at the Church Christmas program. So I didn't learn them quickly. A few days later the girls were sewing on our costumes and we boys worked on making other things to be used in the Christmas program. At other times we practiced singing songs. I was not as interested in singing as in the other work.

Somehow I was good in learning my pieces to read, so I was asked to act in two scenes. We were all so busy the school hours ran by. They used to drag sometimes before. Our teacher told us boys to come back in the evenings to work some more on the thing we were making. No one said no; we were all glad to come. That all was lots of fun. But at the same time I was almost just as unhappy. How was I going to get presents for my friends and relatives? What would I wear on the day? I had no good clothing. Days were slipping by and the big day was not far now. Maybe the clothing that I wore every day would be good enough when I washed it real good, and the nice reindeer fur boots my Aunt Bessie was making for me to put on. Those would be plenty good enough for me, along with three or four packages for my best friends. Yet I was sad (or bashful) when my classmates talked about what they were going to wear, or how many packages they would have to pack for their friends. Some of them even asked what I was going to wear, or how much I had to do in packing. I just said I didn't know, and turned away. Some looked sorry when I said that, but some others laughed at me. So I kept away from talking about clothing and presents.

Some of those persons kept on talking about the package of things we were going to get from the Junior Red Cross. One of them even told me that he had packed one for me, too. I asked what it was, and if it was really true, but he only said, "Some good things," and that he couldn't tell. I wasn't sure but what he might be telling me that so I would be disappointed and he could make fun of me.

David asked me to come to his place and say our pieces to each other. I liked that, so we did it almost every night. Somehow his parents gave me a funny feeling one night. They looked at me a little too much and whispered something to each other. I wondered what they were saying, or what they were up to.

Sometimes I wished I had gone to camp with my Dad. But I was having fun at other times, mostly at school. I was to see what Christmas was like. I had just heard about it before. Another thing I liked was keeping secrets about what we were going to do in the program. I liked to keep secrets and use them as surprises later. We didn't even let anybody in the other school room know what we were to be doing in the program. They did the same to us.

A week or so before the big day my aunt finished the boots she was making for me. Boy, I liked them! I felt very proud. At least I was going to have nice boots, which were as good as those of any of the boys who made fun of me. But I told no one of them yet. Ann, Aunt Bessie, and I were all busy. Aunt Bessie was making something to trade to the store so she could get a present. Ann took over all of the housework, and I was busy with other things and school work. I very often thought of my Dad and Mom and brothers now. Sometimes I longed to go back to camp.

At last it was only two days before the school's Christmas program. We had decorated the school room and had been helping the big boys fix the platform. After we finished the platform, we came home and were planning to pack what little we had for presents.

While we were having our dinner we heard the dogs barking. I knew what caused them to bark—it was my Dad coming in from Southwest Cape. I looked out to see if it was him. Sure enough, there was his lead dog at the front of the door. I helped him unharness the dogs and bring out the dog feed. I always had dog feed ready on hand for this purpose. While he was feeding the dogs, I unbound the load on his sled, with happiness in and outside of me. There was a big piece of reindeer meat with plenty of fat on it. Oh boy! We are going to have some tonight! And there was a bag of something soft and light which I hoped for so much if it was what I thought (fox skins). With them we could get some presents for my friends and relatives and get something for ourselves, too, because we were running out of groceries. We even had had to go for a few days without coffee and tea and sugar.

But that wasn't all I was happy for. I was happy because my Dad would see me in the program now. He told us that Kenneth Nagotak had come with him; he was at Akoak's house. I liked him around, too, so he could see the Christmas. I wished that Mom and my brothers and cousins were there, too.

We got back to our dinner. We had some frozen raw reindeer meat and fat. Boy! That was good. As we ate, Dad told us what they had done and caught. They had caught many foxes and seals.

I told him all about us. Finally he said, "I used more dogs this time. I expect to have more, too, on my going back trip. Are you going back with me?"

Of course my answer was, "Yes, I'm going this time."

He said, "If you want to go next time, that will be all right, too, because I have to take quite a few other things."

"I still want to go this time."

Then he said again, "Is it okay with your teacher?"

I hadn't thought of that before, so I answered that I would ask him.

After dinner we opened the bag. Oh boy! It was almost full of fox fur. He rested a while and then we went to the store. The little store was overcrowded, but we pushed through and were pushed back a few times ourselves. At last we got to the counter. We got what we wanted, but it wasn't as much as I wished for. But we got our arms full and I had to come back for the rest of what we got by trading the fox furs. Now I had something to pack for my friends and relatives.

The next day was just a day before the school Christmas

program. We rehearsed almost all day. During the rehearsal David told me that his Dad wanted to see me right after school. He was smiling and looked happy when he told me, but he didn't tell me anything else. I had been suspecting that his father was up to something. I was worried about what he was going to do. Was he going to punish me for something? I feared him more than my Dad because he was more rough when we did wrong than my Dad, even though he was good and gentle. So I went to him that afternoon.

When we went into the house, Margaret [Akoak's wife] was taking something out of an old trunk and Rachel and Lydia [Akoak's daughters] were busy packing gifts. Akoak was doing something else. Margaret put back something she was taking out of the trunk and closed the lid as soon as she saw us. Akoak looked up and said, "Come here before we go to the program tomorrow—be sure to come."

I said, "Yes," but I still wondered what they were going to do with me.

At last the big day came. As the first thing in the morning, I took to school with me the bag of packages we had packed. There was a big pile of packages in the school office already. Two men were sorting it out. The Southsiders' packages [i.e., people living on the south side of the village] went to one room, and Northsiders' went to the other room.* We had the final rehearsal that morning. This time everybody in the school was present to watch the program. It was the very first time I had appeared before the others. I was very nervous already. On the singing part it was all right, because we sang in a group, but my voice was very low. My legs were shaking a little. The room seemed to be warmer than usual. Every eye looked on me. I was very glad that some others had a strong voice. It was lots better to watch the others in their part of the acting, and lots of fun, too. Then when the scene that I was included in very suddenly came, I was struck with some

* This distinction between "Northsiders" and "Southsiders" made little sense in terms of the Eskimo kinship system and residence patterns. Although it was true that clansmen tended to live in close proximity with each other, the division of the village into two parts (a division apparently started by the teacher) tended to split some of the clans and in other cases lump together people from antagonistic clans (see Hughes, 1960).

kind of strange feeling. I could hear the beating of my heart above every other noise. I was sure it would thrust out of my chest very soon. I was shaking and the floor seemed to shake under me. Before I knew it, I was on the platform with the others. I sweated in my face and was cold on other parts. It was very hard to keep myself still. My legs trembled with nervousness when my turn came to say my part. I couldn't find the words to say that I had learned so well. Not a sound came out of my throat. Then at what seemed to be a voice—speaking right behind my head—I almost whirled around to see who was speaking. But at the same time I came to myself, and it was my own voice. I said the last sentence at too long last. I walked to the other side, much surprised and relieved. I could breathe easier now. But I still would have to go in another scene, and the worse was yet to come, when the people would come to watch in the afternoon.

I wished I didn't have to be in the program. I should have been at the camp. But I was very excited and happy, scared and anxious in one way, yet partly proud. I always feel proud when I have a new experience.

At the end of the rehearsal both of our teachers said we all had done very good. They said that they wanted us to do as well when the people came in. "Keep in your mind that we'll be very proud and happy if you do your parts nicely. Above all, make the people happy, especially your parents. They will want you to be good in doing your parts."

As we went out of the school, David told me to come over to his home before the program. "Oh no, what in the world are they going to do?" But if I didn't come, his father would be fiercer than a wounded wild animal, so I would rather come before he got mad.

The program for the Northsiders was to be in the late afternoon and in the evening for the Southsiders, so my folks were coming in the evening.

A couple hours before the time, I put on my newly washed clothing and my pretty new reindeer fur boots. I walked and stamped around the floor and felt real happy. But I was going to my uncle to face him in whatever he was going to do. I said a prayer of some kind as I went in through the

66

outer door. I hesitated a moment or two before I dived into the room under the reindeer fur curtain. They were having some tea. Everyone looked very happy; all of their faces shined with beams. There was a cup of tea ready for me. But I still felt a bit like a stranger.

After tea, Uncle told David to stand before him. I wondered all the more what was coming up. He looked him over and said, "Dirty behind the ears and finger nails; hair has to be combed real good."

It was my turn to stand and he looked and said, "Clean, but hair too long. If you don't want to have pigtails, I'll have to cut it."

He clipped it quickly while David was being washed (with the help of his sisters). I thought he just wanted to see that we were washed and ready to appear before the people, but the best was yet to come.

After I was brushed and washed, Margaret got a big cardboard box for me, and one for David, too. Uncle told us then, "Those are for being such good boys, and I want both of you to do your best in the program." He meant I and his own children. "Now put those on."

Then we opened our boxes. I couldn't believe my eyes for a while. What did I find in there? The most beautiful brown suit I have ever seen in all my life—and there was a blue one for David. I thought I had the best uncle in all the world. They helped us dress up. I couldn't even know how to begin to thank them. Oh, how good the suit looked! How comfortable they were, and they just fitted too!

David and his sisters, Rachel and Lydia, and I went to the school some time ahead of the time for the program, as we should. The desks and chairs had been cleared out of one room. There was a whole roomful of happy, heartful school people making lots of noise, with laughter and all kinds of cheer. All wild and completely out of control. The older folks were trying to calm down the light-hearted and too much delighted smaller children. Too much noise and too wild for me for the few first minutes.

As soon as we pulled off our parkas the other children gathered all around us and "Ohed" and "Ohed." I felt proud all right, and somehow I felt funny; they hadn't done this to me before. I hadn't been in such good clothes before. I tried hard to smile but couldn't find a word to say. I just stood there and looked around shyly. Suddenly I noticed something that made me have enough to talk about and join the wild crows. Those who had been laughing at my clothing before tried to keep away from me, and those who had seemed to feel sorry for me cheered and danced around us and sounded very glad. I tried to make friends with them, and I did.

Without a single bit of notice our turn to act came. So suddenly it came, it almost scared me right out of my skin. When we got on the platform, oh, what a sight! A whole sea of faces and about a hundred pair of eyes looked at me. "Oh no! What could I do?" I felt like I was in a flame of fire, sweat running up and down my neck, but at the same time I felt a strange kind of chill shooting up and down my back. My legs had no more feeling. Suddenly I thought I heard a little voice speaking in my ear, saying, "I want you to do your best in the program." I tried hard to gather myself and my turn came to speak. Somehow I felt good and relaxed. The words came into my head some way and out my mouth. When the last person had spoken his or her piece, and after we bowed to the people, there was a clapping of hands so loud it drove us swiftly to the other room. I got through it better in my next act. The program lasted about three hours. We would have to go through it all over again, but it was going to be the last time. And this time it was going to include my folks and Uncle Akoak.

The teachers let us out before the next program for about an hour. I just ran over to Akoak's to pick up my old clothing and then to my house as fast as my legs could carry me. I rushed in to show what I was wearing. I threw down the bundle of duds I was holding without saying a word, and threw off my parka. Nobody said anything. We just looked at each other with our mouths open wide. Then all at once everyone said, "Those are real nice."

I answered them, "From Uncle Akoak. David has them, too."

Then I told them the time and told them to be there before

the seats were taken. I saw that Ann had a nice dress, too. She had made it at school by herself. And she had nice boots on.

A cup of tea, and I rushed on to school. This time the school was overcrowded and everybody was squeezed very tightly, but I got through my acts all right. I did the very best I could do, though I felt better than the first. The program seemed to be longer—but more fun, too, and then it was over finally. The Northsiders stayed in one room and the Southsiders came into the other. I was a little tired when we sat around the room after the performance. Then some boys passed around the gifts; they handed a few to me. I could hardly wait to open them. Last of all they passed around some packages to all the school pupils from the Junior Red Cross. There was one for me, too. The guy who told me he had wrapped the package handed it to me. He said, "I hope you'll like them." The teacher said a few words, and then we were going home at last.

We went out into the dark and cold but clear night. The night air smelled very fresh. There were stars twinkling all over the sky above, and flashlights shone brightly. We sang the Christmas songs that we'd sung in the school. They sounded sweeter in the cool, calm night air. Oh my! I think that was the best night in all my life and the Merriest Christmas I ever have had.

The next day it was December 25. I and Dad talked to my teacher about whether he would let me go back to camp. He said that he wished to keep me in school, but would let me go if I wanted to go badly. I did. Dad said we would go, but that I'd have to come back for the boxes of things I got and the box from the mission which we were to get that evening.

There was the Christmas service in the church. The church was very beautifully decorated. There was a program, too, but entirely different from the school program. I was in a singing group and had a verse to read with the other Sunday School children. I felt very much like I did in the school program, but I was a little better.

There was a nativity scene acted by some adult people. I

didn't much understand what that meant, but I knew it had a very deep meaning and it was very strange but very beautiful to me. I thought that those who were acting it were very important persons—that they had been chosen for the scene and that if I ever grew up I'd be an actor for the nativity, too.

The choir sounded real good, indeed. I thought there were no songs so good as those carols. Then all was over too soon. It passed so quickly. The packages were passed around, and after the packages came the mission boxes. The boxes I had always longed for before. I learned how we got it from our church but still don't know where they come from.

This all was fun but not as much as I had in the school program. But I thought it was far more beautiful and I felt happier, too, in some way that my words can't tell.

When we got home we opened our presents and Ann and Bessie opened their boxes from the mission. They found some things they liked and passed around some popcorn and nuts and candy. Oh! How good they were. I and Dad didn't see what we had in our box; only Ann and Bessie saw theirs. I planned it that way, because I wanted to share the surprise with my folks back at the camp.

We were very busy getting ready for the trip that was going to be the next morning. I put away my beautiful suit, because I didn't need it at the camp. As we were putting the things that we were going to take with us in some boxes, Akoak came in to tell us he was going, too. He was going to do some trapping at our camp, and help us with our extra load. Now we could take all our needed things. Kenneth was getting ready, too.

He and I took some boxes over to his house so we wouldn't have to do that in the morning. David and his sisters were surprised to know that I was going back to camp with Akoak and Dad. I hadn't told them about this until then. They all said, "Why are you going to leave school?" I told them I wanted to go home badly now.

I got back to our house and finished my packing. Like other times, I couldn't sleep that night. I worried that the weather might not be good for the trip and we would have to stay. At the same time I was anxious to go home again.

Like other times, I'd told my folks the evening before to wake me up early.

The night seemed to be long and too quiet; the minutes lengthened to hours. I listened to the ticking of the clock, with its hand seeming to stay in one place all night. I tried to look at some magazine, but my thought wouldn't turn on anything and kept on being anxious and worried about every little sound around, like wind blowing.

I did not need to be wakened up. I started to prepare breakfast an hour or so too early than it should have been when I couldn't stand the slowest moving of time. I couldn't wait any longer for morning to come. I looked out for the hundredth time to make sure the weather was good. I looked out through the little round clear space I made on the glass by blowing on the frost. It was dark, but the stars were twinkling and there was no snow blown by the wind, so I thought it was calm and clear.

Maybe it was four o'clock when I woke my folks when the breakfast was ready. My Dad asked, "Why wake up so early? It's only four o'clock."

I told him about the weather. Then he said, "All right. I think it is better than to hurry."

After breakfast Aunt Bessie put our lunch in a paper sack and a can and filled our thermos bottles with tea. I put my sealskin pants over my reindeer skin ones and the boots that Aunt Bessie had made for Christmas. I wore two parkas, one over the other. The outer one had the fur side out, which was brown and white without a snowshirt.

Dad told me to go out and check on Kenneth and Uncle Akoak. They were having breakfast. Akoak told us to go ahead and start when we were ready. David handed me a package and told me not to open it until I got home. "Be sure not to open it." And he said it was from him and his sisters. I tried to run home but my clothing was too heavy and stiff.

My Dad wanted to wait a while for the others, so we waited for almost an hour before we harnessed our dogs and strapped our load to the sled. Quite a while before daybreak we were on our way at last. We were the first ones to start. I found out that our dogs ran better than before. They pulled the sled faster than they had before, and I was really glad for that.

It was still dark when we stopped at Kazighia's camp so that Kenneth and Akoak could catch up with us. I half wished that we could go on, but at the same time I was interested to look around the cabin. I looked all around the cabin but didn't look inside. I didn't feel like doing that for anything— in the dark. I was scared to do so.

When I got tired of looking around, I came back to the sled. Dad was walking back and forth beside it. We waited a long time, but nobody came. The day was breaking in from the east. The Savoonga mountains and Mount Taphok were silhouetted against the dim light of daybreak. Above, the stars were shining brightly all over the sky and the air smelled cool and very fresh. Once again I was touched by the beauty of nature.

All the while I thought of Uncle Akoak and cousin Kenneth as slow pokes. When they didn't show up for an hour or so Dad got tired of waiting, too. So he started the dog team again. We were to wait for them farther inland. I watched the mountains showing clearly against the clear blue-green sky as the daylight grew brighter. My Dad pointed out the way we were to take and told me the names of the places. He told me that I would be traveling by myself in time to come and it was the time to study the way now—all that I could learn.

Finally we stopped on top of a hump to wait for the others. I stood up and looked all around and tried hard to study the places, but what drew my interest most was the wild beauty of the surrounding, which was covered with white snow. Spotless white country, which seemed to have no end at all.

Again we waited a long time. This time Dad showed me how to use the compass that we always take along whenever we go on a long trip. I thought the compass just pointed out the village or the camp. For the first time I learned that it points to the north at all times and we have to figure out the way by it, not just follow it. He said that it is the most precious instrument for traveling.

It was complete daylight now after more than an hour of waiting. We saw two black specks moving along, just leaving the shoreline and coming toward us, so we thought it was them. We waited for them until they were quite close and then we started on again. For a while they were within sight, but we stopped again before they were too far behind. We saw that we had a better team of dogs than theirs. This time we let them catch up. We let their dogs rest for a while before we went on. Kenneth and I talked about good times we had had the past two days until Dad and Uncle Akoak called, "Let's go." So we went on again for a mile or so.

Kenneth and Akoak kept up with us, and then they fell off behind again. We let them catch up before they were too far behind this time, and Dad told them that we would wait for them at the place where we would have lunch. We went on. Again they lagged behind, but not too far. We came to the place where we were to stop for lunch. I recognized the place where we always stop for lunch on our way to the village or the camp, right beside a hill among the mountains. Kenneth and Akoak were not far behind, but still we waited a while for them.

It was afternoon when we started out again and the days were at their shortest, so it was getting dark before we got to the camp. It was snowing lightly. Finally there was a light ahead of us shining brightly from the window. The good old camp at last! The barking of the dogs brought out Mom. I didn't feel like helping with the dogs, but still I had to. I wanted to go right in to see my brother, but I had to help Dad and Uncle first. As I was trying to unharness the big dog I heard somebody call me. I looked up and saw two figures coming toward me in the dark. I didn't see well enough to see who they were. But they came right up. They were Marian and Debby, my cousins, and the next thing I knew we were having bear hugs.

At last the dogs were done and the boxes we brought were taken in. I dived in under the reindeer skin curtain that was the entrance to the warm room. Oh! How brightly the seal oil lamps burned. I squinted and blinked. There was another round of bear hugs. This with my brothers, Douglas and Martin. They tugged on my heavy fur parka as I tried to pull it off. Then my seal skin pants. Oh! How good and warm it felt to be at home again, because this was more home to me than the one in the village.

The happiest time came after supper. It was the opening of the boxes we had brought. First they opened what we had brought and then came the most liked mission box. We were all anxious to see what was in it, including my Uncle Akoak. There was a picture puzzle, towels, some clothing, toys, such as a coloring box and crayons, jacks, candy, nuts and popcorns, and books to look at, plus the package that I got from David Akoak and his sisters. Then there were red yarn mittens, socks, and some good things to eat.

The next few days were happy ones, like the other Christmas we had had. I had lots to tell my folks about the Christmas I had had in the village. For a few days I didn't feel like working. I worked just a little, but most of the time I played and looked around the camp. Some evenings Akoak and I worked on some picture puzzles, and he helped me read the book I got from the school, and do a little bit of arithmetic just so I wouldn't forget what I had learned at school. When all the excitement faded away, I started on trapping and the other things I used to do.

# 4. War

During that winter when I was back in camp from the village, my Dad finished his new sled and the old one was so fully broken that Uncle Nagotak used some parts of it to repair his old sled. When he had taken all he wanted from that old sled, he left the runners still on it; both of the wood runners were broken so they were about four feet long, with one longer than the other. The steel parts were still on it, but not good for any use. I looked it all over, and it gave me an idea. Those runners would make a good pair of skis if I took them off and did a little work on them, but I knew Dad wouldn't let me use our tools for such things.

One day he made a trip to the village. He and Akoak and Kenneth. Uncle Nagotak wouldn't say anything if I used the tools. He even had given me some junk to play with, such as old outboard motor parts or a very old rusty rifle or shot gun. To me those were the best of all my toys, so I played with them more than any of my things.

Well, my Dad was gone, the tool box was all to myself now, so I took out a hammer, hacksaw, and a cold chisel, and I took off the runners from the old sled. I bent up the steel part of them, rolled them up in the front, nailed pieces of boards the size of my feet in the middle of the runners and as the last thing, I fixed straps of an old harness. Now I had a pair of skis. "Lots of fun awaits me," I thought.

I put away the tools hastily and ran out with my skis. I strapped them on my feet and tried to move. All at once, before I knew it, I landed on my back. I started to get up. Very much surprised, the next thing I did was a nose dive. Picked myself up again. Oh boy! That was the biggest fun. When I wanted to go one way, my skis went the other way and I fell to one side then, or the other. Then on my back and then a dive—but who cares? This was lots of fun. Besides, I could learn if I kept at it. I got hurt sometimes, but it didn't hurt much. I went right on again. "It will be all right in a while," I always thought.

I took them off to rest for a while when I got tired. I stood up and saw Debby Nagotak laughing very hard at me. I didn't like that much, but she came to me and begged to try. I knew what would happen, so said, "Yes," and helped her put them on her feet. She hung on to me for a little, but I let her go all at once and she fell and landed on her nose. I couldn't help her now—I was laughing too hard to help. She ran home, crying, as soon as she got them off her feet. That was what I had wanted, so that she wouldn't bother me.

I was proud of them, because I'd made them and proved how to use them, too. I thought of another way to use them— sliding down the hills. So I took them on my shoulder to the smoothest hill. The snow was soft all the way down. I chose that one so I wouldn't get hurt too hard or too soon. I'd learned a little from the first falls; it hurt some when I fell on hard snow. I strapped them on once more on top of a hill. As I attempted to slide down, I landed on my back, half-buried in the soft, fluffy snow. I tried to get up, but I fell back to the same position again. I sure was surprised! I tried and tried, but all the way down I repeated the same thing. I finally got on my feet and slid a little bit. This time my skis crossed one upon the other, and the next thing I knew I was struggling to get my face out of the snow. When I finally got up I found myself at the foot of the little hill, the snow way up to my sleeves, in my mittens, melting on my face and running down my neck. I looked up the hill, brushing the snow off my face and ruff. I saw I had made funny tracks all the way down. As I looked at the tracks which I had made, a story came into my mind that I had learned in school. Oh what funny little tracks in the snow! I did that over and over again all day, until I was all tired out. At last I got too tired and hungry and was beginning to be cold. I unstrapped my skis and started to walk home. My clothing was wet and started to freeze at some parts. I put my skis away carefully so nothing could happen to them.

When I got in, Mom was cooking some meat. Oh boy! It smelled very good. At the same time I remembered I hadn't eaten anything all that day since breakfast. They had been calling for me, but I hadn't heard them. The smell of the food made me more hungry, and it felt so good in the warm room that I was sleepy as I ate the good supper.

The next day Uncle Nagotak saw me trying to ski. He came to me and said, "Oh, you have made yourself good things to get hurt with." I think he meant that he didn't want me to be hurt, but I didn't feel too good about that. It didn't sound good.

When Daddy came back, he and Akoak tried to stop me, but Kenneth was interested in them, too. I am ashamed to say that none of them stopped me. I just kept on doing it whenever I got time to ski—that is, when all of them were absent. Soon I learned a little better how to use them. After a long time I could ski on level places and down the sloping small hills. As for Debby and Marian Nagotak, they enjoyed using them when I was away or didn't have time for them. Debby tied them together side by side and used them as sort of a narrow toboggan. Surprisingly, they were very good. Marian could ski a little. Kenneth was as good as I was. At first he did a happy landing like I did. At last they all quit trying to stop me and instead they liked to watch me. All they could do was to tell me not to do it on steep hills or in dangerous places.

On very windy days I had lots of fun on those skis. I sailed with them, using a piece of old walrus hide as a sail. The first try wasn't so good, though. I got up toward the strong north wind with my skis on my shoulder and tugged a piece of cardboard. At first I went slowly, but then I went faster and faster—at last as fast as I could. How could I slow down or stop? Before I could do anything (or I was too scared to do anything), I smashed against the house. I got up, trying hard to hold back my tears. There were sharp pains in my nose, lips, foot, and knee. The straps on one of the skis was broken. That was a good thing, for I would have sprained my ankle. My nose was bleeding and, spitting blood, I limped around the house to the door. I met my father at the door coming out. He asked me what had happened, but I couldn't speak. There was a big lump in my throat. I just went in and had them wash away the blood. I learned that my lip was broken and I had bruised my knee.

Dad found my skis at the back of the house and knew what had happened, so he came in and told me that that was what

I wanted and desired, that he had warned me enough. He was not a bit sorry, he said. "That's what you get out of disobeying us." I guessed so, too, but it was not enough to stop me. Soon I was skiing again; it was too good to quit.

On another windy day I tried again. This time I walked up farther. I strapped them on, held up the piece of walrus hide, and was on my way again. I gathered up some speed. Before it was too fast, I let go of the sail. But I fell on my back. It hurt some, but not so bad as if I hadn't let go. Later on I learned better, but I still was not so good. It was lots of fun anyway.

I didn't want anybody else other than the folks in the camp to see those skis. I thought they were too funny for anybody else to see. So when there was somebody from the village, the first thing I did was to push those skis into the hole under the floor where they would be hidden.

The rest of the winter was very much same as any other and nothing much happened as far as I can remember, except I got letters from David and Lydia Akoak and little packages of dried fruit and things like that from Ann and Bessie, my aunt. But one day early in March, after a long windy storm, it was a clear calm morning, and my Dad had gone out early to check on the weather. Maybe he and Uncle Akoak were to make a trip to Gambell on that day? Akoak and I were drinking our breakfast tea when Dad came in very much delighted. He said there were some dark spots on the edge of the shore ice. "I think they are walrus or something; I didn't see them clear enough in the dim light."

We just pulled on our parkas and rushed out. Sure enough, they were there, less than a mile out. When there was enough daylight to see, they made sure they were walrus. We saw them through telescopes and binoculars. As soon as they made sure they were walrus, Dad, Nagotak, and Akoak took out their rifles, leather ropes, and harpoons (with many heads). They were going out to shoot them.

Just as before, I went to Dad and asked him if I might come along. His answer was not good at all. He said, "You don't have to; we don't need you. What could you do?"

I said, "I just want to watch and join the fun."

He said, "No, you might cause some trouble. You can watch from here."

Uncle Akoak added, "You can use my telescope" (which he would not let us touch at other times). That made me feel better, but there was sadness filling up my heart. As I turned away I could feel that lump coming up in my throat.

"When am I going to be grown up?" I thought. "I'm going to show those fools some day that I'm not a baby." Well, like I always do, I obeyed; I thought that was best thing to do.

I watched them walk away in line, one behind the other. Nagotak in the lead, then came Akoak and last of all, Dad. Nagotak was the oldest, next to him Akoak, and Kakianak, my Dad, was the youngest. I wondered why they walked that way? They all carried their own rifles and harpoons or ice tester poles. I watched them with very hard feelings. I went into my cousins' house to talk to them and ease my feelings.

We talked for a while as Debby and Marian dressed. When they were through, we went into the warehouse to get Nagotak's telescope and we looked at everything through it. After a while Marian and Debby went back into the house when they were called to do their chores, so I had the telescope all to myself. The men had told me they would wave if they killed a walrus. The telescope was a powerful one, so I saw that there were five walruses. I promised myself while I watched that I'd go after walrus in a short time—my feelings were turned from bad to good now. They were quite close to the game now, and I kept my scope on them every little moment. They were walking carefully, keeping low. Boy! They looked sort of funny that way, dropping down and lying still when the walrus stirred, and then on again. Now they took their positions, resting their rifles on the piled ice.

Suddenly some of the walrus slid into the water, but two of them lay motionless. One of the men stood up and waved both arms toward me. I jumped up and ran into the warehouse, almost dropping the precious telescope, and then ran on to tell the good news to my folks. First I poked my head in my cousins' door and shouted. "They got them! They got them," and I then rushed to ours, ran up the little stairs, dived in under the curtain, and poured out the good news. Debby, Marian, and I went back to watch them as they butchered the walruses.

When they finished and started to come back, I told my folks to have lunch ready. When they were down on the beach I skied down to meet them. There was not a bit of my hard feelings left; just watching them was being with them. I found out they had killed three walruses, but one had slid into the water and sunk.

I and Marian started harnessing the dogs while they had their lunch. Kenneth came in from his traps just as they were leaving to go for the meat. He had a hasty lunch, and then he, too, went after them. He was real sorry that he had gone to his traps too early for the hunt, but he brought in three or four foxes, one of them Dad's.

While they were all gone, I got lots of dog feed because they'd need it that night. They went back for more after each trip while we cut up the meat into smaller pieces and brought it into the house. That was lots of meat.

In two or three days they had brought in all the meat. The next day after that they all went back again. I didn't know why they were going back; they said they had brought in all the meat the day before. And they took a long time. Finally they came back all loaded with meat again, I ran down to meet the first team; it was Akoak. I asked if they had killed another walrus. He said, "No, we just retrieved the one that was sunk."

I thought he was kidding like he always did, but they had gotten the walrus—I saw the tusks on the sled. I was very much puzzled, but my Dad had some answers to my questions. I had wondered all that day if they really had retrieved the one that was sunk. But how? That evening at the supper I asked Dad, "Did you really retrieve the sunken walrus?"

He replied, "Yes. From where did we get the meat if you don't believe that?"

I asked, "But how, Dad? Did one of you dive down to get it?"

82

Then he and Uncle laughed out hard. I asked again, "Is that funny?"

They laughed more. Then my Dad said (when he could speak), "That's why we didn't want you along with us when we're going to shoot them—you would scare them with your funny actions."

At last I found the answer to my questions. They said, "We fished for it with a seal hook, not dived for it."

"But seal hooks don't sink; they float on the water."

They said again, "You will have to know lots of things before you can hunt with us. We tied a rock to it to make it sink." I thought they were really smart.

Not long after this Dad and Akoak took sled loads of meat to Gambell. Dad went to Camp Collier with his sled loaded, too. Ahigik was in that camp with his family. Dad returned on the same day; he had very good dogs at that time. Meanwhile we were getting ready for the trip to Gambell, since the closing of the trapping season was near.

Like other years, Mom was busy with our new clothing. The trip was no longer new, but still was kind of exciting to me. Nagotak and his family were to stay in the camp, but he was going to help us on the trip. Victor Kazighia, Louis Kogoyak, Akoak, Gordon Annanak also came to help. As was my duty, I helped them by taking care of the dogs, sleds, and all.

This time I rode with Victor. He took me right to our little house. There were David Akoak, Francis Oalateetak, Herbert Kogoyak, and Ralph Magpa to meet me in my house—my old school mates who had been writing to me all winter and sending me packages. Oh, we had lots of things to tell each other! Yet we didn't much hear from each other, because mostly we spoke all at the same time. Our little house was overflowing with visitors who wanted to welcome us. It was good to be with the old friends again.

Within a few days I was back in the good old school. I didn't feel too new, like I had the other times, but I found out I was way behind from my classmates. I felt a bit sorry, but the good teacher let me do a little extra work at home and I caught up not too long afterwards. The teacher might have put so much work on me that I would have had a hard time, but I got most of my work done with his help.

The time passed on quickly. Soon the spring hunting season came along just like in other years, and my desire to go out hunting was getting stronger. Just like the other times, I cared much less and less all the time about school.

The war with Japan and Germany was going on and they said we might be in danger; it was mostly rumor, but if it was rumor there was lots of it. The ATG's [Alaska Territorial Guard—a militia in which many Eskimos served] were started and trained. We were proud of them, the village's own soldiers. Of course I was going to be one of them as soon as I got old enough. Our school teacher gave out orders for everybody to have a bag of extra clothing and some food and other things we would need badly in case of evacuation, and so we did. I myself was too lively to worry much about war. I cared more for the thrill of the spring than wars, but to do something about that was a big thing and manly, so I wanted to be a soldier, too.

Before I knew it my birthday had passed by, so I think I was eleven years old now (but I don't remember exactly). It was in the spring of 1942, on a morning in the middle or last part of May. The snow was getting very soft and it was raining lightly. Somebody woke us up and told us that the village was evacuating. We dressed quickly and rolled our beddings. A sharp fear pricked me when I thought of my brothers, how the poor things will be when they get wounded, along with Mom, Dad, and Sis. I never cared for myself; I thought it would be a better thing if I got killed than to see other people wounded or to leave me half dead. I kept quiet, but I trembled as I helped the boys pull on their boots. Maybe all my folks felt the same way. My mother must have known my fears; she comforted and she calmed me. She herself was a brave little woman; she didn't show any fear at all. Then Dad and I hastened to harness our dogs. Mom and Sis loaded our stuff on the sled. The lake was spotted with dog teams and some people on foot. Robert Sakigak came around and told us to be calm, saying that there was nothing to be excited about, but we'd have to be out of the village. I was very

84

brave now, not because of this but because of my brave Mom. Dad went to check with Akoak and his family and others before we left. He came back and told us that Akoak and his folks had just left. We were going to Annatuk's summer camp on the other side of the mountain. I was glad to have a chance to see that place; I'd been just past it on trips to Savoonga.

I was amazed at how our sled could have room enough for so big a family. There were six of us in the family, I, Dad, Mom, Ann, Douglas, and Martin, plus our rolls of bedding, a big bag of clothing, a cardboard box of meat, a can of kerosene, a little tent, and a primus stove. But the strength of the dogs was more wonderful; they were pulling the overloaded sled and the runners were cutting deep into the soft snow, yet they seemed not to have any trouble. We took one more passenger on the way—that made seven of us, plus her small bag of belongings. She was Celia Angatok. I was glad that we had a little room for her, since she was weak and not well. She and somebody else had been resting on a little bare ground somewhere at the other end of the lake. They had got that far from the village and she was very tired. Another person I felt sorry for was May Akpalleapik. They didn't have a lead dog, so she was leading the team through the wet soft snow. I wished to help, but my family wouldn't let me separate from them. The ground was very wet and swampy, so it looked hard for those who were walking. I was no longer afraid now, but I felt a lot of sorrow for those who were having a hard time. I wished once more and for the rest of that time that I was old enough to be a man and help some of those people.

I was a little disappointed when we got to the camp. I expected it to be real nice. What a place! All wet, rocky, and muddy. The shore ice was still there. The water was coming down in streams almost everywhere, and where the snow was, it was soft, wet, and knee-deep or deeper. We were to stay in the cabin that belonged to Igalok. There was already a crowd of people in it, so we had to squeeze to get in. Then there were the Akoaks, the Sakigaks, Igaloks, Seuaks, and Danagiks. Some put up tents and some went to Kazighia's summer camp. There were David Akvak, Francis Oalateetak, Ralph and Christine Magpa and other playmates of mine, which made me feel happiness.

Dad was one of the ATG's, so he was to go back to the village. I wished that I could go, too, but it was too much for me to be one so I thought I would have to be a sissie and stay with the women and children. I helped Dad turn his dogs around. Oh! I wasn't feeling good. "Dad is going back to danger. What if he is killed or something happens to him?" This was the first test of danger and war I had had. It was not a bit good. I looked into his eyes in the silence of fear.

He looked back at me and finally said, "Be a man. Take good care of Mom and the children. Let nothing happen to them; take as good care as much as you can. I have to go back." He turned around and went without looking back.

That gave me something to think of and made me shake off my fear. For the first time he told me to be a man and for the first time I had been trusted. "A man, be a man—that's something great! And a family to take care of and protect! I haven't any weapon of any kind, but I'll do all I can"—those were my thoughts.

The cabin was really full. It was really a poor one, too. The floor was only muddy earth and very sloppy. One little bench to sleep on, a leaky roof, and not much light because of tiny windows. Besides that we had not much meat to eat, bad tasting water, and not much firewood to burn. It was cold at night, and my boots were badly soaked up as well as my other clothing. What a life! I got a little used to those hardships, but other troubles came up, such as homesickness and worry. And sometimes some boys teased and made fun of my brothers and caused me to have lots of hard feelings. Women quarreled among themselves. Those were not all good. At other times we had fun playing tag, or hide-and-seek, but the men kept a close watch on us and told us not to wander away, because of the danger. I'm sure the adults with us had a worse time than us; they had more worry than us, the children. They knew what danger meant better than us. To us it was mostly fun and would make heroes of us if we went through it. We were sure of ourselves.

Some of the ATG's (those with us) did some hunting on their off-duty. Some got birds, and one of them killed a seal and somebody else killed a mukluk. There was not much for everybody to eat, but it lasted a few days. We got a little bit of dried fruit and pilot bread sometimes, which was supplied by the store, but I wouldn't take my share, so that my brother would get enough. I had to be a man in our family, and I was responsible for them. I had better not let them go short on that.

We got the news from the village only once in a long while—whenever one of the ATG's got a few hours leave from their leaders and came to see his family in the refugee camp. But my father didn't come to see us. We only heard that he was all right and was too busy in his duty to come. I still was very much worried; they might be keeping back the truth. I got worried more and more, and at last I couldn't stand my worry, because I had had a few sleepless nights already.

One day we had a visitor. It was Edward Aiyaksaq. So we heard the news from the village. He said everything was fine, and that my Dad was okay, too. I begged him to take me in his dog team to the village, but he wouldn't, because children and women were not allowed in the village. So I was still in doubt about the news. But I had to be brave. I had a family under my care.

At last one day Robert Sakigak brought us good news when he was visiting his family once on a few hours leave from duty. He was one of the NCO's (non-commissioned officer) and a squad leader of the ATG's. Well, the news was too good to be true, maybe especially for a worried boy like me. It sounds funny when I think it over nowadays. The news this time—"There is no more danger, for a while, at least; our enemy has run out of bombs to drop." So we were all going back to the village as soon as it was made sure of. But they wanted to keep us in the camp a while longer just in case. My Dad also had sent some meat and other needed things by Robert. When I found out that my Dad was all right, I felt somewhat better but had still unhappiness to bear. As for Mom, she cheered up a little, because Robert was a sort of brother to her, a half-brother, but in the Eskimo customs that doesn't make any difference. So she trusted him for the news and words from Dad to be all true, and I believed she was glad to see him out of danger too.

Robert stayed with us and his family for a couple hours, maybe, and Mom sent words about us to Dad. He was still too busy in his duty to visit us. But he was hoping he might. I could have crossed my fingers for that, but I don't do such things. Instead, I breathed silent prayers whenever I paused from what I was doing, telling myself that my prayers would be answered, even though I didn't know much about religion and what it really meant. All I believed in was that religion is a sort of great magic power of all goodness; it would work for perfect persons.

All the while I was getting more sorry for my poor little brothers. They were getting dirty from rolling all over the muddy ground, and worse was that the older children made fun of them and made them cry often. Now I wished I could take the family to a nice quiet place! But that was too much to do, and the grown-up people wouldn't permit us to do it.

On some places the ground was free of snow and was getting dry. We were now permitted to take short walks in groups. We had some fun once in a while. It was the best part of the year; I mean the part I like the best. The hunting was supposed to be at its best, but most of it had passed already. On those short walks we played with the soft, clean moss, the first blades of grass, tiny buds of light green willow leaves and other greens. Sometimes we pulled up roots to eat, and that was fun, too. So I found some pleasure as well as gloom, worry, and hardship.

One morning it was just another day to bear. Aiyaksaq asked me to get some water for them. He told me to get the water from the shore ice (on top of the ice some fresh water gathers in puddles melted from snow). He told me to taste it first. I did as he told me, but my sense of tasting must have failed me, because when I tasted it by drinking some (a full cup), it tasted good and fresh. So I filled up the bucket and took it to their tent. As soon as the tea was ready Mrs. Aiyaksaq poured some in cups and I was the first one to drink. At the very first taste, I didn't like it. Funny, silly tasting tea; I'd got some salt sea water! How in the world did I taste it the first time? Or the boiling must have brought out the salt? Everyone of them looked at me as they sipped their cups. All the while I was trying to find some words to say. They might think I was joking with this, and that is not good to do. Finally I started slowly. "It was fresh when I filled the bucket." When I finished my words, everyone burst into merry laughter. I felt better, but still sorry, and they melted snow for water.

After our tea, I went back to the water to solve the mystery of the fresh water getting salty after I had tasted it. I tasted it once more. It was fresh! But how did it get salty in the bucket? I got more puzzled. Then I saw that a hole in the ice had melted down to the sea water. On top, the pool of water was fresh, but there was salty water at the bottom. I stirred it up and got salty water! I laughed to myself when I had solved my mystery.

To be sure that would not happen again, I looked for another place to get water. I found a little running brook of fresh, clear water running down a little gulley among the rocks a little way from the cabin. We filled up our water buckets with the cold, good-tasting water.

Afterwards we chopped wood for the fire. As I was preparing the fire to start it for the lunch, the women were slicing the meat and getting the food ready. The children were playing, crying, and laughing as on every day. Those who were grouped just around the cabin suddenly shouted joyfully that a dog team was coming down the hill. I just kept on with what I was doing. One of my brothers rushed to say, "It's Daddy!" I didn't believe him. But a delightful sight met my eyes as a dog familiar to me, our old gray brown lead dog, came into view through the opened door. I was still not sure it was Dad. I had a thought that somebody might have borrowed that lead dog, because many people liked it and often borrowed it. And I didn't want to be disappointed. But I was curious enough to go out and find out who the visitor was. I slowly stood up in front of the old oil barrel camp stove. As I looked outside the door, I found all our dogs. But who was the driver? He looked like Dad, but I was still not sure—still digging for the truth, in case it might be only my imagination. Yet those dirty little rascals clinging to him were brothers of mine. I had a great desire to do the same, but I was too grown up; I'd be embarrassed. Just the old Eskimo ways again.*

Sure enough, it was Dad. Not an imaginary one, because he talked to me and asked me if everything was all right. We told all about the camp and the uncomfortable living. He said that we had only short time to stay in the refugee camp. What good news that was! His looks and what he told us about himself made me have a big feeling of pity for him. He looked very tired; around his eyes was blue from loss of sleep. He was on three hours leave from his duty. He had come to see us while he should be resting and sleeping.

He told the same story that Robert Sakigak had told us— that the enemy had run out of bombs to drop and of ammunition, but that we were to be kept at the camp a little longer just in case this was a rumor, and to be sure that this news did not lure us back to the village and give the enemy a chance to jump in and attack and destroy the whole village.

The fire was going now and the crowd was busy with lunch. Other refugee people came around to hear the news from the village. Eager people they were to get the news.

Time slipped by. Soon it was time for him to go back to the village. I loaded on his sled our extra stuff that we didn't need right away. He was on his way back to the village now, which could be a war front at anytime. Still much worry was with us, but we had more hope than worry now. It seemed kind of quiet after Dad left.

When it came around for bedtime, it was most unpleasant for some of us. We had only hard rough boards to sleep on, and a short piece of round drift wood as a pillow to lay our heads on all night. I didn't mind too much about that. I was used to rough living, but this one was even more rough—and a little too tough. At home I would sleep on a nice reindeer-skin mat and in a warm house. But at camp when it was windy we were chilled at night from the drafts from one of

* An example of culturally structured restraint of emotional expression, in conformity with kinship norms for relations between a son and his father.

90

the thousand and one cracks in the wall, even though we lay down full-dressed, and for a blanket a heavy tough square of tarpaulin was all we had. A few of us rough, crude boys were doing that so that the younger children and women could be comfortable and warm.

The mud floor of our cabin was nicely patted smooth with the soles of mukluks and was dry, as well as the ground outside. Most of the place was free of snow and covered with young grass and good smelling moss and other growing things. The sun was getting warmer every clear day, and we went on our exploring in groups—a happy group when time came around to such things. Another pleasant time was on Sunday worship services and the midweek service led by church elders—a get-together when everyone in the camp was there, in a dry spot, sitting on rocks and benches made of old lumber and logs placed on crates and bones. Hymns were sung and scripture translated by some girls or boys who had learned how. The prayers gave more hope and strength to my mind than anything else. Now I had a strong belief in religion, because of my fear and worry. So I felt safe and protected after the service.

Most of the shore ice was breaking off, so the Bering Sea was quite close to the shore now. Once in a while the men killed a seal or oogruk. I once went fishing with Aiyaksaq. We caught a few bullheads, but luck wasn't with me, too, in this. I was using Aiyaksaq's fish hooks. After catching a fish or two, the hook snagged in the bottom of seaweed or on whatever there was to be snagged on. I couldn't loosen it, so I made up my mind to call Aiyaksaq even though I was very much scared of what he would say. At first I couldn't even let out my voice to tell him what had happened. Then I polished up a few carefully selected words and finally told him. He sort of scolded me, all right, but mostly had a joke about it. I felt better now. But he couldn't loosen the hook, either, so he had to pull on the line until he broke it. Well, that was the last of a pretty, artificial bait fishing hook. We were rewarded that evening with a nice fishy supper with rich, hot fish broth.

On the next day (or later than that) we were wandering

around and explored ground which we hadn't seen before, I and David Akoak with the Chuka children. There were Arnold (to look after us), Erich, his brother, and their sisters, Alberta and Hannah, and some other kids. We played hide-and-seek among the dry rocks, and played tag. It was a nice warm, calm, and bright day. The Bering Sea glistened, like a mirror—icebergs of different size, clean, light blue-greens once in a while and some dirty pieces broken from the beach drifted by lazily with the slow current.

One of the kids discovered a human skull, dried into a pure white bone. When we looked it over, we saw that one of the upper front teeth had grown very long, reaching to the hole where the right eye had been. We thought that tooth must have killed the man or woman whose skull we found. There was a crack leading to that overgrown tooth. We tried to guess the name of the person. Alberta was very much frightened by what we were doing. I felt a bit creepy myself. I still believed that ghosts really exist and the ghost belonging to the skull was still hiding somewhere under the rock, maybe. That was my thought, but I didn't say so. I didn't want the others to know it. If I did, they would scare me as they were doing with little Alberta. She was funny, wearing her big rubber boots over her mukluks. The boots belonged to one of her sisters, older than she, and were over the knees for her. To keep up with us, she had to kick them off and carry them instead of wearing them, but they came in very handy when there was fighting. They were excellent weapons and they kept her mukluks dry and clean over wet places.

Not far from the cabin where I stayed we sat down to rest. The warm sun made us sleepy and we were worked out of most of our energy. We chatted. The warm sunshine, the cool gentle breeze, the music-like song of birds on the water like a lullaby sent us into a good nap. I myself dozed off to a nice deep sleep until somebody patted me on my shoulder. It was Arnold Chuka. I sat up, rubbing my funny-feeling, sleepy eyes. When I looked at him questioningly he told me to listen, motioning with his arm to be quiet. I did so; a humming sound of a motor entered my eager ears. Not the sound of plane motors or any other type. We were sure, because it was the very familiar hum of an outboard motor coming closer and clearer. My heart went pitter-patter-pat. My mind twirled trying to figure out why. "Whose boats are coming? If they are ours, for what are they coming? Are the people who are still alive fleeing?"

Arnold and I just kept on looking at each other without saying a thing, when suddenly a watchout posted on a highest point close by shouted, "Skin boats are coming." We hollered at the other kids and stampeded them. They screamed, running to every direction, very much like a herd of reindeer stampeded by a bumblebee. At last when the frightened children were gathered together, the boats came into sight. There were two of them with three crewmen in each one. Then there was a race as fast as each pair of legs could carry a body.

The women and other children were squeezing by each other, trying to look out at the boats through the little door and the windows. We rushed by them out to see the skin boats landing. One of them was Igalok's. In the boat were Igalok himself, Robert Sakigak, Edward Aiyaksaq. The other boat was Poduk's. They said the other boats were coming. As soon as we pulled the boat out on the ice they told us to go back to the cabins and pack up. We rushed again, and the women started packing. We boys carried down rolls of bedding and bags of clothing to the boats, loaded them and came back for some more. Everyone was doing his best to be fast. Everything was taken care of and carried to the boat and the cabin, which had been called home by a few families for about four weeks or so, was straightened up. Two families stayed behind in the camp because there was not enough room for them in the boat, but the boats were coming back for them on the same day. They were Aiyaksaq's and Larson Igalok's families. They looked lonesome and quiet as they watched us go down to the boat.

The boat was full from end to end. I and Francis Oalateetak were in the bow. It was good to be on our way home. We watched big and little pieces of ice broken off from the shore floating quietly on the glass-smooth water. The crewmen of the boat still hung onto their rifles, and every one of their eyes was as watchful as an old owl's. The speed of the boat was fairly fast, powered by a twenty-four horsepower outboard motor, but to us homesick, anxious persons, the speed was no more than that of a baby crawling. I myself had enough desire to go home, but somehow I was sorry to leave the camp. I was beginning to like it, or at least was getting use to it.

The day was warm and clear—just right to get home on. Other boats passed by on their way to get their families. At certain places of the mountain bunches of auklets were flying around in circles crying and screaming. Francis and I talked of when we would walk up to the mountain to catch those little sea birds with poles and nets.

Some more boats passed by; every boat had three crewmen in it. They all had their 20-30's with them. One in each boat had binoculars watching all around. One operated the motor, and the third acted as captain. We found out the boats were sent out at fixed intervals so they would be passing each other at the midway for certain purposes.

Finally we went around the last point of the mountain, from which the village was within sight—all free of snow. I thought at that time it was the most inviting village one could see. A great big cheer rose from the homesick refugees as their homes came within sight. When we got closer to the beach where we were to land there were men waiting for us. When I was close enough to see, I saw that they, too, had their rifles and were in homemade white drill uniforms. It was kind of a strange sight to see them carrying around their rifles, and to see the uniforms they were in. They were sort of soldiers, all right, or had to be. Taking their parts to fight for the freedom of our beloved country willingly.

As we approached there was the little school tractor ready to take our stuff home on the sledge. The men welcoming us home pulled our skin boat onto the gravel beach and a dozen pair of hands unloaded it quickly onto the sled. But I asked Dad if we could carry our stuff on our backs, because I thought the tractor was too slow. My Dad was in his white drill home-made uniform, too, with his Winchester on his shoulder and a homemade ATG shoulder insignia and a cartridge belt

94

around his waist. He looked like a soldier, all right, and something to be proud of. I was going to be one someday, I was sure. The cartridge belt, which was made by the ATG wives, caught my eyes better then anything and gave me a new idea. It would be a very handy thing for shotgun shells for hunting, even if not for fighting.

Once more we were a happy family, and this living was much more to my personal liking. Dad and I walked behind the rest of the family with our backs laden with bedrolls and belongings. Under the hot sun I got thirsty. Oh, how good the ground felt—good, level gravel with short green grass. I asked Dad to give me the uniform he was wearing, and the cartridge belt. I meant when he finished being an ATG! In reply he just glanced at me without a word, but I knew that it meant "yes." That was his way of expressing agreement.

As soon as our dogs saw us every one of them started barking in invitation and delight. They looked a bit thinner than they had been, for lack of the care they needed, because Dad was too busy and tired to care enough for them. I dropped the things I was carrying home and passed the dogs a shovelful of snow. How hungrily they gobbled up the snow!

Another strange sight met me as an old man came around home from his guard duty, carrying a rusty, old double-barreled shotgun. From his shoulder hung down a wooden box full of re-loaded brass shells and from his waist, hanging to his belt, was a heavy axhead with a strap of leather rope, a cargo hook, and leather thongs made for hurling rocks. Those all were his weapons. What a funny sight (if it were not for the war), his walking around the village that way!

After looking a bit around the house, I went inside. Most of our meat which had been left there without being taken care of was badly spoiled. The room was a nightmare. Having left without straightening it up, Mom and Ann were already busy. Martin and Douglas were in the way of Sis and Mom, as they always were. As soon as they noticed me they had me go and fill up the waterpails—my old task again, but I was quite willing to do it to see the changes in the lake, to see how much it would have melted while we were absent. Douglas and Martin begged to come with me. I tried to turn back, because they always took the fun away by getting in the way. I liked to have some mischief, which is lots of fun, but those brothers always let my parents know, and they scolded me. So I didn't always like to have them around; they told what I'd done even if I had made them promise not to do so. But this time they wouldn't turn back.

We saw some of the water that was clear of ice, and we made little boats and floated them for a while. I filled the pails with both clear ice chunks and water. When we got home the house was in order once more. The dinner was almost ready. A nice dinner it was, mostly because we were at home with no one to boss us around.

The next few days were busy ones, because our work was piled high undone. No hunting was allowed until we got word to do so. Still the watchmen were posted every day and night. My Dad had to pull guard duty like the others, a six-hour guard duty. I thought that it must be lots of fun to do that, and longed to do it myself. When my Dad slept I pulled on his uniform and those funny weapons as he did when he pretended to be a soldier, making motions of fighting make-believe Japs.

One nice day Kazighia came over with the word that we could go out hunting within the International Dateline. He was the commanding officer, the village president, and my father's boat hunting captain. I became bold enough to ask to go along. I asked both Dad and Kazighia. They looked at each other for a moment and Kazighia looked at me saying, "If you are not refusing, I need an extra crewman."

Whoopee, my first real boat hunting it was going to be! I dug up my hunting clothing and jumped into them as we were having a bite to eat and hastily sipping our tea. Also, stuffing our belongings that we would need during the day, such as an extra pair of mittens, a jar of cooked meat chopped and ready to eat, and our walrus gut raincoats. All in one little walrus hide bag. Full of hunting spirit and the delight of spring, sweating under heavy clothing, we walked to the boat on the rack at the same time as Kazighia and his boys got to the boat. His family was there to help around, too, and each one of them gave me a good luck greeting.

Finally the boat was pushed into the water and we were on our way. Dad ran the little motor (twelve horsepower), Victor was the bowman, and Kazighia himself steered the boat. Daniel and I were in the middle as the handy crew. Daniel told me the things that were new to me—how and when to use the paddle, what to do when we went through the icy places, and how to keep dry. Victor told me a strange warning: to be real careful not to fall overboard or into the water any other way, because they would make me borrow and put on the oldest's women's clothes in the village and go into the public places for several days. I certainly didn't want to do that if I could help it, so I was fully taking care. It was only a joke, mostly, but it really worked to make me be careful.

Every crewman was to use his eyes to spot any game. Soon Victor caught sight of a walrus with a baby through his glasses. We chased it for a while, Victor and Dad shooting every time the walrus came up for air. I watched with my hands tight, wishing for something to shoot with. Even if I had something they wouldn't permit me to handle any fire-arm, because they didn't trust me; I was too young to be trusted with dangerous things which require much care. But I was getting enough sport by watching. As always, I was promising myself I'd be a bowman, too, when I grew up.

The walrus was finally floating, harpooned and lifeless. I felt sorry for the little baby walrus barking around its motionless mother, so I was glad when it was harpooned and shot quickly. The little calf was pulled into the boat, and the good-sized cow was towed along the starboard to a nice flat iceberg. Slowly we got nearer the chosen butchering place. As we approached, the men whetted their butcher knives to razor sharpness so that the butchering could be done well and in as short a time as possible.

Soon we were on the ice. There were little pools of water that was fresh, so we had fresh, ice cold water. It was good tasting on the warm day. The men prepared blocks and tackles to pull the hundreds of pounds of walrus onto the ice for better butchering. Only a few of us were needed to pull the big walrus by the block and tackle; I was amazed at our strength in pulling out the nearly ton of walrus onto the ice. The butchering was started and I helped. I tugged on strips of meat while the men cut away with sharp knives, sharpening their knives once in a while on a flat rock. Some hungry white birds gathered around, so whenever I had a chance to grab a knife I cut off pieces of blubber and threw them into the water. Every time I threw them closer and closer, so that the birds would come closer to get them because of the sport of watching them eat and fight each other for the pieces. But a bit of bad luck was still with me, for as I was pulling hard on a strip of hide as Victor was cutting it, it broke off, making me fall backwards. The ice where I landed gave way, but Victor was quick enough to drop his knife and grab me before I could fall into the water. I had his warning in my mind all the time. My face flushed hot, and I breathed deeply when I realized how close an escape I had from becoming a laughingstock of the whole village. He said that he almost thought he should borrow Paugoyuk's mother's clothes. The rest of them giggled.

The butchering was done and they washed the meat in the water, pulled it back on ice, and threw it into the boat. There was room enough for more but Kazighia wanted to go back. So we did. On our way we ate our lunch of raw walrus heart and the cooked meat we had brought with us. Our beverage came out of thermos bottles—the hot tea which we are fond of.

The village was beyond sight. The mountain looked low on the cloudless light blue-green skyline, and we were going slowly toward it. The boat seemed slower when it was heavily loaded. I felt sleepy. The hum of the motor sounded like a sort of music. Finally I'd dozed off, when I was wakened by a rifle crack. I jumped up and saw a young mukluk just killed by Victor on a flat piece of ice just ahead. Dad cut the motor and we pulled in the dead animal and dropped it on the top of the load.

I spotted a black speck on the ice, and told Victor to take a look at it through his glasses. He said it was another young mukluk. He got that one, too. The rest of the way seemed long, longer than we had taken going out. I got tired of sitting on a hard boat seat. My legs felt funny and my feet tickled.

At last we hit the beach. The Kazighia family was waiting for us on the beach. They turned the boat along the gravel beach on the side, and when I stepped out, my legs were very weak. I hardly walked; the gravel seemed to give way under my feet. But it was nice to stretch them after curling up for hours in the boat. With hooks we unloaded the meat on the beach. The women worked as hard as the men—even harder, because they were fresh while we were kind of worn out.

I was proud of the first hunting day in spring hunting as I went home to harness up our dogs. But I was more tired than proud. I found David Akoak had been hunting, too, with the Chukas. After the meat and the calf were taken home and cared for I was completely fatigued, very much willing to go to bed right after supper. I saved all the story I had to tell until I was rested the next day. From now on I was to be in the boat hunting. But it was too bad the hunting season was almost over now, with only some sporty hunting to begin, such as duck hunting, fishing for bullheads, and catching auklets with poles and nets.

I'd forgotten all about school now. Maybe it was closed anyway; even if there was school I wouldn't be a bit interested in it. Too many interesting things besides hunting and work were happening, so it would be a very poor thing to be in the school house, stuck in arithmetic, spelling, and English. I would have had a hard time, too, because my mind would be too busy to pay any attention to such things.

# 5. Fourth of July Footrace

In the spring of 1942 I was in my early eleventh year. The hunting season had passed; most of our spring work was done. The only hunting was for birds and fishing was for bullheads. On one of the nice calm days I and Day went fishing in somebody else's boat. Maybe there were eight of us in the boat. Dad still wore his homemade uniform top. The bowman shot birds for bait and meat. The place where we were to fish was off the point of the mountain. There were other boats there manned by fishermen. Our motor was cut and soon we were side by side with the first fisher boat we approached. They said, "The fish are biting." Sure enough, some of them were pulling them in. Already one of them had caught a big one, about a three footer, and it must have been around sixteen pounds. We went further up the current while we baited our hooks. This was the first time I was to fish from a boat, so I didn't know what to expect or do. I made up my mind to do what the others were doing. I threw my hooks and sinkers over the side of the boat, the way they did. I let out my line until the sinker hit the bottom, then pulled it in about a couple feet so the hooks wouldn't get snagged on the bottom. One of the men jerked his line and started pulling it in suddenly. I felt a bite jerk the line, and pulled in my line hand over hand. All twenty yards of it. At the end was an ugly old bullhead of a very good size. At the very first bite I learned that fishing was going to be lots of fun!

Dad and I filled up our walrus hide bag quite quickly, and so did the other fishermen. Every once in a while we pulled in all our lines and started the motor to go back to the place where we had started fishing, because we had drifted along with the current while we fished. My Dad caught a whopper, which must have been over three feet long and around eighteen pounds. Then I had a bite. I felt it was a big one by the strong jerks it made. I drew in my line, taking extra care with it. It tired my arms as I pulled it in, foot by foot with the line. The water was quite deep, and it seemed deeper than it was, and the fish, heavier than I had ever caught before. At last my catch came within my sight. I even forgot to breathe at the sight of the huge fish, still a way down in the water. When I glanced at the others in the boat, every eye was on me, but no one made a sound. I felt my face get warm. I could even hear my heart beating. When at last my whopper was at the surface, a couple of pairs of helping hands reached out at the fish. It was quickly grabbed by the gills and thrown in the boat. I breathed deeply in relief from my tightly tense feeling. "Maybe it is the biggest catch of the day!" I felt proud—but more bashful, as the men said things to me. I unhooked the fish and threw my hooks over the side once more.

After a short while of fishing I felt a real big one, lots bigger than the first one. Wow! The line loosened and then gave in; I still tugged on it, but it was pulling in more than I was. "It must be a really big one," I thought as I tried to hang onto my line. I no longer could pull it in; I just let out the line slowly. Couldn't think of what to do now, so I hollered at the man next to me. He drew in a few feet of his line and tied it to the boat and grabbed my line. As soon as he grabbed the line he said my hooks were caught on the bottom. How they laughed, because they knew all about it—that I thought I had caught a real big one. I didn't answer any one of them when they asked me if I thought that I had caught a fish. Somebody asked: "Did you think you had caught a whale?" I was mad but I kept it all to myself.

The sun was getting lower and cooler. I began to be cold. My sleeves and pants were wet, my hands soaked and scratched by the gills and horns of the bullhead. My pleasure and sport were fading now. Anyway, the men were talking about going home. The wet and cold made me much glad to go home, to our nice warm home.

Just as we arrived at the north shore, the sun was sinking behind the horizon. We warmed up a bit by working hard at unloading the boat of the walrus hide bags full of fish. Now we had to carry our catch home on our backs for quite a distance. I wished we could do that some other way, but there was none. Dad carried the big bag and I put on my raincoat and carried a string of fish, including the big ones

I and Dad had caught. The lights from the windows shone brightly from the village. We met a lady on our way home, getting water. We asked her if she would like some fish. She would, and I was more than glad to give her all she wanted. I thought she appreciated that, because the village was short of fresh meat. We rested once before we reached home.

I saw mother's outdoor, open cooking stove flaming. She had some water boiling, and so she prepared some fish and dropped them in the pot while we rested.

How good I felt after I had changed my wet duds and washed! I was rather tired, but I wasn't permitted to rest much. The old folks always were trying to harden us in every little chance they had. I thought it was kind of wicked, but really it was for my own good, to prepare me for hard, raw living. I always felt like throwing myself down on my old bed, but I couldn't help it much.

The fresh boiled fish tasted very good after living on old and dried meat. We stayed up late after supper and slept late the following morning. The warm sun shining on my face through the window woke me up. I jumped into my pants and made some coffee for breakfast on a little primus kerosene stove. After breakfast of a cup of coffee and a piece of bread, I ran out as usual. I was going down to the beach to look for some sea plants and weeds.

All at once something caught my eye. There was an extra boat on Igalok's boat rack. I stood still for a moment trying to guess to whom the boat belonged. I was sure that we had a newcomer. "Is it one of the Savoonga boats? But it should be over at the north shore. If it belongs to somebody in the village, it should be in its own rack." Then I gave up trying to guess it and made up my mind to go over to see if I could recognize it. I told my folks about the strange skin boat and I went over to it. As I was going around the corner of George Danagik's house, I ran into Ben, Debby, and Uncle Nagotak. They had been down at the camp at Southwest Cape since the last spring a year ago. I was so surprised I must have just stared at them with my mouth wide open. Both Ben and Debby had changed much. They were taller than they had been the last year.

The strange boat was Uncle Nagotak's. Finally he spoke up, asking, "Where are your folks, and how are you all?"

I told them we were all fine.

They were coming over to my house. They had come in very early that morning, coming for supplies and to get news of the village.

The news was exchanged while we chatted over a quick meal. They said the spring hunting was very good at the camp. Oh! It was a happy get-together after a year of not seeing each other, and there was lots to tell.

Ben and Debby threw themselves down to catch their sleep while Nagotak, Kenneth, and Marian walked around the village visiting relatives, shopping in the little store and getting ready and talking things over with the teacher. They got their school books, since they didn't attend school, but they were keeping up by themselves by reading books.

During the day they painted a number on their boat for identification, and supplied themselves with anything that went with it, in case the war might come around. They were still on the alert. They were to stay in camp the year through, even though the teacher and the people wished to keep them in the village, because of the danger. But my Uncle was a stubborn little man. He paid not much attention to what they said.

The few days of their presence in the village made these days pleasant ones for me. I showed them what had changed in the village and told them all about what I'd done. The sea conditions kept them for a week or longer. All the while they gathered up whatever they could get from the village. We gave them what we could spare. I helped them with their packing. I stuck with them every day because I knew I would not see them for a long time.

One morning Nagotak came to tell us that they were to leave. It was a nice morning. Ben was sleeping with me; he was homesick already and didn't have much breakfast, so very eager to go home. But to me, it was kind of too bad to be parted from them. How I longed to go with them, but it couldn't be helped. My Dad wished to go by the village rules. Besides, we didn't have a boat and nobody would be much willing to take us in their boat, because that would be against the rules.

There was a bunch of us helping Nagotak and his family, carrying their packing and their stuff down to the beach. Others were loading the skin boat. When everything was finally loaded in and checked to see if anything was forgotten, they jumped in the boat and we pushed the boat into the water. At the same time as the boat was pushed, a hard lump came into my throat. We waved until we couldn't see each other's arms. I felt like crying. I wished to be going with them and be back in our little, quiet, beloved camp. As I sat, much sadly, on the beach I watched them slowly disappearing out of sight, hardly keeping back my tears. Then I looked around. Oh! My! I was there all by myself. Everybody had gone home. I hadn't noticed that I was in an awful mood. The sun was shining and quite warm, but I was cold and the world was dark for me. I went home slowly.

When I got there it seemed too quiet, but it was all right, because I didn't feel like talking or doing anything else. I just lay down and didn't want to be bothered by anything. My tears forced their way through my eyes. Without knowing it, I fell asleep. I slept all morning. When I woke up it was late in the afternoon. They hadn't wakened me up, knowing how I felt. When I sat up, I felt weak and dizzy. My head felt funny. It seemed light and hollow, with ringing in my ears. My eyelids were heavy, and my thoughts were dim. This continued the rest of the day and the following night. I couldn't sleep; I burned with a high fever. I stayed up all night and in the morning Dad went to the nurse to tell her of my sickness. She came over to take my temperature and pulse. She didn't tell me anything, but she gave me pills to take. I couldn't eat much all that day, but in the evening I felt much better. The night was a nice one, with a deep sleep. I felt well in the morning and had a big breakfast. Even though my legs were kind of weak and wobbly, I felt fresh.

From that time on the weather was not very good—wet and windy. The village was getting more and more short on meat, especially fresh meat. I and Dad went hunting for birds but didn't have much luck, because the hunting was quite poor, on account of bad weather and not much game. Sometimes I went with Ada [Nathan's mother] and Ann and our kids when they went to the mountain to gather roots and greens to eat. I was with them to look after the boys while Ada and Ann gathered greens, and to help them carry home what they had gathered. The other women were always there, too, and their older children with them to take care of their brothers and sisters. My brothers kept me awful busy; they both were full of high spirits to wander around. My! It worried me. They might have gotten hurt among the rocks. I did the best I could to keep them together. Douglas, who was older than Martin, liked to pull from my hold and run away, running here and there, and he was quick despite being very slim. While I was busy chasing Douglas, trying to catch him before he could get hurt, Martin, who was not so quick as Douglas but husky and strong, gathered all kinds of plants and tasted them, even grass or moss. This kept on almost all day. I wondered how they were so full of pep and energy while I was worn out. They were still as lively as they could be.

At lunch, or maybe we should call it a picnic because there was a whole gang of us gathered together sitting around on rocks with pieces of cloth or paper spread on the ground, we ate whatever we had brought and drank our tea or coffee from thermos bottles. We had a nice time. I liked it very much, myself. After that, the women went back to their gathering of greens until it was time to go home. The day was far spent when the women had filled up their bags with greens and roots. We strapped bags full of greens on our backs and started walking home. When we got home, most of the work at home had been done by the women's husbands, as far as they could.

After filling up my belly, I felt like doing nothing, but I had to do my work or my Dad would chase me to work, as every father did to his boy. Oh! That was tough, but without notice I was learning to take it. There would be water buckets to be filled up, wood to be chopped, and whatever else they had saved up for me to work on.

By this time my longing to go back to Southwest Cape had

faded away or had been forced out of my mind by something else or by any sport or work that I could find.

Not too long afterwards the freighter came and we were all full of delight at having a new supply for the store. The usual work had to be done, but I believe everybody was in a working mood. I myself was going to work quite willingly. Everybody had gotten ready when they heard that the freighter was at Savoonga. So if the weather was right for the working, everybody who was to work rushed to the north beach when it came around the point of the mountain. Also, the whaleboats were there, ready to be pushed in the water. As soon as it was time to do everything, we went into action like an automatic. The boats were pushed in. The school tractor was there for pulling a heavy wagon or a sled after it was fully loaded with boys and girls who liked the pleasure of riding. I myself liked riding it very much, but the men always kept us away. I didn't want to be kept away from it, because it was great fun to ride it.

We sat or ran around the beach as we anxiously waited for the first boat to come back from the ship loaded with boxes and many other good things. Then the first boat hit the beach. It was unloaded quickly by children, men, and women. The heavy boxes were loaded onto the sled and the boxes that were not so heavy or were light enough to be carried on our backs were grabbed and carried up farther and strapped to one's back. Like in everything else we do, we grouped up with our friends and relatives in our group. We were David Akoak, Margaret (my aunt), Rachel, and Lydia Akoak. And maybe somebody else. When a box weighing twenty-five pounds was carried to the store, we got three cents for it, and four cents for a sack of flour, and so forth. I remember the two pennies I was paid for carrying a piece of lumber; that was awful cheap, but to me it was something and was big business.

I don't know how the men working in the whale boats were paid, or those working with the tractor. Our teacher, Mr. Riley, drove the tractor. He liked everyone so well he let us jump on the sled and let some ride with him in the tractor seat, along with what we were carrying on our backs.

He let us get off just a little way from Oshaweetuk's house. So we had to carry our load from there to the store, and earned our pennies by riding most of the way! The sled was unloaded by some men and the boxed things were sorted out by the store workers. Then we took our pennies from the storekeeper or his clerk, and went back for some more boxes.

As we worked, there was also some fun and some fights. I remember when Austin Omian and I played with our ropes, lassoing each other while pretending to be cowboys on our way back to the north shore, or juggling with oranges that were given us by the storekeepers—and all sorts of fun. When it comes to fighting, there would be a group of us doing it, or maybe only a pair of us. I was carrying a two-by-four on my back about sixteen feet long. One of the boys started throwing a rock at me, and picked up handfuls of gravel and threw them in my face. I told him to quit throwing, but he just mocked at me, and kept on throwing. I was getting hotter all the while. I warned him: "If you don't stop throwing, I'll make you cry."

He just back-talked me and out-talked me. When he hit me with a rock about the size of a ping-pong ball right above my right eye, I lost hold of my temper. I swung with the lumber I was carrying and hit the boy on the back of his head, and he dropped to the ground with his face down.

"He dropped dead," was my thought. A cold fear struck me. I didn't mean to hit him that hard, but I didn't really know what I was doing. I didn't know what to do now. I looked down at him fearfully; then I made up my mind just to go on as if I didn't know what had happened. As I was turning away, he began to move and cry. I stepped back, ready to defend if he fought, and I felt better—at least he was not killed. He ran home, saying he was going to tell his mother and father. Oh! I felt awful. With my hand I felt where he had hit me with the rock. There was a lump. From that time on I felt very uncomfortable. I felt very wicked because of what I had done.*

A short while afterwards during that day, I looked for his

* A clear statement of the extent to which Nathan had by this age internalized the cultural norm against intragroup aggression.

mother. Sure enough, I saw her with that boy. I went over to her at once and explained what I had done, even though I was very much afraid I would cry if she said one single hard word. But that woman was a kind one. She made us friends again, and she said that if she saw us fighting again, she would tie us together and beat us with a rope. She made us promise definitely not to be mean to each other. Now I felt happy once more.

Then lunch time was on hand. I walked to the store with Dad. He carried a box on his back; I carried something else. I showed him the coins that I had earned. Dad was working in one of the boats. I was kind of worn out now. My shoulders ached where the rope had been cutting in, and my back was sore, rubbed down by the hard boxes.

When we got to the little store, it was overflowing with people and supplies, and there came a good smell from the fresh fruits. We squeezed in and got our pennies. Then Dad told me to pick anything I liked to eat; but I didn't know what to take. There were too many good things, so I just said, "You had better do the picking. I would like anything you take." So he just filled paper sacks with fresh oranges, apples, pilot bread, and so forth. When we approached our little home, Douglas and Martin ran to meet us—happy rascals they were when they saw what we had brought. It was a happy meal we had, but I was tired.

My Mom and Dad talked to me saying not to work too hard or tire out myself, or not to carry too heavy stuff. But I went back to work anyway. I felt like I'd better go home and rest, but every time I looked around in the store, I saw lots of nice things, such as good-looking shirts and pants, which would be real dandy for school clothing, or some slick rubber boots, and some good eating stuff. So I kept them in my mind and worked on. Many other people told me the same thing as Mom and Dad. At the end of the day the men made the boys and girls quit working, but I made a few more trips, ignoring what they said. Then I went home all run down. All I did was grab a candy bar, and take off my clothes carelessly. I might even have dropped down on a reindeer skin mat asleep, I was so tired.

I slept until I was awakened by my Dad talking. Mom, him, and the kids were having a midnight meal. Dad was still working. Oh! I felt awful. All of my muscles were sore, and my shoulders and back and stinging pain. They asked me if I wanted something to eat, but I just turned over and tried to go back to sleep as quickly as possible to forget my feelings. Anyway, I was getting what I had earned by disobeying what my parents had said, and I learned one more lesson the hard way.

I felt worse when I woke up late in the morning. All my muscles were tight and sore. I found Dad sleeping. Mom told me that almost all of the work was done and the ship was gone already. There was no more work for boys and girls now, but the men were still working. I was trying to hide how I felt, but it was no good. I did light work around the house, but I dragged myself to whatever I did. After my work around the house was mostly done, I went over to the store. I saw the boys who had been working with me the day before. We were proudly telling each other about how much we had earned the day before. We looked around at the good things, telling each other what we would buy and sharing with each other some chewing gum, candy, dried fruit, or whatever we had. We watched the store workers unpacking many things. It was big fun to watch them. Every time some good thing was pulled out, there rose voices, "I will buy that kind." "I'll ask Dad to get me that." "Me too, I'll buy one of them." Once more the empty shelves in our little store were filled up with canned goods, candy of all kinds, clothing, and many other things which we all wanted.

Out of doors the men were still working, some with the tractor, hauling boxes, barrels of oil, gas, and sacks of coal. Some worked in the store and around the store, sorting out or taking to the proper places what the tractor had brought from the north shore. Some worked at the school, taking care of the school supplies. And then I remembered that I had some work to do at home. Still my muscles were aching. I pulled away from my friends to go home. They all tried to keep me, but I just told them I had some work to do. I didn't wish to part from them, but that was much easier to do than to

112

take the punishment from Dad for not giving some help to Mom.

When I got home, oops! there was some work waiting for me. We were running low on water—oh! It was not a bit easy to get myself working. As soon as I got the water buckets, my two rascal brothers dropped their toys and both shouted in unison, "May I go with you?" No matter how many times I said "no," they got hold of me and if I forced them away, they would cry and make Mom scold me. And when they were along with me, they watched what I did and told our parents when I did what I was told not to do, like something that was fun but dangerous. Anyway, we had fun together, too. I would have to call them many times when it was time to go home. When we got home, we received our reward—candy bars for each of us, or something else if we had done good.

The next few days when the work was all done, pay-day came around, and it was a happy day for me and the kids. I, Dad, and the kids all went to the store. The little store was full of people crowding in, buying the fresh goods. The women and girls bought bright-colored cloth to make snow-shirts and the men bought something also needed, or just got what others were getting. When our turn came for buying, I was the first one to do the buying. I proudly placed my coins on the counter in front of Mr. Kapugan, our storekeeper. As is our old custom, I first got something for Mr. and Mrs. Aiyaksaq; and then for myself I got a shirt and some cracker-jacks. Dad picked some more clothing for all of us for school, and a box of fruit, hardbread, and so forth. We saved some money for other uses and some for Mom and Sis. Then we went home, each one of us with something to carry, full of happy thoughts. On our way home, we stopped at Aiyaksaq's house. I and the kids had something to give them. They happily took what we gave. I felt real proud and the kids felt the same way.

Then we went on home. Ann and Ada were waiting for us. Then they both went shopping and came back with arm-fuls of what they wanted. Shiny new pots and pans, a dress for Ann, or boots for each of them. They were sure glad to get the fancy cloth to be made into snowshirts, and bright red to trim it with. We tried on our new clothes. They looked fine to us, even though they were just plain blue denim overalls and blue work shirts. Then Mom put them in flour sacks to put them away until school day or Fourth of July celebrations, the biggest holiday of the summer to everyone.

Then the big meal came. We happily sat around our oil-cloth covered board that was used as a table but was on the floor. Some of our relatives were with us, especially the old people. In this way is shown our appreciation of our relatives, that we (the children) are grateful to those old people for taking part in caring for us. Or we think that they may be present in place of another beloved member of the family who had passed away sometime before and would be missed in such time. Those who are with us now mean a very great deal and add to our joys. Every time when good things are happening we call up relatives or friends, or just neighbors, and the good things are shared with much enjoyment.*

The village was all supplied and the summer's greatest entertainment was to be held—the Fourth of July. Whether on the fourth itself or later on it was arranged by the village council and welfare committee, depending on when the store was supplied with things to be used as prizes for the winners of the games or the contests that were held. Just as on the other holidays, everybody was busy getting ready for the day. The women made new snowshirts and new komaks (sealskin summer boots). At that time this kind of boot was made not only out of skin, but also out of other things. Somebody had thought of a new idea—to make them out of old woolen jackets or other fabric material. I was to wear a pair of that sort of boots. They were made just the same way as the sealskin ones, with long wide laces, but on the top they were fancied up with brightly colored trimmings. They were made by one of my cousins. I was proud of them but later I got bashful of them, because they looked like some of those

* In this passage Nathan is referring to the cultural belief in reincarnated souls. It is a widespread Eskimo belief that the soul of a deceased member of the family returns to inhabit the body of an infant born soon after the death.

114

the girls were wearing. But some of the boys wore them anyway.

When the bell rang in the morning, the people gathered in front of the school building. Maybe everybody in the village was there, and some people from Savoonga were there, too. I was kind of bashful and shy, but I had to be there with other school students for the ceremony of the day. It was a nice day. Everybody was dressed the best they could—the girls and women in their bright colored shirts with rabbit skin ruffs, and men and boys with white snowshirts and many in jackets of different colors.

The school students were standing in one group and the other people in another group. Our teacher and missionary made lectures on the Independence Day. After our teacher spoke, explaining why the flag was saluted, we said the pledge, and we sang "My country 'tis" and the national anthem. When the ceremony was over, then came the foot races, starting with the small children. My brothers joined in the race. Douglas was the winner in his group, but Martin was way behind. He didn't even know what it meant to be in the race.

When the older boys were called for the foot race I heard the men call my name. David Akoak and I were sticking together as usual. He was called, too. Oh, no! I didn't want to be in the race while there were so many people watching. I wished that I was not there, but I had to be there. I wished to refuse, but my folks wouldn't let me. Now I had no way out of this, so I had to run a race. There were so many of us, and my friends were there, too. I didn't care a bit about winning it. I jointed in the line, bashfully, with my head hanging low, and took my position along with the others. I half-listened while Kakoktok told us what to do and when to start. Finally I was wakened by his loud counting: "One, Two, Three and then Go!" Then off we went. I just ran. I didn't care to know if I was ahead or behind. I ran at full speed, anyway. I didn't know I was in the lead until I approached the finish line. I looked up again and glanced around and heard the people cheering at the finishing line. I looked back and realized that I had won the first prize. Oh! I felt more bashful now. A prize was handed to me. It was a box of something—candy, a pair of socks, and a pair of gloves. Now I was very sweating. I seemed to talk to my parents a funny way. David was the second winner, so he won something, too. I handed the box to Mom and slipped away to a quieter place, because the old folks were pestering me with praises and congratulations in our own way, which I didn't like much. But I didn't get much out the way of that. Whenever I went there was somebody doing the same, even my best friends. So I had to take it. I was getting more bashful.

Then it was time for the grown-up young men to have a foot race, an old-fashioned one. There were several runners. They started from the village, following the north shore all the way up to the mountain, and then followed the foot of the mountain to Lake Troutman, and returned to the village following the shore of the lake. "Gee!" I thought, "All of them are good runners. Because they ran all the way." When they got closer we made out that Clyde Oshaweetuk and Dennis Chuka were in the lead and next was Don Napartuk. Now my bashfulness was fading slowly and I was getting thrilled little by little. I even joined in the cheering at the top of my voice.

After some other games were played, it was time for lunch. The prizes I won were given away to our old people. Our little house was full of joy, because my mother's sister and cousins came to eat with us. Oh! again I got bashful, but I enjoyed the company of my cousins. The lunch seemed too short, but still I didn't want to miss what was to go on in the afternoon. The bell rang and there was a crowd gathered in front of the school almost instantly. I ran to join the crowd of people as fast as my legs could carry me.

When everybody was there the men on the porch announced what was to go on that afternoon. Very interesting things followed, one after the other. Some I had never seen done before in all my life. Now I forgot all my being bashful. I was full of thrill, and the beauty of the day soaked into me. On the houses were flying little flags and against the deep, blue, cloudless sky, our Old Glory showed its bright colors waving lazily in the light breeze. All the village was a beautiful sight, with nicely clad, happy people all full of spirit. The warm sunshine warmed every heart, or at least mine.

At times we gathered in the shade of the buildings. Later that afternoon even the light breeze died down. Everybody now pulled off their outer clothing and were wiping the sweat off their foreheads. But the contests were still going on very active. We boys and girls must have been in everybody's way. Whenever we could, we pushed in immediately and imitated what we had seen done by the older people, until we were pulled away from it.

All my bashfulness was turned into thrill now. Almost anything that was going on was lots of interest to me. And it was a lucky day for my family. Ann and Ada were in the winning team in the tug of war, but Kakianak lost in everything he tried.

The walrus hide jump looked like lots of fun.* I tried to do it, but they didn't permit the boys to do it. They thought we might get hurt. But we saw how it was done and whispered to each other that we would do it sometime. Once they made all the children get together and they threw out shovelfuls of peanuts. We gathered them from the ground as fast as we could. I thought I had filled up my cap, but when the thing was over I found out I'd filled my cap mostly with rocks and only a few peanuts.

Then there was a skin boat race. Several boats were taken to the lake, which was as smooth as glass. There were five crew members to each boat, and they paddled to the other end of the lake. We played as we waited for them to return. We threw rocks at the tin cans in the water, and made games, like guessing whose boat would win the race. I was so thrilled that sometimes I forgot what I was doing. Once I ran in the water and soaked and spoiled my fancy boots while I was chasing another boy. Sometimes we even dunked our heads trying to beat each other in staying under water the longest time. We were doing all sorts of things—doing

---

* An ancient recreation resembling a "blanket-toss."

whatever our hearts contained and having a real great pleasure. We were especially playing games against those boys from Savoonga. We stuck together in groups. I guess every child had everything he wished for on that day. I felt that way myself. It was a perfect day. Everything went fine.

Suddenly there was a loud rifle report to signal the racing boats to start. They were white specks at the far end of the glass-smooth lake. Their paddles glistened in the sunshine. After about five minutes we could hear their voices chanting in rhythm to the paddle strokes, yet they were still quite a long ways away. After a short while they were midway. Some more rifle shots were fired and the high cheering was on now. The loudest cheering came from the children. The closer they came the higher the cheering raised. Now we were very wild. Maybe out of control. Several times I found myself wading into the water. Some other children were doing the same. The first boat made it in a surprisingly short time. As soon as it hit the shore of the lake it was extra quickly pulled out of water. Even the crew members didn't have a second of time to get out of the boat until it was quite a way up on the shore. We did the same to the other boats. Then some lost their guesses on the winner, including me. An argument went up, followed by a good fight, until somebody was pushed in the water to cool down his tempers, maybe, or until we were pulled apart by the grown-ups.

My legs and feet felt wet, all right, but who cared? I didn't want to miss any part of the day. When we got back to the front of the school, the benches had been fixed by somebody. We asked one another what were those for? There were boards in front of the benches. We didn't get any answer until we saw the singers come one by one with their drums under arms and sit in a row on the bench. It was going to be the village's most favorite old entertainment—the Eskimo dance (*atook*). The narrator announced that everyone who had the spirit was to dance to the nice old as well as new songs.

In a short while the song started. The air was filled with voices and tunes of the drums, and then the dancers actively took their places, dancing to their favorite songs, or songs of their fore-folks and grandfathers' songs. Some danced with partners by groups in a row, and some by themselves. I'd been in such a dance before, so I thought it was lots of fun to watch and hear the old songs. I was filled with a thrill and a strange desire that was entering me, or it might have been the spirit of the thing. I couldn't keep still now, my interest was so high. I found my arms in movement and my feet stomping in rhythm to the tune of the drums. I couldn't stand it now, so I dashed in front of the singers, all full from inside out of the sport of dancing. The music haunted me greatly. I didn't know what I was doing, and I didn't care to know—until at the end of a song I gathered myself together and all of my dancing spirit had been used up so quickly. "Oh, no! What have I done?" For the first time I noticed the solid wall of faces watching me, the high roar of cheering and clapping of many pairs of hands. I was a big show-off, all right, but suddenly some funny warmth shot into me. I was completely ashamed of what I'd done, half-knowing what was going on. It seemed there was no way out of the solid wall of people. Even my legs felt weak and wobbly, and I shook a bit. I wanted to get the heck out of there, but I didn't know which way to scram! Then somebody called, "Hey, hey, get your prize." Well, I got at least something out of all the mess. It was a bag of peanuts, candy, and dried fruit. I'd got myself in a mess; the other boys and girls gathered around me, giving me some hot words concerning my dance. But I learned a lesson— to stay out of such a thing if I am not bold enough to take the ending. It was a good beginning but a tough ending. From that time on I kept behind the crowd.

When everybody had no more dancing spirit or the singers had worn out their throats, there followed a rifle match, in which we boys and girls had no way of taking part, except to watch and wish for just one shot, at least. But we were far from being trusted with such a dangerous thing. The marksmen showed off their skill in shooting. I willingly left the firing line when my parents asked me to go home for a cup of tea, and then came back for the movie, which was announced by the narrator. Now the sun was getting low on the horizon, and it was beginning to be cool. I was kind of tired out when we got around the table and pulled out my bag of prizes, and shared them with my little brothers, parents, and sister.

For the first time that day I noticed what a mess my boots and pants were. In the morning they were very pretty, but now they were wet and awfully dirty. I shouldn't have noticed them until later if it were not for the punishing roar of my Mom and Dad. They were fierce as wounded wild animals, especially Dad; but Mom always took it easier on me. It was what I deserved. I got my reward by having to change into my old clothing, and then went to the show.

The rifle match was just about to be over. I don't remember who was the best shot. My father was not interested so he didn't shoot. Or maybe it was that he had lost in all that he tried that day, and called it his unlucky day.

It was an interesting movie of cowboys and others. Any kind of movies were interesting, because we had them only once in long whiles, and just silent movies.

Now the big day was over. I was much satisfied as I cuddled under our blankets on reindeer mats with Martin and Douglas. All three of us slept together, each of us munching a candy bar. We were all happy. We always slept together, like that. It turned out either to be a happy bedtime or not so happy, because sometimes one or both of my brothers picked on me, or I on them, until I had no more patience and hit them or they hit me with an elbow, or I slapped them. Then we were in for trouble. The worst came from our parents, scolding us and making us stay up and waking us very early the next morning to make breakfast. But when we were getting along well I told them stories or we played games that lulled us to sleep, and the best part of it came in the morning. We would be wakened to a nice breakfast after a good long sleep. What I call the good breakfast is when it is of store-bought grub. Not of any particular food, but plain pilot bread with jam or butter. And sometimes canned stuff or dried fruit would be a most delicious meal.

We had the habit of washing up after breakfast, which we didn't like sometimes. My brothers would be coaxed to be washed by Mom or Ann. I did my washing myself. My Mom was clever, because she wouldn't give us any candy or wouldn't let us do anything we wanted to until we washed up.

From that time on we were back to our normal everyday living. Sister Ann and Ada turned back to their everyday chores. Dad started his usual ivory carving, or any other means to provide for us, and I looked after Martin and Douglas and jumped at every little chance to have some fun and pleasure for myself. We still enjoyed the visit of my Mother's relatives for a few more days. They stayed in other people's homes, but they often came to visit in our home. Their children and we were always all lost in fun until they had to go. Then we were sorry to be parted from each other.

A few days or so later those people from Savoonga left for their homes. I, Dad, and the boys helped them carry their things up to the north shore and helped them all along. There were a bunch of us helping them. We helped until the last boat was pushed into the water. Then I, Dad, and the boys started walking along the beach, picking up sea weeds and plants that were washed up. We followed the beach until we got to the south shore, and climbed right to our little house, hands full of sea weeds of all kinds.

From that time on the living was just the same as other times, except the village was growing low on meat and other food. I was getting tired of eating the old stuff and the dried meat. Many a time I and Dad went bird hunting, but with not much luck. Two or three birds wouldn't be enough for one day's meal in our good-sized family. But even with no luck I liked hunting just the same.

# 6. Bird Netting with Kakianak

During that summer some ships anchored and Dad sold his ivory carving for candy, cigarettes, or other things. In one of those boats some engineers had come and they surveyed some places and left stakes. We didn't know what they were for. The engineers and their instruments were a very new sight, so we boys gathered around them, along with some of the grown-ups, too, trying to make out what they were doing and what their tools were for. But none of us had the right answer. Some days they were working on the ground at the south of the village, and other days on the north of the village. The stakes on the south of the village marked a long strip of ground, and we made out that was going to be a landing field for the airplanes; and those on the north, we still didn't make out what they were going to be for. Lots of gossip went up about it. Some people said it was going to be for war equipment and some said it was going to be a place for raising a farm with animals. We didn't get the real truth for it, and the men who were working on it left the island. I thought it was going to be very interesting to see what we had never seen before—some cows, pigs, and so forth.

The summer went on with not much happening, but the food supply was going down rapidly. The women were going up to the mountain to gather plants for food. Sometimes I and Dad went to the face of the mountain to catch auklets with a pole and net when the wind was from the right direction and it was good weather.

When I first did this kind of bird hunting, it was new and and filled with lots of sport. It was late afternoon near evening. I'd filled the water buckets and chopped the wood, and Kakianak (Dad) had just finished feeding the dogs when he called me to eat. The sky was blue and the wind from the west was not so high, but not so low either. The ground was dry. Maybe this was the day Dad had chosen, because the conditions were right. When I got in the house he had a large flour sack. Into it he put a length of leather rope with some short pieces of whale baleen tied to it, which he had made a day before. I had wondered what that was for, but he hadn't told me. As he always does, he let me learn it for myself. Then he put in some dried meat, rolled the sack and tied it up, making a strap to be hung on the back.

I asked him, "What are you going to do?"

He just glanced at me and looked away without a word— left me still trying to solve the mysterious thing by myself, until he said, "Let's eat."

Why were we eating so early? And it was a big supper. After the meal was over he put on his hunting clothing. He told me to get ready if I was going. Of course I was going, but get ready for what? He said, "Just get ready."

I jumped into my hunting clothing and rolled up our rain coats. Mom handed me a paper wrapping. I didn't know what was in there, but I didn't look, because I always liked to have a little surprise at lunch time.

I didn't know what we were going to do. And at evening, too. We always started hunting as early as possible in the morning. I was still more puzzled. At last I found out what we were going to do when Dad took the bird catching net while I waited for him with the roll of rain coats hanging down my back. He handed me the long pole, saying, "You carry it first. I'll take over at half way."

We walked up to the mountain and then close by the graves. I always felt creepy when I went near the graves, because I still believed in ghosts and I thought they really existed and were invisible; thought they were there and could be heard. Every little noise brothered me. I didn't even want to look around. I might see some ugly, scary figure that must be unearthly. I just kept my eyes on my Dad's back or the ground. Once just ahead a squirrel chatted nearby and I really jumped high, giving my Dad a good laugh and me a real scare. We had been very quiet, except for the noise we made by walking on the gravel.

When we got up to the mountain he took the pole I was holding in my hands. We followed a mountain trail that climbed part way up and around the point. I had followed the same trail with some boys at other times but only part way, and had been wondering to where it led and how far it went around the point of the mountain.

126

The beauty of the place and the nature always drew my attention. So it did this time, too. It made me forget my creepiness and scared feelings. The sun was very low over the horizon, the sky was deep blue, and the water sort of rough and ripply. A few birds were flying around. The mountain showed many tones of color, from darker green to lighter. The rocks and boulders, big and little, showed natural colors, some mixtures of yellow, brown, and gray. The sun was getting red and gold when we looked down at the surf splashing into white foam against the rocks. We were sitting at a point on the high rocks to catch our breath. Another part of nature I liked was the fresh cool wind as it blew through my hot hair and heavy sweater. Boy! It felt good and smelled very good. Around me the big and small rocks looked as if they had been placed one upon the other by a giant mysterious hand. I was sure it was done by the maker of nature or the creator.

After about fifteen minutes of rest we stepped along, I panting for breath at times and catching handfuls of greens, eating them as we walked. Following the old trail, we passed by some rock piles. They were used as blinds to catch auklets. Dad told me they were not the right places for the direction of the wind. All the time the birds were increasing and their music-like calls were growing louder.

I'd learned how to catch the little birds from under the rocks before, so I was poking into the hole while I dragged behind a short way. Then I caught one auklet and showed it to Dad. He said, "That will be a good decoy; keep it alive."

I didn't understand him clearly, but I did as he said, anyway. I pushed the bird into my big pocket. It fluttered its wings once in a while in my pocket. And then I forgot all about it until just a little way from our place. The place he showed me was a short way ahead. I felt something fluttering on my side. I began to reach in my pocket to find out what it was, and felt a sharp pain from the beak of the bird. It hurt me and scared me at the same time. I yowled at the top of my lungs and then shouted, "There it goes!"

Dad whirled around to see what was eating me. "What's the matter? And what goes?"

I replied, "There!" pointing to the bird.

He asked, "What? Where?"

I said, "The bird. It escaped." Maybe I looked serious; he did.

He said, "I thought it was something serious. You scared me."

Then he laughed heartily. I joined in. The little bird was having a nice cozy ride and I paid for it with a painful bite on my finger. I felt sort of mad. But now it was impossible to get even with that bird.

We got to our place when the sun was just above the skyline. Dad sat next to the piled rocks, fastening the net onto the end of the pole. He told me what we were to do. I sat behind him. He told me to watch him closely. Of course I did, because this kind of bird hunting was very new to me, and I wanted to know how it was done. I wanted to learn to do this new way of hunting, which I could do without cost of ammunition. The flock of birds flying in a circle was getting to be larger. Oh! I wished to pour on questions, but I knew I couldn't get any answers, so I bit them back and waited for him to tell me. He watched the birds flying by, but he never attempted to catch any, even though some of them flew by so close. He just watched them. If I were in his seat I would have caught about a dozen already.

He kept on that way for some while, without trying to catch any, until a little flock flew by at what seemed right under our noses. Then in a flash, in a split second, he swooped up his net. With a steady, and carefully aimed swoop he caught one of them. I thought that was very surprisingly marvelous. Now I didn't trust myself to catch any, because I thought, "That is for the trained hunters with eyes that are trained especially to watch the fast flying birds that are too many to watch." I couldn't figure which bird to keep my eyes on, or how to aim the pole and net.

Then he told me to put on my gloves and handed me the live bird. He said, "Now keep it alive. Don't let it go." I did as he said.

I wanted to try the pole, but I was far from knowing how to do it. After he had caught three birds he stood up and took out the leather rope that had the short pieces of baleen on it. He tied one end to a rock and stretched it out like a clothes line, and tied the other end to another rock.

"Now what's he up to?" I couldn't keep back my questions, so I asked, "What's that rope for, and what are you going to do with those auklets?"

I got the answer, the same old answer I always got from him: "Just watch; you'll see," was his reply, as he took one of the little birds from my hand.

I'd been trying to guess what those short lengths of nicely fixed whalebone or baleen were for. Oh! No! He tied the bird to it through the nose. "Oh! a poor thing, hanging by its nose, wildly fluttering to free itself." But it had no way of escaping. It bothered me very much in my heart, and he did the same thing to the other bird.

The live decoys did a very good job of luring in some birds. Then Dad gave me a little instruction. He told me to keep my eyes on a bird that was flying close enough to catch, and to estimate its distance to the length of the pole. I tried his instructions in a few swoops, but I didn't do it fast enough, or else I raised the pole too soon, and scared the bird away. When the speed of the net was correct, something else was wrong. My aim was not so good. The net passed the bird on one side. The funny part of it was that some birds I tried to catch were as far away as twice or three times the length of the pole. They looked closer than they were.

But no matter how I did at it, it was great big fun. I surprised myself when I caught one without trying to catch it. I swooped the net at a bird, and another one flew right into the net and got caught itself! The one I had tried to catch was too far away. When I caught that one, Dad said, "See how easy it is?" I didn't really do it, the bird got caught by itself, but I kept that to myself.

Then he said, "Now let me do it. I'll let you try again after we catch enough to eat."

I willingly let him take over, because my arms were tired already and I couldn't trust myself, even though I wished to do it some more.

Now I wasn't too sorry for the birds when I had had the sport of catching them. Afterwards whenever Dad left the pole to replace the worn-out decoy, I got hold of the pole and net, and used it until he got through. I caught one or two more after dozens of tries. Now I got a little surer of myself—and thought that I would learn to do it if I practiced.

I still had my old personality. I was very proud of my catch and kept them separated from my father's so I could show them off when we got home. The proudest part of it was when I would hand them to the old folks. I was not only proud. It made me feel good when the old folks' faces lighted up with joy when they received what I gave them.

My Dad went on catching birds and I was getting in every chance that I could to take my seat in Dad's place. But somehow I was getting tired and sleepy. Even though I was getting lots of sport, some thoughts kept flashing and turning in my mind, no matter how much I tried to push them out. It bothered me a lot when I looked at the birds that had got caught as they flew and met their death, and those that were tied to that line struggling at what seemed to be their hardest, but with no way of escape. When I placed myself in those little birds it really bothered me. The best help to ward off such thoughts was when I thought of my hungry brothers, mother, and sister. How happy Mother would be when we brought home our catch of birds!

Now I began to nod, getting colder and colder. The call of the birds was lulling me. Once I might have dozed off, and was getting deeper and deeper into sleep, until a sharp slap on the side of my thigh. Dad growled at me, "Wake up, hunter. That stuff is not for hunters. Or we will call you a big sissie. You ought to be ashamed of yourself." And he added, "Put on your rain coat before you are too lazy and cold."

His gruff words worked in my mind. I got ashamed and snapped out of it, but it was only for a while. It had kindled up a fire in my mind, but when I settled down from moving around, some sleep and cold gripped me again. The cold forced me to keep still. As soon as I stopped moving around the drowsiness took over. I shook my head to keep awake, bit myself, but both became useless. My eyes got heavy and were hard to keep open. Then I would doze off to a nice sweet nap—even dreamed a little—then wake up suddenly as if by something. Then I would glance at my father, pretending that I had not been sleeping. Oh, it was so good. I closed my eyes for a little more nap.

I kept on doing that. Then Dad had to wake me up again. This time he made it in such a way that it made me wide awake. He almost shouted at me; maybe I was in a deep sleep: "Hey! Hey! What's going on with you? If you are going to be that way, you are not worthy to be trusted as a hunter." He added something which I never wanted when he said, "I will not take you with me again if you are that way. You have to be with babies." That didn't taste any good, but it did a good job on me. From that time on I was far from sleepy.

Again whenever he laid down the pole I grasped it and did my stuff. Sometimes I made him laugh. Maybe I was very funny trying to catch the birds that were too far or those that were too quick, and I was too slow. Still, some of those too close made me mad. It was hard to guess the distance. I shouted at them, "Hey, you fly too fast!" Or, "Come closer, you wise bird!"

When he called me to take over and said, "Let me show you how to do it," I would say, "Let me try just once more," until he had to pull the pole from me.

Then he said, "Watch closely; I'll show you how to catch them."

I did watch closely and became sure I would catch some now, and begged to try, saying, "Oh! I see now. Let me catch one." But when I tried the staff, I found out that thought could do it far easier than one could do it by himself.

But catching or not catching, it was really filled with sport and lots of fun. Another thing we laughed about was when the birds got caught by themselves when they flew into the net at the same time that I raised the net trying to catch the birds that couldn't be caught. Anyway, I caught five or six of them—something to be proud of.

One thing I noticed about those little birds—in spite of

the fact that they were small, they were very tough. They stood what a person couldn't take; real tough, indeed.

My father was not an expert with the pole and net, because he, too, missed his marks by not having a very good aim. He sometimes hit the bird with the pole or frame of the net. It made a loud thudding sound that would knock out a person very cold or even kill the person. But the small birds whirled around and flew right away, full of life—not all of them, but most of them. They were flying at a good rate of speed, and the pole is swooped with much force in order to make swift swoops. Some of them were killed that way instantly, but most of them took it and some of them would be knocked down to the ground. But we had to be quick to grab them, because they came to fast and flew right away, or ducked into any hole nearest them as soon as they came to.

I had been cold, shivering and chattering my teeth, but now I was warmed up and wide awake—the way I should be.

Before I could have enough fun, the flocks of auklets were getting smaller and smaller, until there were only a few. And then no more. It seemed very quiet now. I missed their call; they had been calling, "Look! look, look, look." It was too short. I hated myself for wasting time sleeping.

Another mystery came into my mind: "Where do all the birds go?" I asked Dad, "Where did they go?"

He said that he didn't know. Maybe some went to sleep and some went to eat somewhere.

While Dad was getting our catch ready to take home and rolling up our rain coats, I wandered around, peeking into the holes and under and among the rocks, looking for eggs and birds. I found three eggs when Dad called me, holding up a paper wrapping. He asked, "What's this?"

"Oh, yes, that's what Mom packed for us," I said. I had forgotten all about that until then.

"Let's eat them now," Dad called.

I went back to him. From my pocket I pulled out the eggs I had found and laid them down on a flat rock where we were sitting. Dad asked me in a surprised manner, "Where did you get those eggs?"

"Down there," I replied.

132

Now to open the surprise package. In the magazine pages were some dried meat all cut up, ready to eat. Oh, I felt hungry when I saw the food. There was another wrapping in the paper sack. My mouth watered as Dad said our grace before the meal. The meal that didn't taste very good at home was good eating now. When we finished the meat, my appetite had been built up by it. I opened the other wrapper. Oh boy! There was some pilot bread with jelly, dried fruit, and two bars of candy. Boy! I enjoyed the little lunch.

The night was chilly, so whenever we sat still we got chilled. Yet Dad told me to take off my warm rain coat. I told him, "Oh, I'm cold."

But he said, "You don't need it. You'll be warm on the way."

I unwillingly pulled it off and rolled it up with other rolls and tied it. Now I shivered with cold; my fingers were stiff. I pushed in the eggs I had found in my pocket.

But Dad said, "No, no. You'll break them. Let me have them." He wrapped each of them in the paper and put them in his hood, which he pulled back, not wearing it on his head. I laughed at him. What a strange way to carry them! I laughed at him, at the thought that he might break them on his head. What a mess he would look!

But he said slowly, "It may be funny, but that's the way we carry them, because it is the safe way, if you don't have anything to put them in."

Then I wondered, "Those old-timers are so full of ideas which I have to learn."

I'd rolled my birds in Dad's coat and mine. He carried the almost full, large flour sack of birds and the pole. I carried the rest. Our way home was to climb part way up the mountain to the trail and then sideways, following the old mountain trail. Dad led the way. I followed right behind, panting for breath already. My legs felt weak. Every muscle strained at every step. Sure enough, I'd warmed up by now, and my body was getting moist from sweat. Dad carried a heavy load, but it didn't seem to bother him as much as it did to me.

I was glad that I had taken off my coat. It would be

torturing me with the heat now. I wished we would stop for a moment of rest, but we just keep on. I couldn't help it; I had to keep up with him. I was having a hard time to keep up with him. I thought we would stop to rest a while when we reached the trail, but we went right on without a moment of rest. But it felt a little more comfortable to walk on it than climbing up straight. It almost felt like walking on the level, but we still were climbing up and down short ways. Now I was sweating very much. The roll of coats got uncomfortably hot on my back and it stung where it pressed on my back. I got more and more thirsty, but there was no water to drink. It was semi-dark, so had to take care where we stepped. My Dad was doing quite a fast step. He was used to walking fast, because he had walked long distances when he was young—even walking all the way back and forth from Southwest Cape to Gambell. And he made round trips, too, on foot in the summer time.

It was hard for me to keep up with him, taking care to watch out for the rocks in my path. Several times I tripped, but I wildly fought for footing and avoided falling. If I fell it would mean bruises, a black eye, deep cuts, or even broken bones.

Watching my step kept me busy, but I still had other thoughts that bothered me, too, and kept me from enjoying our hunt perfectly. No, it was far from that; it made me sorry. As we walked silently I thought of the birds as if they were like human beings. I wondered if they had feelings like a person and thought, talked, had pleasure and sorrow like people. My thoughts were started by the eggs I'd taken. "What will happen when its mother comes home and misses the egg? What is she going to say? She will ask her neighbors, maybe, or she will look for her dear child. Maybe she will be in deep sorrow and weep for her child." I hoped we had caught the mother; that would be best.

Then I thought of the other birds we caught. They were having lots of fun enjoying their families and were happier than when caught and tied up as decoys, all the while waiting for their death. Now they are dead, going to be cooked and eaten. Then I thought of their folks. Maybe their own brothers or sisters had seen them caught, tied up, and then killed? I couldn't stand a moment if things like that would happen to my folks. I thought of human creatures as most wicked beings—like I and Dad now. The thoughts bothered me so much that I couldn't stand it much any longer. I tried hard to ward it off. I started looking for greens, picking those that were nearest to the trail and chewing them as I walked. It helped my thirst some.

When I got tired of picking and eating all I wanted, I looked ahead. There was the village in full view. The lights shone from the windows. I saw the boat racks just ahead. Oh! I had a big hope that we would sit there for a good rest. But Dad just kept on passing them by. "Are we not going to take a rest? Or ain't Dad tired with that heavy load he has?"

I seemed to feel more tired than ever. The net that flopped up and down with every step I took gave me a bad feeling. My mouth and throat were dry from thirst. I remember the water that trickled down the mountainside in a little stream right on our way. I was going to get a big drink from that icy cold water.

At last we got down the mountain, but it was harder than going sideways. I had used most of my strength. When we got to the level ground, oh!, it felt good to walk on it. But the gravel wasn't the same as solid ground to walk on. And it seemed to slow down our steps. Then we got to the place where I wanted a drink, and finally I got what I had wanted all the way. Dad dropped down on his back. "Oh! let's take a rest and a drink of water!"

I just threw down what I was carrying and lay flat on my back. The cool ground felt very good on my hot back. I wanted to drink the water right away. I would drink like mad, too. But my Dad said, "No! No! Rest a while to cool yourself, or you'll get sick."

My sad, awful thoughts came right back into my mind. I started talking to Dad about what I was thinking. I started saying, "Dad, what do you think is going to become of the families and the mother of those eggs and the birds we caught?"

He looked at me surprised, and he said, "Snap out of it. Don't be a sissie. That stuff is not for men hunters." But he asked me, "What makes you say that?"

And I told him, "I don't know, but it bothers me."

He said, "Oh, I see. It can't be helped. But think of your hungry family first before you have such thoughts. Now let's drink water," he said, "but drink just a little or you'll be sorry."

I got down on my stomach to get a drink from the running water. The water was ice-cold. Before I could drink half of what I wanted, Dad said, "That's enough. You drank too much." Sure enough, after I got the drink I felt somewhat lazy and cold.

The next thing Dad said was, "Let's go home."

At the sound of going home, a thought of which way we would take shot into my mind. I asked right away, "Which way we are going, Dad?"

He pointed to the way we came, saying, "That way. The way that goes toward the lake and follows the edge of the lake toward the village."

Oh! No! Not in the dark. I felt very creepy, and wasn't yet even by the graves. I tried to avoid that way by saying to Dad, "Why do we go that long way? Why don't we make a short cut this way, straight to the village?"

His answer gave me the shivers: "That way is short, but it is not easy to walk carrying a heavy load. It is gravel almost all the way. But this long way is easier to walk on, and we can save time, even though we have to walk in a curved way." Jeepers! But I had to go with him.

Aw! The scary place. I wished we didn't have to go through that place, but we were going to. My other unpleasant thoughts were replaced with scares.

I was not so happy. But I was keeping that to myself. I wouldn't let my father know it. So when he asked me why I wanted to make a short cut to the village, I said, "Oh, I just wondered."

Then we went on for some way. I didn't feel good. My legs were a bit wobbly but they went all right. It was my turn to carry the long pole. I held it up on my back. We walked without saying a word, like we always did. I couldn't look around now. I kept my eyes on the ground just ahead of my feet. I seemed to hear voices. Strange noises. I thought I saw some ghostly figures with the corner of my eye. Once I almost scared myself right out of my skin, when I bumped into my father. He had held up his step for a short moment to adjust the bag he was carrying to make it more comfortable. I didn't see him, because I had my eyes fixed down. I knocked him hard and nearly made him fall forward. I just stood still and waited for what I was going to get.

I got what I expected. Right away he looked at me and asked, "What is the matter? Were you asleep? Didn't you see me?"

I couldn't tell him the truth, because I knew he would say that I was silly. So I just made up my answer: "Oh, oh, I was looking the other way. I couldn't see you"—and other excuses, the best I could think out.

I was a bit worried we might stop to rest. After what really was a short time but I thought must be a long time we passed the scary grave place. I wanted to have a good rest now that we were in a better place, but we went right on without a moment of rest until we got home.

Mother and the children were asleep when we got in. Mom woke up as soon as we opened the door. I pulled off my boots and I started picking on my brothers, until I had waked them up. Once again it was a happy moment for our family. It made me happy to see Mom's happy face when she saw the birds and the happy voices coming from my brothers.

In the morning Mom passed out my catch to the old folks, and my friends came over to me. I had lots to tell about my hunt, and my friends were all pleased to hear my story. And I felt proud. We played with the bird catching pole and net, taking turns. One of us threw tin cans and another of us caught them with the pole and net. I proudly showed my friends how it is done.

The rest of the summer passed by without much happening, or at least anything that I can remember. Just our everyday living went on.

For our money problems Dad carved ivory to trade in at the store for our meals, or else traded some oogruk skins that we could spare. Sometimes Ada's and Ann's sewing was sold or traded. In those works I was to take my part to provide for our family. Sometimes I had to give up what I had planned to do with other boys, no matter how much I wished to be with them. Maybe we had planned to play at the lake, or go to the beach to hurl rocks at birds—which I thought was lots of fun. At the lake we would play with toy boats, sailing them, or just wading in the cool water. Or we would take a walk somewhere.

But oh! I felt like I was tied down with work to help my parents. I begged or made an excuse to go on my own. Sometimes my parents would let me go, but almost every time they were firm and very strict. But I felt like helping them when I thought how good they were and are to me. I worked as best I could and had to be coaxed to eat or to go to bed. I was so happy in my work, and had great desire to get it done.

I had more than one reason to get my work done. The best reason was when I got it done I was promised that I would be free to play or do what I wished to do with my friends. The sooner I did my work, the more time I would be with my friends.

When I and Dad were working doing ivory carving, I did the sanding and polishing. I worked hard when I felt like doing it. I knew if we got it done, Dad would get something from the store. I didn't know it much, but my Dad was preparing me for the future in how to provide for the family which I would have. And I was getting the experience of ivory carving. I learned I needed patience, work, and care.

Once in every short while I asked, "How is this? Isn't it done yet?"

And then Dad asked me, "What do you think of it?"

I would say, "Maybe it is all done now." Because I was always sure I had gotten it right and got it done.

But it wasn't done at all. Sometimes at a glance he would say, "Look at that part. You haven't done it yet."

138

So I had to work all over again. Then I showed him again: "There! I'm sure I got it done."

But still more he would say, "Wait, wait. You haven't done this part," or "A little more polishing here," or "Remove the scratches here."

Sure enough, I hadn't touched that part. Little by little I learned to notice undone parts. I learned to like the work. More often, Dad said, "See for yourself if it is done."

Later he got his ivory carving ready to be sanded and polished, and he left the rest to me while he started on another carving or something else he had to do. All he had to say was, "We'll go to the store when you get them done," or "Let me know when you finish them."

When he took them over after I did the work, I waited for what he would say about them. When he didn't say a word, I knew that I had done the work well. But if I had overlooked something or I had done carelessly just to free myself from the work, he had me come over and would say, "See here. It needs more work here," or "It needs more shining." Oh! I had to do it all over again. Still more he would say, "I wouldn't have let you do it over, but if you do your work that way now, you will do careless work in the future, and nobody will buy your carvings."

He was a good teacher that way. It was just to get me started right. Later on I always made sure I'd done the work so I wouldn't have to be bothered by him. What helped me do the work better was a sort of reward I got from Dad. It was that I liked to see him look pleased when he saw the work well done.

The ivory carving made some part of our living and kept us supplied with what we needed from the store—part of our food, such as flour, sugar, coffee, tea, fruit, and milk that we used every day, and many other things besides. But that was not all we had to buy. There were more things, such as fuel to use in the stove and for light. If we had to hunt, we had to get ammunition for our guns, and we needed something to wear. We children needed to have our pants, shirts, and snowshirts replaced quite often, for we played so much in dirty places, and we would get as filthy as pups.

Our other part of living came from hunting—the main part of it—and from the wild plants and roots. Often women took that part, but men had to help along with it. I myself also helped with that part. Besides that I helped with most of the work around the house.

But on other times I was too selfish to be of help. I felt I'd rather have some fun with other boys and girls. Then I was real bad. I just went ahead with what we had planned to do, paying no attention to my parents. We would be having a good time, but all the time something seemed to keep ringing in my mind. It was what I'd done to my parents. The fun of playing was too good to be missed, so I just tried to force away what I remembered and go on with the fun. But when I couldn't stand the thought of disobeying, I would try to pull away from my playmates and they would hang on tight to me, telling me not to spoil our fun or they would not let me play with them again if I broke away from them. And then I would play on with them for some time. But all the time I would get a more and more awful feeling, until I dropped what I was playing with or got out of the bunch of children and ran home as fast as my legs could carry me.

As I ran away I would hear both unpleasant and pleasant words. First they would holler, "Hey! You come back here. You are needed here. We want to play with you." Or, "He is just a big phony; a cheater."

I just hollered back, "I can't help it. I must go to work."

Then the hollering became nice. "Be sure and come back as soon as you get done with your work."

I would turn around and wave, then run on. On my way I thought up some excuses to make when I would face my parents. When I got there, there was my Dad, more like a wild, wounded beast than a dad. Fierce as could be—but his roar was always far worse than his bite. I never received a single spank from either of my parents. Mom always took it easy on me. She often left the rest of my punishment up to Dad.

Now I would take what I had laid up for myself by being naughty. Before I could eat or go to bed, I had to get done or receive what was in for me. Dad would roar at me and that froze me solid with fear. He would say, "Get that thing done," or "Go get some water before you go to bed or eat."

I would make excuses, but none worked, because Dad knew none of them had much truth in them—as plain as daylight. I started on what he had told me to do, trembling or even with a big lump in my throat and a sharp pain in my heart.

More and more, little by little, I learned to realize I was receiving what I very rightly deserved. And there was no way of escaping except by doing my work. My parents didn't mean any bad for me. They were only giving me my lesson, to teach me to live the right way. I would need the lessons in just a few years from that time, because I was to take over to provide for the family—our growing and increasing family. My parents were teaching me because I was the oldest of the boys in our family. Mom was doing the same thing to my sister, Ann, as Dad was doing for me, but in a way that women need to learn.

It was the last part of July or the first part of August and again my Dad was up to something. What it was, I wouldn't know until I found out for myself when we did it. I liked to ask him what he was going to do, but I knew pretty well that I would not get anything from him by asking. I knew all I would get would be, "You'll see, wait and see," or "I don't know." No matter how curious I was I'd have to get my answers for myself by figuring them out or by waiting until when we did it.

Now it was evening. He was making something out of wire and sticks. He sharpened one end of the wire and bent it, making a little sharp hook. Then he fastened the other end to a stick that was a handle for it. He made several of them, some short, some longer, and others still longer. "Are those hooks? What are they for? Are they for fish?" No, it couldn't be that.

My Dad was hard to understand, so I gave up and watched the rest of what he was doing. Now he wrapped them up in a flour sack along with some dried meat. Over it he rolled his rain coat. Then he looked at me. Seeing my seriousness, he just grinned and giggled. Then he said to me, "If you are coming with me, roll up your things. But you don't look willing to go."

Without knowing what we were going to do, I packed up my things. Then we put them away, and we had our supper and went to bed. So I figured out we were to start in the morning.

Dad told me if the weather was good we would go hunting tomorrow. But to where and what kind of hunting? I'd have to wait until morning. I was wide awake, as always when I am anxious.

But I dropped off to sleep without knowing it. When I was called in the early morning, I jumped into my clothes. I didn't feel like eating breakfast, but I had to. Finally, Dad told me that we were going after young birds, to the far side of the mountain. I checked on the weather. It was nice weather. The sun was just peeping over the horizon. It was chilly. The dew on the grass and weeds sparkled brightly like jewels, giving many rainbow colors in the sunlight. The light of the dew pierced me to the heart, and my heart glowed with beams of joy. So I got back in, full of delight and glee, to announce the beautiful weather.

Once again off we went, Dad leading the way. I followed behind. Both of us didn't make a sound, except I was wondering about the tin can which my Dad held in his hand on a wire, swinging it back and forth. I didn't know what we were going to do with that tin can.

Suddenly he stopped and looked back at me, fishing in his pockets for something. I asked him what he wanted.

He asked back, "Did Mama give you the matches?"

I replied, "No, why?"

He told me, "Go run back and ask for them. I'll wait here."

Oh, what did he want the matches for? He didn't smoke. Was he going to start smoking? "Oh, boy! That is something to be proud of." Almost every boy's Daddy in the village smoked a pipe or cigarettes, so it seemed funny mine didn't. Those were my thoughts as I ran back.

Ann was running to us with the matches wrapped in a paper. I grabbed them and pushed them in my pocket, and ran on. We started on our way again when I caught up with him.

The dew wet our new high rubber boots as we walked on the wet grass and weeds. Some white daisy petals, bluebells, dandelions, and other flower petals stuck to my boots. My boots looked pretty, decorated with many kinds of flowers of many colors. Some flies and bugs buzzed by. The birds chattered their songs. Oh! What a peaceful, beautiful world! It made my body full of gay from inside out.

The sun was getting warmer, but it was damp and cool in the shade of the mountain when we got to the foot of the mountain. I appreciated the coolness, because it was comfortable for climbing up. Dad told me to take care in all of my steps, because it was dangerously slippery on the steep, wet trail.

We walked out of the shade into bright sunshine at the top of the mountain. We sat on a rock to catch our breath, looking at the village. We saw some people walking out on the same trail we had taken. We guessed they were on the same hunting trip that we were to do. We heard dogs barking; the school caterpillar tractor was purring on its way to the lake to haul water; and there was the hum of the outboard motor belonging to the boat going to Savoonga, and of others going out fishing. We could see them as white specks breaking the smooth glassy water with the ripples they made behind them. They seemed to go slowly. Things looked golden in the village, touched by the morning sunlight.

I was feasting my eyes on the beautiful scene—the sweet, cheery sound of everything. The cool but not cold light, fresh breeze, and everything that went with Nature, Goodness, and Beauty carried my thoughts far away into the land of paradise, until Dad broke the stillness and spoiled my dreams, when he said, "Let's go now. We have caught our breath."

But my thoughts and enjoyment of nature didn't stop there. There were lots of things to like and enjoy on our way ahead—some plants or flowers that I had not seen before, and the places that were new to me. So it was big fun to explore. I hadn't been to that place before, so I was very much surprised to see the Savoonga mountains. And when

Mount Taphok came into sight, I thought it was part of our camp, South West Cape, so I asked Dad, "Oh, is that part of South West Cape?"

"No," he replied with a laugh. "Our camp is way south that way," he said, pointing to a direction.

Sure enough, I recognized the mountains that we used to go through in winter by dog team when we were on our way to our camp, or rather, my home. All my thoughts of our beloved place came back to me and my longing to go back increased a lot at that moment.

Then we went down the other side of the mountain to a certain place which Dad had picked for what we were after. We left our things on a big rock. Dad handed me some of the hooks he had made, and a small flour sack. He gave me a short hook, a longer one, and a still longer one. He told me what to do, and how to do hunting and catching of those little young birds. He told me to look in the holes and under or among the rocks. He said, "Don't get under the loose rocks; they might fall on you and crush you. And be careful not to bust your hands and fingers. Now have some fun, but be sure to remember to be careful, or we will have a sad hunting."

I started peeping into the dim holes, but I couldn't see anything for some while. But just the same, I thought it was lots of fun. Dad whistled at me every once in a while and held up what he had caught to show me a ball of gray down that was a young bird.

I asked him, "How do you catch it?"

He just said, "The way I told you how to catch them awhile ago."

Then I kept on peeping and looking. In the next hole I peeped in there was just the thing I was looking for right in front of my eyes. It was so sudden and I was so surprised at the sight of a soft, gray ball of down, I just stared at it, not knowing what to do. Before I could make up my mind what to do, it ducked into a hole. Then I tried to hook it, but I was much too late. When all my excitement was over, I looked around to see if Dad had seen what had happened. He was busy hooking another bird. I didn't tell him, because

I was ashamed of my being slow and clumsy. But I had learned something. When things are that way, I had to be quick about it.

In one of the next few holes I looked in I saw something moving. I reached for it with my longest hook and felt something soft. Then I started to pull it out slowly. Pulled it closer and breathlessly, until I got hold of it in my hands. I clutched it tightly, and held it up to show it to my Dad.

"I got one!" I shouted.

He nooded his head, saying, "Fine. Get some more."

I caught a few more after that, and then I saw a grown auklet in a hole, and I caught it right away. I didn't know what I was going to do with it, so I held it and I asked Dad, "Hey Dad! I caught an old bird. What shall I do with it? Shall I let it go?"

He replied, "No! Kill it and we will eat it. It is good to eat, too."

When I got tired of peering into holes I sat down on a rock, leaning back on another one to rest. I felt in my pockets for some chewing gum. I found something wrapped in paper in one of my pockets. What could it be? Hoping it might be some candy or something good to eat, I unwrapped it slowly. Oh, yes! Those matches that I had run back for that morning. I remembered that I thought Dad was going to smoke. But he didn't ask for the matches. I struck one of them on a rock and watched it burn. Then one more. It was fun to do that, but I quit and put them back in my pocket. Oh, it was nice to rest!

I watched a couple of boats passing by. I waved to them and they waved back. I took out one of the birdies that I'd caught from the flour sack and looked it over. Then I started picking the down and feathers. Boy! It was fun to do it, so I kept on cleaning it.

I heard Dad calling me, "Nathan! Where are you? Are you all right?"

I answered him, "Right here. I just wanted to sit down for awhile." He had lost me and had been looking for me.

He said, "I thought you had gotten hurt and were hidden away."

"Oh, I'm sorry. I got tired of looking for birds, so I sat down for awhile."

I still kept on pulling the feathers off the tail, wings, and head. When I was through with it, I held it up. Oh! It looked funny. But it looked like a real baby's soft, fat tender skin. It was a baby of its kind, anyway. Ooops! My sad old thoughts came back to my mind, thinking of the birds as real people. "Oh, no; we are taking away their babies." Such thought built up a sickness in my head and down in my stomach. I pushed the bird back into the sack to get it out of my sight, because it really bothered me.

I was startled by a call, "Yo! Ho!" I looked up, and I jumped. There were some people watching me.

I felt bashful, because they had come right up to me before I saw them. One of them was Aaron Koneak. He had a sack filled with birdies. We talked a while. He asked me what I was doing.

I told him, "I worked on picking one of my birds."

He asked to see it.

I showed him. Oh! How they laughed to see the funny looking, half-bald bird. They did a lot to help me ward off my bad thoughts and get back into the fun of catching birds.

Once more I was going from rock to rock, once in a long while pulling out a young bird from under the rocks. I kept my mind real busy to keep out the sad thoughts that bothered me. There were some women and girls, too, hunting for those little birds. Some of them got quite a lot, filled their sacks almost full. But one of them had only two in her large sack. I felt sorry for her. Then I thought of giving her some of my birds. But I felt too bashful to do that, so I watched for a good chance to do it. I waited behind as she came up, I told her to hold open her sack and I threw in some of my birds. I told her to keep quiet, and I hurried away. I don't know why I felt bashful.

Soon I heard my Dad calling me. Some of the people were starting on their way home. With his arm Dad motioned to come to him. When I got there he had filled the tin can with water. We went down the hill together to a spot where there was somebody's tent frame. He gathered up some trash

146

and sticks and built a fire. A campfire. Gee! I liked the smell of the smoke. We called up to some of the hunters, and sat around the fire while the water was being heated for our tea. We were chewing our dried meat, joking, laughing, and just telling stories around the fire. I enjoyed myself. Maybe so did everybody.

I liked to hear the crackling sound the fire made as the sticks burned. Soon the water in the tin can boiled. I was surprised to see Dad pull out our cups, a small amount of tea, and handfuls of sugar cubes. Soon the tea was ready. It tasted smokey. Oh! I liked it very much. Somebody passed around homemade biscuits, fried in seal oil.

The fire burned down. Our eats were finished up. Dad told me to get ready.

I just asked back, "Get ready? What for? And to where?"

He just looked at me seriously for a moment and he said, "Why? Don't you have a home? Are you going to stay here while we go back home?" He pulled out his pocket watch that he wore around his neck hanging from a string, and showed it to me. It was very late in the afternoon, near evening. Oh, the day had passed by very quickly!

I filled up the tin can several times to make sure that the fire was out. We gathered our things together and then climbed up the mountain side. We walked all the way without stopping until we got to the same rock we had sat on the last morning. We sat there again for awhile. Then we went on until we got home.

The other happy part of our hunting came when Mother and the children saw what we had brought home. I liked to see them happy when they found out our catch. Both our boys liked to play with the birds. But this time they were funny. They both hastily opened our sacks, as always, expecting to find pretty birds. When they opened them and one of them pulled out a downy little, ugly looking birdie, they just dropped everything and screamed in fright and hurried away from the sack.

I asked them, "What's the matter?"

They both replied, "Those birds are very ugly looking! What happened to them?"

147

Oh! Well, I would have some fun with them now. I took one of the birds, and asked them to come and play with me. They screamed some more. I tried to hand the bird to them, and it made them wail. Oops! My fun was over already. I had put myself into punishment from my parents and earned some work to do. I was kind of tired, but I had to get some water for the house, and give water to our dogs, or do whatever else there was to do.

The next morning we helped Mom clean those birdies, and my brothers were no longer afraid of them. They happily picked the birds, sitting around the trash box. They made a mess of themselves; lots of fluffy down sticking to their clothes and hair. We laughed a lot when we found the bird that I had partly picked. It looked funny. The next meal was sure a hunter's reward. The soft, tender meat from those young birds was delicious.

By now I didn't feel as sorry for the birds as I had, and I was picking on Dad to go hunting at least once more. We did go hunting two or three times after that in the summer. Those times I got all the fun and was less bothered from thinking about the birds. It still bothered me, but not so badly as before. So I was catching the real sport and purpose of hunting. I learned that we must have something to eat, and we must get our food at every possible opportunity, and must store up food as much as we could get.

# 7. Nathan Joins the Church

My parents were not Christians. But they were not satisfied in pagan beliefs, either. We held some sorts of ceremonies, according to what the old people had taught. We were doing them just because it was the custom of our people. People thought there are gods everywhere—the weather god, god of the sea, and many others. All of them had to be worshiped in the proper way to please them. To please them, we offered sacrifices of what we had. If the gods were not pleased they would be angry, and cause us to be sick or have other harm. When we displeased the sea god he got angry and caused the sea to get rough with wicked waves, or the bad weather to come. There were many others beyond my learning, because I didn't care much to learn.

Aside from all the other gods, people had the belief that there was a God above all the others—what they called "Grandfather,"* who watched over everything, who caused every being. The God that was invisible but really existed, who watched over poor people and those who had become orphans or unwanted by other people. So our parents always talked to us to be good to such people. They said, "For Grandfather watches over them. You'll be punished if you do bad on them. And if the punishment is not on you, think of your brothers or sisters. They will be suffering for your cause." There were many rules that were to be followed. Never to steal, never to cheat anybody, and others. They said, "For what you have done to your fellow person, will be done to you by Grandfather."

There were many, many others, some funny and very foolish but they had to be carried out. Some funny medicine was believed to cure sickness. For boils they used beautifully made and designed ivory cups made by holy people. A cup was placed over the boil so the boil's spirit would feel proud and pleased and wouldn't do harm; the patient with a boil

* A literal translation of one Eskimo term for the creator and omnipotent deity—"Apa," which is the kin term applied to father's father, mother's father, and all males of their generation. There is another, more esoteric, term for this deity, Kiaganak, apparently used only in a ritual context.

was to take it easy so he wouldn't make the boil angry. Some plants were gathered to be used as medicine, some that were no good to eat, but had to be taken to cure sickness. There were some foods that people with certain sicknesses couldn't eat, food that would do lots of good to the patient. There are hundreds that I don't remember, or so many that I can't write all of them.

Women who were pregnant were on a special diet. They had to omit lots of kinds of food and were not allowed to watch or attend several things. And men wouldn't allow any pregnant women to ride in their hunting boats. Some of them were right and useful to do, but most of them were not all necessary to do. Growing boys were not allowed to eat certain foods or were not supposed to do some things that would have done a lot of good for them, but must be followed just because if a boy believed in them, the spirits would be pleased with boy and bring him out to be brave, strong, swift, and able to do lots of things.

I myself didn't believe most of them, and I didn't wish to follow them closely but I did it just to obey my parents. I wanted to be just a plain person. I did have some beliefs in both religions, and I was getting interested in Sunday School. We all liked it, but to me it was too mysterious. Some of it was very hard to understand.

Slowly our old beliefs and customs were fading away, and we were taking up the new religion, until we all took up the whole thing in one summer when a preacher came to our village to baptize the people [this was 1941 or 1942]. And we attended, too, because we had become deeply in religion now. I didn't know a thing about it, and it was the first communion we had had. All of it was very strange to me. A very new experience, it was. I wondered while we stood before the minister in a half-circle; I watched very closely as he dipped his hand into the water and held it on our foreheads and said his prayer. "What a strange thing!" And it looked funny to me. I felt awful, trying to keep from laughing and keep my face straight. Every time I glanced at David Akoak he was grinning, and I felt worse. Suddenly Dad noticed what I was doing and he nudged me on my shoulder. At once my feelings changed. I felt different. I felt as I was changed in person, too, even though I didn't understand what it really meant. As always, I felt as bashful as I could be. My face was very hot. I was glad when it was over, and I had to sit back on the bench with Herbert Kogoyak and somebody else. I felt the sweat running down my back. It felt uncomfortable. I didn't dare look up. I just stared down at the floor. Herbert's words were very soothing when he whispered in my ear. He said, "It's really good for you. I'm glad you did."

Then the minister uncovered the communion table. Turning around with the Bible in his hand, he read the scripture. He took the bread and blessed it, gave thanks, and then broke it, saying, "This is my body, broken for you."

I didn't understand a thing about it. How can such things be? How can the body of Jesus be broken for us and eaten?

When the plates were passed around, I just stared at it. It looked like bread cut in squares, just bread. But it must be very holy, I thought.

When the thing passed by I looked at Herbert Kogoyak questioningly, but he didn't say anything. And I didn't know how to ask him. I just murmured: "What? How? Could be?"

But he whispered back, "Just believe." Maybe I did.

After the bread had been passed around, the minister read the scripture again. In one hand he held the Bible and in the other hand he held a tiny little cup. He read, "In likewise he held the cup and gave thanks. This is my blood which is shed for many. Drink ye all of it."

I anxiously waited to see the tiny cups passed around. When it came to us, I looked at it carefully. It looked very much like blood, and must be, too. But how can the blood be kept that long? I wanted to pour on questions on Herbert, but I remembered we were told to keep quiet, so I bit back my questions. Oh, what a big mystery it was! I knew I must believe, but how and why are these done? It was tough. Too hard to believe, but I knew it was a must.

I was sweating; the church was warm and stuffy. I was glad when it was time to go. As Herbert and I got near the open door the fresh air smelled very good. The minister was by the door, shaking hands with the people. I felt bashful, especially because of the ragged, dirty clothing I had on. The minister held my hand tightly and spoke to me, but I couldn't find any words to say, so I just looked at him and smiled. At last it was time to ask questions of Herbert. I trusted him to know lots of things of what had been done, because his Dad was a very religious man (Kogoyak), an elder of the church.

I started asking as soon as we were out of the crowd. "What does all this mean? What is going to become of me now that I am baptized?" He looked at me thoughtfully for a moment. Then he said, "You have become a Christian, and you are saved; never to die."

Oh! I felt happy. I thought he meant that I would never die from this mortal life. I replied, "That's fine, but what was the meaning of the drinking of blood? Is it real blood, and does it taste good?"

He answered me again, "You've just got to believe what the preacher said. It is the symbol, and the cup contains not the blood. It is grape juice. Of course it tastes good. Now just let the things be and just believe. If you have some more to ask, ask my Dad."

I felt happy to be called a Christian like many people, even though I didn't know what it meant. But it was not for long. A few days later some boys and girls began to make fun of me. Even from my best friends and playmates I received such things. "Hey! You big Christian. Hey, you big believer. Let's hear you pray. Pray for that and this. Let's see you perform some miracles."

Gee! It was getting rough on me. But there were others that comforted me. Some said, "Let those say what they wish to say, but pay no attention to them. They don't know what they say."

But it was more than I could take, so I made excuses when Sunday came around and stayed home, mostly all by myself locked in our house. My parents asked me why I was acting that way, but I wouldn't tell the reason. Sometimes I would say I was going to the church, but then I would keep away from the village until the church service was over. Sometimes David Akoak or Francis Oalateetak stayed with me. Then we did some experimenting with things that we shouldn't. Other times we had just clean fun. We made little bombs of gun powder wrapped in paper, with a candle-wick fuse. It was lots of fun to blow up piles of sticks with them. Or we would half-bury them in gravel to make holes by blowing it up. Then we had beach fires by them, and boiled sea weeds just for the fun of it. When we had clean fun we made little wooden boats and sailed them in the lake; or we would have target shooting with our air guns. Every time we had our fun.

My relatives didn't want me to smoke. My parents were very strongly against it. Twice my Mom and Dad told me it would make me sick. They told me not ever to touch that thing, that it would spoil my lungs. My Dad said if I ever smoked he would not buy me any good things to eat or good clothing. Of course I didn't like that to happen, so I kept away from smoking. But I didn't hold that too long. Uncle Akoak let David smoke for some reason, but he talked to me that he wanted me to save my lungs to be a runner. He said, "David's not to be our runner; he is spoiling himself. But you I will always be proud of; you are to be our runner who will have strong lungs and run without running out of breath, and even if you run long distance. So leave the pipe and cigarettes alone."*

He himself didn't smoke (like my Dad), but my Uncle Nagotak was a very heavy smoker. I thought he was the best smoker on the whole island. So he didn't talk to me like my other relatives. He even handed me some cigarettes, but I turned them away. Then he would say, "Good boy."

Most of my friends smoked, even though we were nothing but kids. When people went to church, we gathered together somewhere. They would have picked up some cigarette stubs. One of them would have stolen matches, and some of them would have grabbed some smoking tobacco. Others would

* In the past, athletic contests were a characteristic feature of relations among the clans. Aside from prestige, such contests also served the function of intimidation and, by that, curbing of interclan violence.

have made crude little pipes out of wooden thread spools with copper tubing or feather tube stems. In one of the deep holes or somewhere on the beach they would puff away, passing the cigarettes from one person to another, or the crude pipe from mouth to mouth. One person who would do it best was chosen to light the cigarette or pipe. Otherwise the matches would be used up before they had lighted one cigarette. For payment he would get an extra cigarette stub. They offered or insisted on making me smoke, too, but I always refused. I didn't like it; even the smell of it would make me sick.

After I turned them down, they would ask me why I didn't want to smoke. I told them that my parents didn't want me to smoke.

They said, "Oh, go ahead. Your parents are not here. They won't know it."

When I told the whole story, they only told me, "We smoke always but we still can outrun you. Nothing has happened to our lungs. Your parents only tell you that to scare you."

I still kept firm, and I got the worst part of it when they said, "Let's leave him alone. He is not a guy. He is just a baby. He won't do any manly stuff. He is just a child. We don't want a child with us."

Now I was driven away with my head hanging low and my heart heavy. But I always cheered up because I'd obeyed my parents. Even though my friends said, "You don't know what you are missing," I still wanted to wait until I had grown older. I thought the use of tobacco and smoking was strictly adult stuff. That was not only my thought, but my Dad talked to me that way, too. He said that when I grew up and became a man and when I was old enough to provide entirely for myself, I might smoke or use tobacco if I wish. But the best thing was to leave that thing alone. I promised myself I would try it when I was old enough. I thought that was for men and something to be proud of. I admired the men with pipes or cigarettes in their mouth.

But I was tempted to experiment with that thing and was overcome by it. I became impatient and decided to try it.

I wanted to become really one of my gang of friends. I got tired of turning them down. Above all, I was tired of being insulted—that I was a baby and afraid to do the adult stuff. "I am old enough now," I thought; "I might as well start what real men do."

It was one Sunday morning. People had gone to church, including all of my family. As always, David Akoak and I were in my house talking about what we wanted to do. But we couldn't think of anything to do. At last I told him, "I know what to do. I know where Mom and Dad keep their chewing tobacco."

I opened the walrus stomach bag and I found some Black Bull chewing tobacco. I stuffed some into my pocket and I tied up the bag as it had been. Into the other pocket I pushed in a small handful of kitchen matches. Then I called, "David, come. We're going to do something."

He asked, "What are we going to do?"

I told him, "Just come with me; you'll see."

I ran to the nearest and deepest ditch. He followed right behind. We jumped into the hole. In the bottom, I pulled out the bunch of black tobacco from my pocket. Oh, it smelled strong.

"Oh Boy!" David exclaimed. "Do you have the matches too?" he asked.

"I sure have," I replied, as I patted my pocket.

He made an odd-shaped cigar. But I had trouble making one. Every time I rolled one it would unroll, or break in two in the middle.

Then he said, "Hey, let me have it. You are wasting the smoking material."

I handed the whole thing to him. He quickly made me a cute little cigar in a jiffy. I sure like it. Now to light it. I put the strange smelly thing between my lips. I struck a match, but I burned my finger and dropped it. I struck another one. It went out before I held it to my cigar. I couldn't do it.

Then David kind of insulted me. "Hey, you big baby. Let me show you how to light it."

I handed him a match. He struck it and started puffing

157

my cigar. The blue-white smoke shot out of his mouth and it smelled very strong and awful.

Then I took it back and drew my first puff of smoke. It tasted worse than it smelled. Boy! It was very bitter and the nastiest thing I ever tasted in my life. I blew out the mouthful of smoke right away. David asked me how I liked it.

Knowing what he would say, I pretended to like it and said, "It's good."

I accidently inhaled the second puff and I coughed like everything. It stung my nose very seriously. When I recovered from my coughing, I was not sure if I'd like to be a smoker. But David just urged me to smoke some more. He said, "Ah, come on. Take it like a man. Don't be a sissy. You'll learn with a few more puffs. It won't hurt you any."

I felt sorry to have started such a bad thing. But it was all my fault, so I kept on trying. Every time I attempted to draw in a puff it made me cough. It stung my lips, tongue, and nose. But I kept up the thing so I would become somebody by being a smoker. I already felt a sickness in my stomach and I felt dizzy and more dizzy, all the time coughing seriously, but still trying to puff my cigar—until the daylight seemed to grow dimmer and dimmer, and David's voice was getting fainter. He seemed to get farther away from me, and it got blacker. I reached out my arms to grasp his hand, but all of a sudden I completely blacked out.

I didn't know how long I stayed that way. The next thing I knew there were some funny noises ringing in my ears, and then a speck of light getting closer to me and bigger. Then I made out the funny noise to be my name. It was David talking to me, asking me if I was all right. When I got the full sense of things around me, I was down on my stomach and breathing fast and violently. My head burned with aching and felt hollow and light, but my stomach was awful and sick. The ringing noise kept steady in my ears. I felt like vomiting, but I couldn't. David just told me that I would be all right in no time. I hoped that he was right, because I felt awfully sick. After several tries, I vomited and felt a little better. I swayed from side to side as we walked to my house. Hoping a drink of cold water would make me feel better, I sipped a can of water. Oooh! My tongue burned as if it was on fire. And I vomited the second time. I forced myself to throw out all the contents of my stomach but I felt no better. I didn't bother to undress. I just dropped on a mat even with my shoe packs on.

At the same time my folks came in from church. Right away they noticed my sickness. My Dad asked me why or what made me sick, feeling my forehead.

I told him, "I don't know. I just felt very sick all of a sudden."

Then he said, "Maybe I know why you are sick," as he sniffed around. "Isn't it nice for you to get what you deserve by not keeping what I told you about smoking?" He knew right away that I had been smoking.

He asked me some more. "How do you like smoking?"

But I gave no answer. I was too sick. He looked at me for awhile, and standing up, he went out and came back with a package of cigarettes in his hand. Oh, no! What's he going to do?

"See what I got for you," he said; "Good pack of Luckies."

At the sight of the terrible thing my sickness increased. I turned the other way, facing the wall.

But he held the cigarettes in my face. Then he said, "Turn over. Let's smoke and have a good time."

I tried to refuse, but he kept firm. He said, "Now I get the proof that you have been smoking. How many times did I tell you not to smoke? Now that you want the thing, let's smoke and enjoy it."

Oh! I knew the worst would come if I refused him. So I had to take it. I said, "No," once more, but he went on and lit one for himself and he put the other between my lips. I just tried to hold it in my lips. I didn't dare draw a single puff. My sickness got worse. My head ached as if it would kill me. I felt as if I had no stomach at all.

When he got what he wanted out of me he pushed the cigarettes under my blanket. He left, saying, "You can have the cigarettes. Be sure to smoke all you want."

As soon as he closed the door I got rid of that ugly thing I had held between my lips, and threw the unwanted pack out of my blanket. Oh! What a punishment! But that was what I rightly deserved. I was sure I would never try to smoke, no matter how much anybody insulted me.

Dear Mom soothed my sickness the best way she could. She took it easy on me, as she always did. She said, "If you hadn't done that thing, you wouldn't have sickness now. I hope you will do better from now on." Nothing interested me—no food, drink, sleep, or anything. There I lay, trying to bear my sickness the best I could, trying to avert my unpleasant thoughts of tobacco and smoke. But they seemed to creep back to my mind. I even smelled the stale tobacco odor in my own breath. Oh! What a dreadful experience I had gone through.

After some time Dad came in grinning. He looked at me for a moment. Then he asked me, "Did you finish your cigarettes yet? Now how about some cigars or a pipe? Shall I get some for you? That's what I'm going to buy for you from now on—cigars, pipes, smoking tobacco, and cigarettes. Nothing else—no more candy, fruit, good things to eat, or good clothes."

Self-pity overcame me, and I couldn't hold back my tears, so I cried.

Within the next few days I recovered from my sickness. But I was tortured by the smell when some smokers came in and smoked in our house and lighted up and puffed away. All the unpleasant experience of my smoking came back to me at such times. Of course in my mind I didn't want anything like that, and so I paid no more attention when I was insulted about smoking. I just let them go. I kept firm when I turned down their offer, because I knew pretty well now that it would hurt me more if I smoked than being insulted. When my friends got together and whispered in each other's ears, I already knew what they were up to. I knew they had collected some cigarette stubs or had stolen some from their parents, or their older brothers had given them some as reward for doing their work. And at once I got the heck out of there, because I knew I would be invited to the dreadful stuff. That was not for me.

# 8. Unloading the Ship

The rest of the summer went by just as usual. The fresh meat shortage was high and the store was running low on everything, because for some reason the freighter was not coming. The whole village ran low on almost everything. Sometime in the summer a little boat (*Trader* by name) came around and supplied the village with flour, sugar, tea, or whatever little it had to trade. We traded some sealskins, ivory, leather ropes, and so forth for whatever the man had to trade, and it helped the whole village some. But it didn't last long. Within a short time the village had used up the little supply and had to go on as best as it could.

Every little thing was shared in the village as far as it would go. To me this life seemed hard and dull, without such things that we were so much used to having. Our food had become very nasty. I could hardly eat it. But is was better to eat it than go with an empty stomach.

Before I knew it school started. It felt kind of funny, but I liked to be back in school. The first day we were in school our teachers, Mr. and Mrs. Riley, carried in a big box full of neatly packed packages. "Oh! What can they be?"

Then Mr. Riley picked up package after package, calling out the names written on the packages. He told us not to open them until every one of the people got theirs.

I hardly could wait for mine. Then finally I heard the teacher call my name. I tiptoed up front to get my package. It was a heavy one, wrapped in blue paper, tied with a cord. Something in there rattled when I shook it. Oh! What could it be?

The minutes lengthened as I anxiously waited to open my surprise package. Everybody around me felt the same way. Some had bigger ones than the others. Mine was a big one, too.

At last everybody had gotten a package. Our teacher said, "Now open up your packages!"

My fingers trembled as I tried my fastest to untie the knot that tied up my package. Then I ripped open the paper wrapping. I found out what was in there. They were just my books! It was the pencil, an eraser, and a ruler that rattled in there. I looked over my writings in my note book and other papers. My writing was real funny, and there were some funny drawings.

Now I remembered that those packages were what we ourselves had packed up the last day of school. Some others also hadn't remembered and thought they were sent to us from somewhere. We laughed when we found out the truth.

Then our teacher passed out some additional things, such as fresh writing paper, new pencils, toothbrushes, and new books. Then came fancy boxes of candy or other sweets. When everything had been gotten in order for school, our teacher gave announcements of what he had heard through the radio. I thought it was the best and most exciting announcement that he made; what we had wanted to hear for a long time, what we were starved for. He started, "Now, we are all set for school. Everything is in order now. Do you have anything to say, or anything you need that we missed out in supplying you for school?"

Then came the sentence; after some moments of waiting, he went on, "If you don't have anything to bring up, here is the rest of what I have to say now. The school is going to be excused so you can help with the work with your parents and friends and neighbors."

Questions came up into my mind. "What work? Where? When?"

Before I could ask, he went on, "Tomorrow a military ship is due with supplies for the store and school."

Then came a very loud cheering; the room was filled with a roar. Our teacher had a bit of a hard time quieting down the people. When it was silent once more, he finished what he had to say. "Put away your books in your desks neatly, and go home and get ready for the big work. But do not forget the school safety rules. Keep away from the tractor. Keep out of the workers' way, and so forth. Now you may go."

Now the children got out of control. Everybody rushed to get their coats and parkas. Some desks and chairs were overturned. Then the wild people were caught and held back until the last desk and chair had been taken care of neatly.

When I was clear through the door, I operated my legs at full speed to carry my good news home. And so did my school mates. They ran wild in every direction, loaded with the best news of the year. I ran past people all the way home. Some people tried to stop me to learn what I was rushing about, but none stopped me. I was too excited for that. I shot in through the door and ran into Douglas, my brother. The can of water that he was holding flew out of his hands and landed upside down on the floor. I didn't even pay much attention to that. I first glanced from one surprised face to the other in my family. Dad was sitting on the floor with a vise between his legs, bending over his work with white sawdust all over in front of him, humming his queer little Eskimo song, and his cheek bulking full of tobacco. He looked up from his work in a scolding manner and exclaimed, "Hey! Hey! What's the matter?"

Douglas struggled to gain to his feet. The floor was wet and slippery under him. When at last he gathered himself together he first looked up as if he was going to cry. I hoped he wouldn't because I would be scolded on account of him, and he was Daddy's boy. But he looked different in the next instant. He looked back to me with his jaws dropped wide open, his eyes as big and round as a silver dollar. Martin was taking his usual nap. But now it was too noisy for any nap. He jumped out of his corner with puckered lips. But it was not the right time for that, either. Everybody was in an excited, happy manner. Mom was cooking whatever little we had to eat for our midday meal.

I was trying to spit out my good news. But I was completely out of breath and didn't have a single spare breath to use for news telling. Besides, I couldn't find the right words to say. I began, "Puff, puff, puff. Ship—puff—freighter—puff—tomorrow—puff—the store supplies—puff—will bring goods." I looked from one person to the other.

Mom dropped her fork. Douglas stood still drying his wet hands on the side of his pants. Martin forgot that he was about to cry. Dad was very surprised, but he just calmly and slowly chewed his tobacco, sucking on the juice.

Nobody got what I was trying to tell until I caught my

breath and told the story clearer. Then the good news drove my brothers crazy. They held each other, jumped up and down, yelling at the top of their voices. Daddy quieted down the crazed children and me, by shouting, "Quiet! Quiet!" Then we focused our eyes and attention on him.

He said, "We won't get our supplies as soon as the ship gets here."

My brothers asked, "Why?" in unison.

I added, "Why not?"

Then he replied, "Why? Don't you see the weather?" as he pointed to the window to find out the answer for my question.

And it was not a very pleasant answer. For the first time I realized it was a very windy, stormy day. How come? I didn't see the storm on my way home from the school. I must have been too excited and too full of happiness. That must be the reason for not noticing the wind and storm. My spirits sank when I stared at the stale weather through the window. My bright amusement melted away. But then I became brave and cheered everything up. I put in, "Let's get ready, anyway. We can't tell what tomorrow is going to be like." Everyone gave in.

I pulled off my wet rubber knee boots and damp clothing. Dad said, "Yes, let's get my carvings ready for trading in before tomorrow."

Mom cut in, "Let's have some tea before we do anything else. We can't get anything done on empty stomachs."

Yet while we were sipping our cups of nice strong tea, some boat captains dropped in to ask my father in whose boat he was going to work. Zachary Naciknak beat them all and he was the lucky one, because Dad said he'd work in his boat. There were several of them that went after Dad. I was to work on the shore. It was the hardest and toughest job, but they always arranged our age group in that job, and the reason was that people thought even though it was hard, it was safer than working in the boat.

Mother dug out our ragged, warm work clothing. Dad and I stuck our noses to the pieces of ivory. Before I knew it it was late in the evening when I did the final shining up job on the last ivory. We went to the store to get some needed things and to sign up for the work.

The ship was due in the morning the next day. After a hasty meal we lay on our mats. We three boys talked about nothing but the ship and the store supplies, turning over, picking on each other, laughing, playing with each other until our parents told us to be quiet and go to sleep. My little rascal brothers dozed off quickly, as soon as they were quiet. But me, I was too far from dreamland as I lay there. My ears seemed to be wide open. I wanted to listen to the wind blowing and to the whipping sound the rain made on the roof and the wind side of the house. Some of my family snored. It helped drown out the noise the wind made. Then I couldn't keep myself still. I turned over, tossed. I put my hands over my ears to drown out the noises that bothered me, but I was still wide awake. I got anxious about what the weather was outside; then I carefully and quietly slipped out of my covers and stood up to the window. I lifted the curtain, but I could see nothing but darkness. It was very dark, so the answer to my question about the weather was plain—it was very bad. On returning back under my covers, I made a noise that woke up my Dad. Looking up, he saw me and said, "Aren't you asleep yet?"

I told him I couldn't sleep.

But he insisted. "Try to sleep. Otherwise you might sleep late tomorrow."

I lay there staring at the ceiling and listening to the whistling sound of the wind. After some time of being in that mood I noticed the sound of the wind changing and the pitter-patter of the rain fading away. Slowly anxiousness increased. I got up several more times to look out the window. Every time it was too dark to see anything. I tried to think up something to do to cut the time, but there was nothing to be done quietly. Once again I looked out the window. I saw some stars twinkling brightly in the sky. "Oh! It's clearing up."

Then I looked at my brothers. Martin was sleeping with his eyes half-closed. I wondered if he was seeing things. Well, I thought up some fun. First I looked at my parents to see if they were asleep. Their stillness and steady breathing told me they were sound asleep. I got in front of Martin's eyes and passed my hand close to them. His eyes followed my moving hand. I saw that he was conscious of things moving in front of his eyes. Now for some fun, I flailed my arms, making a funny movement. First he just groaned in his sleep and then he laughed. Then I wanted to know if I was really making him dream. I got closer to him. I made awful faces, making movements in a scary motion, and making a low growling sound deep down in my throat. First his face wrinkled and he gave a short sobbing. As soon as he stirred I slipped under my covers and pretended sleep. I heard him scream, calling "Mom!" Mom asked him what was the matter, comforting him. He said that he had had a scary dream.

At first I giggled, but then I felt very sorry, remembering the bad dreams I'd dreamed. It bothered me. "Why do I do such a bad thing to a dear little brother?" I felt like crying. I promised myself I would make up for that by buying him something real good when I worked.

I didn't know that I'd fallen asleep until I heard somebody calling Dad. I snapped out of my sleep at the thought of the ship, and forced my sleepy eyes open. It was Zachary Naciknak. He said, "The ship is due to arrive in a few hours." He wanted Dad to help to get ready for the work before the ship arrived. He also said, "It's too rough for work, but the boats are to be ready anyway."

I snapped out of my drowsiness and helped get breakfast and got into my work duds. I took a long look at my brother Marty (as I called him). I felt sorry for what I'd done to him last night.

Soon we were out of doors. The wind had changed to north, and the rain had let up, but the waves were kind of high. We went to the men gathering around Zachary Naciknak's whaleboat. As soon as we got there they moved the boat to the shore. Other boat crews with their captains were getting their boats ready. But there was no ship yet. As in everything else, the kids were around, being helpful and bothering at the same time. When all the boats to be used for the work were ready, some men went home and some stayed around their boats to chat with old pals and buddies. After a moment Dad asked me to walk home with him. When we got there the boys were getting up and having their breakfast. We had a cup of tea ourselves.

When we were just about through David Akoak ran in with much excitement. He almost shouted out his news. "Here it is. It's arriving." We knew what he meant, so I just pulled on my rubbers and rushed out. He showed me where it was. Sure enough, there was the long-awaited ship. It was not a big one, but it was bringing our supplies anyway. We ran to Zachary Naciknak's boat.

The weather was not very good. The waves were high—too rough for working. Strong, cold, north winds blew, and the sky was all darkened with heavy clouds. When the ship came around to the south side and anchored some distance off shore, the whaleboats were pushed out. The working crews got in their boats and the other men waited for the right time to push out the boat. The big waves looked very dangerous, and they made a loud noise. Some men got wet when the boat was pushed out at the wrong time.

When the last boat was pushed out we sat on the beach with the cold, stinging wind to our back. Some men said that we wouldn't get our supplies in this kind of weather—that was clear enough. Everyone knew the weather was too tough, but most of them still had lots of hope. That included me.

The boats stayed at the ship a long while. We played tag or ran around to keep warm. At last one boat came, but it didn't have anything in it. The crew cut their motor, without hitting the shore or nosing in. They made signals for us to go to the far end of the lake or even farther. They thought the waves were low enough over there for doing some work. While we were walking, the workers' boats were taken up on board the ship and they went the same way. They went all the way to a place called Oyneck. The ship and the whaleboats got there first and some men got there, too, running on the shore. While we were on our way it started raining. I put on my walrus gut raincoat.

There were three of us walking some way behind the rest

of the people. We were Nusalaq, Edwin Nanok, and I. We ran sometimes, or stopped for a while, and walked. It seemed a long way. All the way Edwin bothered us. He was a very bothersome rascal. Once when Nusalaq lighted up his pipe, Edwin snatched it out of his mouth and ran away with it, puffing on it. In spite of his being thin and small, he was swift. Nusalaq ran after him, but couldn't catch him for some distance. Every time he was close enough to catch him, Edwin made a sharp turn to one side, and poor Nusalaq was not quick enough to get hold of him. He finally caught him, but Edwin wiggled himself free before Nusalaq could get his pipe back.

As he is ill-tempered, Nusalaq was kind of mad. When at last he got a good grab on him, he first took back his pipe. Then he sat down with Edwin on his lap, who was giggling at the joke he had played on the old man. But Nusalaq pulled down Edwin's pants and spanked away. Slap! Slap! Oh, I had a good show. I thought Edwin was still laughing, but he was crying with the very first slap. Served him right. When Nusalaq was satisfied, the place where he had been spanking was red. As soon as Edwin pulled up his pants he grabbed some rocks and started throwing them at us until we had to run for it. Some of his rocks missed us by only an inch. We were glad when we ran out of the throwing range.

Edwin caught up with us, but he had cooled down. Now we were close enough to see the men on the beach and boats going back and forth from the shore to the ship. But there was about half more mile to walk before we got there. The closer we got, the faster we walked. We made out that the boats were unloading some boxes, but they were having a tough time at that work, because the waves were very high. But it was a little better than the other place.

All of this time it was raining like everything. At last we got there. First of all Nakak called us to come to his tent, which he used as his portable office, because he was a store director, in charge of some things in the store. So we went over to him and signed in to start our time for work. After he got our signatures in his note book he passed us some pilot bread. Oh, boy! We hadn't had a crumb of anything in so long a time, it tasted just great. Just simple pilot bread, but going without any white people's food for so long, even the simplest thing tasted good to us. Nakak said as he passed around the stuff, "Have a bit of those to build up your strength for the hard work you are to do."

The little tent was cozy to get into out of the merciless downpour of cold rain. When the last bite of good-eating stuff was swallowed, we ran out for work, I wringing my badly soaked gloves that clung to my wet hands. To my surprise the waves were much higher than when we first got there, and some boats were turning back to the ship with their load of cargo, because they couldn't nose in to unload, or if they did, their boat would be filled with water and the most-needed cargo would be soaked.

But we got busy piling boxes and sacks of flour and sugar into a big pile and covered them with heavy tarps. The village caterpillar was hard at work, too. It was taking home some of the cargo, as much as the sled would hold for a load each trip.

When the water got too rough for hauling in some cargo, the boats towed in some lumber in big timbers bound with rope. When the boats got close in they anchored offshore and threw us a line. Then we pulled in the timber. We untied it, then carried it up farther on the shore, making piles of that kind of lumber here, and this kind over there.

At the change of current the waves got lower, but they were still too rough for the boats to nose in. But they did bring in barrels of oil and gasoline. A line was tied to the barrel, the other end was thrown to us, and the barrel was dropped overboard. We pulled it up on the shore, far enough up so the waves wouldn't wash it away.

As we passed by the leeside of the kitchen tent, a whiff of the wind brought us a real good smell of the food the cooks were making for lunch. My right shoulder was getting sore from carrying lumber, the rain had soaked through my walrus-gut raincoat, and my hands were wrinkled from soaking.

Kazighia and Nakak, who were in charge of the work, came

out of their office tent and told half of the workers to get their lunch while the other half carried on their work with the boats. Some more of them stayed at the ship to get some grub. I went with the last half of the workers to fill my tummy. Oh! It was real nice to be out of the rain. The camp stove was red hot. The big coffee pot was boiling away. Some of the cooks wrung out our wet gloves and hung them up to dry while we ate. They served us boiled reindeer meat, coffee, and some bread. Gee! I don't know what was better than that lunch. A thought popped up in my mind while I was sipping some coffee. I remembered how I had scared my poor little brother, Martin. I knew I was going to make up for that so my thought would be smoothed out. I asked for a paper sack and I stuffed some of my lunch into it—some of my bread and dried fruit. One of the cooks noticed what I was doing and she asked me what I was doing that for. Besides, she and my Dad were pals. I told her I was saving them for my brother.

She thought for a moment, then she said, "Go ahead and eat those yourself. I will save some for you to take home."

When our time for lunch was over, we got up. My legs were already numb from soaking and fatigue. I got my gloves from the drying line. They were dried and they were comfortable and warm—but only to be soaked in the next few moments.

The work was carried on with lumber and barrels. All the while the rain poured on. I was wet from inside out from sweating and the rain. Just before dark Nakak and Kazighia gathered our age group. They told us to get our coffee at the kitchen tent and start for home. While we were in the tent it got dark. There was Victor Kazighia to take us home, to see that each one of us got home.

Just before we went that same woman handed me a nicely tied paper wrapping. I thanked her and put it under my coat. The cooks were going to ride home on the sled pulled by the village cat.

We started for home, led by Victor. My feet felt heavy from fatigue. The way seemed long. The lights seemed to get no closer as I watched them while walking on. Finally

172

the rain stopped and the dark blue sky was dotted with bright stars and the wind became chilly. Even though I was walking almost as fast as I could to keep up with the others, I was cold. The Mala girls were with us, Connie and Louise. To kill the time and distance I kept my eyes just in front of my feet, because when I looked on ahead the village lights seemed to go farther instead of get closer. After some time of doing this I looked up and saw that we had covered a lot of the way. I got back to what I was doing and the next time I looked up we were just about there. There was the edge of the lake, closest to my home.

The boys were asleep but Mom and Ann were up. I was worn out. As long as Dad wasn't home, I pulled off my wet clothes and dropped into bed. But Mother served me some tea and other eats. She wouldn't let me sleep without eating. I remembered the paper wrapping that the kind lady had packed for my brothers. I cut the string. It was kind of wet, but the contents were all right. Martin was sleeping on his side. I held the open paper sack in front of his nose and called softly in his ear. Before he woke up he sniffed in the paper sack. He opened one eye; then the other. Rubbing his sleepy eyes he got hold of the sack, sitting up. Then he forgot he was sleepy. He squealed with joy. "Ohoo! Where did you get them?" Oh, I was filled with affection and I got the rewarding hug around my neck from both of the boys. Then I took up my rest and slept.

The next morning when I woke up there was Dad with us, and the morning was bright. Dad told me almost all of the cargo was brought in from the ship during the night, but the waves had gotten high again, so the boats were pulled up and they had quit working for rest. All of the lumber had been taken onto the shore and most of the store barrels were still at the ship. The water was too rough for any work at all. And the north wind was strong. The boat captains called up their crews and the rest of the working men went after the whaleboats. It was too rough at sea. So the boats were pulled on land and paddled across a lake and pulled on the ground to the next lake, until all of the boats were on the shore of Lake Troutman.

We boys had been running with the sticks that the boats were pulled on. I was very glad when the last boat was at the edge of the lake. We had a boat ride across the lake, but we were drenched from the spray the boat made as it hit each wave with the force of the bow and the wind blew the spray into our faces. We made it to the other shore of the lake. Again the boats were pulled on the ground to their places.

After another day or so of the same tough, windy weather, the village got word from the ship skipper that the remaining barrels in the ship were to be dropped overboard to see if they would be washed up on the beach, and if the first one got washed up, the rest of them would be dropped. We watched the barrel that was dropped from the ship. It drifted away with the current and was washed up on the shore during that day some miles from the village, somewhere east on the other side of the mountain. So all of the barrels were dropped into the sea.

After the ship had gone it was payday—the happy part of the time when we were supplied. I was surprised when I found out that my pay was more than half as much as my Dad's pay. With the money I got us some nice looking red sweat shirts. I proudly gave the shirts to my brothers. When everything was settled down once more, we started to school again. I proudly wore the new red shirt that I had got myself. Our teacher made a short speech that made everybody happy, too. The speech concerned how we had been loyal to the school safety rules, and how hard we had worked. He said that he was very glad to see that we had earned our own school clothing. Oh, I hadn't felt so proud before. After the speech new books were passed around and fresh papers and pencils. I thought that made the school more pleasant and enjoyable.

The next few days we got our promotions. Now that included me. Boy, oh boy! That made me feel like somebody special. At the close of school for the day I asked our teacher to let me take my books with me for home work, but that was not the real reason why I asked. It was that I wanted to show them off to my folks. He let me. I proudly showed them off and, as I had promised, I stuck my nose in them that evening before bedtime and did some work. And Dad liked looking them over.

To my displeasure, when I got farther into the school and my new, pretty books, my proud days and happiness were almost over. My proudness turned the other way; my books became very wicked—too full of hard work to do, and of mysterious questions. The school became a gloomy, dull idea again. I lost all of my interest in it.

# 9. The Dream Seal

Now all of our meat was very low and old. Only once in a while we had some reindeer meat—that was most welcome. But the promising north wind blew, which would bring in the ice, and it would be good hunting. It blew harder and harder and cooled every day, until it began to snow. And then it was very stormy. When the storm let up, some icebergs were seen. As always, men got their hunting gear ready. As for my Dad, he made a new toboggan out of whale baleen, and an ice tester pole with a sharp hook at one end, and at the other end was a sort of blade made of an iron pipe sharpened and shaped to test the young ice for safety.

After a day or so the Bering Sea was white with ice. The men went hunting. I went to school. I didn't do any good that day in school, because it was hard for me to put my mind on what I was to do. Instead, my thoughts went with my Dad out hunting. I wanted to make believe that I was shooting a seal, mukluk, or even a walrus. But I dragged myself around in school all morning. Every little chance we got, David, Francis, and I got together and chatted about hunting. We told each other if the weather was good on Saturday we would ask our Daddies to let us go with them out hunting. We talked on until a rough, gruff voice or a high pitched voice called out, "Boys! Get busy." After the usual classes, we would be excused for lunch. I was poor in my work in the class, but who cared? It didn't bother me. All I wanted was to be released from that unpleasant, sissie school.

A little before noon our teacher had news for us. He told us that Poduk and some others had been lucky and killed a walrus. Now I felt more hungry—so hungry that I could hear my stomach crying. I couldn't keep still. Several times I visited the toilet unnecessarily, just to shorten the time, but I couldn't settle down to my work. Nor could the other kids. Not only were we anxious for good food, but it was far more than that. We wanted to see the smooth-as-glass ice to see if it was thick enough for skating or coasting on slopes with our handmade, crude sleds, or whale baleen toboggans borrowed from a hunter-father. Somehow I pushed away my strong, delightful thoughts and got busy with my work and forgot about the time. I was so busy I never noticed the minutes dropping by.

After what seemed like a few minutes but really was an hour, our teacher stood up in front for short story announcement, or just a little talk to take up the last ten minutes of the school day. This time he had a short story that ended by someone saying that he was hungry, and our teacher added, "I'm hungry, too. How about you?" Then came the answer from everyone. "We are hungry too." Everybody liked the last ten minutes best of all.

We were very much under the control of our teacher. We were made to leave the room in order, row by row. Otherwise a person got a sort of penalty for violating the rules. So while we might have been as wild as stampeding cattle, we marched out row after row, until we were clear out of the door. Doormen were posted to report anyone who had not gone out as the rules told them to do. Then he or she had to stay some extra time after school for punishment. But it was hard to do as the rules said that day. I didn't know that I had started running when I was halfway through the hall.

Boy, oh boy! It was a nice day. The sky was blue and bright sunshine. Francis Oalateetak and I ran all the way to our houses. We saw some blood-stained snow in front of the houses. That assured us of the luck of the hunter-daddies. As always I dashed in through the door, and landed on a mukluk skin that my Dad had brought home. When I opened the inner door, my sniffer caught a whiff of a good smell. Mom had been cooking fresh meat. But it was a funny thing; Mom served only a little bit of the fresh meat, and served some of the greens and nasty meat.

So I asked her, "Why, Mom? I don't want to eat this old stuff. I want fresh meat."

But she only said, "No, no, you'll get sick if you eat your fill of fresh meat. We haven't had it for a very long time. It is too strong for us."

It was the same with our lean dogs; Dad fed only a small piece to each dog. He said, "If we feed them more, it will kill them."

180

The story Dad told kindled up a flame of desire in my mind. He told how some of the men had shot a walrus in open water, and told of the mukluk he had killed—how close it was when it came up in the water, and how he hadn't needed his seal hook to get it. He had got it with the hook on the ice testing pole. When I thought of it, I was sure I would kill something that close. I wished that I at least could try one day of hunting. But I knew that Dad would only say, "You must go to school. Besides, I want you to wait a little longer." So I bit back my words and went on to school.

The first thing in the school in the afternoon was spelling. My mind was too far from that, and I didn't do any good in spelling. I had plenty of words that I had to work over. Next came arithmetic. I was worse in that. After the class was sent back to their seats and desks, our teacher wanted me with him for a moment. I sat by him at his big desk. My heart hammered against my chest. I knew he was a rough person, but to my surprise this time he was very gentle. He spoke to me at almost a whisper. He started, "I don't know what is wrong with you. You have been the best student in your class, but all of a sudden you fall back. Surely something is wrong with you. If this goes on I'm going to lower you to the next lower grade. But if you tell me what's wrong with you, I will do my best to help you over that thing that's bothering you."

I was very much stunned. I couldn't find a word to say. All I said was, "I don't know."

Then he told me to go back to my desk and get busy and he added, "We will talk this thing over later on."

When I sat back at my seat, I put my opened book in front of me and pretended to be busy. Others just in front of me and one to my back poured on some questions, but I couldn't hear any of them. I sat there thinking, thinking, and thinking until I dreamed up an idea. I made up my mind to write a note to the teacher before going home. It was not the first time that I wrote him a note. Several times I'd been doing that to get help from him over any rough spots. But this time it was going to be a special note. So

I got busy and wrote a note and read it over; then tore it up, and made another note. And I went on until I thought I'd done my best. The note read: "Dear Sir, I want to go hunting very much. Please, shall I go with my father tomorrow? That is my trouble. Please answer me. Nathan K." Then I waited for a chance, putting the note between the pages of my book.

When the teacher left his desk for a moment, I wadded up some scrap paper and walked to his desk, pretending to be getting rid of my trash. And I dropped my folded sheet of paper where he could see it. When he returned to his desk, I watched him with the corner of my eye. I saw him pick up my note. After he read it, he glanced at me, and started writing something. It was near time for us to go to the other room for our ivory carving class. When he stood up from his desk, I fixed my eyes on my book. My heart beat as if it would break out through my chest. I even sweated a bit. As he passed by he dropped a folded sheet of paper on my desk. Without drawing any attention from other students, I opened it carefully. I read it, holding it in the page of my book so I would look as if I were busy reading my book. The note read: "Please see me after your ivory carving class. We will talk this thing over privately. Thank you."

I went to our carving class. I did nothing much. My mind was too concerned about the talk with my teacher. I didn't get my work on ivory any farther. Our ivory carving teacher, Magpa, kept asking me, "What's the matter? Are you all right? Are you sure you are not sick?"

"I'm fine; it's nothing," I said.

And he said, "Then get busy. You are wasting your time; and remember you need money from that ivory."

I pretended to be busy, but I was really doing nothing with my carving. But my mind was busy polishing up some words for my talk about my hunting.

I thought it was the longest hour of the whole day. My being in this mood worried Magpa. After urging me to get busy several times, he said, "Something is wrong with you. As I am responsible for this, I don't want you to carry on as you are. And I don't want to get into trouble with your parents if I make your sickness worse, if you are sick. Now you had better go home and lie in bed."

But I kept firm and refused to be excused, and I didn't tell him anything about that talk with my teacher that I was anxious about. I didn't want anybody else to know it.

At last 4:00 came. As soon as I put away my work and tools in their proper places, I went to see my teacher. He was in his office and was too busy with his radio talking to other places. I sat in the office, waiting for him to be through with his business. He nodded his head at me in a friendly manner.

Some people asked me why I was sitting there, but I didn't answer anybody. When he was through he asked me to go with him to the school room, where we would not be bothered by people as we talked. He said he wanted this privately. My heart started beating harder and harder. He asked me to sit in front of him while he sat down in his chair behind his big desk. Then he began: "I want you to learn in school very much. We need you here. We can hardly spare you just a day."

I kept silent as a mouse.

"But I have been thinking about it this afternoon. If you're thinking too much about hunting, you won't do any good in school. Does your father want you to go hunting with him?"

I answered, "I don't know. But I'm sure he wants me to learn about hunting, and I want to go hunting more than anything else."

He asked me, "Are you tired of school?"

I said, "No, I'm not, but I like hunting very much."

He said, "Oh, I see. Tell you what. If your father really wants you to go hunting, I will let you go. But I will give you extra homework, and I wish you will write a story about your hunting every time you go hunting while in school."

I hated to write stories, but I said, "Yes! Yes! I will do that."

"Now remember—I will let you go hunting only once a week."

Again, I said, "Yes." Now I was full of joy, but I had to work on my father, now that I was cleared with my teacher.

Just before he excused me he told me not to tell anyone of my schoolmates. He said, "Be sure to remember to keep this thing to yourself only. If you tell them they will want to go hunting, too, and hunting will take away their attention from school, as it has done with you. Now you may go, but take your books with you."

Oh boy! My mind was so full of good stuff, I started to run; but I stopped short when I ran across a thought that wised me up. If I ran I might attract people's attention, and make them ask me what I was so excited about. So I slowed down my legs. But my thoughts were in a big hurry and way ahead of me.

It was getting dark in the short days of November. Men were getting in from hunting, busy taking care of the meat they had taken home, and unharnessing their dogs. My mind was so full of good news to tell my Dad, it felt as if it would burst open. Just as I thought, on the way home I met Francis Oalateetak and David Akoak, waiting for me, full of questions. I quickly made up my mind to fool them, and thought up something that would conceal my truth. They started, "Why in the world did you stay in after school? What did you want from the teacher? What did you do?"

I answered, "Oh, it was just to work over the wrongs I made today."

One of them asked again, "Then how come you stayed so long a time?"

I still kept back the truth. I didn't want to tell a lie, but I was doing it in a good cause. So I told them I had had a hard time.

Then they started insulting me. They said, "Oh, yes. We forgot you are a big dope." That didn't hurt me a bit, not a little bit; rather, I just grinned because the truth behind what I had been talking about was too good to make me feel bad, even though they said dirty stuff to me. Besides, it was not the first time they'd done such a thing to me, and we were used to being that way to each other. So we just went on to my home.

When we got there my Dad had just come in from hunting. We helped around. When things were taken care of Francis and David skipped along somewhere, but I insisted on eating with my family. They had asked me to go with them, but I turned them down, no matter how much they asked me to go with them somewhere. Partly I wished to go with them, because they had said something by our secret code in speaking. They said, "We have some 'Thank you,' and 'You are welcome.'" (We used words "thank you" for cigarettes and "you are welcome" for matches.) We thought nobody would suspect anything out of those nice words and we were right. Nobody knew what we really meant when we talked in our secret code talk.

I had a strong desire to be with my folks that evening, so I kept firm until they were by themselves, and I went in with my Dad. My folks asked me, "How come? Why do you bring your books with you?"

I answered, "Why? Of course, to work on them." I don't know why I didn't let out my news until after supper.

My Dad told us that he was awfully unlucky, or that something was wrong with his rifle. He said that he had missed a lot. Now I had a chance to go with him. After some waiting, at what I thought was the right time, I spoke up. I let out what was in my mind. I began, "Dad, may I go with you when you go hunting tomorrow?"

My Dad was very much surprised, because it was the first time I'd asked to go. He only asked, "What do you mean? What are you talking about?"

I said, "I mean, I want to go hunting with you tomorrow if it's good hunting."

But he asked me, "What about the school?"

I answered him. "I'm going to do my school now," I told him as I held up my books.

Again he asked, "What is your teacher going to say? I will be responsible if you miss school without his permission."

But I had something to say for that, too. I told him I had been responsible for myself. I had been talking with my teacher, and had cleared everything.

But he still was in doubt. He said, "I don't trust you. Are

you sure you have talked the things over about your hunting?"

I kept firm; I was backed up with lots of truth. I told him, "If you don't believe me, go see my teacher for yourself."

At last he gave in. He said, "If you have cleared the things up, I will be glad to have you along with me, then. But I will go ask your teacher tomorrow morning before we go."

He and Mom told me to wear my warm fur clothing. But now I didn't like to be in those old furs. They were too warm, stiff, and bulgy. I sniffed my nose in refusal, but Dad said again, "If you will not wear that clothing, it is best for you to stay home and go to school." Oh! How many things did I have to do before I could go hunting! But I was glad enough to do anything, as long as it would help me to go hunting.

Just before Dad went out to get some ammunition for the rifle from the store, I asked him, "Now do I get ready?"

He answered, "If you have told the truth, you may."

As the first thing I took my own rifle from the corner. It was nothing much but a pile of junk, rusty junk. It was a Remington .22 long rifle, so old that it very often misfired, and sometimes I had to take it apart on the spot, because it got jammed and wouldn't work. And by the time I had put it together the game would be way out of sight. But when it fired my shots would almost always count. It still shot quite straight, and maybe that's why I loved every screw pin and rust scale on it. I liked its looks but to other people it was just funny junk that was too old-fashioned; way out of style, but I cleaned it carefully and lovingly, and placed it back in its corner carefully.

Then I worked my dry, hardened mukluks and other bits of clothing to soften them for better comfort. Last of all, I did my school home work while I lay on my reindeer mat with the light from a kerosene lantern. Many times I had to tear up my work and do it all over again. I kept that up until quite late, to make sure I got every problem right to the word and letter and every figure, without a single mistake. Checked them and rechecked them. I had been working so hard it tired out my mind and I slept quickly as soon as I had put my books away to a safe place, where my little rascal brothers wouldn't get them.

I had been sleeping very soundly when I was awakened by something. I was sitting up when I woke up. I wondered what woke me up, because I was very sleepy, rubbing my eyes. Then I remembered that I was going hunting that day. It was not time to be sleepy, but I saw it was only 3:30 in the morning. "Oh! It is too early. If I don't get enough sleep, I will be too lazy in the morning." So I lay back again. For a few minutes I had a little hard time to get back to sleep. The sporty thoughts of hunting kept on rolling in my mind, and I wanted to listen to something, but I didn't know what. Every little sound rang in my ears.

I was dozing off finally when a loud noise wakened me up. I snapped out of my sleep. The noise was made by a dog shaking off the snow from its back, a dog that was chained to one corner of the house. When he shook, the chain whipped against the house, making lots of noise. But I dozed off quickly in the next few minutes.

Back in dreamland I was walking with my father on the white ice at the edge of a small pool of open water. Dad handed me a rifle and a few rounds of ammunition, and walked off to some place. I sat there in wait for the seal to come up. After just a little while a big seal came up. I slowly and very carefully took my rifle up and pushed in a round of ammunition, and closed the bolt and then cocked it, keeping my eyes on the big fat seal. Then I brought the butt of the rifle up to my shoulder. Then I lined up the sights on the seal, resting my rifle on the pile of ice to make it steady. I even held my breath. When I was sure of the alignment of my sights and sure of hitting the seal, I squeezed the trigger and kept on pulling it as far as I could. Pulled it harder and harder. When I applied my strength on the trigger I knew something was wrong when the rifle didn't fire. I wondered, "What's wrong?" I opened the bolt and I pushed in a fresh round of ammunition this time, and I fixed my sights once more. This time it fired but it only made a funny little report, and just merely dented the fat seal. "Oh! What going on?" I was very much startled when the seal laughed at me deep from its throat.

Now the seal crawled up on the ice, roaring, telling me, "That gun you have is no good. Don't ever trust it." When it came closer, showing its sharp white teeth with long sharp fangs on the lower and upper jaws, I couldn't figure out what was happening. But it was a good thing that my rifle had become an automatic. I poured bullet after bullet at the scary-looking seal. Some of the bullets bounced off the seal, some went right through it, but that didn't seem to do any harm to the monster. Now I fired my gun like a madman, while the scary monster came on roaring loudly and getting closer. Then to my relief it lay motionless, but still full of life, groaning in pain, begging to be killed quickly. I felt very wicked now, but my bullets didn't do any good in killing it; so I grabbed my rifle by the barrel and was raising it to hit the horrible thing on its head, when I snapped out of it and I sighed in relief. It was all just a nightmare, but it was so real I thought it was real.

The tea for breakfast was just about done. My Dad had started a primus stove. The noise it made might have been the roar of my monster. "How's the weather? Is it good for hunting?" I asked Dad.

He nodded his head in answer. "Have your breakfast and start getting ready, if you are sure you have cleared it with your teacher," he said. "But I still don't trust you. I don't want to be blamed for this if he hasn't given you the permission. I want you with me, all right. You might be a better shot than myself, because I'm having very tough luck. I missed almost every shot." He added, "I'll go ask Mr. Riley. I'll take Sakigak with me to help me. If you haven't told the truth, I'll send you right back to school."

I was not a bit afraid, because I had cleared with him already. I told my Dad, "He told me not to let any other boys know about my hunting except you and myself."

Dad told me to harness up our dogs. I did that while he went to see the teacher. First I pushed my ammunition into one of my pockets, and in the other I pushed in some cubes of sugar for our tea. Then I harnessed up our dogs.

It was snowing and the wind was kind of strong. Because of the weather I was not sure if we would go. But I got everything ready anyway. When my father returned he was happy that I was going with him. I asked him, "Are we going in this weather?" I was surprised when he told me it was perfect for hunting.

It was still dark when we started. My Dad had never believed me when I told him that I could go faster than some dog teams by skating. This was a good chance to prove it to him. I asked him to let me strap on my skates and go ahead of him, but he wouldn't let me. He only said that I would waste our time. But I took my skates with me anyway.

On the way we caught up with some other hunters that I knew well. One of them was Edward Aiyaksaq. He was surprised to see me going hunting, and he bid me good luck in our own way and words. And there was Sakigak, catching up with us.

The daylight was getting brighter when we went down the other side of the mountain. Down we went to Igalok's summer camp. And the snow had let up and it was not so windy on the other side as it was near the village.

There were many other hunters, but there was not any of my age. I was the only boy going hunting. Most everybody was surprised to see me, and they asked me too much— like why I hadn't gone to school. I kept quiet, as I had been told to do. Soon we found a place for our dog team and secured them with the anchor and tied them to a big rock. And there was Louis Kogoyak, Dad's brother-in-law. I was glad he was around, too.

While Dad was busy with the dogs, I untied our hunting gear. Those were our rifles, a small sealskin hunting bag that contained our extra mittens, clothes, ropes, sealhook, and other things. Dad had an ice tester pole and he had tied up a stick. I didn't know why he was taking along that extra bothersome stick. And he had a toboggan which I wished to have for myself for coasting down the small slopes on the snow. It was a slick thing for that purpose. When he got through with the dogs he picked up his rifle and the other things that he had brought with us and he handed me his one pole. I didn't know why I would need the ugly-looking stick. I didn't like it a bit. So I said, "I don't need this awful thing."

He gave me a gruff answer, "You dope. You need that thing. Take it or stay behind," he said. So I went along, with my .22 Remington rifle on my back, and held that stick.

Dad led the way. We passed by some hunters, some at the edge of open water. No sooner had we done that but we heard somebody fire already. I was really full of thrill as we walked, and I wished I could shoot something. Now I knew the importance of the ice tester poles, as we followed the safe ice. I couldn't tell any difference between the safe ice and the thin ice. I couldn't test the ice, but Dad did. He knew the ice, and he told me many things about ice. But I didn't catch a thing about it. It was too mysterious to me.

As we walked he stopped and stared at a particular place and said, "Look, there is open water over there. We'll go there."

But I never saw any water. To me it was ice, ice, and ice all around us. I asked him, "Water? Where? I don't see any water."

He said, "I didn't see the water, but I knew where the water is."

Oh, my! How did he know? He looked at me a moment and pointed to the ducks flying at a distance. "See them go down at that place?"

Sure enough, they went down and disappeared into the ice. Well, I learned two things about hunting now: the use of the ice tester pole and how to find the open water by watching the ducks. But I was not going to believe this until I saw the open water myself. On we went to that place. I lost the location already, but Dad knew it. He had remembered the place by the mountain at the sky line. He kept the place in his mind.

I was surprised when we saw the water; it came into sight just dead ahead. There were some men close by. We recognized them; Chuka and Edward Aiyaksaq were right next to us, and there were some others, too.

When we got to one of the small open patches of water, Dad piled up some pieces of ice for me to rest my rifle on while shooting. There were some small ducks on the water. Before he left he looked at my rifle thoughtfully. He said, "You have a very poor rifle. I don't trust it."

I told him it was good—"See me get that duck." And it was a good-looking duck too. I wanted it very much.

Dad said, "OK, let's see you shoot it."

I worked the action; pulled and pushed to close it; then rested the gun on the pile of ice. I next lined up my sights carefully, held my breath, and applied pressure on the trigger. I was expecting the "Pop!" of the rifle, and a light recoil; but there was only a low "Click!" of the hammer. It had misfired.

My dad started saying, "Your rifle is no good," but I told him to keep still. I wanted the pretty duck. He did keep still. I pulled back the hammer to cock the rifle once more. I fixed my sights at the base of the duck's neck. Again I pulled the trigger. "Pop!" went the little gun, and satisfyingly, I felt the recoil jerk and the duck flattened its wings in death agony. I still counted my shots with the little rusty shooting piece.

The current brought my bird to the edge of the water, and Dad reached out for it with the ice tester hook to get it for me. I grabbed it and looked where the bullet had hit the duck. I proudly told Dad, "Right through the head."

He said, "It's all right, but I still don't trust that rifle. It's nothing but a lead spitter; but it's better than nothing." All my dreams came back to me botheringly ("Don't ever trust that gun; it's no good"), but I warded off these thoughts and took up the sport.

Dad told me, "You stay here. If you shoot something, wave your arm at me. Don't ever try to hook it. You don't know how to do that, and it's too risky for you yet. And look at me often. When I wave my arm, come to me right away."

I said, "OK."

Then he walked off to open water near by. I saw him take a position, but he didn't fire. I waited for something to come up in my water, but nothing happened. Slowly the water froze into a smooth thin film of ice. My feet got colder and colder, but I kept my patience and sat there with my rifle ready.

Then there was movement in the ice. The ice moved with a groan and a grinding sound that partly scared me. The thin ice on the water wrinkled up and broke. I looked from one man to the other, and of course at Dad, too. I looked at him more often, but he didn't seem to notice the movement. He and the other men kept on waiting for the seals to come up, but nothing came up from the water in front of me. I slowly lost my interest and wished something would happen.

Soon something happened, as I wished. Somebody fired and reached for his seal hook, then pulled up something on the ice. Next he waved up his arms for us to come over to him. My Dad came to my place. He asked me, "Did anything come up?"

I said, "No."

"Chuka got a mukluk. We'll go over to get a share," he said.

I replied, "Why should we? We can get something by ourselves."

He only said, "Come on. We are not sure of getting something. We must have a share of that meat."

I gave in and followed behind. When we got there, Edward Aiyaksaq was there too. He asked me if I had seen any seals.

I said, "No."

He said, "Hmmm. Too much sugar, huh?"

I asked wonderingly, "What do you mean?"

He said, "I mean you added too much sugar in your tea this morning. That's why seals are scared of you."

It was too hard to believe, but I sure did use lots of sugar in my tea that morning. Maybe that was it—but I still hoped something would happen later in the day.

While they were skinning the mukluk I was watching a young mukluk come up from the water at the same time. I heard somebody say, "Quick, somebody shoot him."

I looked around and found somebody's rifle right next to mine. Thinking it was Dad's, I grabbed it. I was used to the feel of his rifle; somehow this one felt a little different, and the sight looked different, too. I thought it was only because

I hadn't fired that gun for a long time. But the trigger pulled seemed heavier and it kicked harder. I missed in spite of all my careful aim and steady trigger pull. The bullet went over the mukluk's head. But no wonder—it was Edward's rifle!

Edward came to me, saying, "Hey you? That sugar hasn't worn off. You are too sweet, yet. I never miss with that rifle. Why don't you let somebody shoot them who doesn't use so much sugar?"

I answered him, "I . . . I . . . I don't know."

Everybody laughed.

"What's this? What has the sweetness to do with my hunting luck?"

Chuka told me with a laugh, "Remember, my boy; don't use so much sugar the next time you are going hunting."

"It must be . . . but it was too awkward to be true, and I hadn't tried my real luck yet," I comforted myself.

The ice changed, moving while we fixed the meat to our toboggans. My Dad didn't know much about the current and ice movements himself, so Chuka instructed us. He gave my Dad "Do that's" and "Don'ts." He told us not to stay at the large open water. He said, "The current is changed. Now it will take away your kills. So go over to those small open waters."

We did. My Dad had shot a few times, but had missed every time. I hadn't got a chance to shoot any seals, except the one I missed with Edward's rifle. Dad said, "You had better use my rifle, as long as you are a better shot than I am, and maybe you will have better luck."

When we got to the open water he fixed me a gun rest. While we were at it somebody got another mukluk. My Dad said he would get a share of that, as we hadn't had much luck. He told me again not to attempt to hook what I killed. He said he would show me how to do that later. He said if I got something, to wave my arm. He told me some more things to do—not to make a noise if the seal is real close, and to make any movement slow but steady. I took his words.

He was a little way off when a seal came up, a little seal. It was looking away from me. I slowly brought the rifle up to my shoulder. I didn't dare breathe. The air seemed very still. And then I pulled back the hammer to cock the rifle. It made a loud "click" that really was a little click, but it seemed loud. Next I fixed my sights right on the back of the seal's head. When I was sure of the steadiness of the rifle and the alignment of the sights, I pulled the trigger. When it went off, it was like the breaking of a thick rod. I felt it hit my shoulder with a satisfying "Bang!" The bullet churned up the water. I thought I had missed again, but to my delight when the splash settled down there was my seal. The bullet had gone through and hit the water, churning it up.

Jumping up, I looked at Dad. He had turned to me when he heard the shot. I waved my arm delightfully. He came running. I would have hooked the seal by myself if I hadn't been told not to do it. But I must obey. When he got there I pointed to the seal. I told him, "There it is."

He just hooked it with the pole and pulled it up on the ice. "Oh! What a fine seal," he said. It was a fine time to be proud, and I sure was proud.

He told me, "I still want to get some share of meat from that mukluk." He added, "Get all the seals that come up in your water." Then off he went.

I was glad to have the open water and the high-powered rifle all for myself. I stared at the diamond-shaped open water in front of me. Every little unusual movement in the water stirred me up so that I grabbed my rifle, but mostly the things that stirred up the water were pieces of ice that broke off and came to the surface of the water and fooled me, or the current that made some ripples that looked like they were made by some animal. My shooting hand would be reaching for my rifle, as if pulled by a super magnet in the iron, and then was followed by disappointment. But my disappointment would soon fade away, and new hope and interest would take over.

And then I got very anxious. When I looked at the men, they were still at the mukluk they were skinning. Then I looked at the little seal I'd killed. Some thoughts came up as I looked where the bullet had hit the seal. Right where I had fixed my sights. The thought was, "You used too much sugar. That's why the seals are scared of you." Oh! It must be wearing off at last; but I still didn't believe it wholly.

Then I saw something come up at the far end of the open water. It looked big to me; I didn't know it was a mukluk. I grabbed my rifle and took a position, but I was too slow. Before I could line up my sights on it, it went down. Oh, no! It sure is a shame to let it go even without a shot, but I still held my rifle and kept my position. I watched the little ripples it made. "Darn it." I hated myself for being too slow. But then to my joy and delight it came up again, and closer too. I made quick aim and took a pot shot.

"Missed!" I thought, but that was not it. I saw some blood in the water the animal churned up as it made a quick flip over. I had wounded it, but not killed it. Some hard feelings came up within my mind and I worked the action of the rifle to load the chamber with a fresh round of ammunition. It was a model 95 Winchester 25-25. I slammed shut the bolt with some sort of fury in my mind, hoping the animal would come up once more. I glanced around and saw my Dad coming, but way off yet.

It came up again. Sure enough, it was wounded, and badly, too; bleeding from the wound. I took a careful aim and made a nice, clean shot that finished off my mukluk. I watched its body come to the surface, lifeless, but it was going to be for a mere few seconds. I grabbed for the seal hook that Dad had put on the ice ready for use. But I heard him shout, "No, No, Hold it. I'll get it for you."

I turned around and told him to hurry, but he couldn't come fast enough to draw in the meat. And when I looked at my mukluk, it was not mine anymore. It was sinking. I watched it disappear and bubbles came up. By the time Dad got there it might be quite a way down already. Along with the kill I had made, my heart sank. I couldn't say a word to Dad. The lump in my throat was too hard.

When he got there he asked, "Where is it?"

I just pointed to the place without a word.

He looked at me and said, "Too late; and it's my fault.

195

But don't be a sissie. Be a man. It has happened that way to every hunter. You've done a man's work." He must have guessed how I felt. And he guessed it right.

He comforted me some more, pointing to my seal. He said, "We have lots to take home now. Remember, sometimes we can hunt all day without seeing a thing, but today we are very lucky." He told me how to approach the open water. Some, or most of it, was very surprising to me and very confusing. And how to use the seal hook; and many other things. I couldn't get them all straight, but I had to.

After some time three ducks landed on the water. I had my .22 long rifle. I asked Dad if I could shoot them. He said that I might. I waited until all of them dived down. Then I watched for them to come up. One by one they came up. All met their death as soon as they showed up on the surface. I waited for them to dive down so some of them wouldn't fly away when I fired at one of them. It mended my hurt mind a little, because I got four ducks.

Dad's mouth smiled at my good shooting. He wished that I'd go with him every hunting day. I nodded my head. But I couldn't; I must go to school. I enjoyed my day, anyway, even though I was far from satisfying my hunting sport hunger.

My father pointed to a man going in the direction of the shore, drawing a meat-loaded toboggan. He asked me, "Where do you think he is going?"

I replied, "To the shore."

He said, "That means we are going to do that too."

I was surprised. "Why this early? Why can't we stay a little while longer?"

Dad answered, "Because we have to go home and it is not early." He showed me his watch. It had gotten quite late before I knew it.

Dad had fixed the meat to the toboggan while I was having my sport, and had fixed a rope to my seal and ducks. He told me to draw my own seal. Oh! I felt proud as a person could be, with my rifle across my back and an ice tester in hand and drawing a seal. When I looked around I was surprised to see every hunter heading toward the shore.

Soon we joined the rest, and there was a long line of hunters drawing their catch home.

We joined after the last hunter. Men were surprised to see me hunting. Everyone said good things to me, praising me for good hunting. I felt proud. The hunter next to us stepped aside and told my father to get in ahead. He said, "You have a young hunter to take care of. Get ahead." So we did.

It went the same way until we were next to the leader. He told us to get ahead, too, but my Dad wouldn't. Some of the hunters teased me that I was a little pup training to be a hunter. I thought that was real funny, so we laughed. Lots of them asked, "How come you are not in school?" but I never answered. Some guessed that I'd run away from school. Still others asked my Dad why I wasn't going to school. He only said, "I don't know." So nobody got the right answer. I kept my secret.

As we walked, men chatted and told stories. I had to half-run to keep up. Sometimes my seal got stuck on some ice and I had to tug at it to free it. The man behind me helped with a smile, and one time when the seal was freed suddenly I nearly plunged forward and I became the laughing stock of the group. But I didn't mind a bit. I was too thrilled to mind such a thing.

I sweated like everything under my heavy warm clothing. The ice was good and smooth. On the way near the shore I listened to the men talking to each other, and soon I thought how the boys would be surprised to see me coming home from hunting. How I would tell the story of the seal I had killed!

Soon I came to reality when we reached the slope of the shore. I was pretty worn out, but I never let anybody know that I was very thirsty. By the sled we took off our rifles and other things. I grabbed for a piece of snow to eat to quench my thirst, but Dad kicked my hand. He said, "No, No. Leave that alone if you don't want to be sick!" I dropped the snow and started working.

When we were through packing our meat and seal onto the sled, Dad gave me a small piece of raw frozen meat. He said, "That will get back your strength that you have used on the way."

I ate the raw meat. Oh! It was good; it had gotten salty. When I finished it I reached for more, but Dad said, "No, No," again. He said "You are too tired. You'll be sick if you eat too much."

I told him I was not tired, but he kept firm. He said, "Yes, you are tired. You don't feel it." Oh! How many "No's" was I going to get? But that's hunting.

Next he pulled out our thermos bottle of hot tea. I called Edward Aiyaksaq, who was near by. I asked him to have some tea with us. He came. Dad poured him a cup and I pulled out the cubes of sugar and handed them to him.

He asked, "What's that?"

"Sugar," I said.

I was somewhat embarrassed when he said, "Ahh, no. Sugar is not for hunters. It brings nothing but bad luck."

He took a piece of bread. I watched for my chance to even up with him. It was getting dark, but still daylight. He put down his cup to cool it off, and he looked around. I dropped some cubes of sugar into his cup of tea.

He took the cup and started sipping it. He looked up after a few sips, but I acted as if I didn't know what was happening. Then he asked, "How come? This tea is sweet."

I answered, "I fixed it myself and I didn't add sugar."

When he came to the last sips he said, "Oh, no! What's this?" There were some cubes of sugar, or what was left of the sugar that I'd dropped in. He said, "Oh, no. You will spoil my hunting luck. You big sweet tooth. I'll get even with you sometime." Then we laughed.

I knew it was not true, but still I was not sure of it, so I would just have to see for myself. When my turn came for drinking tea, I sat down on the snow, only to be shouted at by my Dad. He said, "Get up! You are asking to catch a cold!" I stood up. My legs were somewhat tired. Soon the tea was finished and we were just about to leave. Dogs barked and howled from many teams, and we went up the hill. I rode and Dad half-rode, but mostly ran. We passed by some teams and some of them passed us by.

The time seemed shorter when we skidded down the slope near the far end of the lake. As soon as we were on the level, I tied on my skates. I wanted to show my Dad that I could make faster speed than dog teams. The wind that was blowing at a good force was to be partly on my back—just right to help me along. My father asked me if I was sure that I wouldn't lag behind. I assured him I wouldn't. I decided to have some fun at the same time. I tied a small piece of meat to a length of cord. There was rough ice for some way, so I didn't get off until we reached the smooth ice, which was slippery for the dogs. I knew the dogs wouldn't run very fast on slippery ice, so luck was with me. I took my rifle from across my back and left it on the sled. When I first got off, I skated by the dogs to see if I could match their speed. I easily went along with them. When I saw that I could easily go faster than the dogs, I put on more speed. At once I got up ahead and held my speed. To make sure that I could keep the lead I used only half of my strength to lead the dogs, as they were trying to keep up with me. I slowed down to let our lead dog smell the piece of meat, and he yipped delightfully at it. I kept it just ahead of them. I kept doing that for a good distance. I was doing it on purpose—so that the dogs would use up their breath and strength in running after the meat foolishly. It worked; after a few moments of running furiously, I saw them stick their tongues out and grasp for breath.

Now was my chance. I let our lead dog catch the meat and waved goodbye. I didn't want to make fun of my Dad, but I wanted to prove to the old-timers that I could make such good speed by skating that any old-timer swift runners couldn't match me.

I put all my strength into my legs. I had a good head start. I dropped my Dad far behind, as if he were keeping still. I caught up with Edward Aiyaksaq, who was quite a way ahead. I didn't slow down for him. I just hollered, "Goodbye, slow poke," and passed him by. He was with my Dad in not believing that skates could match the speed of the dog team. When I got ahead, I wanted to wear out his dogs as I had done to our own dogs. I whistled so the dogs would come after me. They did. I skated, zigzagging, giving him some trouble, and gave extra work for the dogs. Then I waved to him "Goodbye" once more and used all my strength and soon lost him behind in the semi-darkness.

It was a good thing that I had sharpened my skates a few days before; they worked fine. Soon I approached the crowd of people skating. Most of my schoolmates were there. David Akoak, Francis Oalateetak, and Herbert Kogoyak came to see me, "How come you didn't come to school?"

I lied to them, again just to protect my secret with my teacher. At first they didn't believe me when I told them about my seal. David and Francis each held one of my arms and pushed me all the way to the edge of the lake. Almost everyone of them treated me like an old hunting champion, and I felt that way, too.

Their questions were kind of tough; but every time I told them that I had run away from school. They said, "How are you going to face Mr. Riley?"

I just said, "I don't know," and pretended to be afraid.

Boys gathered around me as I sat down to untie my skates. But that was all I did, for all of my friends took the skates off from the champion.

Among them was my old pal Daniel Kazighia, who was the loudest when they gave me a congratulation cheer. I had a big story that the boys were all ears to hear, but we were interrupted by a dog team. It was Edward. He stopped for a moment to tell me that he would see me when he was going without a load on his sled. I challenged him again, and called him "Slow poke." I was half-carried from the edge of the lake to my house.

Soon Dad came in. All hands helped him taking care of the meat and dogs. I invited them all for dinner. The dinner was enjoyed by all of us, but my friends were interested mostly in my story. They listened seriously, saying, "I wish I could go hunting, too!" "Maybe I would shoot a seal, too!" "Oh, how fun!"

After a heavy meal I felt tired for the first time. My legs were numb and felt weak. Forgetting what my Dad would say. I settled down in one corner comfortably, and surrounded by my friends, told my story to the eager boys. I was just about feeling nice and drowsy, and had begun to enjoy a good rest when my Dad rolled his displeased eyes over me. He frowned at me. Then came his voice: "Hey, you tired old lady. Aren't you going out to enjoy the nice evening air?"

I didn't care for the air, but I didn't want to be called an old lady. So I jumped on my feet. My legs were stiff with fatigue already. "Owwww!" I thought I had snapped my muscles. But sure enough the evening out of doors was very pleasant—a full moon shone almost as bright as daylight. We walked around. Soon my legs felt okay, and I forgot some of my tired feeling.

Some other boys joined us. Again I had to hang onto my secret. Unwillingly I told a dozen lies to protect my secret.

Next we went to the dark corner and one of the older boys lighted up cigarettes. He handed me a roll to celebrate my hunting day and the seal I'd got. I'd gotten the taste for smoking by now, so I liked it. When it was gone we kept on chatting about hunting. We came around to the point that each boy planned to ask to go with his Dad on Saturday. Then it was time to go home. First we played tag for a while. That was what we always did, just before going home; an old-fashioned game that we thought of as big fun.

Then first Francis and I took David home, then we went to Francis's house. Last I walked myself home. When I got there Mom had fixed the bedding for us and Dad was making bedtime tea. I didn't pay much attention to the tea. I was more interested in bed. But before that I had a word with Dad. I asked him to let me go on his hunting next Saturday, because we wouldn't have to go to school. He said, "Oh, sure, but we got to see about the weather first. If it's good we will go ahead." Oh boy! that was what I wanted to hear.

Douglas and Martin were having a good time playing with the ducks I had shot. I watched them, lying on my stomach. Their chattering lulled me quickly to sleep.

The next day Dad went hunting and I went to school. As we were gathering around, my schoolmates came to me and told me that Mr. Riley was going to scold me. I paid no attention to them. I told them, "He won't say anything."

When we went into the schoolroom, lots of pairs of eyes stared at me and Mr. Riley.

I felt bashful and I felt my cheeks grow warm. After we were seated I passed my homework to the teacher and got to my other work. I found myself interested in my work, and I busied myself until I heard Mr. Riley calling my name. I tiptoed to his desk. I looked in his face, and I felt fine when I saw him looking pleased. I'd done a good job on my homework, and my present work was all fine, too.

On the following afternoon I wrote a short story of my hunting, and my teacher rewrote it and he was pleased with it. When he found all my work satisfactory he said he would excuse me every Friday from that time on.

But I became the envy of my schoolmates, and it gave my teacher a hard time. After a few weeks he was losing his school boys.

That was only the beginning of my nice hunting days— not only hunting, but good fishing added to the hunting. And when I got more confidence with my teacher, I learned to handle him when I was AWOL. This was the beginning of my hunting days—of nice, thrilling, but sort of boring and tiresome ones, too.

From that time I went hunting mostly two times a week. Once during the weekdays and then on Saturdays if the weather or ice was in a good condition for hunting. Now I had got the feel of the sport and how to take care of hunting gear, the dogs, the meat we got, and everything that went with it.

# 10. A Hard Lesson

From the beginning Dad and I had been lucky, so I started to expect to bring home something from every hunting trip, and something that I had shot, too. But it didn't turn out to be that way at all. Even though I had known that many times even the best hunters came back after a hard day without a thing to bring home, I expected to get something, at least a duck or something. But even if we didn't shoot anything at all, we got a share from somebody else's walrus or mukluk.

In a short time I learned my lesson from nature itself, helped along by my Dad and other fellow hunters. It was one of those days—must have been Saturday, or a weekday— when we woke up to a nice day, just right for good hunting. I was full of spirit and glee and so was my Dad. As I got ready, as on the other hunting days, I had all the dreams and thoughts of getting a seal, walrus, mukluk, or some ducks. My pockets bulged with ammunition for my well-loved .22 long rifle.

I helped Dad harness up the dogs. Now I knew what to do, so Dad left it to me to do. Every once in a while l looked up at the dark blue morning sky dotted with bright twinkling stars, and got a whiff of the fresh, cool north wind that seemed to be scented with good hunting. My thrill leaped up high with that and I worked as fast as I could. Yet time seemed to drag. My spirit was so high I let out yelps of delight with the frisky dogs that howled and leaped against their chains. Finally we were ready. I sat on the sled with Dad's and my rifles across my lap. While we were yet on the way daylight was breaking. As always, some other hunters were ahead of us, and some were coming after us. The dim blue morning daylight showed the surroundings. Dad and I took turns warming up by running at the back of the sled, holding on to the handlebar.

Soon we got to the place at the top of the hill where we go down to Igalok's summer camp. He told me to stop the team; then he stood up to scan the ice. We usually went on ahead, and this time I wondered why he was doing that. He showed a bit of disappointment, or something that looked like it.

I asked him, "What's the matter?"

"Hmm," he said. "The ice is not in very good hunting condition."

I asked, "What's wrong?" hoping we wouldn't turn back from there.

He replied, "No open water."

I swept my sight over the white ice that extended until it was out of sight in every direction, and there were some dark blue patches in many shapes and sizes that I thought were open water in the ice. So I spoke up, pointing at them, "But what about those?"

He shook his head, saying "Those only look like water. But they have been frozen over. That was open water yesterday. The ice hasn't moved, so the ice didn't break open."

I insisted they looked very much like water to me.

But he still said, "They are not water at all. But let's go down. The current might come in and start the ice movement."

I saw some other men gathering by the little cabin, just standing up and talking. They weren't going out on the ice. We joined them as soon as we secured our dogs with the sled anchor, and to a rack. Some were saying the current might move and break up the ice sometime during the day. But some others said it would not. I was with those who said it would, even though I didn't know anything about the movements of the ice and current. All my thoughts were to go ahead, go ahead. I wanted to go out. To heck with those who said it was not good for hunting. I didn't sense a bit what others did—that it was a very poor hunting day.

Some men started going back up the hill, but three or four started out on the ice. My mind went with them, and I looked at my Dad, pleadingly, to go along with them. At least to try our luck for the day. Understanding, or on purpose to remove the edge off of me, he said, "Let's go with those to pass the day."

I didn't have to be asked the second time, so we went. I, still mindful of game and sport and peppy too, followed Dad as fast as I could walk, right at his tail. There was four or five inches of snow on the ice. That would be tiresome to walk on, on our return. But now I didn't care or pay attention to it. All I had in my mind was what we were going to get.

We walked on and on until we came up to a place that I thought was open water ahead of us. But to my surprise it wasn't. Dad was right; it was frozen over. He tested it for thickness, and he turned around. He told me, "This is safe enough to walk on for one person. Don't come too close to me. Walk behind me at a distance of ten paces."

I did so. I watched him walk on it. Another surprise—this ice was only overnight old and it was thick enough to walk on safely.

I saw the ice give way at each of his steps as if he was walking on a starched bed sheet. I slowly followed at a safe distance. When we got across to the far side he told me, "Young ice that looks as thick as or looks thicker than this one may be only an inch or even thinner. And we have no way of telling it except by testing. So don't forget to use your ice tester to make sure."

We kept on climbing out to some pressure ridges here and there to have a better and farther view of the place around. James Taganik had joined us. He and Dad talked a long while, while we looked over the ice from one of those pressure ridges. Their talks were discouraging, and I was getting that way, too, from the way the ice looked. But I always pushed out the discouragement and still hoped for better luck.

We were way out. Every time I looked back, the cabins were getting smaller, until now they appeared to be only small dots in the far distance.

Slowly some bored and discouraged thoughts were forcing their way into me. But then, we came to a big berg. At the leeside of it was a small crack. It might have been a little over a foot wide, not any longer than an ice tester pole. We stopped there. I didn't know why we stopped until my Dad said, "We will cool off here." We were sweating from the long, hard walk and I felt my calves and thighs tiring, so

I was glad to sit down and lay down my rifle and other things I was carrying.

I was laying them down carelessly, and I was surprised to hear my Dad say to me, "Have your rifle ready. They might come up."

Instead of getting my rifle ready, I asked him, "What might come up?"

He said, "The seals or something. What's the matter with you?"

But I still didn't get it, so I asked again, "Where are they going to come up?"

He replied, "There," pointing to the small crack in the ice.

I must have shown an expression of doubt on my face and in my actions, but he and James Taganik knew how to handle me and make me interested. They glanced at each other with sly grins and Dad reached for his rifle and said, "You'll be sorry. I'm going to get your seal if you don't want it."

I suspected their glance and their grinning; but just in case, I pulled out my rifle and leaned it against an ice cake by me while I sat down in wait for a sleek head to come up in the small water.

A brisk cold wind cooled us off quickly and my hopes faded away, along with the warmth of my body. Until "no hope, no hope" seemed to tick, tack, tick, tack in rhythm to the beating of my heart. Slowly, or it seemed slow, the water froze to a glassy crust of ice. My feet got colder and colder. I closed my fists in my mittens to keep them warm. I kicked and jumped up and down, and did everything to keep warm. Less and less I paid attention to the glassy spot that had been a wide crack. Now and then I brushed off the white frost that formed on my fur ruff from my breathing. Not a bit of hope or interest was left in my mind. It was all boring, and cold, and my empty stomach was growling. I began to imagine getting into our warm little house and having good warm boiled meat and some nice hot tea. But I tried hard to push that out of my mind, and tried to think of something better, because all those thoughts made it worse for me. But the thoughts kept coming. The only thing that interested me was Dad and James talking. Telling stories about nice, good hunting days in the past. I liked to hear the good stories, but when they came around to gossiping things over in a language that was too deep for me to understand, that, too, became boring stuff.

It was all phooey for me. What a day! The time dragged— it even must be stuck. I knew they might say something about it to me. If they said a word about going home, it would be the most pleasant thing of the day.

I hung on to my patience the best way I could. The idea of going home became a very strong desire. But just as much I wished there would be something to shoot at. It was hard to let a long day pass without shooting at something. I thought of shooting those black specks on the ice just for the fun of it, and to satisfy my want. But it would be just a waste of precious bullets.

Every time I looked at Dad and James they were always just chatting. They didn't seem to mind the boring day. The biting cold didn't seem to bother them at all. They were very much concerned in their story or in whatever it might be. Sometimes they both climbed to the top of the iceberg and scanned the vast field of ice that looked endless all around. Maybe on the tenth time they did that, they both turned to me and gave me some hunting lessons talk. Because even though I tried my best not to, they had sensed or seen it very plainly—the expression of my distaste for the day.

They lectured in turns. "This is only one of the countless days ahead for you or any hunter that will turn out to be this way. But there are good ones as much or more than the poor ones. Good hunters never let poor hunting days take the sport or spirit out of them. No matter what the day is, a real hunter enjoys it. At the end of such a day he just looks forward and hopes for a better day ahead. And nobody can help such days like this. So take away the hard feelings and cheer up."

But I was much too bored and discouraged to cheer up. I never expected the day to be this way. I even felt my throat tense or tighten, forming a hardness that was hard to swallow. At the end of their sermon, one of them mentioned about going home. What a delight! But I kept calm, just so they wouldn't know my feelings. But they both already knew.

James led the way. I followed last. It was nice to walk when I was cold. James told us he had seen some meat left over from a walrus that had been caught by some hunters a day before so late in the afternoon that they had left some meat to save time. He was going to take us to that place. I was glad, because I was hungry. I felt sorry I hadn't eaten much of my breakfast that morning. I had been too delighted and was not interested in eating then, but it was part of my lesson.

After tramping on some thickening snow—must have been about a mile—we came to the left-over meat that James had told us about. I was warmed up, but I felt my legs tiring. Yet we still had about two or three more miles to walk.

We salvaged some of the good meat, then we chipped away some almost rock-hard frozen meat to eat. I found a chunk of liver frozen in the shape of a saucer. I leaned it against a protruding iceberg. My, it looked like a good thing to shoot at! I still wanted to shoot. I asked Dad, "How powerful is your rifle?"

He looked at me puzzled and asked, "Why? It has lots of killing power."

I asked him, "Let me shoot this piece of liver and see how much power the rifle has."

He didn't like the idea, but I begged, "Let me try that. I never shot anything today. I might get out of practice."

They laughed at me merrily, and he handed me his Winchester 25-35. I carefully aimed and shot the chunk of frozen liver right in the middle. Some fragments flew and the remaining broke into four equal parts. We gathered around it to see how much damage the bullet had made. The bullet had gone through and broken it into fragments and cracked the ice.

Laughing jokingly, Dad put the broken pieces of liver into my leather hunting bag and said, "Here, take these home for supper. That is what you shot today to take home." I laughed at his joke. My craving for a shot was a little satisfied.

When we had eaten our fill and cooled off we started

again. I felt a little better and a little peppier with a filled stomach and a little rest. We walked on and on. Maybe at nearly the end of a mile's walk I began to mind the snow. It would be far better for my tired legs if it was not that deep. The balls of my hands and toes got sore. Oww! My poor thighs and calves were aching with fatigue. All over under my clothing I was very damp and hot with sweat, but my cheeks, chin, and nose were stinging from frostbite. My fingers were stiff, cold, and numb from holding the ice tester pole. That was bad enough, but the thing that hurt me most was going home without having shot anything to take home except that frozen liver. It was a shame and discouragement and distaste to have such a day.

More and more it got harder to keep up with Dad and James. Sometimes I lagged behind, but as soon as Dad noticed that he would exclaim, "Catch up! You are not supposed to do that."

He gave me no mercy. They didn't stop for me to catch up. They just kept on walking even without slowing their pace a bit. I forced myself to run to catch up. Sometimes I stumbled over a jutting piece of ice, and plunged into the snow. That maddened me some, so I jumped up, gathered my scattered things and ran until I caught up. Then I would follow, keeping up with them mostly by doing my best. Then I would start reading my mind: "What a poor day . . . No game . . . No sport . . . Nothing but heart-discouraging labor and a fatiguing day. I will never go hunting on days like this one. Only on good days." Then, Whack! My feet would get hooked on jutting ice. I would struggle wildly to stay on my feet. Sometimes I won and prevented a fall, but nearly always I plunged into the snow and realized that I'd lagged behind. Ohoo! Then I would have to put on whatever little zest I had and run to catch up.

In my mind I cursed the snow. It was using up my energy; good-for-nothing torturer! I wished a giant snow plow would clear it out of my way!

I was just about to make up an excuse to have my Dad stop for a while for rest when he did. We sat on a good pile of ice. "Let's cool off a while."

Thank their goodness. I brushed the snow off a block of ice and sat on it as if it was a nice sofa. I'd been keeping my eyes off the shore, watching it coming too slowly, which increased my sadness. I looked up at it for the first time at about a mile away. Maybe this cheered me some, but bad thoughts of a no-good day were killing me.

James looked at me. He had a mocking grin all over his face when he asked me, "What's the matter? Are you tired out already in a short, slow walk?"

I forgot my sadness, but took up lots of madness. I said, "Naw!" right in his face. But I guess he wanted me a little more mad.

He said, "How come?"

Then I got up and went up to him, until I caught myself telling him, "I'm not tired! Now I'm not. Do you hear me?"

I looked away from him quickly and looked at the shore. My, oh, my! It was less than a mile. Maybe three quarters of a mile.

One of them said, "Let's go."

James glanced at me. I looked him in the eyes and almost shouted, "Yessir!"

The madness burning in my mind made me stick right to their tails all the way. Either the rest or the warmed-up temper put new strength to my tired legs. And I kept up with them all the way. I felt worn out when we got to our dogs, but that madness kept me going. I helped along to get the things ready. When everything was ready James brought his thermos bottle of tea or coffee. We sat on our sled and enjoyed our good hot drink.

The bad thoughts of the day flowed into my mind as we sat there. James gave me a little apology for what he had done. He explained, "I knew how you felt while we were coming. I wanted you to forget the discouragement that was eating up your energy. I knew you were strong enough to take a hard day, but the poor day is what you haven't learned to take. And I knew that madness would do a good job on you. That's why I made you mad."

I asked him, "Do you mean you knew how I felt all along?"

He replied, "Sure, why not?"

212

I was surprised. "But how did you know?" I asked.

He said, "It's very plain. I have had the very same experience as you have. Some days that were worse than today. Now forget the day and cheer up. Your disappointment won't do you any good. Just start thinking of those nice days ahead of us."

Soon our hot drink was finished up. Our dogs were howling and our bottles put away into their places. I asked Dad to sit on the sled while I would half-run up the hill. At first James was just ahead of us all the way up the sloping hill, but when we got up to the top his team ran faster. Soon he was out of sight. He had a better team of dogs than we had. When we got to the top I rode hanging onto the handlebar of the sled. Our sled went bumpity-bump over the humpy, hard-packed snow, sometimes making me lose my grip with our newly trained pups helping in their delighted running. Oh boy! That was just the kind of ride I liked.

Soon we went down the other slopes nearest the village. Some powdery snow streamed up as I applied the snow brake to keep the sled right. In the next few moments we were at the foot of the slope. Dad got up and let me sit down on the sled. He wanted to warm up. I hadn't said anything much. Dad had been talking to me about something, but I had not paid much attention. All I'd said was "Ah huh! Is that so? Maybe, I guess so . . ." now and then, but my mind was full of thoughts of the not-so-good day. He still wanted to keep me interested.

The first time he drew my attention was when he asked me, "Do you have your skates with us?"

I replied, "Yes, oh, a . . . but I didn't file them yesterday, so they are not very sharp." I clearly was making excuses. My skates were sharp enough even though I hadn't filed them. The real reason that I said that was that I was just about tuckered out.

He started to say just what I was afraid he might say, "Now is a very fair chance for a race. I'll race you to the village."

"Oh, no," I thought. I wanted to ride this time. But I said, "All right," as I strapped on my homemade skates.

Strapping them on was not easy to do in this cold windy day. I was all stiff thumbs at the job, but I did the best I could so they wouldn't get loose and slow me down. We were to go against a quite strong wind. It was brisk and hard on our faces.

I was all no hope again. What my father meant by a fair chance was that we had no load except those few good-sized chunks of meat that we had salvaged from the walrus carcass we had found for dog food. I wanted to make more excuses to make Dad let me ride at least part of the way. I pushed that aside on second thought. I knew it would be of no use. My Dad was stubborn.

At some distance before we got to the edge of the lake I studied the speed of our team. Right now they were making a good speed, but when they ran over the smooth lake they would slow down some. That would give me some chance; that is, if I were not so tired. I was going to try it anyway; I made up my mind that I would do all I could and take a ride when I couldn't go on anymore.

I rode all the way over the rough ice without saying a word. With not much delight I got off the nice comfortable sled. Oww! My poor muscles, tense and sore from fatigue, were stiff. I wished that I hadn't taken my skates with us. I wouldn't have had to have that race. Well, it had to be that way. But I didn't dare follow the sled. Instead I hung on to the handlebar to limber up my legs for a short way. Then I let go of the team and managed to follow. I did, and kept up that for quite a while.

Unexpectedly I felt better when I had warmed up and limbered up my legs, but I had quite a way to go. I was sure I would not make it. When I steadied my breathing and muscles, I put on some more of my little left strength and started gaining. Then I took the lead, but our pups came after me then, gaining on me until they caught up and hung onto my tail.

I put on all my strength and made the best speed I could make for five minutes. Then I looked back over my shoulder. I was gaining until I got out of breath. When I slowed down to catch my breath, our team gained on me. Whew! But before they could catch up, I had caught enough breath to go on at top speed. Then I went on again. The next time I had to slow down I saw that I'd got a good distance ahead, so I could go slow longer to have a good break.

Now I'd warmed up my body, and mind, too. I got interested in the race, rather than griping and groaning with every thought. I got so much fun that my tired feeling eased off. When I figured out I would make it to the edge of the lake way ahead of Dad with his team, I just went on at my relaxing speed.

When at last I got to the edge of the lake nearest the village, Dad and his team were far behind. That ought to make him believe that on skates one can go as fast or faster than dog teams.

And thank goodness there was nobody around at the lake getting water or ice. I didn't feel like talking to anybody to tell of my poor day. I didn't want to tell that kind of story to any one of my friends or cousins yet, until the taste of the not so good hunting day had faded away. When I unstrapped my skates, my feet were very sore, aching at the soles. But my legs, body, and mind felt somewhat nice.

I walked from the lake to our house with thoughts of Douglas and Martin. Oh, how good it is to come home to the happy company of little brothers after a boring day! It was still daylight—earlier than we were used to coming home. I helped take care of things. I even went on and fed the dogs, which before I would lay aside until I was well rested. But this time I wanted to get everything done so I could rest without interruption. I wanted it that way; besides I had some school home work to do. I saw that we had enough ice for water and everything.

When we got inside Mom noticed that I was tired. Oh, her soothings were, as always, far better than Dad's. She smoothed out the roughness gently and softly, while Dad had to do it by forcing me in a way to harden me. That is quite hard to take before one learns to. And those brothers, the pride and delight of my heart, made the thing thrilling. I watched them with affection as they giggled when they pulled my mukluks and sealskin pants. Ann was of not much help when

I felt that way. She was always quiet and didn't want to get into anybody's business (unless to complain once in a while when she got more than her share of around-the-house tasks or chores).

Soon the supper was started. For the rest of our family it was a nice time, as always, but me—I was quiet from fatigue and boredom. Dad and I laughed when Mom took out some of the broken chunks of frozen liver from my hunting bag. The folks didn't know what was so funny until Dad told the story. At first they didn't understand—especially Douglas and Martin. They thought it was not a joke. They both looked at me with their mouths wide open, questioningly.

Mom asked, "What is so funny about the frozen piece of walrus liver?"

Dad told her, "That is what Nathan shot to bring home."

The kids got more serious and interested. So I touched Dad to leave the story for me to tell as a tale to the boys.

One of them asked me, "Was that liver alive and moving? And you shot it to kill it?"

I told them, "It sure was alive and it moved very fast. While Dad and I were standing on the ice, it came sliding on the ice real, real fast and I grabbed Daddy's rifle and I shot it."

Mom got puzzled and the boys got more interested. One of them started saying, "Oh, when I am old enough, I'll go hunting for livers and shoot many of them!"

I laughed, and Dad laughed, too. They both wanted to know what was so funny. I told them, "You both are funny, because you can't hit the fast-moving livers. Only good shooting marksmen like me can get them. Even Dad can't hit them."

The boys exclaimed, "But you can teach us how to shoot straight. You are a good marksman," as they grabbed our air rifle.

I said, "No, you can't learn." I told them, "I'm the best shot in the family, even better than Dad."

They looked disappointed but then Dad said, "Boys! Let Nathan go hunting for livers; you hunt for seals and other animals."

216

But they were very interested. They said, "But the liver is very good to eat. We must hunt for them, too."

Dad and I had our amusement. I told the boys, "We will start practicing at the next fine weather."

"Oh, boy! That's fine!" they both hollered.

After supper I was thinking just to start on my school work and keep at it until it was time to sleep. But I had decided to go out for a while, as I had been forced to do by Dad. Now it had become my habit. It had become a pleasant thing to do at my own will. But I didn't wander around the village as I usually did. I didn't want to do that for fear someone might meet me and ask me how the hunting was. I didn't want to tell the unlucky story.

I had to wait until Douglas and Martin slept before I could do my school work, because they wanted my books and papers. I was expecting to sleep quickly after I'd done my work. But I was wide awake; I lay there, still thinking of the day just past. I listened to the ticking of the clock as the minutes ticked by.

When the early morning came by I got mad without any reason to be—except for having had trouble in going to sleep. At too long last, I finally had slept. The next morning my mind cheered some, but my bad thoughts came back, along with my daily things to do. But I averted them finally, when I joined my schoolmates and cousins.

The school seemed interesting after a tough day of the other hard lesson. But some days of it helped bring back some desire for hunting, no matter what the hunting would turn out to be. Every day of school was not very good. I always wanted to have something else to do for a change. Doing the same thing for days easily bored me.

That was my first unlucky winter hunting day. Many of them after that became just another day of no luck, which I learned to take as they were. Even though days like that didn't make me sad anymore, lucky hunting days were happiest of all, and none of them felt like hard labor. Even the labor of drawing the meat home was sporty to me. But when we had nothing to draw home on unlucky days it seemed like just hard, tiring work.

Our everyday living went on and I learned more things about hunting. The unlucky hunting days became just like other, easily forgotten things; but the nice lucky ones took their places in my memory and I enjoyed telling about them over and over to my friends.

# 11. Truant Hunter

As December came by, the school became very interesting, but not very new to me anymore. But it was always the best part of the school year, because we always laid aside our regular work and began practicing and preparing for the Christmas programs. I didn't mind missing the hunting and staying in school until Saturdays, when we didn't have to be in school. Then I went hunting, but only when the weather was nice and good for hunting. I usually filled the day with work at home, such as replacing the week's supply of ice. I liked that too, because Dad let me have the dog team for myself when he was not using it. I mostly made several trips getting sledloads of ice—not only for ourselves, but also I got some for Aiyaksaq and his family. Even though they were not really our grandparents, they did to us as grandparents, so we acted to them as their grandchildren.

Sometimes I did some cleaning with the house, helping Mom. Other times, when I had nothing much to do—and when I felt that way—I just had a good time with other boys playing or taking walks on nice days, especially with Herbert Kogoyak, Francis Oalateetak, David Akoak, Ralph Magpa. The girls who mostly played with us were Barbara Danagik, Amelia Seuak, Frances Danagik, Virginia Nusan, and some others. We always played that we were grown-up people and pretended that we were families.

My parents didn't want me to do such playing, but I liked it so much I disobeyed them often and went ahead and had my fun playing with a happy crowd. Some of us would make believe we were parents, and our sons and daughters were getting married. We held a make-believe marriage ceremony.* The groom's parents paid the bride's parents lots of things. We collected lots of old tin cans, bones, cardboard fruit boxes filled with snow, and whatever we could find. Oh, what a

* This imitated the customary marriage form, which was a matri-patrilocal residence pattern in which the groom's parents sent gifts to the bride's family when the groom began his period of work for his bride. After a year or so, the married couple would return to live permanently with the boy's parents, a move accompanied by gifts from the bride's family to the boy's family and kinsmen (see Hughes, 1960).

sight! But it was lots of fun to pretend to be grown-ups anyway. What a laugh the adults would get when they came upon us! Some said we were not supposed to do that. That it was strictly for the adult people; but others said it was all right for us to be educated early. Some still said it was a big mischief; that we might carry it too far. But to us it was great fun to experiment with adult things. It made us feel grown-up to call somebody Mrs. So-and-so, Mr. So-and-so, or Mr. and Mrs. So-and-so; and we felt proud when we were called that way by our playmates.

In school our teachers divided us into groups. One group worked on preparing the room; another group practiced singing. Still others practiced acting out their parts in the programs. The next day the groups shifted around. The girls sewed some costumes. Virginia Nusan was sewing my costume. I liked helping her, and trying on my costume.

Also the Sunday School had become interesting. We memorized some Christmas Bible verses and practiced singing some carols. The days seemed shorter than they really were, they were so full of nice things to do.

Dad had been making trips to Southwest Cape for trapping. Sometimes he stayed there for a week or more. He was not very lucky. He brought a fox or two, or nothing at all on each of his trips. On most of his trips I often packed a package of dried fruit or some other things, such as a writing tablet, pencils, color crayons. I wrote notes to each one of my cousins every trip, telling all about the school and my hunting most proudly.

Kenneth also came to the village for supplies. When he came for dinner I pestered him with questions. I made him tell me what all they had been doing, until he would have nothing more left to tell. I always told him I would be with them someday, and do away with the school—and do lots of hunting, trapping, and other things I used to do at the camp. How I longed to do that! Before, I liked our little quiet camp far better than the big, noisy village. But now I'd learned to like the village as much as our camp. It was not too big anymore.

While Dad was away I took over the work a family man

222

had to do. Dad had taught me how to handle most of his work. So I always knew where to start. Before I could go to school in the morning I had to do some of the things, and then do the rest after school; and then the time would be all for myself.

On one of his trips Dad had forgotten his rifle and all of our hunting gear was in its place. He hadn't told me not to go hunting, and he didn't tell me to go, either.

One morning when I went early to do some morning chores, the weather was a perfect one for hunting. Oh, I wished Dad was here. I was sure we'd go right away. I had a very strong desire for hunting. In the next few moments an idea popped in my head. Maybe my Uncle would let me go with him—Robert Sakigak. I thought up a plan carefully so it wouldn't go off at any place. Then I ran over to see if Robert was going, or if he had already gone. I made up my mind I wouldn't go with anybody else except him.

He and Francis often went with Dad and me for hunting. Francis didn't go with his Dad on weekdays. He was in school. So I thought Robert Sakigak would go by himself. I ran over to his house to see him. Sure enough, he was busy getting ready to go hunting. I was a little afraid to ask him what I wanted to do, so to attract his attention I ran up to him pretending to be in a hurry.

He looked up and asked, "What's up?"

I was nervous but I tried hard to control myself and my words. I asked him nervously, "Are you going hunting and to where?"

He replied, "Well, where is Kakianak?"

I told him, "He's at Southwest Cape."

"Did he say you might go hunting?" he asked.

I said, "He didn't say anything about it."

Now I was hoping that he'd let me go with him, and he did. He said, "Go ask your folks and hurry."

Oh, boy! I ran as fast as I could, but instead of asking my folks if they would let me go with Robert—I was afraid they might try to keep me back—I lied to them. I told them, "Don't miss me at noon. Ralph Magpa invited me for dinner, and after school we have some more practice to do for the Christmas program. So I will be late." They okayed everything.

Carefully but quick as I could I took out my hunting gear: my hunting bag, toboggan, ice tester pole, and Dad's rifle. I ran to Uncle Robert again.

He was waiting for me. He said, "My, you are quick. Are you sure your folks permitted you to come with me?"

I lied again, "I'm very sure."

He said, "If you are telling a lie, I'll never take you with me again."

Oops! I pretended I hadn't lied. I didn't say anything. I thought it would be all right if I went with him today, at least.

"Now you must do exactly as I say; I'm responsible for you. I'll be blamed if anything happens to you."

I assured him, "Sure, I'll take every one of your words for it."

"Come on, then; let's hurry and go. We are kind of behind our time."

We were going to the face of the mountain on foot. We walked, pulling our toboggans behind us. It was nice to walk on the hard-packed snow, packed to ice hard by foot hunters. As we got to the north shore I heard the first bell for school. It sounded as if it were calling and coaxing me to school. I did my best to ignore it, and kept my mind on the hunt. We walked up to a high-piled pressure ridge. We climbed up on top to get a better look at the ice conditions.

We caught sight of a bunch of men gathering at one place far out on the ice. Also sighted several small open leads—just the right places to wait for the seals, walrus, and mukluks to come up.

Although I should have been happy and excited about the nice day and every good thing that went with it, I was bothered by the untruthful things I had told my folks and Robert. But I made up my mind that I wouldn't mention a word about it until we came home. I knew it would spoil everything and make Robert worried. But oh! I felt guilty.

After he had studied the ice we were to walk over, he said, "Everything's pretty good. If we are not too late we will get our share from the walrus that somebody killed." We could tell that somebody had killed a walrus by those men gathering at a place.

He continued, "If we are too late we will go to one of the open leads and see if we can get anything. Come on, let's go."

When we climbed down from the high place we couldn't see the men we had seen, but Robert had studied the location, so on we went. We walked on many places where the ice had cracked into pieces of many different sizes and shapes. It looked and felt risky to me when we jumped from one piece to the next. We had to catch our footing very carefully. One slip of a foot would mean an immersing in the freezing water, and probably death from drowning or freezing. I always felt better when we got across that and onto solid unbroken ice.

After an hour or so when we had covered more than a mile and a half, we met some men returning home, drawing their toboggans loaded with walrus meat. We talked to some of them. They told us the meat was all gone already, and some offered to share their meat with us. But Robert wouldn't take any; we were hoping we might get something ourselves. We climbed up on an iceberg to look around again. There was a small patch of open water nearby and another one a little farther on. We went toward the smaller one first. As we walked, Robert told me to stay at the nearest one; he would go on to the other open water. We were just a few paces from the water I was to watch when a brown head came up. At the same instant we dropped to our knees, reaching for our rifles. In the next few seconds I worked the bolt of my rifle and lined up my sights at the back of the walrus's head. I was ahead of Robert in doing that, and then I was waiting for him to shoot. I would have fired as soon as I had steadied my rifle and lined up my sight, but I was taught by Dad to wait for someone better skilled in shooting big game, so I wouldn't be blamed for it if I missed or if I spoiled the whole. Since the walrus had to be shot at a particular spot for a clean kill, Robert was careful and calm, while I was anxious and excited. It seemed endless, waiting for Robert to shoot. It was hard to keep my finger from pulling the trigger. But at last he shot. I let go my finger and our bullets hit their marks. The walrus floated lifelessly. I was amazed by the quick actions of Robert. In less than a moment he got it with his seal hook. While I held it by the line, he cut a loop in the skin and pulled a strong leather rope through it. Now we felt it was secure.

For the first time since we spotted the walrus he spoke up, "We got it! You sure bring us good luck." Examining the head, he told me, "Your shot was a perfect one; mine was way off to the left. So you did the killing."

I was so excited and pleased I had forgotten to speak. I still didn't know what to say, except for a smile. I must have been quiet for a while, because he asked me, "Ain't you glad we got a walrus?"

"I'm glad," I replied.

He handed over the rope to me, and pulled off his snow parka shirt and waved it to attract some hunters so we could share it. A group of men came soon. They were talking, asking questions and telling each other what had happened, and saying how lucky they were. Robert told them I took a big part in getting that walrus. As each one praised me and congratulated me, I felt bashful.

A group of us pulled the big animal on the ice. The men pulled out their sharp butchering knives. I reached for mine, too, but Ah! I'd forgotten all about it. Some men teased me about it, so I had to help in other ways. In a short time the walrus was butchered and divided among us. I loaded my share onto my toboggan, and bound it tight. I had had a nice time, but the lie I told to my folks and Robert was bothering me. Just before we started back somebody mentioned it was some time after 2 p.m. The time had passed very quickly.

We started going home in a line, following one after the other. Robert was leading, with me following him, and after me there were several men. Robert took it easy on me. He asked me once in every while if I were tired. Then we stopped for a rest. Maybe at near the end of a mile he told the other men to go ahead if they wanted to. Some did, but there were three or four with us. As we rested, he told me to let him know whenever I was tired. We went on again, pulling hard on our toboggan full of meat at the rough places.

After maybe another mile, Robert asked me, "Ain't you tired yet?"

Even though I was getting tired I said, "No."

Then he said, "Well, I am; let's take another break."

We sat down on chunks of ice. Again he told me, "I don't want you to over-work yourself. You might injure your good health." I liked that, because my Dad always gave me no mercy. He would have me go on no matter how tired I got.

It was roughly four miles from the village where we got the walrus. We had about two more miles to go. The other men went on while Robert and I rested. Then we were all by ourselves. We went on until we reached the shore. I was quite tired now. We rested again. The rest of the way to the village was level and on hard-packed snow. I was glad for that. It would be easier when I was tired.

Some men joined us. Some had gotten seals, some walrus, and mukluks. When we got quite close to the village, I asked Robert to stop for a break. But he said, "Oh, we can make it; it is a short way more."

I told him, "I have something to tell you."

He stopped and looked at me. I was afraid he might scold me, but I had to tell him about the lie I had made. When I didn't say a word for more than a moment, he looked worried. Then finally he asked me, "What's the matter? Is something wrong? Or did you get hurt?"

I said, "No . . . But, but . . . ah, my folks didn't know I went hunting with you."

He looked at me worriedly for a moment. Then he said, "Oh, my! your folks must be worried about you. Don't they know where you are?"

"No, but I told them I would not be home until late," I told him.

"Go on, then. They are going to scold you."

I went on to our house without a word. They were sure to scold me, but I was going to face it. It was starting to get dark late in the afternoon.

When I neared our house I saw somebody by the house,

and when I got closer I saw that they were busy. Then they saw me. They all looked up at me. When I got there, Dad had just arrived from Southwest Cape. They were busy unharnessing the dogs and taking care of his things. Dad and Mom looked very surprised. Dad looked at me. Then at the meat I had brought home. Then at Mom. He looked cross, as if he was going to scold me. I felt about to cry.

Dad began, "Where have you been?"

I didn't say a word.

Then he turned to Mom and asked her in a scolding manner, "Why did you let him go?"

Mom told him the whole story—how I had fooled her that morning. Oh no! I was in a very bad place. Robert came and talked to my Dad and calmed him down. Soon he looked pleased. Now everything was fine.

Dad showed me, saying, "See what I caught." He had a couple of foxes, and he had some more in his bag that he had skinned. We were the happy family gathered around for supper. David Akoak and other boys were with us. I told my happy story.

Dad talked to me while we ate. "You deserve a good scolding and punishment, but I'm going to let that go, since you have done lots of good in one way. But you should have let Mom know about it—and the worse thing is fooling her."

I told him I did that because she might not let me go. And she wouldn't have let me go.

Dad said, "From now on, don't go hunting or anything without letting us know about it before you go or do anything. We will let you go when we feel it's all right for you to do it." Now I felt real good. And they were very pleased with the meat that I'd brought home.

# 12. The Christmas Program

The days seemed to pass by quickly before Christmas. We were busy in school, going earlier in the mornings and staying an extra hour after school. I liked that. I didn't mind being in school, because the teacher let us practice for the program, and decorating the room was nice work. Our teacher let us do that work mostly by ourselves, only giving us ideas here and suggestions there, and then we were to be on our own. We needed to be quieted down while making some Christmas cards and so forth. Most of the time we talked about what was in our Junior Red Cross packages. We hoped to find what we wished for in those packages.

My everyday chores at home seemed to become dull, and it was too bad that I had to do them. But if I didn't do them, and just kept on doing something for Christmas, we would have to do without our needed things, which were even more necessary than the long waited Christmas. My brothers and I were busy with the furs, cleaning them so we could buy some presents for our friends and relatives. Dad was planning to go to check his traps and take care of them so he could stay with us for Christmas. Even ahead of time we fixed packages for our cousins there at Southwest Cape. We packed some of our used clothing and a few things bought from the store.

Kenneth had said he would come to the village with Dad for Christmas. I was looking forward to seeing him. I wanted him to be present because I wanted him to see me performing in the school Christmas scenes.

While Dad was away we got the fox furs ready and cleaned and got whatever had to be ready for Christmas. I longed for my cousins who were at Southwest Cape, Debby, Ben, and Marian Nagotak.

The days went by quickly and then it was just a few days before Christmas. We were rehearsing like everything in the school and church. But it had become cold, windy, and quite stormy, and Dad was storm-bound at Southwest Cape. Mom and I were much worried that the storm might last so long that Dad couldn't be home for Christmas.

It was still quite stormy two or three days before Christmas. I was awfully worried now, because I was sure Dad wouldn't be home for Christmas. After school at four o'clock David Akoak and I walked to his house. It was kind of dark. We were talking about my Dad and, of course, Christmas. Suddenly we came upon Kenneth getting in from Southwest Cape. We were very happy to see him. We grabbed him, asking questions and talking as fast as we could, until he had to push us aside, exclaiming, "One at a time!"

When finally he succeeded in taming us down, he told me Kakianak had got in, too. My heart leaped up. Soon as I found out how his folks were, I ran home. I found my folks just about done taking care of the dogs and other things. My worry turned into happiness. Dad asked me, "No hunting this time, huh?" He was not scolding, so I told him it had been stormy; besides I was more interested in school this time.

My! Mom and I were feeling fine—relieved from our worry. Dad had been lucky. He brought in two foxes, but he and Kenneth had had a tough trip. It was windy and snowing all the way from Southwest Cape. They had been coming against the winds and whipping snow. Poor Dad. But he was tough and hardened, so he didn't mind the weather much. Now we were happy once more. But we had to be real busy, packing gifts for our friends and relatives.

He pulled out a bunch of notes from his pocket—a bunch of "Thank You" notes from my cousins. I liked them better than anything else.

The next day after school Kakianak and I were to take our furs to the store to get our needs and presents for our friends and relatives. I made a list of our own needs so we wouldn't forget them. When we got in the store it was very crowded. We had to squeeze to get to the counter, and we waited a long time. Everybody was getting their presents. When we finally got our shopping done, it was dark, and I was tired of standing and pushing and being pushed for a long time. But I was happy as I could be, for we had two big cardboard boxes full of things. But happier than me were Douglas and Martin when we brought in our big boxes. I carefully chose the best of the things we got for our friends and we packed away until quite late at night. I was busiest writing names on each package.

The next day slipped by, and then it was Christmas. All day we carefully rehearsed the program that was to be performed twice that day—once in the afternoon and again later that night. In the afternoon there were not many people, but it was exciting, because it was not until then that we had much chance to see other groups from the school who were taking part in the program. It was fun to watch, and most exciting to be on the platform in front of a crowd. I had my former feelings, but this time I was calmer and more myself than the other year.

Then the evening, there was a bigger crowd of people. When my part came, I felt warmer and it seemed harder to be in front of people. I didn't seem to know exactly how I'd performed, but I liked it. And I was glad the fun was not over yet. It was fun to sit while the big pile of presents was sorted and passed around. Some men and older school boys passed around the packages. In spite of being shy, I wanted to do that, but I was too shy to speak up for that. Besides, we small boys were not trusted for doing that. They promised to let us do it next year when we were older.

Sure enough, they passed around some familiar packages; those were our Junior Red Cross boxes. I got one myself. I heard it rattle when I shook it gently. At last the pile of presents were all given out, and it was time to go home. The crowd left the school with bags full of packages over their shoulders, like a crowd of Santa Clauses.

It was late at night when we got home. The house was cold. Dad lighted the heater and Mom got our clay lamps going. Douglas, Martin, and I gathered around the heater to warm up our hands. Douglas and Martin imitated what they had seen in the school Christmas play. Next came the time for popcorns, peanuts, and candy. As I was the only one who could read, I passed out the presents to my family from the bag. Then there were "Ohh! Ohhh! Just what I need"—and so on, as every package was opened.

Now the Christmas happening was over at school, but we

looked forward to the pageants in the church—caroling and all. That was to be just the next day. Again I had to take part in the pageants. In the church program I felt much different from what I did at school. I can't describe it exactly, but the joy soaked into my heart very deeply. It was calm, easy going, but deep joy and more real. I thought the Nativity Scene was very real. I couldn't really recognize the persons acting for who they were, and I thought they came from somewhere, not from the village. It was something mysterious that I couldn't solve. Do they come down from Heaven? No. But they were real live persons, even a real live baby that cried. My mystery went on until the end of the pageant, when they removed their costumes. Noah Kogoyak was Joseph, Jean Magpa was Mary, and the baby was somebody's baby, and the rest of them—Oh, I was really surprised!

Once more there was a good pile of packages. And a box for each family from the Mission.

As we walked home in a cold, calm night, my friends and I sang over the carols we had sung in the church. The carols seemed to sound heavenly in the calm, clear night. The voices lowered and rose slowly and sweetly, especially "Silent Night, Holy Night," which sounded best to me. At each house we went by we said a "Good Night," and "Merry Christmas" to friends and relatives. I said "Good Night" to Frances and Barbara Danagik, and then to Napartuk's family, our good next-door neighbors.

I could hear Douglas and Martin chattering their teeth as we got into our house, but in the next few moments was the happy time once more, sitting in a family circle opening our packages.

Then we opened the big cardboard box that came from the Mission. There was some clothing for each member of the family, some coloring books, crayons, some good eats, such as popcorn, nuts, candy, and some dried fruits. We tried on our new sweaters and other things. Oh! It was a happy time. Our little room was almost half-full of paper wrappers and strings. That was some work for Mom and Ann.

After a light supper we went to bed, but we were all too excited to sleep, especially Douglas and Martin.

I know we didn't have to worry about school until the next month, so the next day was a whole day for play or work. I hoped for nice winter weather. My friends and I would go for a long walk on the lake, visit around to friends' houses, go skating, get a supply of ice by dog team, or whatever we wished to do.

My father talked about going to Southwest Cape in a day or so to take care of his traps. I started writing notes to my cousins down there and packed small presents for them.

The next day was a nice one. I went out early. There were my friends. We were a happy gang, walking around in the dark, cool morning. The sky was dark, blue and starry. Francis Oalateetak asked me to come to his house to warm up while we waited for daylight. We did. His father was gone already to check his traps that morning. His mother fixed us some hot tea. She was a very kind lady. How we did enjoy that tea and her home-made biscuits while Francis showed us what he got for Christmas! We played fine games until it was daylight. I went home to see what work I had to do that day, telling the boys I'd be with them after I got my work done, if I had some to do.

At home I asked my folks if there was anything to do. But Mom and Dad only said, "You are old enough to do things without being told what to do. Look around and see what's needed to be done."

They were right, and I felt a bit ashamed for my acting like a kid. I did look around, but what's to be done? Sure enough, I found something to do, and the work I like to do. Our supply of ice was low. I must get some while the dogs were at hand. We needed lots of it, because for several weeks Dad would be away with the dogs.

I harnessed up our dogs and started for the lake. It was hard work to get pieces of ice. I sweated under my warm clothes in the cold day. But just as it was much work, it was also fun to do. I liked that work. On the first trip I cut up several sled loads of ice so I wouldn't have to do that every trip. Besides that, I helped some ladies get their ice. Then I hauled in the ice to the house, trip after trip, until we had a big supply of it, enough to last us three or four weeks. As

I usually did, I got an extra sled load of ice for Aiyaksaq. It was noon before I knew it, when I got that work done. We had a big pile of ice. It meant I didn't have to worry about that for a long time. Now I had all afternoon for myself.

My father was getting ready. A thought came to me as I helped him around: "What if I ask to go with him?" Since I didn't have to be in school until the next month, he might let me go with him. My! How good it would be to visit my uncle and his folks down at the camp.

I started thinking, "How am I going to ask for that? If he might let me, oh boy! But if he wouldn't let me, I know how I'll feel disappointed, very disappointed. So I'd better not ask for it." I was thinking hard, trying to gather enough courage to ask. It might be worth trying.

My father noticed that I was thinking hard. He asked me, "What's wrong?"

I told him, "Oh, oh, nothing."

But he insisted to know. "Yes, something is wrong. You are sad and worried. What have you done that you are afraid to tell me?"

My heart hammered against my chest; I felt the warm feeling come over my face. But still I couldn't find any way to tell him what I wanted to do. Finally I collected myself and blurted out some words: "The school is out until next month. I wish I could go with you to see my cousins."

His serious look on his face turned into tender kindness. He said, "I've been thinking about that myself. But then I came to think of your mother and family. They are very helpless without you. Remember, you are the man of the family when I'm away. Besides, our dogs are not very good. They can't take two of us that far. Just think of how much your mother needs you here. There will be a time when you'll have your own dogs and go any place you want to." I felt disappointed all right, but the way he talked of me as a man of the family made me feel better.

He continued, "Sometime in the future when you finish your school you and I will take the whole family down there and we will stay there all we want to. Just study hard and

236

learn quickly." That was something that he hadn't mentioned before. It really gave me something to think of.

He went down the next day with Kenneth. I felt somewhat sad. If I had gone with him I would have a very nice time with my cousins. Probably I would catch a fox or something. Why was I the one who was to be responsible for the care of the family?

In a day or two that feeling faded away, because it was not the first time I had to take it as my father had said. I'd learned to respect my parents deeply. So I was happy again, as I ought to be. I gathered my friends into my house and had good times with them on those times when I had done my work.

The time went by quickly. My father went back and forth from the camp, sometimes got stormbound down there and had to stay down there a couple of weeks or longer. He was always pleased to see how much good care I'd done to the family, even though I'd done nothing much. He did that just to make me feel better after he had disappointed me.

# 13. A Crewman for Kogoyak

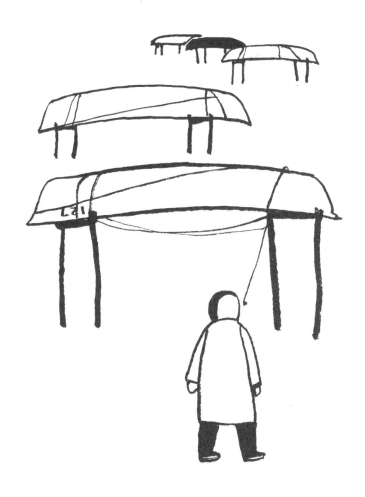

Now my parents were doing something that was strange to me. They always bought us (the children) whatever they were able to buy from the store. But now they never did that anymore—they bought only what was really needed. Where did the rest of their money go? What did they do with it? I never saw them buying anything for themselves, either. Sometimes I asked Mother why they were doing that. She would answer that it was a secret, that I must not know.

Many times when I saw the other boys in their fine, new school clothing that their fathers had gotten for them, I came to my father and asked him to buy me a pair of blue jeans, or a fine new shirt. He would say, "I'm very sorry; we don't have enough money to buy fine new things. That clothing you have is as good as new if you keep it washed clean."

Of course, he was right, but he used to buy me and the boys new ones long before we wore out our clothing. We were even going without good things to eat that Dad used to buy all the time as long as he had a little money. Now it was only once in a while that he bought small things like that. I knew my parents had the money, all right, but what were they going to do with it?

Another strange thing he had done was when he asked Robert Sakigak to come over to our house to help him with a letter to his friend Ahigik at Savoonga. Why didn't he let me write it for him? He always made me write letters for him, even though I was not any good at writing yet. He always said that it would help me learn. But now when Robert came in with me, he asked me to excuse them. Strange; very strange. What was my father up to? I couldn't figure that out. I excused them, anyway.

It was the year 1943 now. Later on I got very curious, and I got curious enough to ask Uncle Robert what was that all about that my father had to write about to Ahigik?

Now my uncle always fooled me, and had his fun with me. He grinned when I asked him the questions. He said, "Your Dad is going to let Ahigik buy you a girl from Savoonga."

I was stunned. I asked him, "What?"

241

He said, "You are going to get married. He is going to buy a wife for you."

Oh! Oh, no! No wonder he was acting very strange and queer. I was not going to have a wife, even if Dad bought one. No! Not me! If they do buy that girl I'm going to run away, I thought.

Now I had something to worry about. What an embarrassing thing to have; I was even bashful to get near my friends. I felt as guilty as I could be. Everybody seemed to know what was in my mind. I was only twelve years old. They shouldn't do such a thing to me. Just imagine—me going around with a girl as a wife among my friends. I was sure they would tease me as soon as they found out. "Getting married. Phooey! I'm not going to do that. No, not me!" thought I. Oh, well, wait a minute. My uncle always made fun of me. He must be just kidding to have his fun. Yes, it had better be that.

Several days went by. I was worried. My parents thought I might be sick or that something had gone wrong that I wouldn't tell them. I always said, "Oh, I have a hard time in school." Of course that was not true.

One day I happened to be playing games with Francis at his home, when Robert asked me, "When are they going to bring your wife?" Ohoo! Not that again. Then he burst out with his merry laugh, and his wife, Bertha, giggled.

Oh, how good I felt now, because I knew now he was only kidding. What a relief!

He asked me, "Were you happy you were going to have a wife?"

I said, "Naw. Who wants a wife? That's a silly thing to have."

He laughed more. Then he told me, "In a few more years you won't think that silly."

"Humph! It's awfully silly and always will be."

The time went by as usual. The school was dull, but sometimes interesting. Good and bad weather followed on. My Dad went and came from the camp with not much luck from his trappings. They went on saving part of our little income. Dad and I worked hard on ivory carving whenever

242

we had time for it. My parents were saving up for something that must be very important. Akoak, my Dad's older brother, had a private conversation with Dad and none of us children were allowed to hear any part of it. In such conversations children listening or interrupting are considered very bad and naughty. So we always kept out of it. Besides that, they always talked in a language that's too deep to understand by any person such as I.

Akoak used to go down to Southwest Cape for trapping, too, but he was getting ill from a nasal infection—which we didn't suspect a bit, an infection which he was to die from the following summer.

On one of his trips to the camp, Dad brought us very good news from his brother, Nagotak. They were coming for the whole season after trapping season closed. We were all happy about that. We wished the time would pass quickly.

Now I was old enough to be trained to be a boat-hunting crew member. There were a couple of skin boat captains that were after me for a crew member for the spring hunting. One was Magpa, my uncle (in some way of relation). Even though he was closely related to us, I didn't know him much. But he was always very kind toward us. The way he was to his children made me bashful. And what I thought of my second cousins (his children)—they were sort of noisy, wild persons. I was too timid to be with the rough boys.

The other boat captain that was after me was Kogoyak. I didn't know him so much, either, but I was close friends with his boy, Herbert, and his daughter, Joanna. As far as I knew their father, he was a nice, gentle old man, but always very firm in whatever he did, and he was quiet.

Of course, my father was to decide for me to which of those men I would be a crew member. I was surprised when my father asked me which one of them I liked to be my captain. I answered him as I always do when he asks me to decide for anything: "It's up to you, Dad. I'll do as you want me to do."

He said that he would talk it over with his brothers. Later on he let me know that his brothers wanted me to be with Kogoyak's crew for a few years, and they would let me be with Magpa after the next few years, because they didn't want to let down Kogoyak, since he was a very nice man. Magpa himself had agreed with those three brothers, who were his cousins.

I was very happy to become a boat crew member, of course, proud to be a crew member, like a man. The hunting season was a few months away, but Mrs. Kogoyak made a good pair of hunting boots for me. I happily helped the men in getting their things in order for spring hunting. That was part of the crew member's duty for his captain. Herbert and I became even closer friends.

All at once school became dull and boring to me. I wanted something that was for men. These were my foolish thoughts of it—that school is for women and kids, not for me. Anyway, I had to go to school, no matter how I didn't like it. The school hours seemed to be too long, yet the time before and after school slipped by too quickly.

One fine day Kenneth came in from Southwest Cape. He said the folks were coming after he got some dog teams in to help them. It was sometime around the last part of March or early April. It sure was good news, because I hadn't seen them since the last spring a year ago. In the next day or two Kenneth took the rest of our dogs, and several dog teams went with him.

In the next day it was the hardest for me to do any work in school. My mind was fixed on the happy arrival of my cousins. I failed in everything. I used to feel bad when I didn't do well or the best I could, and I would try to do better the next time. But this time I didn't pay much attention to how my work turned out. I was very impatient, hardly waiting for the teacher to say, "Time is up" or "Dismissed."

I laid my opened books on my desk, pretending to read. I visited the toilet just to kill time. The teacher was always alert and watchful, always keeping an eye or rather a corner of an eye on every one of his students. So even though I did my best not to draw his attention to what I was doing, he did notice what was going on with me. As I was his pet student, he never scolded me in the presence of the others. He always wrote his words on a slip and gave them

244

to me with other papers put in my books, and some other ways that wouldn't catch the eyes or ears of others.

I returned from one of my visits to the toilet. I saw my book on the desk was closed—which I had left open as if I'd been studying. All at once I noticed the edge of a paper sticking out of the book. I knew that the teacher had something to say to me.

I took a glance at him at the front of the room. He was seated behind his desk, bent over his work. Then I sat down as if I was unaware of everything. My fingers trembled a bit as I slowly but curiously opened my book. Sure enough, he had scribbled a few lines on a slip of paper. He had written what he usually did, "Please remain for a few minutes after school. I want to talk to you. Important. Mr. Riley."

I got kind of curious. What's he going to talk to me about? Has he noticed what I'm doing? Or what? I went on trying to act as if nothing had happened. I took out a sheet of paper and my pencil and started writing a few spelling words, writing them over and over even though I knew them well.

At long last I heard him say, "Time's up." I pretended as if I didn't hear him and went on scribbling on my paper so the boys wouldn't know I was to stay after school. Then slowly I put away my books, cleaning out some used papers. When the last boy had disappeared into the hall, I sat on one of the class chairs that was arranged in a semicircle for class purposes around the teacher's desk. I was facing him. He looked stern, looking at me above his glasses. The looks of his face caused some chills shooting up and down within me.

Then he asked me, "Are you all right?"

I just nodded my head, because I couldn't find my voice.

He asked me a few more questions, "Are you sure you are not sick or anything?"

I sort of whispered to him, "I'm all right and I'm not sick."

"Then you must be plain lazy?"

I shook my head, saying, "No" in a low voice.

He went on, "I still think something is wrong with you, or have you got something in your mind?"

I nodded my head.

"What's that?" he asked.

I whispered again, "My cousins, my cousins are coming."

"What!" he almost bellowed. "Who are your cousins?"

"Marian, Debby, and Ben," I said.

"From where are they coming?" he asked.

"Southwest Cape," I mumbled as I glanced at his stern face.

He slowly showed expression of interest. "When are they coming?" he wanted to know.

"Maybe today or tomorrow," I told him.

"Oh. I see. Bring them to school when they get here. But you should keep your mind on your work. That's very important. Now you may go. Have a good time with your cousins when they come." His face was once more kind and pleasant looking.

My heart felt faded away as I said to him, "Yes, sir. Thank you."

My legs seemed too short to carry me home as fast as I wished. First of all, I looked at our dogs, expecting to see those that Kenneth had used. But they were still gone. That meant they hadn't arrived yet. My heart sank a bit, but I comforted myself. Maybe they are still on the way. They'll get in later tonight.

As usual my family were getting our afternoon tea ready. At our tea I asked Dad, "I wonder if Nagotak and his family are coming today?"

He shook his head. "If they had started this morning they should have arrived by now. It's too late. Maybe they weren't ready, or the men wanted to rest their dogs, as they always do. So they won't arrive until tomorrow, if the weather is nice."

Anyway, I still hoped they would come that day. I kept looking out of the window to see if any dog teams were coming. Whenever I saw a dog team I ran out, but it always was somebody from Savoonga or some men returning from their visit to Savoonga. I gave up when it started to get dark. Dad was right as he always was.

I had some homework to do; much of it, since I hadn't done anything much in school during the day. As soon as the boys were put to bed by Mom, I took a cloth bag where I always

246

kept my books and papers so the boys wouldn't get into them. I threw myself into my work. I always wished that I had somebody to help me with such work, but there was nobody in the house who could help. My sister Ann had been in school way ahead of me, but for some reason she hadn't learned anything. Now I was far better than her. So I had to do all my work by my own means of learning. I worked and worked, so I wouldn't worry about it in school tomorrow, unless to make corrections. I was always sure to have errors. I worked until Mom and Dad had to coax me to get into bed. I was tired and had no trouble dozing off to sleep.

Next morning I had to be called twice, because I'd been working far into the night before. I went to school ahead of time so I could play with other school boys and girls. I went into our room to put my books on my desk. I nearly ran into Mr. Riley in the hall. He greeted me, "Good morning," then asked if my cousins were around.

I told him they hadn't arrived yet. Then I went out to play with the children gathered around the school. We played our favorite games until the bell rang.

The morning school was all right. A good thing I had already done my work for that day. All I had to do was go over where I had made mistakes. To fill in the time that was dragging, I read some books and wrote notes to my classmates that I dropped at their desks as I passed them by on my trips to the toilet.

Lunch hour came around. It was a welcome hour to be out of the dull, boring school house, but it always slipped by too quickly.

The afternoon two hours of school were long ones again, but this time I tried my best to keep my mind on my work, though with much effort. I did nicely in spite of the way I handled my spelling and other problems. When we did our work nicely the teacher always gave us half an hour to spend for anything we wanted to do. I dug into the library. I found an interesting Eskimo story book written in easy, simple to read English. Just as I was enjoying it the most, I heard the teacher announce that the time was up. Oh, how fast that half-hour had passed by!

Like a flash thoughts switched from the story I was reading to the arrival of my cousins. Then a rush out of the school and a run at top speed to my home. Wow! there were the dogs that Kenneth had borrowed. I flew through the doors into the house. There were Debby and Ben. The next thing I knew we were locked into each other's arms in a tight bear hug, but without a word at first.

The afternoon family tea was enjoyed more than any other time, with some stories all tangled up and unfinished, because one story after another cut into each other. A noisy but happy tea it was. Luckily it was Friday; the next day we wouldn't have to be in school. I told them the teacher wanted me to bring them to school, and that he wanted to see them. That put a little interest for school that I always disliked sometimes with all my mind. Now I had something to bring to school and present to my nice teacher.

I was so happy to see my cousins that I almost forgot to feed the dogs, something that my Dad had asked me to do. Remembering that, I ran outside and started chopping some frozen meat with an ax, throwing pieces to the yowling, hungry dogs, while Ben watched me and kept away the stray dogs that are bothersome while feeding.

Later, when their Dad came for them, I found out they were staying with Magpas. They asked me to go with them right away. I went with them, because they both were timid as mice—just as I was when we first came to the village. One of them clung to Nagotak, their Dad, and the other gripped tightly to my arm all the way, burying his face to my side and under my arm whenever we passed by somebody.

At the Magpa place they wanted me to stay with them. David Akoak joined us there. I begged them to let me go, and they did finally, when they got better acquainted with the Magpa children—Alberta, Erich, Hannah, and Lois.

The next day or so while I was getting ready for Sunday School with my brothers, all three of them showed up— Marian, Debby, and Ben, all ready for Sunday School. In spite of their timidness they were eager to go to church with me. When the bell rang we all went as a group. I was very happy as I introduced them to the Sunday School teacher.

He was very glad to see them and to meet my cousins.

Then the next day was Monday. As they had come the day before, they came again, anxious to go to school—that is, except Ben. He was not sure he would like the school. I agreed with him, but I never mentioned a thing about it. I happily introduced them to Mr. and Mrs. Riley, our teachers. They were very glad to have them in school. Ben and Debby went in the other room, as they were to be in the lower grade taught by Mrs. Riley, and Marian was in our room, as they hadn't had very much school experience.

Marian sort of picked on me. Our teacher didn't like that very much. He had to scold us for too long chats. Quite often. And in not too long a time, Ben was scared of school by some hard work. He refused to go to school. Oh, we had a hard time to coax him to school. He was stubborn, but cried too easily.

His sisters were different. They were earnest and interested in school. Soon Debby caught up with me and Marian got ahead of me, in no time at all. Somehow they made the school a little more interesting to me. But still what I wanted was the spring hunting, especially when I was going to be a crew member or a boat hunter.

The presence of my cousins and my Uncle Nagotak made me happy. The time went faster. Nagotak bought me fine new blue jeans and blue shirt that I'd wanted for so long a time, when he saw that I was wearing quite worn-out clothes. He sort of scolded his younger brother, Dad, for not taking care of our clothing. Dad explained why he did that, saving the little money they got, but I still didn't know what he was up to. At that Nagotak gave him some money—as much as he could spare. Nagotak seemed to be very interested in Dad's idea. He was pleased with it. I wondered the more what he was going to do. But I got no solution for that, so I gave it up and tried to forget it and fix my mind on hunting and school.

On Saturdays and after school Herbert Kogoyak often came to call on me so I could help that crew in preparing their hunting equipment. It made me a proud, happy person. Soon everything was all ready for hunting. Other boats started hunting, but we didn't yet, because Kogoyak said, "It's too tough for us still." He promised we would start when there was more open water.

Dad gave me a few instructions: "Be helpful as much as you can; be quick, but careful in whatever you do. Take good care of everything your captain has—don't break paddles or other things. Obey everything that your captain tells you to do. Never, never try to use any firearms and other weapons unless with the permission of your captain and other, older persons. That is the most dangerous thing that may happen at any time. So don't try shooting." There were some other things also that he wanted me to remember.

I sort of got tired waiting for them to start hunting. Maybe they wouldn't. It was only my impatience. I was very impatient in everything.

I talked to my teacher about it one afternoon—that I had to start the hunting and had to be out of school for that. He frowned about it but he said at last that this may be as important as the school for me, as we must learn to hunt as early as we could. Then he said that I may, and I was very glad.

I told him, "When I don't show up in school, I may be out hunting."

He said, "But be sure you are hunting or else I won't trust you. You may use that as an excuse. If you don't go hunting, come to school, or if you are out of school on account of sickness, be sure to let me know about it. Now, good luck to you." I thanked him.

Ben and Debby had moved in with us, so we were as crowded as herrings in a bucket in our tiny little house. They were scared out of the Magpa's house by the wild, rough children. Anyway, they were so timid, even their own shadows would scare them right out of their skins. Besides, they were getting homesick for the quietness of their home in the little camp at Southwest Cape, and it was getting hard to keep them happy.

One nice May morning Herbert Kogoyak woke me up early. He said, "We are going hunting. The ice has gone far out. Get dressed up in your warm clothing." Then he left.

I found that my Dad had gone earlier that morning with his captain, Kazighia. I was delighted. It didn't take me too long to dress and have a quick breakfast.

When I went out the sun was up, but the snow was still firm and crusty in the chilly spring early morning. I first ran to the place where Kogoyak's skin boat was, hoping they hadn't left me behind. The boat was still on the rack. I was a bit doubtful if it was the right boat. I made sure by looking at the clear, big black numbers on each side of the bow. I waited a while or a few minutes under the skin boat; then I couldn't stand waiting. I went to their house. Oh, no! I found them still in bed and slowly having their breakfast, as if they were not going to do anything. Herbert might have fooled me. But he hadn't. That was only how slow they were. They started asking me if I had my breakfast. I told them I had it. It was not very important to me while there were lots of fun and excitement waiting in the day ahead.

Mr. Kogoyak was very much pleased with my fastness. He said, "Now I see that I'm lucky to get a best crewman for my boat; I don't have to wait for him. But I'll have to see how he does in the boat today. I hope he is good for that, too."

I learned that I had a nice captain. And, too, I was going to see how he and his boys were going to be to me in the day. They asked me if I had packed a lunch with me. I hadn't. Then his wife, Sophie, fixed one for me. She let me roll it in my raincoat.

Herbert was sick. It was too bad, because I was sure to miss him, as I knew him better than the rest of his family. As we loaded the gear into the sled, he wished me "good luck." I told him I was sorry for his sickness and that I'd miss him a lot in the hunt. Also his sister Joanna wished me "good luck." I asked her to tell our school teacher that I'd be away from school that day.

I didn't know much of what to do or how to do it. However, I kept the instructions. My father told me to be as helpful as I could. I did that. There were some other boat hunters getting ready next to us. The men stared at me. Some pulled wisecracks at me. Some praised me. They made me as bashful as I could be. Some said, "Now we see Mr. Kogoyak has a new son-in-law. Ha Ha. He is going to marry Joanna; that's why he is crew member."

Some others said, "That guy is lucky. He has the best hunting captain in the village. He is going to become the best hunter, like his captain." That was some torture for me.

Mr. Kogoyak comforted me in a low voice: "That's all right, Nathan. They won't do that anymore later on. They are doing that because they are jealous of me for having a good crew." I liked him even better—a nice, gentle old man he was. He eased that hard feeling that had built up within me.

I was glad when we were on the water. Our motor hummed, and made our large skin boat seem to glide on the smooth-as-glass water. I tried to keep myself handy around the motor to help Otto Kogoyak tend it. That was what I was especially interested in, something I wanted to learn from the boat hunting. Otto was eager to show me this and that about it. I always watched him as closely as I could.

I had had a little experience of this kind of hunting a few times before this, but hadn't gotten much out of it. We went from place to place among some ice on smooth water, watching for game. At some places Louis, our bowman, piloted the boat standing in the bow, signaling Kogoyak, who was steering the boat, and Otto, who was running the motor. Boy, they knew how to do it! When we went through where there were small broken pieces of ice, I grabbed a paddle and helped keep the ice from hitting the skin boat, which might tear a hole in the skin with the sharp points and edges of ice.

Wow! This is the life for a person; far better than school! I enjoyed myself very much. Now and then I looked back at the village, which seemed to sink from view. The mountain became bluish in color and danced merrily in the heat waves of the rising sun. We kept looking for game. Some black spots on the sparkling white ice kept fooling us—they were easily mistaken for mukluks or walrus by unlearned persons like me.

Once in a while I held the funnel while Otto filled the tank of the motor.

Now the day was far spent. All we could see were some other boats far on the horizon, and icebergs and some ducks. Finally, Louis spotted a mukluk on an iceberg through his field glasses. Kogoyak steered the boat as Louis directed the way by signaling. Soon I could see it. As we got closer to it Otto slowly cut down the motor. When the mukluk raised its head and stared at us, I got worried that we might scare it away before Louis could shoot it. When he was sure of the shooting range, he aimed at it. That looked like a careful aim. I held my breath, as if I were going to shoot it. Then his rifle went off. The mukluk lay motionless. He got it with his square, long-barreled, rusty and junk-looking 30-30 rifle.

We got on the ice to skin it. I didn't have a knife, so I just helped around with a hook. We had our lunch. When we finished loading the meat into the boat, Louis asked Kogoyak what were we going to do then. Kogoyak looked at his pocket watch, then told him, "We must start going home. We have no more time left to go out farther. We got a mukluk. That's enough for the day. We'll have another day tomorrow."

Then we started toward the mountain. The village had sunk out of sight sometime ago. I felt lazy and drowsy. The steady hum of the motor was lulling me. Before I knew it, I had dozed off, until Otto woke me up. "Come on, sleepyhead. Let's fill up the motor before it runs out," he said. He had his friendly, wide grin when I looked at him with my sleepy eyes.

Then I yawned, "Ho, hum." I helped him and started moving around to wake myself up. I stared at the mountain. It was very much closer and I could see the top of the village. I'd slept quite a while.

Otto offered me a cigarette. I wanted it, but I was bashful about smoking in the sight of Kogoyak and Louis. Otto knew that I smoked secretly. I told him that I was scared to smoke. He said, "That's all right. They won't care." So I lighted it up timidly.

I glanced at Kogoyak first and then Louis. Sure enough, just as Otto had said, they didn't even look at me. He said,

"See what I mean? Nobody will scold you for anything here, so don't be scared."

I enjoyed myself again, watching ducks fly out of our way and some other boats at a distance to our left and right, heading toward the village, too. The village came closer and closer. When we got near enough I could see skin boats with men unloading their meat on the shore.

It was hard for me to place where we had launched our boat earlier that morning. There were several places, one like the other. But the men remembered, and knew it very well. I thought we came in at the wrong place. To my surprise I was the one who was wrong. It was just the right place. I felt kind of groggy when I got out of the boat onto the solid ice of the shore.

A group of my schoolmates ran down shouting my name. They all had a bunch of questions for me to answer. I tried my best to answer them one by one, but they kept pouring them on. We pulled up our load of mukluk meat onto the ice and did a quick job of it. Next was to pull up the boat. There was such a crowd of boys that we pulled the boat up the slope of the seashore all the way up to the boat rack without stopping a moment.

When the boat was lifted and put on the rack, Kogoyak told me to get my sled to take my share of the meat home on. I was much too bashful to talk to too many people; I ran all the way home. I just dashed into the house. Mom was cooking.

She asked me what we got. I told her, "We got a mukluk."

She asked me to have a cup of tea or a drink of nice cold water. I told her, "I'm in a hurry."

Ben and the boys were playing around the house, sailing their hand-made sail boats in the puddles of water from the melted snow. Their skin boots were all a mess—soaked up in the dirty water. But they didn't care about a thing. They were having lots of fun with their boats.

I grabbed the toboggan and ran all the way back to the shore where Kogoyak was waiting for his boys and me. I got there way ahead of his boys. I sat on the toboggan, and slid down the slope of the shore and almost plunged into the water. The only thing that saved me from taking an ice cold, salty bath was the high pressure-ridge. The toboggan went all the way to the top of it, teetered at the top, and luckily slid backwards.

Kogoyak looked at me with an unpleased grin and said, "There, my boy. You are risking a dangerous thing. You have to be careful. I'm responsible for you. You'll put me into big trouble with your father. I fear they'll take you away from me if I don't stop you from doing a dangerous thing like that."

I told him I was sorry. He told me to take any piece of meat I wanted, but I let him give me one. He told me that Otto and Herbert wanted to see me tonight. I told him I'd come.

I started home drawing the toboggan behind me. I found out that I had run right past Kazighia's boat unloading and my father had called me, but I hadn't heard him. I took my meat home and came back with our dog team and sled to help Dad. We loaded all of his share of meat onto our sled. We pushed the sled while the dogs were pulling at their best. We had too much of a load on the sled, but we made it home. Dad asked me if I had eaten or gotten anything to drink. I told him I hadn't. I fed the dogs while the family took care of the meat.

My boots were soaked badly, too. I was glad when I took them off and toweled off my sweating feet, followed by washing up; this refreshed me better than anything else. Around the wooden eating platter I was proud and self-satisfied to tell the good hunting story with my Dad to the happy family. Mom was pleased with me for becoming a real help in providing for the family. There were my home-sick cousins, Ben, Marian, and Debby, eagerly listening to my story.

After supper I put on my around-the-village clothing, and went over to see Otto. He needed my help to prepare some gasoline for tomorrow's hunting, and other things that needed to be ready for tomorrow. We did that in a short time. Herbert was much better, but still in bed. I talked to him for some time about the day and told him how I'd missed him.

Kogoyak told his wife that I was a good crew member,

except for one thing—that I had broken the boat hunting rule by sleeping in the boat. He gave me something to remember. It seemed to write itself in my mind. I felt ashamed of myself for doing that. I told myself, "I'll never do that again, for sure."

The next few days were filled with good hunting. I enjoyed that, even if we didn't get anything. It was a nice day away from school.

But my good time was interfered with soon by the departure of my cousins. It was a day not good for hunting. They packed up all day. They were to leave that evening. I was not too happy; I longed to go with them. But the unpleasant truth was plain—that I couldn't go with them. And I remembered what my father had said—that he and I would take the family to our camp some day in the future, without fail. Anyway, I kept myself handy, helping with their packing. The boys and I packed a small box for them for a surprise package.

Three or four dog teams were taking them home. Kakianak was one of them. I sadly watched them go and waved "goodbye" to them, until their waving hands were beyond eyesight. I knew we wouldn't have much of a chance to see each other until next spring. It was going to be an awful long time. Our little house was empty and quiet at their absence. I felt lazy from sadness. However, I had some freedom, free from my Dad's strictness, because my mother was not too strict. So there was an evening which I was to spend just as I pleased.

I asked Mom's permission to stay out that night. After telling me a few "Don't do that's," not to smoke too much, and not to stay out too late, she let me go. I looked for my friends. We played some active games, walking around the village and doing whatever we pleased to do. It was early in the morning when I went home. My family was all sleeping soundly. I just pulled off my shoe packs, didn't bother to undress, then threw myself down to sleep. I was tired from hard playing.

In what I thought was a few minutes my brothers woke me up with their noisy, active play, each other chasing me or playing whatever their game was. Mom told me to get up, too. She reminded me of—Ugh!—school. I had had so much fun I had forgotten all about school. I told my mother that I was too sleepy for school, but she said, "Come on. You must go to school. Nobody told you to stay up all night." She was right. It was all my fault.

I hoped the weather would be good for hunting. I hoped the wind had died down so I wouldn't have to go to school. But no hope. The wind was still too strong. Nothing else to keep me out of school, so I would have to be in it for the day. "Well," I comforted myself, "should I not take hard things, no matter how hard they are?"

I pulled on my school clothes and went out. I was glad to see my friend, Herbert Kogoyak, coming to school. He had got over with his sickness. I threw myself into my work and enjoyed it somehow, although I didn't do as much good work as on other days. One reason I liked the work was that Mr. Riley let me skip some of it and catch up with my classmates.

The next morning Kakianak got in from Southwest Cape early. He went to bed. I went hunting. This time Herbert was with us, so I liked the day better than other hunting days. We were lucky, too. We got three or four mukluks and a walrus cow with a new-born calf. I made several trips to bring in my share of the meat. For my share, they let me have some mukluk skins and the calf we got.

Soon my sadness about my cousins was gone. I was too busy to be sad, having lots of fun.

# 14. Akoak's Death

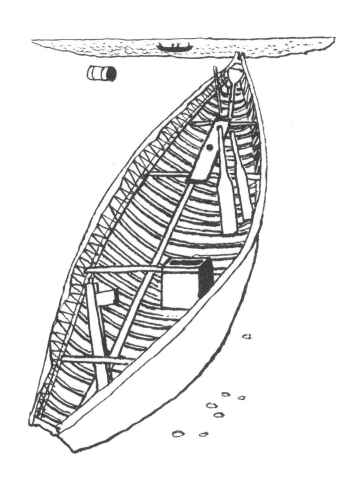

Now I was twelve years old. I hadn't done anything for my birthday. We don't have any kind of celebration, and I didn't think of that, except to feel one more year older. That I was pleased with.

The hunting season went by, with all its fun. But duck hunting took its place. To save money, my father bought me only shotgun shell reloading supplies: gun powder, shots, and a primer, and I had to reload my own shells, instead of buying factory-loaded shells. I learned to like the job of reloading my own shells. My Dad told me never to waste a shell, and I didn't. I shot the birds only when I was sure of getting something, not trying any lucky shots, as I had used to do often.

One morning I was coming home from a duck hunt. It had been a lucky night, and I was tired from carrying my ducks on the long walk from the south of the lake. It was early in the morning. I threw the bunch of ducks in the door and sat down on a crate outside the house to rest. I sat there until I was cool enough to go in the house. Then I pulled off my heavy hip boots and put on a pair of homemade slippers. I got busy getting the breakfast going—just a simple breakfast of coffee, oatmeal cereal, and fine dried fruits. That was really a big treat for me, because I was tired and hungry from the long walk and from carrying the ducks.

When the breakfast was ready and the coffee poured, I woke the family up. Ann took over serving. Dad asked me if I had gotten anything. I proudly told him, "Plenty of ducks."

He was pleased, saying, "Fine. We'll have a feast, then."

Mom was even more glad and pleased. She was going to make goodies of those ducks. The boys also were very glad to see the bunch of ducks. To them the birds were more than good things to eat; they liked them as playthings as well.

While we were sipping our coffee, Dad quietly spoke up: "I'm going to Savoonga with my captain, Kazighia, for a visit and on some business with my friend, Ahigik. You must come with me. I want to take you along."

Gulp! I told him, "I don't want to go to Savoonga. There

are too many people that I don't know over there. I'd be bashful. I don't want to go."

He said, "You must go to see your cousins Pearl and Emily, and your other relatives there, and Ahigik wants me to take you with me so he can see you."

My Dad meant what he said. I couldn't make him change his mind, no matter what I did or said. So I had to go with him. Oh! I was not interested in visiting Savoonga. But I had to now. I packed my traveling sack with my extra clothing and one or two other items.

Sure enough, one of the Kazighia boys called on us. We went to their house. They were loading their stuff onto the big sled drawn by the school tractor. I wished I was not going. But maybe we'd have some fun on the way. We might land on the shore somewhere at a place where I hadn't been before. So I had better try to enjoy the trip. It was not the first one; I'd been at Savoonga last year. At first I had been bashful, but in the next few days I had liked it very much, having fun with new friends.

After an hour or two of the boat trip I fell asleep because I was tired from the hunting the night before. When I woke up, I found myself covered with a warm coat. One of the Kazighia boys had covered me when I fell asleep. I had been sleeping until we were somewhere between Camp Naskuk (Napartuk's camp) and Taphok. We were going close to the shore, following the shoreline. The ice was not all melted on the beach, although most of the beach showed gravel and sand. Some ducks flew up from where they had been sitting, and flocks of them flew past us. Oh, I wished to shoot some, but I didn't have my gun. Besides, Mr. Kazighia wouldn't let us shoot.

The sun shined warmly, making our trip a pleasant one. But I wished we could land and walk around, at least for a few minutes. As I had thought, I was having fun on the way, even though I didn't know if I would like being at Savoonga or not.

I had my wish at Camp Taphok. We landed for some water and I offered to help Daniel to get it. The place was very beautiful to look at. We saw some eider ducks and geese around the pretty, glass-smooth little lake. They took off at the first sight of us. When we returned to the boat, holding the bucket between us, the rest of those from the boat were on the shore. Kazighia told us to walk around a little if we wanted. "But don't wander too far," he said.

Daniel, the girls, and I ran off up the beach to look for sea plants and whatever else had been washed up on the shore. We gathered up a few sea weeds and some plants to eat on the way. We wanted to go farther, but the men were calling and signaling for us to come to the boat. We started running. Kazighia told us we must be on our way. Well, it had been a few minutes of fun added to that we had in the boat. I was so delighted that I hastened to take my place at the motor, and started it, surprising my father and the others. I had learned to run the same kind of motor while hunting with the Kogoyaks, with the help and instructions of Otto during the hunting season. They grinned at what I'd done. After I'd started it I moved to the next seat so Victor could sit at the seat to tend the motor. But he told me to stay where I was and tend it. Oh, boy! I liked running motors for the fun of it. I liked everything about running motors, except filling the tank every once in a while. I didn't like that part. But I felt proud to be one of the important crew members.

Soon they were making some tea and lunch was on. I like meals like that lunch better than any meal at home, even though we ate the same food. It tasted somewhat better. Also the tea tasted good. I didn't know why I liked it that way; maybe I had worked up a better appetite.

Soon I got tired of tending the motor and I let Victor take over. He said that I was a good engineer.

Kazighia and Ahigik were related, so we stopped at his camp for an hour. Dad presented me to his friend, Ahigik.

They talked about something that made me curious. Ahigik told my Dad, "I've been working on both of them, but I haven't done too much to them. One is not very good. It was the only one I could find. The other is perfect."

I wondered what they were talking about, but I didn't dare ask any questions.

Ahigik kept on telling Dad about something. "Come, I'll show them to you," he said as he led us around to the back of his house. I was surprised when Ahigik showed to us two pieces of wood that no doubt were parts of a skin boat. He said to my Dad, "If you are not in a hurry, I'll finish them for you. Or if you want to do the job by yourself, it's o.k. by me."

Dad told him, "You have done lots of work. I'll do the rest of the job myself. But go ahead with it if you wish to help me some more, and I'll take them on our way back."

I looked at my father questioningly, but he never said a word. I still couldn't ask anything, except to myself. No doubt these were skin boat parts. Was my Dad going to make a skin boat? Or was he going to build it for Ahigik? Or somebody else? I couldn't find out.

Ahigik asked us to come into his house for some tea. I went in with them, but I didn't have tea or anything because I was so bashful. While they were having their tea, Dad wanted to pay Ahigik for what he had done for him, but he wouldn't accept anything. He refused because he was a close friend of my Dad. He said, "You have done enough for me; besides, I'll need your help sometime."

Soon we were on our way again. Victor asked me to run the motor again for him. I did that gladly. He himself wanted to shoot some murres. There were plenty of them nesting on the high cliffs. I wished I could shoot at least one. But anyway, I had fun running the motor. I was busy doing that, cutting it down when Victor shot down a bird so he could pick it up out of the water. Then I would get the motor back up to the speed it was running before. That was fun to do. He kept shooting them, hardly missing any, until Kazighia said, "It's enough."

I kept on tending the motor until we were about to land at the Savoonga beach. Then he took over. There were lots of people running down to the beach to greet us. I thought everybody in the village was on the beach. Hmmm! What curious people they were. I shook a bit, not from cold or anything other than timidness. Oh, I wished that I hadn't come!

Lots of helping hands took care of our boat and the other

things in a short time. While I was shying, trying to keep out of sight, a couple of ladies came asking me to come to their homes. They were my own cousins, Pearl Awigiyak, and her sister, Emily. I felt a little better, but still the many people staring at me gave me the chills. At their homes their husbands and their dozen children tried to make me feel comfortable and at home. For the first few moments their hospitality worked the reverse way in me—it made me even more bashful. But their kids were nice. I overcame my bashfulness and began to have a good time with them. Then Dad asked me to go out with him to see other relatives of ours. He said that they wanted to see me. Oh! I didn't want to go out. I was too bashful even with these people who were closely related to us. I didn't know the others very well.

I nodded my head anyway. The children I was playing with didn't want me to go, but I had to go. They all told me to come again, and their father, Awigiyak, said, "Be sure to come back to play with my children. You make me happy." They, too, made me happy, helping me to overcome that bashfulness.

First we went to Joseph and his family. They are my mother's close relatives. We usually stayed with them whenever our family visited in the village, so I had come to know the boys in their family quite well. I didn't remember them much, but they did remember me. We were glad to see each other, even though I didn't remember their names. And I forgot my bashfulness when I found some more of my friends.

Just as we were to take a walk to the places where we used to have our fun the year or two before, Kakianak came to take me to the store. He had taken a few dollars to spend. He asked me if I wanted anything from the store. I didn't. But when some men saw me coming in, they went ahead and bought me some things. I had an armful of things, some that I'd needed badly. I stuffed them into my bag.

Kakianak told me that we were going back early the next morning. He asked me where I was going to stay for the night. I was going to go back to my cousins, Pearl and Emily, and their children. He took me over to their house, where the children were waiting for me. We started all over again with our fun, playing Chinese Checkers and other games. Soon Pearl spread the bedding for us and passed around bedtime snacks. Then we huddled under the bed covers. When Awigiyak turned out the gas lamps one by one, the children told the old stories that they had learned from a grandpa or grandma. The stories went on until their parents told them to be quiet.

In the next few minutes they fell asleep. From the sound of their steady breathing and faint snores, they were all asleep; but I couldn't sleep, because the place felt strange to me. I turned and tossed.

I heard somebody else stirring. Then a low voice asked me from the darkness, "Are you asleep, Nathan?"

"No, I'm not asleep," I answered her, almost in a whisper. "Who are you?"

She was Mary, the oldest girl.

"Let's get up and do something," she said.

"All right. What can we do?" I answered her.

"Come on, I have a flash light."

I got up quietly. We went to the kitchen stove.

"I'm going to make something good for you," she said as she took out pans, bowls, and other things.

I got worried at once. I asked her, "Won't your parents scold you?"

"No, they won't mind. Mother has taught me how to do this. Besides, they are sound sleepers," she replied.

I felt a little better, but still worried. She mixed something in a bowl. She put in into a pan, then into the oven. We sat side by side, looking at a picture book. When the kettle of water starting steaming, she jumped up and quickly made something else. Then she pulled out of the oven something she had baked. Boy! it smelled good. When she had the table ready, she asked me to sit at the table. I did. She whispered, "This is my midnight party." She giggled proudly. She was a smart little girl for her age and size.

When I told her that she made the best cookies and cocoa, I made a proud, happy little girl out of her.

When we finished the things she had made, we started cleaning the pans and dishes we had used. Very quietly at first, but then we started splashing each other and had fun making noise. But nobody stirred. Now we made more work to do, but we didn't mind doing it. She threw me a rag when we were through with the dishes. Then we got down on our hands and knees and mopped up the floor.

We went to bed when we were through. But we still couldn't sleep. She kept on telling funny stories and jokes. Then she was quiet. After a time I also fell asleep.

It was early morning when my Dad woke me up. He said that Kazighia wanted to go while it was still early, to take advantage of the calm weather. I was sleepy and kind of lazy, but I jumped out of my bedding. I was a little sorry to leave so soon. I hadn't wanted to visit the place, but when I knew my friends again, I wanted to be with them. Pearl got up and fixed some breakfast while I washed up. She woke her children when the breakfast was ready. We had a nice time once more. They packed something. They told me not to open it until I was home. Little Beth was sorry to see me leave. She told me to visit again real soon. I told them I'd be visiting in the very near future.

As I walked from the house to the boat, my friends popped out with small packages for me. They all helped us with our things and the boat. In a short time we were on our way, waving to the boys on the beach as the skin boat gathered speed.

When we came to the cliffs, Victor asked Kazighia if he might shoot some birds. Kazighia told him to do so. He gave me his seat at the front of the motor. Then he took his place at the bow. I liked to run the motor while he shot the birds. I would turn it down when he shot down one, then add on some speed. To do that I moved one lever and then another and turned a knob. I had to move them right, otherwise the motor would cough a few times and then stop. Letting it stop once and then having to start it would waste time and the boat captains don't like that. So I was glad I'd learned to do that quite well.

Victor kept shooting until he had used up his shells. We kept going until we came to Ahigik's camp. We stopped there. Dad and I went up with Ahigik to get those skin boat parts.

He had done more work on them. Dad thanked him for his work.

Now I couldn't stand my curiosity or keep back my questions. I asked Dad, "Are you going to make Ahigik a boat?"

He just shook his head.

"Whose boat is that going to be?" I asked again.

He only said, "I don't know."

"Why, is it going to be ours?" I asked him, hopefully.

He just shrugged his shoulders in answer.

Oof! I couldn't get anything out of him. I knew he wouldn't let me know if it was none of my business.

Ahigik asked us to come to his cabin for a lunch, but Kazighia wanted to go on. So we were on our way again. We did what I'd wanted to do on the way: at several places we landed to gather some driftwood, and at one stop we had our lunch. I liked walking on the sandy beach, gathering driftwood. When we got enough Kazighia steered the boat directly toward the point of the mountain, instead of following the curved shoreline to make up for the time spent for stopping to get the wood.

Now my desire to walk on the shore satisfied, I made a comfortable seat of my raincoat and other extra coats. I stood up lazily to fill up the gas tank. I wished it was bigger than it was, so it would run longer, without having to be filled. That was the kind of task I didn't like to do, but had to do it.

In the late afternoon we arrived at the north shore. There were our folks, waiting for us, also the tractor with its sled. I asked my folks how did they know we were coming home, and how did they know about the time we would be arriving? Kazighia had sent a message through the radio that morning before we left Savoonga. I thought he was very smart to do that. I was glad to be home, even though I missed my friends in Savoonga.

Kakianak worked on those skin boat parts until he finished them. Then he started buying some boat building material, so I was certain he was going to make a boat. I wished I knew whose boat it was going to be. The store was out of some of the material we needed for building a boat, so we had to wait for the store's supplies.

Soon there was some work for the men to do at that C.A.A.*
My Dad was hired. He had to work there all day until 5
o'clock in the afternoon, leaving not much time to work
on the boat.

Something made me figure out the boat was going to
be ours—and at the same time solve the mystery of my
parents saving money. They must be saving up for the boat!
I wondered if I was right. I hoped with all my mind, but
they hadn't told me about it yet.

Then one evening Dad told me it was going to be ours.
I was as happy as I could be. The first time I met David
Akoak I told him. Maybe we were the two happiest boys
in town! We started talking about how we would go places
hunting and do everything in our very own skin boat.

By now I had learned to use our tools well enough that
Dad could trust me for some of the work with it. He got
some wood ready for me to saw and plane, telling me how
to do it and what next to do before he went to work at the
C.A.A. I did as he told me to do. Often at noon he came
home for lunch to see all of the work done. Then he would
say, "Fine. You have done the work."

Then he would give me some more work to do. I always
did it with much pleasure, because he made me feel good
when he was pleased with my work and told me how good
a help I was to him.

I wanted to hurry up to finish the boat in the shortest time
possible. But I had to hang on to my patience sometimes,
remembering what my uncles and Dad always said. They
said, "Only careless, lazy people hurry along with their work."
I did my best to do the work well, not carelessly hurrying.

Poor Uncle Akoak was getting ill from that nasal disease.
He came around once in a while to look over the work Dad
and I were doing. He often told me how to do things easier
and better. I appreciated his instructions very much. He
would sit near me and watch me work for some while, then
would go home, telling me to call him when I had any kind
of difficulty. He always told me not to attempt to do anything

* Civil Aeronautics Administration (now Federal Aeronautics Administration), for which a weather installation was being constructed near the village.

that I didn't know how to do, in case I might spoil it and waste hard-earned money. He also promised me if I did my work carefully and faithfully, he would pick me as a bowman when we finished the boat and started hunting in it.

Finally he got so ill he couldn't come around to see how our boat was coming along. Every night when it got too dark for more work, and when our tools were put away carefully, I would go to see Akoak. He asked me how I was coming along with the boat. I told him everything we did to it. He listened, interested.

As the days went by he was losing, until our school teacher had to send him to the hospital at Nome. We were all worried, awfully worried about him. One evening when I visited him to tell him what had been done on the boat, he looked very sick. He was to go to the hospital the next morning. He turned to face me and told me to come closer to him and sit down. I sat in front of him, crossing my legs. Then he started talking to me.

"You are a big boy now, no longer a child. You yourself showed to me that you are old enough to be a man, old enough to take care of yourself and look after your brothers, including David. I trust you that you will always help take care of my family. Please live with my family when I leave. I mean when I leave. If it wouldn't have hurt your parents, you would have been my own adopted son. Remember that you are my own child. You and David help each other in everything you do. In fact, you two should live together. Everything I have here is yours and David's. Since David is not old enough to take care of my tools and other things, I'll give them to you. Keep them real good. They are all yours, but you must keep them in my house. If you take them out, you must bring them back here. That's what I want to tell you before I go. I trust you will take my words and keep them in your mind."

I told him I would do as he said, and would keep his words as much as I could. He touched my feelings. Why did he talk to me like that? I sensed what he meant, but I couldn't bear to think of what he meant by telling me things like that; so I tried hard to ignore the meaning of it.

270

We got word that evening that Jack, a pilot, was coming the next day in his plane. Akoak was to leave on that plane. I came home. I was worried like everything all at once. My folks noticed my mood. They asked me what was the matter with me. I didn't tell them anything. All I could tell them was that I was tired.

We went to bed when the time came around. I didn't even know that I'd ignored my parents when they were speaking to me. They somehow learned why I felt that way, and then tried to comfort me. But their comforting added more hardness and enlarged the lump in my throat. I pulled the covers over my face, then wept myself to sleep.

The next morning Kakianak didn't go to work. As soon as we were through with our breakfast I went to Akoak's house. They were still at their breakfast. Right away Akoak asked me to have a cup of tea. I did. Little did I know that this was the last time we would have tea with him. I watched them as they helped him into his clothing, then laid him on the stretcher.

Soon we heard the plane coming. It landed and came close to the front of their house. We waited while they unloaded the cargo from the plane and loaded the stuff to go. Then they called for the passengers to come aboard. There were several men carrying him on the stretcher. Then they helped him to one of the seats and made his as comfortable as possible. He looked around as he fixed his eyes at me and David. I smiled at him. He smiled through the pain-showing expression on his face.

When it took off we watched the plane until it was out of sight. I never went home. I stayed with David and his sisters. We all didn't feel very good, and we didn't do anything much, just forcing ourselves to pass the time and to keep our minds busy. David asked me to stay with them overnight. I asked him to come with me to my home to get my parents' permission. He did. My parents gladly let me, after telling us not to do any mischief. They said, "You both are old enough to take care of yourselves. Remember, you are young men. Only kids do mischief things." We promised to be good.

271

At his home we gathered some comic books and found some other things to do. We retold some old stories. I was surprised when their mother asked us to have a family night prayer. They didn't believe in Christianity. She asked us to pray for Akoak. Akoak had told them to become Christian before he left.

We did have a prayer. Whether the prayer was answered or not, it gave me a hopeful feeling. I did my best to make the family happy, but had to do the same thing for me, too. It was not very easy to bear that hard feeling I had. Their mother, Margaret, was real nice, as she always was. She did lots to keep us happy. She even gave us cigarettes to smoke. She told us each to smoke only one that evening.

Soon their children, Sarah and Ethan, were asleep, but David and the rest of the family and I stayed up. When we thought that Margaret and Rachel were asleep, David and I did whatever we found to do, even smoking cigarettes. When we got tired of doing things, we started a picture jigsaw puzzle. We fell asleep while working on it.

In the morning Margaret woke us up. We were using the board that is used as a table for our puzzle. We laughed when they woke us up. We had slept right on our work!

A day after that we got a word about Akoak through the radio. They told us he was doing fine and he was sent to Bethel hospital. The days went by. During the daytime I worked at home on our skin boat and came back to spend the night with Akoak's. Later we heard from him again. He was to get an operation. They were looking for some blood to match his, and we felt better about him. And we had more hope for his recovery. Time went by, and we didn't hear from him for some time. I continued to work on the boat, staying at home most of the day. But I came to the Akoak's for the night. I got somewhat tired of the boat that we were working on. My father kindly told me that I didn't have to do that every day. Doing the same things every day always bored me very easily. I like to do something for a change; and then getting back to things I always do gets me back to interest in them.

Not only my being tired of working on the boat delayed

us, we also ran out of wood and other material needed for it. The store didn't have them, so we had to wait.

After some time very awful, bad news reached us. Akoak had passed away. Sorrow hit us hard.

For some days I couldn't go to stay with my cousins. I couldn't bear to see their sorrow, in fear it would make mine worse. It was so bad, it's not easy to describe it on paper or by words. He had been an uncle to me—but good as a father. So his death was a bitter sorrow.

For a long time at nights I cried myself to sleep. I didn't pay much attention to my daily working. Nor did poor Dad. He was moody, but kept on as always. When I got brave enough to bear my sorrow, I returned to my cousins. We bore one another's hard feelings, and that made it a little easier for us.

Margaret was a very brave woman. She always knew how to smooth out our hard feelings, even though being done over with her own broken heart. My sorrow led me to some sickness. I hadn't felt well for a long while. Akoak's last words to me stood out very clearly now in my mind. No wonder he had given me his words. He must have known that he was to depart.

Then along came the freighter to resupply the store. It's always a happy time. Just as every year, we were all busy. Still my Dad was very careful with our pay, buying only what we really needed and saving as much as we could. When I asked him to buy something that was not too needed but that I wanted because the other boys had it, he would say, "I'm sorry. We need our money for our boat. That's the way you'll do in the time to come. When you want something you need badly, there is no way to get it except by saving for it. The more you save the sooner you'll get it."

When all the work was done with the store supplies we were paid. My pay was as much as Dad's. I gave all of my pay to him so we could use it to buy the things needed for our boat. But we never touched Ann's and Mother's money; we let them use it for themselves. I was proud to be of some help to my Dad, because he said I'd be the captain of that boat someday.

273

I still felt the pain of sorrow for my uncle, but Dad comforted me and said that if we threw ourselves into our work we'd give no chance for the sorrow to get into us. Of course he was right. Keeping ourselves busy kept our minds occupied, too busy to let in sorrow.

It was the time near the fall, it must have been in September, when we got the frame of our skin boat just about done. Dad asked me to go to buy some paint for the frame from the store. He told me to choose the color I'd like for it. I chose some light gray. When I came back he told me to go ahead and start painting. I started right away, after putting on some ragged clothing.

While I was at it, along came David Akoak, and he asked to help. I told him to go in and ask Dad. He did. He ran home for a paint brush. Soon we were busy talking about how we would be happy to use our own boat. But now we had two other willing helpers who were much too helpful—my kid brothers, Martin and Douglas. They kept us awfully busy trying to keep them away from the wet paint. We were busy shooing them away, but they kept on coming back. Finally we got very tired and sat down on the ground to rest and talk, unaware of the kids. Then when I heard them giggling and laughing gaily, I turned to see what they were doing. Oh, no! What a sight! They had found the cans of paint where we had hid them and they had painted their faces with their finger tips. They looked something like clowns and Indians in the books, with their war paints on.

I grabbed each one of them in both of my hands at their shoulders, intending to scold them. But I changed my mind at the same instant. I'd better let Mother do the scolding, because I couldn't stand scolding the poor brats. I was trying hard not to laugh when I turned them over to Mother. She looked serious at the first sight of them, but started laughing. I couldn't keep back myself now, so I laughed too.

Mother turned to me. Ooops! She started, "Why didn't you watch them closely? They wouldn't have gotten into that mess if you hadn't let them."

I explained to her the best I could. Then everything was straightened out once more and David and I got busy again.

We had been more than half-way through with our painting and we stayed at it until we finished. We got it done before Dad come home from working, then we put away the paints and put the brushes in cans of water so they wouldn't dry up.

When Dad came home he was very pleased with our work. He pointed out some places that we had missed. He said, "You must be very careful if you want a good boat, and if I don't correct your work now, you'll go on like that all the time. One more coat of paint and it will be ready to put the skin on."

Oh boy, it was almost done now! I asked him, "When will we use it?"

"Not as soon as we finish it," he told me.

"Why not? We want to use it soon as it's ready," I said.

"We can't go out in a boat without a motor," was his reply.

Gulp! I hadn't thought of that. Motors cost lots of money. We were not rich. Besides, motors or things like that were very hard to get at that time, because of the war. They were unavailable at many places. "How and from where are we going to get a motor?" I wanted to know.

He shrugged his shoulders and said, "We have to save up for another year or two."

Oh no! A year is too long a time. It was very plain that we couldn't save enough in one year. Then I remembered that we did have a little motor down at Southwest Cape. I mentioned it right away, hoping that was the answer.

But Dad only laughed at me. I wondered what was funny about it. "That," he said, "is no motor for our big boat. It's just an old pile of junk."

I asked him, "Why not? It's a motor—better than nothing."

He said, "We need a better and stronger motor than that one."

True, that motor was too small for our big boat, which was over 24 feet long, and 6 or 7 feet at the widest part. I asked him then, "Why did you make it so big while we don't have a motor for that size boat?"

"Akoak told me to make it that big. I would have made it that big or even bigger," he said.

"Why?" I asked him.

"We have a big family. We need a big boat," he answered. "We might get a second-hand motor from somebody somehow. So let's hope."

That was fine. As we ate our supper he told me, "We still need another thing for the boat."

"Still more? What's it?" I asked him.

"We have only one walrus hide; we need one more. I know Kazighia has an extra. We'll go ask him if he will sell it to us."

Kazighia and his family were at their camp on the other side of the mountain. I wanted to know how much they would sell the walrus hide for. Dad told me, "Twenty dollars is the average price."

"Twenty dollars! Too much. Can we afford that?" I asked him.

"Yes," he said, "remember you worked hard and gave me your pay. We'll use that."

Oh, yes. Now I felt real good, because I'd earned money for the badly needed part of the boat.

"He may not let us pay him all that in cash. He may want something," he said.

"When will we go to see him about it?" I asked.

"Well, I want you to finish painting the boat, and I'll ask for a day off so we can go day after tomorrow, weather permitting."

I told David when we went to bed that night all about what Dad and I had been talking about that day. He was very interested.

The next day as soon as we filled up the water buckets we started painting. Ann took care of the boys this time, and we did faster work on it than before. Then we changed places with our painted work to check over for some missed spots, going over them until we were sure we hadn't missed any. We hardly could wait for Dad to come home and see how we had done with the boat.

When he came home he looked over our work closely and said, satisfied, "Well done. Good job." We were as pleased as we could be. "Good boys will make good crew members for their captain," he added.

As David and I started to walk home, Dad called me to come home after we had eaten. We talked about nothing but our boat that evening as we ate our supper. David said, "When you become a captain, let me be your bowman. Don't let Kenneth be your bowman. He never worked on the boat. He didn't help us any."

I told him, "Sure. You'll be bowman. Douglas, Martin, and Ethan will be our crew."

Little Ethan was proud, and Sarah spoke up. "What about me? Won't I be a crew member too?"

David answered her, "No, women don't go hunting."

She looked sad. So I told her, "Women stay home to make boots and other clothing for their hunter brothers, and cook food for them. A woman who makes clothing and cooks makes the best sister for their hunter brothers." Now everybody was happy.

After supper I told Margaret that Dad wanted to see me. She told me to go see him. Dad always told me to obey what she said, and said that she would tell him if we didn't obey her. When I came in, he asked me if I would like to go with him to Kazighia's camp to see him about the walrus hide.

"Who wouldn't?" I told him, "I will."

He told me that Tom, Kazighia's boy, was going too, to see his parents. Since his brothers were too busy to take him, they were letting him go with us, so Dad could take care of him. He told me to get up early in the morning and come over to our house.

When I got back to Akoak's home we found out we had forgotten to get some water. Rachel had used up the water to wash our clothing. I wanted to get some, but Rachel wouldn't let me go by myself. So we went. When we did work like that in a group, our work seemed to be lots of fun and pleasure.

I was wide awake when we went to bed that night. I thought of the next day. It was going to be exciting. When would I learn to be calm and patient when I am to do things like that? I am always too excited to sleep, making the time drag.

When I got up to get a drink of water, I saw Rachel was awake too. When she knew that I was awake, too, she jumped at the chance to use me. I helped her take apart a coat; she ripped the seams while I held it for her. I was not very willing to do that. Not much fun to do, but she made me do it.

When we finished it finally, we were still wide awake. We played some games and made some noises, until Margaret scolded us. Early the next morning she woke us up. I was glad she did, because I wanted to be up early.

I ran to our home. I found Tom Kazighia and Dad there, getting ready. I did not have much to do to get ready except to roll up the raincoat that I took with me wherever I went, and tie it up with a rope, making a sling to carry it on my back. Rachel had given me a little wrapping of paper, saying, "Here is something to pay you for helping me with the coat. Don't open it until you are all by yourself." I had put it in my pocket. It was a small package. I wanted to see what it was, but I couldn't because Tom and Dad were walking with me. When we started up the hill, it started raining slightly.

Dad turned to us and asked me, "You boys don't mind getting wet?"

We both replied, "No, not a bit."

"Then we'll go on," he said as he started again.

At noon the rain stopped. We were on top of the mountain. We slowed down to eat some blackberries. We went on, stopping here and there where a bunch of berries temptingly showed. Dad often said, "Go ahead and eat some. We still have enough time to spare." We would stay there a long while, at least fifteen minutes, until Dad would say, "Come on, let's go." Then we would go until we came upon some more berries. Dad always said, "Let's eat some of those."

As we approached the camp it looked pretty. From the top of the hill, the tents stood pure white against the toast-brown withering grass. The sandy beach stretched far toward Mount Taphok. The tide was way out. The low surf washed the shore, where the rocks popped out here and there. While we were climbing down the hill we heard a shot. It was Kazighia himself; he had just shot a seal.

Tom and I threw down our bundles of raincoats when he asked me to go with him to the shore to a place on the beach where the rocks were exposed in low tide. We were having fun looking for little fish and just looking at many kinds of little marine animals. It was fun to watch them in the shallow water and to catch the little fish. We filled a concave place on a big rock with water and put in the fish and other small animals and watched them a long time, swimming around in the shallow water. We must have stayed there for a long time, we were so interested in watching and catching more and putting them in the water.

We heard somebody hollering for us. Then we saw him waving at us to come.

Tom asked me, "What are we going to do with the fish we caught?"

"I don't know. What would you do with them?" I asked him in return.

"Nothing," he said.

"Then let's throw them back to the water so they can go home, and we'll go home," I suggested.

We said "goodbye" to them as we dropped them among the rocks.

Suddenly he hollered in pain and jumped. He scared me so I jumped too. I asked him as soon as I recovered from my pain, "What's the matter?"

"It bit me," he exclaimed.

"What bit you?" I asked him.

"That bit me," he said as he pointed at something that moved on the rocks. I felt kind of creepy at the sight of something that was moving. I stepped down to look at it. It was only a tiny crab that had used one of its pinchers on his finger!

We started on to the tent. When we got there Kazighia and Kakianak were talking in front. Dad said, "We don't belong here. We must find our home before dark." It was long past noon already. How the time went by so fast when we had fun! "Remember, we spent four hours coming. There are not too many hours left before dark," Dad said.

We started to pick up our small bundles of raincoats to

get ready to go, but all said, "No, no. You must not go on an empty stomach. You must eat first." After we had finished a light meal we went on our way up the hill.

Tom and I talked as we walked. He asked me to come to the camp with him sometime again. I told him, "I sure will."

"Next time we will stay here all day," he said.

We walked on without stopping, except to cool off and rest for awhile. Once in a while Dad would ask us if we were tired. He said he would let us stop to rest before we got too tired. Even though we were tired some, we never said so. We wanted to keep on.

At first Dad never mentioned anything about the walrus hide that he had wanted to buy from Kazighia. So after a length of time I asked him while we sat on a big rock to rest a while. I was surprised at him why he was taking it easy this time. He used to keep on no matter how tired I was, giving me no mercy. But I never mentioned anything about that.

I was asking him, "Are you buying the walrus hide?"

His answer was nice. He said, "Yes, he is willing to sell it."

"For how much?" I asked him.

"About twenty dollars," he answered. "But he wanted just ten dollars in cash and wants me to give him a few needed things he can use in his camp. He took all the rifle cartridges that I had with me as part of the payment. I have only five in my rifle."

I wondered why my rolled raincoat was bigger and heavier than usual. But I never mentioned it. Dad might think I was tired. When Tom asked me if I had any string, I fished for a little ball of it that I always keep in my pocket. Then I felt a wad of paper. I nearly pulled it out, but then I remembered the little wrapping that Rachel Akoak gave me that morning. I found the ball of string and handed it to Tom. Then I got behind him and cautiously unwound the paper wrapping. There were a few cigarettes, a couple of packages of gum, a couple of tootsie rolls, and a book of matches. "Bless her," I thought. I wrapped them up again, taking out a pack of gum and stuffing the rest into my pocket.

I opened the chewing gum and passed it to Dad and Tom. They asked me where I got the gum from. I told them I had found it in my pocket.

We made our return trip in a shorter time than the other way trip, because we didn't stop so often as that morning.

That evening we went over to Victor Kazighia's to get our walrus hide that we had just purchased from his father. We paid Victor for it, as his father had asked us to do. We had brought some groceries and rifle shells and ten dollars in cash. Victor and I carried the rolled walrus hide back to our house. My Dad said we would put it in the lake to soak it the next day.

I asked him how long it would take until it was ready to put on over the boat frame.

"About two weeks, at least," he said.

I was anxious to do that. Every morning that I went to the lake to get some water I went to see the hide to check that nothing was wrong with it.

School started the same week. Every pupil was always happy at the first day of school. We unpacked our books that we had tied up in wrappers when the school had closed. We got promotions, too. I knew well what promotion meant. It was really something good and not very good at the same time. The good part of it was that we were more respectable by our fellow schoolmates, and we got the praise of our parents. The other part was more and harder work to do.

When the skin for our boat was ready, I asked for an excuse for one day from the teacher. For the first time my teacher didn't let me do what I wanted to do. He said, "I'm sorry. We can't spare you today. If it was the next two days, I'd let you help your father, but now this week of preparing for school is very important. You can help him after school." I thanked him and went on into the school room.

At noon, when I went home for lunch I told my father that I couldn't be out of school, but I'd help as much as I could after school. Mother and some other women were sewing the hide, which was stretched over the boat frame. There was a cold, September north wind that had stiffened and partly frozen the wet walrus hide.

I had a quick lunch, served by sister. Then I kept myself handy with the women and did what my father wanted me to do. I made a teakettle full of hot tea to warm up our helpers, the women. It was nice to see them sipping nice hot tea while they were cold.

As I was pouring more tea, calling to the workers, "Come in and warm up," David Akoak popped out just as if from nowhere, all thrilled from inside out, evidently. Just as we were about lost in the fun of helping around, the bell rang. It was too bad to drop our fun and run to school. But anyway, the school was exciting before we got tired of it.

The first thing we did in school was spelling. That I liked quite well. Then on to correcting the words we had misspelled or left out, followed by arithmetic, which I thought was the worst part of school. The only thing that kept me doing it was our teacher, who said we must learn it so that we might become the storekeeper. At his saying that, I imagined myself seated behind the counter selling everything. Then I would think I must study arithmetic.

As soon as we were excused for the day David Akoak and I ran to his mother, Margaret, to let her know that we were going to help around with the boat. She said, "Go ahead, but be sure to come right here as soon as you are through helping." We must have given her a hard time in trying to keep us out of mischief that would be harmful for us. To us everything we did was nothing but clean fun. But that was where we were mistaken.

When we got there, the women were putting the last stitch to it. We kept ourselves helpful around the work (maybe too helpful sometimes). Now also my brothers were getting into everybody's way. They were supposed to be boys, but were more like dirty bundles of rags. They got so dirty by getting into every corner big enough to get into, and by rolling on the ground while they played, much the same way as some puppies played.

No matter what they were, they were my brothers. So I couldn't stand seeing Will Napartuk bullying with them. He teased them and made them cry. I nearly lost my temper when he chased them around, scaring them. I didn't even know what I was doing when I grabbed a big stick to strike him right on the head, and I didn't care how hard I was going to hit him. A good thing I had chased him past my father, who caught me by the arm and held me. I tried to wrestle myself free but he held me tight. Then with my free hand I threw the stick at Will with all my might, like a spear. It missed him by a few inches. I was a little satisfied with that, and I shook from my rage.

My father scolded me for that. "You are not supposed to do that. He is a man. He is not your match. You might have killed him if you hadn't missed him with that stick." I felt ashamed when I had settled down from my anger.

He turned to Will and said, "You are a man, not a child. You ought to know what you are doing. Never let him [pointing at me] see you do that again, or else I won't stop him again and will let him do what he almost did." Everything was all right once more.

It was dark when we put the almost finished boat up on the rack that Dad and I had fixed some days before. In the next few days Dad sent me to the store for some white paint. I bought the paint and he told me to go ahead and paint our new skin boat. I was happy to paint our very own new skin boat. When I finished it I asked Dad what more we needed to do with the boat.

He said, "Lot's more."

I was surprised. I asked him, "What more do we need?"

"Rudder, oars, paddles, oar locks, and the keel with a bone runner," he said.

I saw we still had to do much with it. Then I tried to figure out how much it would cost us to build it. I estimated it to be roughly around $250 or even $300. No wonder it took my parents a long time to save up that much! I had only a fractional part in paying for it. But I took a big part in making it—that I was proud of.

The other things we'd need were a motor for it—that was a big problem for us; some oil cans—just simple things, but for us not easy to get. First, we didn't have money for them; second, the store didn't have them, and there was no other place to get them that we knew of.

The winter came and passed very much as the last one. My father went back and forth from Southwest Cape for fox trapping. I asked to go with him, but he found some reasons that I couldn't go with him. When he started going down there I returned to live in our house. My parents thought that if David and I were separated we wouldn't do as much mischief as we did when together. Because we sneaked out at night (even though we did that just to enjoy the moonshine and have clean fun) we were not to be trusted. Who would trust us, we who were looking for trouble all the time? We didn't know the difference between good and bad things to do. All were fun for us.

My Dad took us with him for hunting when he was sure the weather was good. We enjoyed those hunting days the best of all. He did that just to have us with him, because he was always worried that we might get into some trouble.

When the spring came my Dad told me to ask our teacher if it would be all right for us to go to Southwest Cape. In school I was kind of timid to ask the teacher. He was kind of a rough-looking man, but not as rough as he looked. I didn't have to talk to him in person. I was well used to writing him notes about everything and he liked it that way.

When it was about time for class to start, I scribbled a note for him. My note was: "Dear Sir: My father wants me to ask you if it will be all right for us to go to Southwest Cape. Nathan."

I folded the slip of paper and put it among the papers that he was going to check.

When he looked over the papers he lifted up his eyes from them and fixed them on me. I tried to ignore him, but I couldn't help staring back at him. My heart pounded so loud I thought my classmates heard it, too. I even had forgotten to breathe, I realized, when I saw him scribbling with his pencil. It was so silent I could hear the scratching of his pencil on the paper and the ticking of the clock seemed unusually clear and loud.

He handed me my papers and book. I could hardly wait to go back to my desk. My fingers trembled some as I unfolded the paper slip. The note said: "Nathan. Tell your father to come and see me at 4 o'clock. Tell him to bring Kazighia with him. Riley."

When I went home I told my father all about it. He did go to see him with Mr. Kazighia. When he came back he had bad news for me. Mr. Riley had said they wanted to keep us in the village because of the danger of war, but they'd let us go when it was not too dangerous.

During the spring I quit school. I went hunting almost every day with Kogoyak—until the spring season was passed. And so did my father. He was hunting with Kazighia.

That year Nagotak and his family never did come to the village. They stayed down in the camp. My father and Kenneth took some supplies by dog team to them before the snow melted. On his return trip Dad brought the little outboard motor—just a crude pile of rusty junk. But I loved it as if it were a person. I started cleaning it. I took it apart and cleaned its every part lovingly. In a day or two I had put it together in one piece. Then I took it outside and clamped it on the handle bar of the sled. I ran over to Mr. Napartuk to ask for a tin can full of gasoline, and poured it in the tank of the little motor. There were our neighbors watching me—Napartuk, George Danagik, and Edward Aiyaksaq. They were all laughing at me and my old machine. It was not good at all to be laughed at.

But the worst was to come yet. I set it to a starting position. When I thought everything was in starting order I wound a piece of rope around the flywheel and yanked it. It spun around but didn't start. I did that several times, but the motor didn't even cough. What could be wrong? I checked it all over. Everything was in place. Still something was wrong. The neighbors were very much amused. I was kind of mad, but I thought I and my machine must be a funny sight. Even my father was laughing from the door as he watched me.

Then he stepped out, putting down his work of sawing bone for the keel of the boat. He said, "You have been in school more than I ever was. You ought to know things like this." He told me to spin the motor once more. I did, hoping he would help me. Then he asked me to remove the spark plugs.

I did. He held each armature wire and let me pull on the start rope slowly. I did as I was told to do, watching closely what he would do so I could learn it from him. He told me to spin it once more. I did again.

He told me to get the cloth bag that held some tools. I ran in and came out with it. He took out a screwdriver from the bag and opened the top of the flywheel. He looked into it through a hole that I hadn't noticed before. Then he showed me the breaker points. He said as he worked it open and let it snap back closed, "This is the trick you have to watch out for."

He took a tiny wrench and adjusted it to the right opening. He let me hold the wires before he fixed the breaker point while he spun around the flywheel, asking me if I felt anything.

I, surprised, asked him what I was supposed to feel. He didn't answer me. After he worked on it, he held the wires while I turned the flywheel for him. He nodded his head in satisfaction and let me hold them while he turned the wheel. I wasn't expecting anything, when suddenly I felt the sharp of shock.

I jerked my hands and yelled. He giggled and showed me the points after he had adjusted them. "This is the heart of every outboard motor. It is dead if this is not adjusted right." He showed me more. "This is another way to know if the motor is alive." He snapped on the spark plugs to the wires and opened the motor. Some sparks jumped between the electrodes. It was a very new thing I learned about motors.

Then I put the spark plugs in place, tightened them with the wrench, adjusted them to starting order, and double-checked to see if I had forgotten to do anything. Everything was in order as it was supposed to be. I wound the rope around the flywheel once more, and gave it a sharp, quick pull. The little motor caught right away and kept running until I pressed on the stop button. "There." I had the motor ready.

But the boat was not ready at all, as Dad said. I asked Dad, "What can we do with the boat? What needs to be done?"

He said, "Look for the can of white paint that you bought

last year and give it a second coat of paint, if you want to."

I did that. I found the can of paint from where I'd stored it the last fall. Kenneth offered to help this time. I appreciated his help. We did the job that morning, while Dad was busy making the keel and fixing a runner from out of whalebone. He was short of whalebone. He went to his friends, asking if they had some left over or some to spare. He got all he needed, but it took a good deal of time to fix it.

Kenneth, David, and I were very anxious to use our new boat. We kept asking Dad, "May we try our new skin boat as soon as we get it ready?"

He said, "Yes, you may. But you can't."

"Why can't we?" we asked.

"You all ought to know," he said. "We don't have even a drop of gasoline and we don't have any money to buy it with."

Oops! How right. David and I looked at each other without a word to say about that. But not so stunned at that as David and I were was Kenneth; we eyed him closely. He grinned and said, "That means if I buy some we will try the new boat."

"If you do that we will try it as soon as we finish it," Dad told him.

David and I always talked about Kenneth having no right to be a crew member because he hadn't helped make the boat. Now he had a bigger right than we. Well, we each had a share in it. That made us entirely happy.

In the next few days we got the boat ready. With Kenneth's help, everything went much faster. Even though we were without some of the equipment, we had every really necessary thing a boat should have. When Kenneth bought us the gas and oil we mixed it in a can and got it ready. Now all we needed was some good weather. By that time the wind was too strong.

We were disappointed again when some trouble happened that none of us could help. A flu epidemic occurred. We all were too sick for anything for about a couple of weeks longer. Then we were all well again, once more eager to use our new boat.

I was still weak from the flu sickness when Kenneth and I did the final job to get it ready. There was still some ice offshore a short way out. Since we had a small outboard motor we were just going out bird hunting, along the shore. Auklets, murres, and some ducks were flying in flocks near the shore when we pushed out our new boat onto the water. We were Dad, Kenneth, David Akoak, and Nanapin. We each had our shot guns with us. I ran the poor little motor. David sat next to me as my handy man. Kenneth was at the bow, where David and I were hoping to be. But I was not disappointed. I liked being "The Engineer," as we called ourselves. Dad was steering, and Nanapin was a crew member.

I took extra care because I felt that we were being watched. Thank goodness the little motor caught at the very first try. Proudest and most thrilled were David and I. Even though I ran the little motor at top speed, the boat went kind of slow. "Who cares, anyway," I thought.

We were having our fun when we started shooting birds. It was an early spring evening. As it wouldn't be dark, we just kept on shooting birds until we used up our shells. I had so much fun shooting and running the motor that the time seemed too short when we had to go back. I was sorry our shells gave out so soon, leaving nothing else to do except to go back. But we had gotten many birds, anyway. When we nosed in, there were our neighbors to help us with the boat. Everybody had some nice things to say about our first use of our new boat.

Kenneth whispered in my ear to ask Dad when we would go bird hunting again. I asked him. He said, "As soon as you buy more shells for your guns." Oh boy, Kenneth and I exchanged glances delightedly.

Little Ethan was very cross because he hadn't been hunting with us. Dad told him he would go with us when we went out on a real hunt for seals, mukluks, walrus, and whale. He was happy once more. My brothers didn't care much. They were happy.

It was after midnight when we went to bed. A happy person I was. I started thinking of what Dad had said to me long ago—"We will take the whole family to Southwest Cape in the future." Now we had a boat and probably would get a bigger motor in the next few years. But a year was an awfully long time, for no doubt we couldn't go by that time Mr. Riley had said. But I couldn't help hoping we would in the near future. Maybe next year.

I was thirteen years old by that time. Soon I was dreaming we were going home to our loved little camp, Southwest Cape. Little did I know that this dream would come true. Anyway, a dream is a dream, and I soon forgot all about it.

# 15. The Ancient Enemy

In the next few days I kept myself busy carving ivory, even though my friends asked me to play with them. I told them that I was busy. I was no longer satisfied with that kind of fun. I wanted real fun—hunting. I saved up my ivory carvings to buy some shells. When I finished a few carvings—enough for a few boxes of shells—I asked Dad to take them to the store so he could get me what I wanted. But he told me to do that myself. At first I wouldn't, because I was bashful about my carvings; if the storekeeper wouldn't take them I'd feel embarrassed.

My Dad was stubborn. He forced me to do that myself but I wouldn't give in until he came with me. I did when he said, "If you don't do it, you'll never get your shells. With no shells, no hunting." Of course that was right.

Dad and I entered the store and I put the cardboard box on the counter in front of Mr. Kapugan, the storekeeper. I didn't have a word to say. "Well, what do you have here, ivory carvings?" he asked me.

I just nodded my head without a word.

"Let's see them now," he said.

I felt like running away, because there were men looking at us. Nakak, the store's ivory carving inspector, was seated at the other end of the room. Kapugan called him over so he could look at them and make prices for them. I felt very uncomfortable as he looked them over quickly. Maybe he didn't like them. I wished I hadn't made them. But he didn't say anything yet, until he had looked them all over.

Then he looked up at Kapugan. Now was the time for the worst, thought I. But no; his words were too good to be true. "Very fine pieces of work; give him top prices for them," he said. Then he turned to me and asked me, "Did you make all of those by yourself? Didn't he help you?" he asked, and pointed at my Dad.

"Yes, I made them by myself, and nobody helped me," I replied shyly.

"Are you sure?" he asked again.

"Yes, I'm sure," I told him with my eyes fixed on the floor.

"Then make lots more. The store will buy them," said he as he got back to his seat.

"Yes, I'll make some more," I told him, more shy than ever.

Kapugan looked up the price list for ivory carving from his books and wrote figures down. Then he totaled it. When he showed me the total it was hard to believe. It was twelve dollars. A box of shells for my gun cost one dollar each. I had enough for twelve boxes now!

"Now what do you want to buy?" Kapugan asked me.

I told him.

"How many?" he asked.

"All that money's worth," I told him.

He grinned and looked at my Dad, questioningly. Dad said, "No. You better buy three or four boxes."

I chose four boxes, but Dad did get a sack of shot, some gun powder, and primers. He said, "By reloading your own shells, you'll always have plenty of shells." He was right. We still had a small amount of money left. He asked me what would I want to get. I told him I didn't want anything. He said, "Then let's get some groceries with that." He got a few needed items.

At home Dad took two boxes of my shells and said, "I'll keep those for you. I'll give you two boxes only."

"Why? I want to shoot lots of birds."

"Because it is the right time now to put away what you'll need for the time to come. Remember, we might go back to Southwest Cape. Then you'll need your shells very badly."

"Ah, all right then. I'll save three boxes now. Then I'll still have one box and lots of reloading supplies to use now," I said, agreeing.

From that time on I put away what little I had to spare and we—my cousins and I—picked on Dad every calm day to go fishing and duck hunting in our new boat. But it was not always that Dad let us do what we wanted. But sometimes while I was not thinking about that, he would say, "Come on, load up your shells. Let's go hunting."

Then I, all excited and thrilled, called on my cousins, David and Kenneth, "Let's go hunting!" I didn't have to call them the second time.

294

Some men went with us sometimes, so there were eight or ten of us in the boat. We got a young walrus one time on our fishing day; on another time we got a sea lion. Still another time we got a mukluk.

Even though small and crude, our little motor served us as well as a big one would.

All that summer went by filled with lots of fun for me. Using our new boat was the best part of it, but I had many more things to do that summer. Women gathered greens, as they did every year. My Mom and Ann filled up their barrel. I went with them to help carry home what they had gathered, and I enjoyed doing that.

Dad was still a member of the ATG, a U.S. soldier. How I wished to be one of them, too! I always begged my father to let me clean his rifle, a Model 1917 Springfield rifle. It was big and beautiful to me. It looked powerful and mighty. I wished I had one like that of my very own. Later, I learned to take it all apart and put it back together again, when I was all by myself at home. That was always the time when I could do whatever I wanted to do—reload my shotgun shells, sometimes carve ivory, or just get into some mischief, especially when David was with me. We made some fire crackers by rolling gun powder into papers and exploding them right in our house.

During that summer Dad and I did so much ivory carving that we were short on ivory to carve. So mother started digging at the old village. There I had to take part again. I helped her. She softened the solid dirt with nothing more than a home-made pick. I made it for her out of an old file, bending it to the end of a stick sawed at an angle. I shoveled the dirt that she had loosened with that crude tool. It was very hard work, but that was the only way to get the badly needed ivory. With no ivory we would have to go without the things we needed.

Sometimes we would be paid off with only a few small pieces from the whole day's work. At the end of the day I wanted to take a good rest, but I wasn't allowed to do it. Instead of rest, I did the chores until it was time to go to bed. Sometimes, though, we found larger pieces. Mother was not discouraged a bit with our tough luck, while I was very much discouraged. I kept up with my work only because Mother wanted me to.

I thought my parents were very wicked and cruel when they treated me roughly. But it was what I needed. All for my own good. They were trying to harden me for the future, so that I could take the hard life with ease. By now I had learned to take rough treatment, and I was not too sorry for myself anymore. But it was not easy at first. Gradually I started to be grateful for their teaching. They were sure wise, while I had never thought of what I'd need in the time to come.

My Dad told me stories about himself when he was my age. He had had a very tough life. His older brothers and his father had treated him more like a beast of burden. So I learned that is why he was so tough for his size. He always said, "Your life compared to mine is a very easy life. Knowing how hard mine was, I don't want to treat you rough, as I was." I wouldn't take it for sure if he had done that to me.

But I was getting what he hadn't got: the school knowledge. I always mentioned it, in order to have something to say for myself. "Even though we don't need strength for it, school is not easy," I would say.

The summer had gone by. The fall was in. As soon as the ground was frozen solid enough, the long-waited-for mail plane came. We had nothing to do with that, but the postmaster sent for my Dad. He went to the post office and came back with some long envelopes. We gathered around him as he tore them open. He pulled out some checks—his pay checks from the CAA! I grabbed for one of them to see how much they were worth, but he wouldn't let me take them. He never even told me how much they were. It was none of my business anyway.

My father got a good amount of money from his pay checks at the store, and I thought we would be living at ease for a while, getting everything we wanted from the store. I thought we were rich. But no! He got only what we needed badly. We still kept up our ivory carving just as we used to do. He kept on going to Southwest Cape to trap foxes.

He still didn't tell me what he was going to do with the money he got by working at the CAA. I wondered what he was up to this time. Even though I begged him to get me some good new clothes, telling him that all my classmates had this kind of good sweater, that kind of good pants, and that kind of good shoes and so on—that I didn't have any, while they had everything—he wouldn't spend a penny for not very needed things. He always said that those I already had were still good and that as long as I kept them clean, they'd be as good as new. Why should I need some more?

Later on he finally told me that he wanted to get started saving for an outboard motor that the store would get for us. That suited me fine. I gave in to him as soon as he told me that. But just as always, he didn't tell me what to do with my ivory carving money. He let me spend that for whatever I wanted. I always wanted to be of some use to the family, so I proudly spent it for family needs. But once in a while when I saw something very good to eat, I got busy with ivory carving to get that thing I wanted. If I wanted it badly enough, I would give up the fun I would have with my boy friends and keep busy, so I would have enough to get it.

Our normal everyday living went on as usual. The school came around. I paid less and less attention to it because there were too many things to enjoy besides school that were far more interesting. School brought nothing but headaches, and I was discouraged by some hard problems. But it didn't remain that way. Holidays I liked it better, when we didn't have to do our regular study. We prepared for some plays. There was always something new every year.

On this year, too, there was something new, but not a good thing. One day, as I usually did, I dropped in at David's house so we could walk to school together. It was a week or two before Christmas. We happily walked to school. On the door we came upon a notice sign. It read, "No school until the epidemic is over." We didn't understand very well about it, but since it said, "No school," we turned away. We decided to do some work with the help of each other. We got some ice for them first, then for us. As we went along with our work, we noticed something strange. There were no people in the village. Usually the people were doing some kind of daily activity, but today the village looked deserted.

I felt weak and tired all the time. David told me the same thing of his feelings. We would push our ice-loaded sled for a short distance, then would rest for a long while. Soon my muscles were sore all over me.

Finally on our last haul of ice we were really tuckered out. We met Naciknak coming slowly from the village with two buckets hanging down from his yoke. He swayed from side to side as if he were very weak. His face was very pale and his eyes looked tired and inflamed. He stopped to talk to us. He asked, "Are you boys all right?"

We told him we were all right.

He said, "Well, you boys had better be careful now. As soon as you get that load of ice, you'd better go home and go to bed. There is bad sickness in the whole village. That's why there is nobody in sight." His voice was low but hoarse. Then he went on as if he were drunken.

David and I looked at each other. Then we decided to help Naciknak. We told him to wait while we went to fill his buckets. He accepted the offer for help. Poor guy. He sat on the sled and covered his eyes with his hands. We carried his buckets of water all the way to his home, because he was pretty sick. As soon as we finished our work, I threw myself down into my bedding, because I was tuckered out. I even refused to eat at dinner time. All I cared for was some rest, good rest. I lay there for a good length of time, but I didn't get rested. Instead, I got more tired. My mother told me that she had the same feeling.

Kakianak was at Southwest Cape. He had been there for a week or longer. We were expecting him and Kenneth on that mild day. But they didn't show up that nice day. Then we began to worry; they might have the same sickness.

The next morning I was sick, with a burning fever, cold, and headache. My lungs felt as if they were ready to burst at any time. I was coughing and my throat was sore, like everyone of us in the family. We were all sick. I wondered why we were all sick at the same time, as if we were struck by the disease. I was very glad that I'd taken care of the ice supply. I couldn't do a thing with this sickness and very tough weather.

The strong north wind was howling and the snow blowing. I didn't care to get out of my covers for sometime. My sickness was getting the best of me, until I saw my mother. Although she was as sick as I was, or even worse than me, she was up and doing whatever she could to make us feel comfortable and ease our feelings. That was when her brave doings touched me.

"I am a man and Mother is a woman, and she takes her sickness better than I do. Why let a woman take care of me, while I am supposed to care for her?" At that thought I got up and dressed. I tried to coax Mother to get into bed, but she wouldn't. Instead she begged me to get back into bed. No, I couldn't stand seeing her work hard, so I refused firmly.

Then I intended to go out for some ice and to dump the honey bucket, but she held me by my wrist with a firm grip, saying, "No, no. You can't go out into this cold weather with your sickness."

I insisted, "Why not? I must do it. We need it."

She said, "Because I don't want you to do it."

I told her, "I'm not as sick as you think. I'm able to do it."

But she kept firm. "You are very sick. You have always obeyed what I said. Are you going to disobey me now?"

I said, "I have to, to do good."

"You are making me feel bad. I thought you wouldn't turn me down," she said.

I always had promised to be obedient to her. So I had nothing else to do now, and gave in to her; but I refused to get back into bed and I helped around in the house as much as I could.

Now we had not only sickness to worry about; we were very much worried about poor Dad. He still was at Southwest Cape. He might be sick too, and the weather was too rough for traveling. So we were sure he couldn't come. Two days went by while our sickness even worsened, and so was the weather worse. We were more worried. I saw my brothers were very sick, especially Douglas; when I felt his forehead, he was pretty warm. He moaned and groaned during the night, gasping for breath and coughing very badly, and I could hear the wheezing in his lungs. A fear gripped me because he was as if to be choked to death any moment. I looked deeply into my mother's eyes and I noticed her fear, too. But when she guessed my fear she looked brave and comforted me. Her words were so strong that they gave me courage. My! She was a brave little woman.

One day I felt better. Thinking I was getting well, I got up and did all I could to make things easier for the family. But still my Mother wouldn't let me go out of doors. And she was doing the right thing, because I got all of my sickness back the next morning—even worse. We were all very helpless. There was nobody well enough to help around in the village.

One morning when I was refilling the stove and lantern there was nothing left in the kerosene can. So I made up my mind to go out to the store for some more. As I was putting on my warm clothing, Mother asked me, "What are you going to do now? You are not going anywhere if I can help it," she sort of scolded me.

I told her quickly, "We have no more fuel for the lantern and stove. I must get some from the store. If we use up what's left the boys will be cold."

At that she took her clothes, saying, "I'm going with you. I can't stand it to see you go out in this weather alone."

I tried to make her stay at home, but she was somebody that couldn't be out-talked by me. So I had to let her come along.

We went out into the blinding snow and the hard north wind that blew right through my clothes and, it seemed, through my skin, all the way to my aching bones. As we staggered along, the wind blew me down to the ground sometimes, since I had not much strength left to stand it. Mother did better than I did. She stayed on her feet better. Several times we had to stop to rest, because we coughed so much, and we got out of breath quite fast.

We made it to Kapugan's home. He was the storekeeper. He was pretty sick himself, but was about to go to the store to sell what the people needed. We were not the only ones coming to the store. There were others, too. Everyone looked sick and weak. When we got to the store we helped each other pump some kerosene and gas from the barrels. We also got a few other needed things so we wouldn't have to come back for them. I told Mr. Kapugan to charge it to our account, even though Dad hadn't given me permission. I was sure, though, that it was what I must do, for we needed the things real badly.

Mother and I took turns carrying the cardboard box. It was not very heavy, but to us it was quite a burden. Every once in a short while we had to stop to rest. The way from the store to our house seemed an unending distance. We had the hardest time at places where the snow was deep and soft. Finally, at too long last, we made it to our house. I pushed the box in through the door, then beat off the snow from my fur ruff and boots, expecting the boys to be excitedly getting into what I had brought from the store, as they always did. But when I came to the door, to my surprise, they hadn't paid any attention to it at all.

It was plain that they were sick, too sick to do that. Then I got more worried. As I lay down to rest, I thought of an idea. I would go over to our school teacher to ask him if anything could be done for our sick family. But, oh! I was worn out. I doubted very much if I could make it to the school house. I was sure I would collapse on the way. I don't know how long I lay there trying to think of a way to reach the school house, but I couldn't think of any way to do it; I was too weak. The trip to the store had done a good deal to wear me out.

It was the best blessing I ever had when I heard the outer door open and then a knock on the room door. I raised my voice the best I could to say, "Come in." Even my voice was pretty weak from so much coughing and sore throat.

Then the door opened. It was Mrs. Riley, our teacher. To me she was much like an angel's answer to my prayer. I was the most glad to see her. But she, too, looked sick. Her eyes were weak and inflamed, but she had managed to go from house to house, giving out some badly needed pills.

I told her everything about our sickness. Then she jotted down some instructions for me to follow, along with the pills she gave us. I started it right away. She told me the nurse would come from Savoonga that day or the next. That gave me some more hope.

The boys were a little better. Their sickness probably was responding to the drugs given them. But Mother and I were worse than ever. Ann took the whole burden of the family care. Though we had sickness to worry about, we were more worried about Kakianak. He had not come for over a week now. We were worried that he might be sick and that he would try to come in this tough weather, which had been that way for a long time. Mother and I always tried to keep that worry for ourselves only. We didn't want to share it with the rest of the family and worry them unnecessarily.

Sometime that day we were surprised by a visitor that we hadn't seen before—a tall, good-sized and broad-shouldered, manly looking person who spoke with a male voice. "Hmm. A man or woman?" thought I. It was hard to tell which it was. This person was with Mrs. Riley, our school teacher. She introduced her as the nurse that she had been telling me about the other day.

I seemed to feel better right away, for she was the most needed person. At least I felt better in my worried mind. I told her everything about our sickness the best my poor English could do. She gave me some more instructions and pills along with some other medicines to take and give to the family. She told us the disease we were having was whooping cough. I didn't know much about what the word "whooping cough" meant; all I knew about it was that it was a bad, very bad sickness.

She told me to follow the directions she gave me as closely as possible and promised she'd come over to see us day after tomorrow. Her strong voice and encouraging words were a great help to my troubled mind, because some fear had gripped me the last few days. It was the fear that my brothers might die at any moment. They both had been very sick, but now they looked better.

The nurse came to check on us again and told me that the boys were much better and the rest of the family was better than when she first saw us. But she told us never to attempt going out of doors. She said we would get back the sickness if we exposed ourselves to the cold. She gave us more pills and other drugs and left.

Ann was very much well now so she cared for us all, taking all of the chores. She usually complained that she took more than her share of the family work, but this time she never complained. She sang as she worked hard, as if she were pleased with the work.

Under Ann's care we recovered nicely. In a day or two we were able to be up. The boys began to play and fight together once more, and kept us busy trying to control them.

As if it was along with our health conditions, the weather was letting up. Mother's and my hope was that Kakianak would come back safely and well. The next day the weather was still better. The wind had calmed down a little and we could see the blue sky and sun shining through the clouds. The same day the nurse visited us. She told us we could go out of doors for short periods if we wrapped up real good in our warm furs.

Even though I felt quite well, I was very weakened and still coughing a good deal, which used up my little strength and left me nearly breathless.

Since the storm was letting up, Mother and I were watching for any dog teams to come across the lake (where they all would come from). Almost all that late afternoon we kept blowing on the frost on the window pane to keep a small hole for watching. We were worried to death by then. A short time before dark I spotted a black speck that seemed to be moving at the far side of the lake. I squinted and strained my eyes, trying to make something out of it. I made sure it was moving. It was coming closer as I watched it. I called Mother to the window, and I told her to scan the place and asked her in a whisper if she didn't see anything.

Right away she whispered back, "kee-mow-seek," meaning "dog team." She had better eyesight than I, so she was sure it was a dog team. She went back to her work, telling me to let her know when it was close enough for recognizing. I watched it coming closer and closer. I could make out that the sled was loaded; then I could count the dogs. There were ten of them. Kakianak had only seven dogs. I was kind of disappointed, but the leaders looked somewhat familiar to me. But still I was not sure, so I called Mother again. She looked out and told me that he looked like Kenneth. Then I was sure, because I recognized his lead dogs.

We still didn't tell our children, because we were in fear now; I could plainly see that in my Mother's eyes. I whispered to her, asking her permission to go over and find out from Kenneth how Dad was. In a whisper she said, "Go ahead." I pulled on my warm parka and mittens and went out of the house into the cold, dry weather.

The wind was still quite strong, or maybe it only seemed strong because I was weak. My knees felt rubbery as I staggered on the hard-packed snow. Now and then I had to stop to catch my breath because the wind blew all the air out of my lungs, and I had to gasp for air.

I finally made it to Kenneth at David's place. He was just through unharnessing his dogs. He looked up and smiled at me. I smiled back. He looked pale and his eyes were inflamed and looked tired. When he talked his voice was very low—so low I could hardly make out the words he was saying. At that instant a fear and worry gripped me; its horrible teeth clenched at me. Then I could make out that he said that Kakianak was fine now, that he, too, had had the sickness. He told me Kakianak was coming and not too far from the village. I was chilled to the bone by the cold weather and worry. I didn't know which chilled me worse.

Then I told him I must go home and tell my folks. He said he would see me later. As I walked home I tried to pray, but I couldn't even pray. Not knowing what to do, I tried to hurry home. I knew I would feel better when I talked it over with Mom. I knew she had some way to comfort me.

When I got to our door before I went in, I thought for a

moment or two how to tell Mom about it. Thinking about that helped me to calm down from my shock and recover from it, too. Then I went in, trying to act as if I had not heard anything and that nothing had happened; besides I remembered we hadn't told the children about it. When I came through the inner door, Mom looked at me questioningly. I made signs that everything was all right. I didn't tell her, because the boys were around me, tugging at my parka and asking me where I'd been. Then when they settled down I whispered to Mom everything I'd heard about Dad. She looked worried for a moment, but she said that everything would be all right. And so I felt a little better.

As we waited the time seemed too long. It was a little before dark, but with the full moon, it was almost as bright as daylight through the window. We had been watching for any unusual spots or movements, sometimes going outside for a few minutes. We were worried to death then. I was just about to go to our neighbors to see if they could do anything if Dad didn't arrive; I was sure they would send out some searching dog teams. Then Mom thought she saw a black speck that was moving. She was sure it was a dog team, but it was off the trail and slow. Soon as she was sure, I asked to go to meet whoever that dog team was. But she said, "Not until it's closer."

I turned away from my watching the dog team, so I wouldn't get too anxious. But even when I was trying not to, I was getting very anxious. Mom noticed that, so she told me to get in the house. Even before I said anything, she said, "Do as I say. Get in the house." I didn't really know why she said or did that, but I did go inside—unwillingly. I didn't go into the room where the family was. I stayed in the storm shed until I heard the dogs barking, and then I rushed out.

There we met Dad. He was sitting on his sled with his head hanging low. I ran to him with all the little strength I had. Mom and I helped him out of the sled. None of us said anything; we just helped him into our poorly heated room. Then we asked how he was. He was so weak he couldn't raise his voice above a whisper, but he told us he was all right—at least he was alive. I started a fire in the little stove to warm him up. While I was at it, Larson Igalok came to see if everything was okay. He had heard about it from Kenneth and he, too, had been watching for Dad's arrival. After we talked a while, we went out to take care of the dogs and sled.

Larson helped Mom and me, even without offering to do so. It was the kind of help I appreciate most, because I wanted to get the work done in a hurry. Besides, we were awfully weak and cold from our long wait.

Larson left even before we could thank him. He must have been cold and tired himself, since as far as I knew, everybody was sick. We didn't bother to tie up the awfully lean dogs. We just turned them loose, threw out some scraps that we had been saving for dog food, and went into the house.

Poor Dad. He was very weak, but his voice was stronger now than when he had first arrived. As he warmed up, he looked better. He had not been very clear in his mind, either, but he was doing fine now. When he was more able to talk, he told me that if he had had to go on a few more miles, he would probably have met his death. And that was certain, with the way his condition was. He'd die from freezing rather than from sickness, because he was too weak to keep himself from freezing. He had frostbite all over his face and wrists and parts of his toes.

When he had some hot tea he recovered better. Then he told us he had lost two of his dogs, leaving him only five. It was a good thing that those five dogs held their strength to bring him home. I hadn't noticed the loss when we were unharnessing them. They had been two of our best dogs.

Then he told us of his hardship on the way. He had started all right that morning from the camp, but when he had got tired out, the cold took on. He was kind of unconscious, and some strange drowsiness and foolish warmth had made him unaware of the danger of freezing. We thought that he had made it just on time. Then he told us that Nagotak and his family had been sick, too, but when they got better he had tried to come home, because he was worried about us, too.

306

The reason why Mother told me to get in the house was that she had thought from the way he sat on his sled that he was dead, and that I might be badly shocked. She herself was very brave in the face of the ill fate that we thought we would have met. Thank goodness, in spite of our sickness, in the next few hours we formed a happy, thankful family.

Fortunately, we all recovered from the whooping cough in a few weeks. But something else took over. Since we were having tough weather, the food became scarce in the village. Besides that, people were unfit for hunting.

Later that winter we heard very shocking news. The Kusauyaks had been lost on their way to the village from their camp, Taphok. Both of them were missing. Only their adopted son, Bert, was found some miles south of the village. His hands and arms had been frozen, especially his left arm and hand, which were badly frozen. Otherwise he was in satisfactory condition. His good warm clothing and cleverness had saved him from a terrible death. For five days he and his mother had been in the weather. Before that his father had died on the way, and he and his mother had buried him in the snow. Then they lost their dog team. After they lost that, his mother forced Bert to leave her. The weather was so bad that Bert didn't know where all this had happened.

The terrible story hit me so bad that I couldn't sleep at the idea of how ill-fated the poor persons had been. I even wept for them that night.

We were quite well by then, but still unable to do more than just carry on around the village. The hardest part of the family chores that I could do was getting more ice supply when it gave out. Some of our poor dogs had died from scurvy and starving, leaving us only three of them, which were little better than skeletons covered with skin and fur. And with only three poor, lean dogs to help us, a sledload was awfully heavy now, although I used to handle it without much trouble. Now it would take me nearly a day to do it.

One day—it was one of our many hungry days—Daniel Kazighia called on us, bringing a big hunk of seal meat, what we called mukluk. They had been hunting by skin boat and had been lucky to get a mukluk or two.

After Mom had cooked some of that meat, how I wanted to eat my fill! But Mom gave us each little more than a bite and some of the rich broth for that day. The boys and I begged for some more meat, but every "No" that Mom said was very firm. It was all for our good, because we would kill ourselves if we ate too much.

As time drew on, more people recovered from the sickness and so did my family, except Dad. Even though he was well, he was weak. So he didn't go hunting, but Mr. Kazighia kept us supplied with meat. When they had been out hunting they would call us to get our share of meat. Ann and I would get it with the help of our three dogs. Later that winter, Mr. Kazighia gave us two more dogs. He was a very kind man, especially to Dad, his boat crew member.

Still later we were finally back to our normal health, so Dad went back to Southwest Cape to take care of his traps for a week or more. Then he came back and told us Nagotak's family was getting better, too.

That winter, on January 5, 1945, was a big day for our family. My little sister was born. A new member of the family, who brought light, warmth, and joy to the whole family. My parents called her Eskimo name after my Grandmother, and we called her English name, Lucy. Martin, the youngest of us, was my favorite brother, and he took a large place in my heart. I loved Douglas, too, but I paid more attention to Martin because Douglas was Daddy's boy. Now little Lucy found her way into my heart and took a place there. Later on she became really a joy and pride of my heart. She was a blessing to our home and extended the happiness of our family. She was the center of the joy of our little family.

Since health had returned to the village, including our family, we were happy once more. But not entirely. Two things kept the family from being completely happy, although we tried to be as cheerful as we could be. The first thing was that our poor Douglas had recovered from the disease, all right, but he was not healthy as he used to be. He was thinner, pale, and caught colds easily. We didn't suspect anything about the tuberculosis he had. Dad, also, seemed to be not in his good former health.

The second thing was that we all weren't able to work as hard as we needed to keep up our poor income. Without the care and attention it requires, Dad didn't get many foxes out of his trapping. Physically disabled and with no time for it, we also didn't keep up our ivory carving. We had used our time to care for our family because the need for it was rather bad. Although we kept down on everything except what was a strict necessity for the family, we had nearly used up what we had been saving for—a new outboard motor for our boat.

I was very much discouraged by that, but my Dad didn't take such a situation the way I did. Whenever we conversed about it, he just comforted me. He said that things like that were just beginning in my life. He told me that in his early life it was worse than now. He hadn't had most of what I had, and he had to face lots of situations worse than this—so why did we let it discourage us, since we didn't know what was in the future for us? Things wouldn't be the same all the time; they might change and turn out better and we should have lots of hope for that.

He promised: "When your brothers grow up to be old enough to help us like you do now, we will be more able to have what we need. Just take care of them, to bring them up as good boys by being good yourself; and take your responsibilities for them and yourself like a man."

He got me back to my courageous and hopeful ambition, even though some hopes didn't pay off much.

But I had lots of hope, anyway. And I had to face the unpleasant facts. It would take us several more years to save up for our future, badly wished-for, new outboard motor. That also meant several more years of hardship.

The family didn't fully regain the most important part: its health—especially Douglas and Kakianak.

Without the motor and good health, we wouldn't accomplish our future plan of returning back to our loved camp at Southwest Cape. That I was looking forward to, and didn't want anything to interfere with. I often talked about it with Dad, but he didn't pay much attention. All he had to say about it was, "Wait and see." It is not necessary to talk about it now while we can't accomplish such a thing. That's too far away in the future.

Of course, that was the fact, but I was very much concerned in it, so I thought, "Why shouldn't we enjoy at least talking about it, anyway, even if it doesn't really happen?" One other very mean factor that would prevent us from doing it was the war, since it was too dangerous to be away from the village by ourselves with no means of defense, as our teacher said. It was another thing that nobody could help.

Finally there was a little improvement in the family's health, and the happy arrival of the spring with all its pleasant happenings helped to take away my thoughts of going home to our camp. Those numerous dreams of it were reduced somewhat, but still were coming on.

That spring when the hunting came around it was, as every year, the happiest time of the year for me. It meant fun in hunting. The best part was good-bye to the tedious old sissie school. That was my biggest mistake, but it didn't seem so at that time, because it was more necessary for me to have more hunting experience than school. In fact, every boy needs knowledge of hunting, since it is our chief source of living. Just like a student getting into higher grades, I was taking more of the position in being a boat crew member: they thought of me as more dependable in the way that they acted toward me.

I was very happy that day when we were just about to go out in the boat. Mr. Kogoyak handed me a box of shells and a rifle, saying, "Today, I want to see how good you'll be as a rifleman. This will be your rifle. If you can shoot it straight, it'll be yours every hunting day. But if you don't shoot straight, or if you handle the weapon carelessly, you'll not touch any weapon, since it's very dangerous if you are careless."

It was quite a challenge to me—a very new lesson I was to take up. I was much thrilled at the idea and I fell in love with the rifle that they handed me. It was a rusty old thing, a Winchester model 94, .44 caliber, that probably had never been cleaned since it was purchased. Its stock was like a piece of firewood, except that it was shaped like a rifle stock. I thought its shells were the prettiest ones I ever saw. They were shiny brass, with cute copper colored bullets. They really were too fat and too short, but I loved the rifle, with its funny-looking shape, the rust, and all, and its bullets. Also, I was very proud of it. If I had known such things then, I would have been crossing my fingers to fire that rifle.

As we prepared to push our boat into the glassy water, I got very anxious to use my rifle. I even started daydreaming of shooting a seal, mukluk, or walrus, or even some ducks. Soon we were on our way, plowing the glass-smooth Bering Sea. "Will we be lucky enough to come upon some animal to shoot at?" I really hoped we would. That day was an exciting one in my spring hunting days. I was usually more interested in tending the motor and other things while hunting, but on that day I kept my eyes on the water looking for anything to break the glassy surface of water, or any specks on the ice that meant something to use my rifle on. But no matter how anxious I was to shoot it, the instructions of Kogoyak stood out clearly in my mind: "Keep the gun in its case until you can use it." If I broke any of his instructions, I'd be disqualified from my riflemanship.

Now the day was half-spent with no game. "Is this going to be another gameless day? No, we'll come upon something. Never give up," I kept asking and telling myself, and kept a sharp lookout. Finally my eyes were not playing a trick on me. I spotted a mukluk, or if that wasn't that, it was a duck looking like a mukluk. Whatever it was, I signaled Kogoyak, pointing to it. Sure enough, it was a mukluk.

As Otto cut down the speed of the motor, I reached for the rifle, looking up at Kogoyak to see whether he would keep me back from doing it. He nodded his head, meaning "Yes, exactly what I wanted."

Otto gave a few more "Don't-do-that's" about shooting in the boat. He said, "Don't attempt to fire at it if it comes up at the other side of the boat, because you might accidentally shoot one of us. You can shoot it if it comes up on your side."

"Sure, I'll be careful," I assured him.

Every time it came up it was on the wrong side of the boat. I kept a close watch out on myself. I might foolishly try to fire at it. Louis, our bowman, shot at it a couple of times, but he missed. Strange way to feel about that—I was glad every time he missed, because I would have a chance to shoot it.

As I was watching my side of the water, up came the head I'd been watching for. All at once I had got ahead of myself. I had raised the .44 and jerked off a shot without lining my sights on my target. Even before I knew it, it went off with a kind of mellow, flat bang, not a crisp, sharp shot, as the 25.35 would, the gun I'd used before. What? I couldn't believe my eyes at first, because the mukluk's body came to the surface lifelessly. It was a very lucky shot. I rolled my eyes on the faces of the crew and met eyes and mouths curled up in pleasure and amusement. I felt bashful and turned away from them; but I could feel their staring on my back. Then I felt the chills shooting up and down my whole body, and fell more in love with the .44.

I watched Louis drive his harpoon home into the lifeless animal with a powerful thrust of his right arm. Soon as it was secured to the side of the boat with a rope, we headed for the nearest suitable cake of ice for the butchering work. I always liked butchering animals, but this time I liked it more. As we happily skinned it, I tried to avoid their praising, but they kept pouring it on me. At the same time, I tried to explain to them that it was just a lucky shot. But they wouldn't believe me. "We will let you shoot more from now on," they promised. I liked that part better than their praising. Now I had a big story to tell my friends in the school and that evening when we got together.

When we got home, my Dad was among the men awaiting to help us on the seashore. There was a crowd; I felt as bashful as I could be as we approached the shore. It used to be my glad moment—when I could stretch my numb, cramped legs. But this time I had something to face which was not very pleasing to me. We were the last boat coming in, so there were men who had reached home before us coming down to help us and exchange the day's hunting news.

I kept my face down as we worked unloading the meat onto the shore, while they told the story over and over. Kogoyak bragged to my Dad, "We have a new rifleman today; and a sharpshooter, too." He offered the skin to my father proudly.

Dad accepted the skin, and we gave it away to Aiyaksaq, as was the old custom. We still kept the custom for its common goodness. He was pleased, and so was I. It is always my best pleasure to do that.

That evening after I had refreshed with a good supper and changed into nice, light, dry clothing, I looked around for my friends, and we formed a happy gang exchanging the thrilling news of the day, each one acting out his story as he told it. I did mine, adding some ingredients that weren't really there, and extending the story beyond its truth. But it was believed, anyhow!

My parents told me not to stay out too late, but the nice, cool night was too pleasant and refreshing after the heat of the day, and I forgot about their words and had a good time with my friends. But then one of them mentioned what his Dad had said, and we broke up the gang and left with a short game of tag and "You're It."

When I came in the family was already in bed, and Mom and Dad were still awake. Dad looked up and said, "You've stayed out pretty late. It's past midnight. I'd scold you, but you'll get your penalty soon enough, when your captain wakes you up and calls to you."

Sure enough, it was late—around 2 A.M. Without a word I threw myself down all the way to sleep. Tired but happy was I. I thought I had hardly had a wink of sleep when I woke to the gentle tap on my shoulder. It was Herbert Kogoyak. He whispered, "A perfect hunting day."

Ho hum! It wasn't very easy getting out of good, sweet sleep. The first words that ran in my mind were: "You'll get your penalty when your captain calls on you." It helped to wake me up, but remembering the .44 woke me better than that.

After a breakfast and putting my hunting clothes on, I was ready to start again. The nice, cool, morning fresh air was so good and it helped to wake me up. I hoped that we would come upon lots of animals to shoot this time. The Kogoyaks were usually slow, but this time they seemed to be slower than ever, while I was more than ever anxious to go.

Once more we were on our way. No matter how thrilled I was, I was somewhat sleepy. I moved around to stay awake, standing on the board boat seat, and scanning the water through field glasses, trying to spot any black specks on the ice that would be walrus or mukluk—or else watching for the surface of the water to be broken by a bobbing head. But that was not the answer for keeping away the drowsy feeling that was just about to get the best of me. Besides, it was tiresome, and with dizziness it became difficult to keep my balance. I had to sit down to rest every once in a while. And one time I sat longer than I should have. I really fought to keep sleep from coming, but it turned out to be a losing fight. I pinched myself, shook my head, but my eyelids became heavier all the time. I tried to hold my eyes open with my fingers. I kept them open, all right, then things doubled, and all at once I had fallen off to sleep for I don't know how long. I'll never know.

Then I was awakened by the crack of a rifle, making me snap right out of my sleep and jump to my feet. It was warm, but I was shaking with cold. Now what did he shoot at? I didn't see anything. I asked Herbert and Otto. They didn't pay any attention. They only laughed and made fun of me. Whatever it was, I reached for the .44 that I had placed on the seat in front of me. I was going to shoot, too. Pulling it out of its case, I filled up the magazine, worked the lever, pushed and pulled it shut, then got the hammer to a half-cocked position for safety, going over my safety rules.

Just as I had done that a walrus broke the water's surface, blowing spray and making a dull whizzing sound. Half-knowingly, I pointed my .44 at it. Again getting ahead of myself, I jerked off a shot. I didn't even know where the bullet had hit, and I didn't care to know. All I wanted was as many shots as I could make. Then I heard the pop of Louis's and Herbert's rifles, and I released another slug myself.

314

Once more I watched Louis sending his harpoon home into the half-dead mammal and then he finished it off with his .30-30.

As I was told to do, I double-checked my rifle to see if I had removed the shell from the chamber, and then pushed it into its sheath. Otto cut off the motor and the walrus was pulled alongside the boat. It was a young and small one. While Louis and Herbert cut a loop on its forehead to secure it to the side of the boat for towing, Otto and I refilled the motor tank.

Now again they picked me as their subject in their talk about shooting. I didn't even know it, but they said my two shots had scored and found their marks in the walrus. Both Herbert and Louis had missed. I helplessly tried telling them I was the one who had missed, and they were the ones who got it, not me. But they insisted it was I. They said, "Then we will see whose bullets are in it when we butcher it."

I told them, "You'll not find my bullets in it. I missed with both shots."

Then Kogoyak said, "You hit it with both shots. I watched closely. Now you are our rifleman."

I said no more.

As soon as we had pulled it onto the ice with blocks and tackles, I filled the pot with snow, started the little kerosene stove to make some tea, and then joined the men cutting up the walrus. Kogoyak showed me the wound, saying, "That was your first shot."

Sure enough, there was a .44 slug that had fractured the shoulder blade.

Then he showed me another wound. He said, "This one is your second shot." When we looked for the bullet, we found a fat, stubby slug belonging to my .44. It had broken a rib and torn into the lungs.

Then I was willing to accept what they said, and I felt proud. He said, "If you had shot it in the head, that would have been a clean kill, but we didn't want that, because it would sink as soon as it was dead. So we like the way you shot it."

I grinned to myself. I hoped my luck would hold out, because yesterday I had done very lucky shooting. They were aimless shots, but with my luck they all counted.

Herbert called me, "Nathan, cut out the heart and I'll make it into a yummy."

I cut it out and sliced it at the center to let out the blood, and then gave it to Herbert. He cut strips from it and cooked it in a tin can of salt water. Then I added a piece of meat. When we had loaded the meat into the boat we sat around the stove to devour the yummy Herbert had cooked for us. It surely was a good lunch, especially when we had worked up a bull-sized appetite. And the tea was the most welcome part.

Kogoyak made us hurry up. Soon we were afloat and going lazily. With our heavy load the boat went slowly on the smooth water. With the going like that, I seemed to be under its strong spell making me very lazy and drowsy.

But the spell was suddenly broken when Louis called me, "Come forward with your rifle." Who wouldn't? When I sat beside him, he told me, "You are going to shoot every seal within eye sight." Oh boy! Just what I wanted. Better than anything else in the boat. We went along without seeing anything except ducks (which I would have liked to shoot if I could—but we had to save our shots for the big game).

As I was looking the other way, Louis tapped me on my shoulder. And when I spun around I saw a round, sleek head. Then I worked the lever of my .44, pushed and slammed it shut, and raised the barrel, bracing my legs. Lining up the sights, holding my breath, and at last I applied pressure on the trigger with a steady, controlled squeeze. I released a shot, going off with a thudding bang, which sounded very pleasing to my ears. That part was good and satisfying, but the most important part was not good at all. I was expecting the animal to come to surface lifelessly like the others I had shot. But unlike the others, I saw the plowing up of the water beyond the seal. The slug had gone over its head and the frightened animal had flipped over and disappeared under the surface!

Oh, my luck was giving out now! I was sure I had every-

316

thing just right, but I had missed. "How come?" I wondered.

I rolled my eyes to Louis, to see what he had to say about that. Sure enough, he had something to say. He said, "That was pretty close. Maybe you'll get it next time it comes up."

But the next time was the same. I took extra care, but missed again. The slug hit too low. With the next shot, I hit on one side; then the other side. Several shots one after another were without score. What's the matter with me and my .44? My luck had really turned me down.

I was full of despair, but they still encouraged me. Then I called Herbert so he could try a shot, and I attempted to draw back from the bow. But they told me to go ahead, to keep on shooting with Herbert. I just pretended to take aim, because I was really discouraged. And that was the first time that I felt I had just a rusty old piece of iron called a gun in my hands, with funny looking slugs supposed to be bullets. I had emptied the rusty iron junk of its shells maybe twice or more, I didn't know. Soon Herbert and I were side by side on the bow seat. On maybe his third shot with his bolt action Remington .22 long rifle, he made a hit on a young mukluk. He had to shoot again to finish it off. Before I was told to do it, I grabbed for the harpoon and struck with all my strength at the mukluk. The pole felt light and I though I didn't push it hard enough, but when I jerked the rawhide rope it didn't give. I felt sure it was fastened good.

When Otto cut the motor Herbert and I met each other's eyes in pleasure and amusement. We got it! All the men were pleased with us. It did some good for my despair, but the way I had missed so many times didn't taste good in my mind. Everyone of them was trying to encourage me, but still I felt awful. Even Herbert had some sweet words, and I accepted his words better than the rest. We were doing a competent game of the hunting, and we were getting more cooperative. When we pulled up the animal on the ice, we told each other "our mukluk," because he had done shooting, and I the harpooning.

When we were just about through, Kogoyak told me, "I think the poor shooting is not your fault."

I didn't understand. I asked him, "What do you mean?"

He said, "I think your rifle is not very good, but I'll see. I used to count almost every shot with that rifle when I was young like you." He took it from the bow and pulled it out of its sealskin case.

"When he was young like me? Did he mean that the gun is as old as him?" I thought. I watched him look it over, then blacken the sights with a match.

"Shiny sights is one of the faults to cause your missing," he said.

Then he asked for some shells. I gave him a handful from my bulging pocket. He loaded the gun. Then he took aim, resting the barrel on a piece of ice to steady it at a duck on the water close by. Then he shot. He missed. He shot several times at ducks, but he missed every time. His shots went wild, like mine. Then he looked up, grinning.

He said, "I'm still young enough, but this rifle is much too old. So you might be a good shot yet if you use a younger rifle than this one."

Now I understood what he meant when he said that the bad shooting I did might not be my fault. I got a little more hopeful. It could have been that, but I still wasn't sure.

He dug for something from the bottom of the boat, and pulled out more junk—a big rifle with a big bore. He said, "You are a big fellow. A big rifle will do for you, maybe. This one is as big as you are. Try it."

How they laughed when I held it! But I always went for shooting pieces, no matter how they looked or what they were. The shells they gave me for it were striking sights. They were as fat as the shells for the other rifle I'd been using, and much longer. It was a quaint rifle I had. I looked closely at the rear end of one of the shells. It read "405."

Then I looked at the grinning men. One of them said, "It will kick you hard and good." I felt a bit scared. But I felt brave when I thought that I was no child anymore, "I'm a man—and this is really a man's rifle."

We were on our way once more. They placed Herbert and me at the bow with my rifle to try another shot. As I kept my eyes peeled for anything breaking the water surface, I couldn't help imagining myself kicked down by this mighty, giant gun, with my feet coming up in the air as I came down with my other end.

Suddenly I spotted a mukluk surfaced quite close, and a big one too. I didn't lose any time in sending a big shell into the chamber. At the same time I felt relaxed, not excited and jumpy as I had earlier that day. Somehow I kept good control of myself. It could have been that little fear of the kick from the big gun that kept me from getting ahead of myself. I lined up my sight steady as I could, then squeezed the trigger. It went off with a man-sized report and kick as heavy as a bull. Not as bad as I'd thought, though. Oh, how good the recoil felt on my shoulder!

Then I heard the men cheer and laugh above the hum of the motor. "Did I miss again?" I thought. "No! I got it this time."

I grabbed for the harpoon, keeping my eyes on the mukluk, but I heard somebody say, "Hold it. You don't need that." I wondered why. When we got close and the animal was just about at the bow, I was awfully surprised.

It wasn't a mukluk at all. It was a tiny seal a little over three feet long. It had looked so big! My eyes must have played a trick on me.

When I got hold of its flippers, I pulled it up and a sight met my eyes. I had shot the whole head off. "A powerful rifle—I'm going to love it if it always shoots as straight as now!" That was what they were so much amused and cheered about: a big gun for a pint-sized seal.

Just as Otto was about to start the motor, Kogoyak saw something on the ice just on our way. He said, "It looks like a walrus on the ice."

"Oh, boy. If it is a walrus, I have just the right gun for it," I thought.

Louis looked at it through his field glasses, and he was sure it was a walrus. On we went, and when we got closer, we saw it was quite a few yards away from the edge of the ice. That was not very usual, since they kept close to the edge of the ice for safety's sake. And it lay motionless. But I didn't suspect a thing. I jumped on the ice with the rest of them, holding the big .405 in my hands. We (Louis,

Herbert, and I) sneaked up to the animal until we were only a few yards from it. Then Louis instructed Herbert and me. He told me to take the first shot, since I had a big rifle; and he told Herbert not to shoot until he, himself, fired. I was surprised at that. The best shot was supposed to fire first, because of the good chance of his getting the game. Why should he trust me for that? I had been doing very wild shooting. Anyway, if I missed, it would be his fault and not mine.

We were coming up, with our rifles ready, their safety buttons on; but mine was half-cocked for safety. I rested the barrel, pulled back the hammer and lined up the sight on the back of the walrus' head.

"Ready?" I asked them.

"Yes," they said.

Then I fired. The walrus didn't stir an inch. I heard the crack of Herbert's .30-.30, but still the walrus was very still. Louis laughed a bit. Herbert and I were surprised. He told us that it was a dead animal. We had shot nothing but a carcass!

We were kind of disappointed. I asked Louis why did he not tell me it was a dead animal. He said they had suspected it was dead, but they weren't sure. No wonder it was so far from the edge of the ice and hadn't made any movement.

Louis comforted us, "Why feel bad? You both hit it. If it was alive, it would be killed by both of you anyway; and it was very good practice. Now let's get busy and cut it up."

We did. I worked on the head to see where I had hit the walrus. There was a wound right where I'd aimed, and the heavy skull was smashed by the big bullet. I liked the gun a little more.

We didn't take all of the meat, just the best part of it. When we got back underway, Kogoyak told us, "We can't take any more meat in the boat. So put your rifles in their cases. You'll do more shooting another time."

I settled down on the seat next to the motor, asking Otto if I might take over to tend the motor.

"Go ahead. I want you to do that," he said.

I sat there, much satisfied with the day's hunt, and started thinking of getting home and how we had had a very thrilling day to tell about—so many seals and mukluks I missed, how I had harpooned Herbert's mukluk, and shooting a walrus that was already dead.

Now the sport of the day was about over, and lots of work was waiting for us; but the work part, too, was not bad. I liked doing it, and when we were through with that, some good and gay times with friends would take over after having refreshed myself with Mom's good food and nice light, dry clothes. But for now I was lazy. The steady hum of the little motor was like sweet music—unless it needed to be adjusted. Sometimes it would cough a few times, then die down. "Oh, no! I forgot to check the fuel tank, and let it run out!" I wished it had a bigger tank than it had, one that would hold enough fuel for a whole day of running.

While I was feeling lazy, it was too much bother to keep on checking it and refilling it. Also, the heavily loaded boat was going much too slow, slower than I wanted it to go. Everybody in the boat must have been as lazy as I was. They were all so quiet. Only once in a long while Herbert and I exchanged a few wise cracks. Then Otto or Noah would join us. Then on again being quiet.

It was late in the evening when at last we hit the shore. I was always glad when we got home on late evenings, because it was usually too hot for working during the day, and Dad kept the dog teams ready and harnessed for me. Often nice old Mrs. Kogoyak would be waiting for us on the seashore. She always had nice things to say to me and Herbert—not the wild praises that made me bashful, like that from the men; but tender, motherly affection that was simple and felt good in my mind.

When we spread the meat on the shore ice it looked as if there was more of it than it had been in the boat and I knew I was to get a big share of it. The hardest work was pulling the boat up the sloping beach. With the boat put up on its rack, I ran home, avoiding the people as much as possible, who would riddle me with questions about the day's hunt. And I then met Ben, my cousin, Douglas and Martin, my brothers, all wet and dirty but a most cheerful and happy trio that pricked my heart with affection.

In the house were the good old folks and my little new sister, Lucy, whom I kissed to death when I got home from a long absence. Then I shouted my story to them and went out to my dogs. I coaxed Ben, Douglas, and Martin, all to go down to the beach with me to get my share of meat, but they were too shy.

With the meat taken care of, the rest of the evening would be as usual. After refreshing myself, I didn't feel like lying down to sleep. I had been sleepy during the day, but at night, when it was time to sleep, I was too wide awake. Before I went out, my folks would ask, "Are you going to sleep again?"

I'd answer them, "No, I'm not sleepy. I want to go out for a while." That "while" was usually all night.

Then they would say, "All right, but please be good. Don't get into any mischief."

I would promise I wouldn't.

On another hunting day we came upon a couple of walrus cows with calves on the ice. There were only four of us in the boat: Kogoyak, Otto, Louis, and I. Herbert and Noah were sick with a cold, so they stayed home. I missed Herbert that day. When we got close to the walruses, I filled up my .405's magazine with its husky shells, because for sure I was going to shoot with the men. We got onto the ice and sneaked up on them, keeping a little pressure-ridge between us. Then we were very close—about fifteen yards away from our targets. I was sure of getting them. I lost control of myself and shot before Louis could take an aim, shooting down both walruses, one after the other, one shot each. Boy, I felt good, but I got ashamed of my careless shooting when we found out that I had shot off a tusk from one of them. I learned I must be careful where I aim.

When we had skinned them, we went to one lone walrus that we saw just a little way from these we had killed. This time they wanted me to shoot that one by myself. I trusted that the "Big Brother" (as I called the rifle) wouldn't miss. It was my best walrus rifle now. So, expecting another walrus,

322

I took a position at the bow. It was a young walrus, so I thought I'd kill it with one shot for sure. Being careful when I was certain I was close enough, I shot at it, but missed! The second time, the third time, the fourth time the bullets found their mark. But it was too late. I had hit it while it was sliding into the water. It sank. What was the matter with me this time? Why should such ill fortune spoil the day's hunt like that?

I turned around, expecting the men to be sorry and feel bad as I did, but they did not. They only said, "Things like that could happen to anyone. Why feel bad? We still have two walruses and calves that you shot."

I felt better, but it was going to bother me again all that day. That was another lesson on how to take hunting, no matter how it turned out.

# 16. High Seas to Savoonga

Nagotak and his family had come from Southwest Cape. With them around my spring happiness was complete. But they were soon to go back.

While they were here, Dad and Nagotak had their private conversations. No matter how curious I got, I left them alone, because I was not wanted there. But once, to my surprise, I was invited to their conference. Dad told me, "When Nagotak comes today, we want to talk with you."

What was this all going to be about? I hoped not about women and making me get married. Anxiety was getting the best of me. I even felt scared because they hadn't done such a thing before. It had always been none of my business. I wanted to ask my father what it was about, so I could make excuses and avoid the talk. But it might be something very important.

I was restless and I wished the church service would hurry up. In the Sunday School our teacher thought I was sick and sent me home a little before it was over. When I got home, Nagotak and Ben were with us. We had our dinner, and it made the dinner more pleasant. When it was over they excused the children so we could have the talk. I felt very restless as I waited for them to start the discussion. But I dared not start it, in case it might concern me. I felt like making an excuse to go out, but on second thought I decided to stay. It might be concerning something very important and pleasant.

Finally, Nagotak began, "Nathan, you have been in school a good deal of time, long enough to be able to help your father and me to talk about the idea we are thinking of, to see if we could accomplish it with the teacher. We expect you to have good English now."

I told them, "I shall try the best I can. Yes, I'm able to talk to him, but I'm sometimes not too sure. And what is it you want me to talk to him about?"

"Well, maybe you want to go to Southwest Cape badly enough to ask Mr. Riley to permit us to go—something you have wanted for so long a time," one of them said.

"If it's that, I will see him about it tomorrow when I go to school," I said. And that was what I was going to do.

I wished it to be Monday, so I could do it right away. I thought if we really could go to our nice little camp, how wonderful it would be! Now we had the boat big enough for our big family. We might have enough savings for our grub, and ammunition for our guns. But we lacked something that was one of the most important things: the motor. We didn't have one, and for sure we couldn't buy one. We didn't have money for it. Besides, the store didn't have any, and there was no other place to get one. The only motor we had was that little pile of junk. I was sure it would not do to take us to the camp. I asked Dad, "What are we going to do for a motor? We don't have one."

He told me, "That's taken care of. Nagotak and I talked about it, and he is going to let us use his. I'll go get it tomorrow night if Mr. Riley gives you his permission, and if it's not a good day for hunting."

I hoped it would not be good for hunting tomorrow. I wanted to push aside the hunting that I had always valued so much. And for the first time in so long I was eager to go to school.

The evening dragged on while I was busy thinking. My friends came to me, asking me to join them for the night's get-together to have fun. But I didn't want that while I was so concerned in what Dad and Nagotak told me, so I told them I had things to do at home. Of course that was only an excuse.

When bedtime came around, I went to bed with the rest of the family, unlike the other nights, when I was usually somewhere else with the happy gang of boys. It was not a night for sleeping, and it certainly was a long, long night. Besides, it had become my habit that I didn't sleep well at nights. I tried to search my mind for a way to pass the night, but I was much too concerned with what I was to do whenever the next day came.

I hoped it would not be a good day for hunting—"Oh, well, I'd better stay home if they are going out hunting," I thought. "But how can I make the excuse for it? Maybe I could tell my captain I'm sick, or should I say that the teacher wants me to be in school that day? No, no, that would be telling lies. Should I tell him I just don't want to go hunting that day? That still would not do. I'd be ashamed to say that, since I'm an important crew member now for shooting game." Thought after thought came into my mind, but none would do.

In the corner of my head I finally found one that I was sure would do. I'd tell them what I was up to. If I told them everything, they would let me stay home for it. I knew Kogoyak, my captain, would understand and let me do it. Now one worry was taken care of, but there were still more. I wondered what Mr. Riley, our school teacher, would have to say about it when I asked him. He liked me doing that because some boys and girls said I was his pet student, because I often talked the things over with him. To keep from attracting their attention, notes did a better job. That was what I would do.

My patience trying to get to sleep gave out, I threw off my covers to get up and look out of the window. I looked over the peacefully sleeping folks. I came upon two extra family members. "Who could they be?" I wondered. This one was Debby and that one was Ben. "How come? Why were they with us?" Oh, yes, they were leaving tomorrow night. They usually stayed with us the night before they went back to the camp. I had been too busy thinking to notice them.

I glanced at the clock. It was after midnight. Not so bad. Maybe if I found something to do, the rest of the night would not be so long. But I couldn't think of anything to do. I forced myself into bed once more. Then I became aware of a sound. I held my breath to listen better. It sounded like the wind blowing. I was assured of this when it became louder and louder. It must have helped me to sleep, and it was a good sleep, for I didn't wake up until Douglas and Martin got on me.

I grabbed one of them by the wrist and pulled him under my covers like we always did. I locked him in my arms, until he had to say that he was sorry for waking me up. This one was Douglas. He always would try to wrench himself free before he would tell me he was sorry. Sometimes he did free himself. In spite of his being so small, he was so quick sometimes I couldn't catch him.

Remembering what I was to do today, I took one look at the clock and rushed into my school clothes, because it was 8:30—fifteen minutes before the first bell. I asked my Mother why she hadn't waked me up earlier. She said, "You have lost too much sleep, so I let you catch up with it." My thoughts of last night zipped into my head, making me rush even more.

I flushed my face with icy water and started for the door. But I heard Mother's extra-firm, "No—no."

"Why?" I asked her.

"You are not going anywhere on an empty stomach," she said.

Why, she was right. That first long night of sleep in a week or longer must have done something to me. I had forgotten breakfast. In the several nights past I had been getting only two or three hours of sleep. I felt terrible—a ringing in my ears, my head felt hollow and light and the rest of my body seemed too heavy for my muscles, and my mind was dopey.

"There's some coffee and tea. Take anything you want," Mother said.

"Just a cup of coffee will do," I told her.

"Aren't you hungry?" she asked me.

"No, just fix a big dinner and have it ready at noon," I told her.

"How would you like a little company at your cup of coffee?" There was Marian, my cousin. Oh, I had even become unaware of my cousins. There were the three of them: Marian, Debby, and Ben. "Oh, sure! Have a cup."

"How about you, Curley? Won't you join us?" I asked as soon as I discovered that they were up. "Curley" was a nickname we gave Debby because she would be curled up in a corner busy doing some sewing, looking in a book, or doing her home work.

As we sipped our coffee I asked them, "Are you coming with me to the school to say goodbye to Mr. and Mrs. Riley?"

"Yes, but not to say goodbye," they replied.

"Not to say goodbye? Why?" I asked them.

"We are not leaving tonight," they said.

"I thought you were leaving tonight," I said.

"Nagotak told us this morning we would not go until tomorrow night, but we don't know why."

Well, I knew the reason, but I never mentioned it because it was our secret until we could be certain whether we could accomplish it, for their disappointment would be more than we could stand to face if we couldn't.

Finishing my coffee, I stood up. "Now, let's go." They both came after me, but Ben didn't pay any attention. He just kept on playing with Douglas and Martin. I asked him, "Hey, what's the matter with you? Aren't you coming to school?"

He just shook his head, to say "No." He was like me, not very interested in school. He was rather shy and stubborn at the same time.

"Come on, the teacher will miss you," I tried to coax him.

But still he hung his head and said, "No."

I held him by his wrist to begin to drag him to school, but I let him go when he puckered his mouth and tears filled his eyes.

The rest of us went on to school, chattering on our way. They said I was way behind in everything, but I didn't care much. I was a bit shy, too, because I hadn't been in school for several weeks. I was kind of scared to see my teacher.

Just then the final bell rang. I met him at the door. He greeted me very kindly, not as I'd expected. It was so good to see him. With a warm, friendly smile on his face, he asked me, "Do you have good hunting stories for me now?"

"Yes, I'll try to write them," I replied to him. Then we went on into the school room and on to my desk.

There on my desk I found a little folded piece of paper. Picking it up, I looked at the next person in front of me, because I could see it was from her—she was grinning, which told me that she, Mildred Kangalik, had dropped it there. Mildred was my special classmate. She looked especially pretty to me after not seeing her for quite a while. But I looked down to my desk, avoiding her eyes.

Then I looked in my desk. It was nicely straightened up and clean. I looked up at her again. She was still looking at me. Then she whispered, "I cleaned it for you."

I could feel my face warming up and thanked her for it.

"How many walrus did you shoot? I hear that you are a shooter now," she spoke up again.

"A few of them. Yes I started shooting," I told her awkwardly, and then I became tongue-tied.

I was glad when footsteps coming from behind me made her spin around to her desk. Then I pretended to be writing, but the sound of the steps stopped next to me. I looked up from my paper and met Mr. Riley's tough-looking face, which had such an expression that it pinched my spinal cord. After a moment of staring, he grinned and nodded his head, winking at me. I tried to smile, but I felt serious.

He motioned with his hand in commanding me to his desk, as he picked up my book. I felt limp and my heart was about to choke me. I thought I would black out at any time. To my relief, his kindness never failed. He placed my book on his desk and went through the pages, and he asked me a few testing questions and let me read a few things in there, and let me skip some pages and start on the page my classmates were on. He even did the first two or three problems for me, so I could know what to do.

We were very good friends in spite of my poor attendance. But I wasn't as relaxed as I had used to be. I had something in my head. I looked into his eyes before he sent me back to my desk. He understood me, because he could tell when I had something that I wanted to present to him or had an unspoken request. He looked at me questioningly, but I didn't say a word. Again understanding me, he made signs for me to write it down. Then I tiptoed to my desk. Sitting down, I got busy on my work, until the last problem was done. My classmates envied me because I had skipped lots of pages. I felt bad, but didn't say a word.

Now I started a note to Mr. Riley. I started several times, but I never finished a one. The last one as best I could remember was: "Dear Sir: My father wants to go to Southwest Cape. He wants to go this summer when the school stops. Nagotak wants all of us to go. I want to go, too, very much. Truly yours, Nathan."

I slipped it in my book along with my other papers so the teacher would find it. But oh! here was Mildred in the way. She had been watching me while I was writing the note. She asked me, "Where is the letter? I thought it was for me."

"No, it's not a letter. It's my work," I told her.

"I'm sure it's a letter. I saw you write 'Dear' on it. To whom is it?" she went on.

When I got no more chance I had to tell her, "It's a very important letter to Mr. Riley."

"I don't believe you," she said, "and I won't until you show it to me."

"All girls are too stubborn," I thought. "If you will keep my secret, I'll tell you and let you see it, and you must promise me to keep the secret," I told her.

"I always keep your secrets, and I never keep a secret from you. Yes, I promise," she said.

Then I let her read the note. After she had read it she looked up from it at me with a surprised expression in her face. I smiled at her, but she didn't smile back.

Just then I heard Mr. Riley say, "Class Number 2." We were Class Number 2. I took a seat in front of his desk with the rest of the class. We handed in our books one by one. While doing that we were not allowed to talk unless he spoke to us, but we would whisper to each other. When my turn came to hand in my book, I got some of that funny feeling. I kept watching him as he went over my papers. Then we exchanged winks when he had read my note. I noticed him write on a slip and fold it, then put it in my book. When he handed it over to me, I wanted to look in it, but it was our secret, so I had to wait until the class was excused and I had returned to my desk. I wished he could hurry up with the rest of the class.

When we were excused I went to the bathroom to read what he had written for me. I opened it after I had locked the door. It read, "Nathan, I like your note. It's very important. Come to see me at 4:00 with your father. We will talk it over. Riley."

I got a feeling like steam pressure was building up within me. I read the note over again so I could read it for my father. It had one word that was too big for me—"important." I didn't understand it so when I came back to the school room, I looked it up in the dictionary and read the definition over and over, but I still didn't get it. "Oh, well, I'll skip it," I thought.

Oh, what a bother—Mildred picked on me again to see the answered note. I had to give in again, but made her promise me to keep the secret. I could trust her; she was a good secret-keeper, but I wanted to be sure she would keep it this time, too, because it was very important to me. She didn't like the idea very much.

Along came the recess time, but I didn't go out with the other kids. I wrote a story about my hunting days for Mr. Riley. I finished it just as he was coming into the classroom.

He asked me, "Why didn't you go out to play?"

"I was busy," I told him.

"With what?" he wanted to know.

"With this," I answered, handing him the sheet of paper I'd been writing on. He was pleased with it. Just then the kids came in. My friends had lots of questions about my staying inside while I should have been out with them. I told them I'd been working to catch up with my arithmetic.

The reason I had stayed in and kept myself busy was that I might be tempted to run home and pour out to my Dad what my teacher had answered to my note.

Now I was getting hungry. I wished I had had more than just a cup of coffee for breakfast. But how good it would be to have the good stuff Mother would have fixed while I'm this hungry!

With arithmetic I had done fairly well. but I had made quite a few errors. Mr. Riley didn't mark off our errors; he wrote just "3 wrongs," "4 wrongs," and so on, so in trying to correct them without knowing which ones to correct sometimes I increased the number of wrongs. When it came around to those corrections of our work, that was when I liked my special classmate. We compared our answers secretly and got the right answers from each other. And that was how we became special classmates. Soon we had our work 100 percent correct.

Then came the time for our own reading in the school library, which was in one corner of the room. I sat on the reading table and pretended to be reading until we were excused for lunch. My cousins Debby and Marian walked home with me. They were to leave that evening—I was kind of certain about that now. I kept my hand in one pocket, holding the note from Mr. Riley. My cousins were always more dear just before they left, because it was always a year before I could see them again. So I wanted both of them to have lunch with me.

Sure enough, Mother had fixed a good big lunch. Nagotak was with us, too. I was glad of that, because I wanted to present the note to him, too. Even though I liked the dinner, it lasted too long.

Then finally the children were excused. We were Nagotak, Kakianak, Ada, and I. I took out the note and read it to them. They were interested, but they said I should ask him and get a permission.

"Maybe that is what he is going to do when we talk to him," I said.

"Very well, we can see about it, and you come with us when we go to see him," they said.

Who wouldn't do that? "I will!" I said.

Just then it was time for school. We ran along to school, Marian, Debby, and I. But Ben was not around, As before, when it was time for school, he slipped out of sight. On we went to school. First was spelling and then English; then last, writing practice. That was all of that, but we had one of our ivory carving classes after school, and then it would be 4 o'clock.

I liked the ivory carving class best of all, because I did as I pleased and was all to myself, except when I didn't know how to do this or that part. Then our teacher would show me how to do it. But it was not every time he did that. He would say, "It is best to learn by yourself, and you are old enough to do it." He was right, of course, but it was hard to learn by self-teaching.

When the class was excused, I sat in the office waiting. Mr. Riley was at the radio. Some men passing by asked me what I was waiting for, but I didn't answer.

Nagotak and Kakianak came in just as 4 o'clock came around. Mr. Riley greeted them and asked them to sit down on the office chairs. With his hands at his back, he walked around the room thoughtfully, as he always did. Then he sat down behind his desk, and started, "I know what's on your mind. Nathan told me all about it."

I interpreted for him to Dad and Nagotak. I could already feel the dampness of sweat on my forehead, because I was not very good at interpreting, yet I had to do it.

Dad or maybe it was Nagotak answered him, "Yes, that is what we are coming here for." I passed their words on to Mr. Riley.

Then he continued: "I'm very glad that you asked me instead of just carrying out what you wanted to do." He paused a moment, then went on. "Since we are quite safe from the war, everything you want to do is okay with me. If I were you I would talk about it to Kazighia, your village president." I interpreted his words the best I could, skipping a word here and there that I couldn't translate into my own words. I sweated more, not only from effort, but also from the excitement of what he said.

"When do you think you will be able to go?" he asked my Dad.

He replied, "As soon as the ice is all gone and the freighter brings in some supplies to the store."

Mr. Riley nodded his head, then said, "That'll be fine, but I shall need Nathan in school."

"I will come back next winter by dog team," I said before anyone could speak up.

"I wish you would. Let me know before you go. I'll give you some books to take along to study," he went on, looking up to my father and Nagotak. "You may go ahead with that, but be sure to let Kazighia know."

"Yes, we will," they said.

The same day Kakianak sent me to Kazighia to ask him to our house for a talk with him. It was in the evening when

336

I went to their home. I was always shy, but I felt even more shy that time. It was another tough time I had. I went in their house as if I was going into great danger. I could hear the beating of my heart, but it seemed it would stop at any time. I even was worried they might be hearing it, too. How silly I was!

I was welcomed by the family, as always I was. Mr. Kazighia was a nice, kind fellow. As soon as he saw me he asked what they could do for me. My tongue stuck.

I began, "Oh . . . Ah." I paused for long time, trying to find usable words to say.

Then he said, "Oh, don't be bashful. Just tell me. I'll help you and it might be something important. Did Kakianak send you to me for something?" he went on.

His question gathered me together. I was helped by what he asked me. I said, "Yes, ah, he wants to see you and talk to you," I replied.

"Of course. I will go to see him right now," he said. "Give me my boots," he asked one of his boys.

The children wanted me to stay for awhile, but I told them I must go home right away. I promised them I would come another time when I wasn't too busy. (Really I was not busy then, but I wanted to hear what he and my Dad said.) They told me to be sure to come again. I assured them I would. We always had a fine time when I visited and came to play with them.

In our home, not being sure if I'd be welcome if I stuck around, I was not surprised when they prepared some tea as if it was for a tea party. They were getting together. They always started their conversation with strong boiled tea. I helped around with cups and serving the tea, just to be sure I was around when they mentioned our camping, so I would know how to feel about it.

They talked while the tea was started, but they didn't bring up the purpose of the talk for some time. I drank my tea as slowly as I could.

Finally, Kazighia asked my Dad, "What could it be that you want to see me about?"

"One thing I want to see and talk over with you is what

337

my family and I have wanted to do for so long a time," began my Dad. He paused for a moment or two. I acted as if I was not listening. Actually I was all ears.

He continued, "Since there is not too much danger of war, we want to spend a summer, at least, at our camp."

I watched Kazighia with a corner of my eye over my cup, and I was certain they didn't mind me being with them at their important talk, because they didn't say so. They would usually ask me to leave if they did mind.

Kazighia was silent a while, and the expression of his face changed. He looked interested.

"Oh, is that it?" he began. "Well, I need you very badly during the hunting season, but why should I hold you back?"

I shifted my looks to my Dad to wait for his reply. He just nodded his head in agreement and said, "That doesn't have to be now. I'm thinking after hunting season is the best time."

Kazighia's interest deepened and he said, "Then everything about that will be all right by me." He paused and then added, "I'll do my best if I can be of some help." My heart overflooded with joy and I felt like cheering at the top of my lungs.

Then Kazighia said, "You have one thing to do that I advise strongly. Before we go any further we better get a permission for you from Mr. Riley." He cast his eyes on my Dad.

And my Dad glanced at me and said, "Nathan said the teacher would permit us—if he is not lying."

I got hot at once when Kazighia looked at me and asked, "You wouldn't lie, would you?"

I shook my head and moved it, "Of course not."

Kazighia said, "Yes, I believe you, but Kakianak and I'll talk to him just to be sure and find out if you are telling the truth," grinning at me. I didn't say anything. I was eager to go with them, but Kakianak looked at me, which told me I was unwanted there.

I watched them as they went out together and tried to wait in the house for them, but I was impatient. Then when I couldn't stand my anxiety I looked for Ben, Martin, and Douglas to seek their company, thinking they would help kill the suddenly lengthening time. I found Martin and Douglas, but Ben was too busy getting ready to go home, and so were Debby, and Marian.

I coaxed Douglas and Martin for a walk to the beach to gather some sea weeds for our next meal. They really didn't need to be coaxed. They were always ready. I asked Mom's permission and she granted it after she checked to see that my share of chores was done. I had quickly taken care of my work in my excitement.

We went away on our pleasant tramp. I thought we were the three happiest brothers wherever we went, even though we came upon some arguments that sometimes led to fights. Also, competitions were high among us, and losers were not happy losers. But back to the story: we walked on the gravel one way, picking up some rocks to throw at gulls and kittiwakes. I walked behind the boys, trying to keep in mind my responsibility for them—"Am I my brothers' keeper?" It certainly was hard to do that when I was deeply concerned with something else, the desire of my heart.

They gathered some sea weeds. I just kept them tied to a string I had brought along for the purpose. We didn't go too far. I called them to go home. Like they always did, they made it hard on me, wanting to go on farther. I didn't blame them, because we had gone a shorter distance than we usually went. I had to repeat that Mom wouldn't let us go out anymore if we didn't come home early. At last they came, stopping now and then to play or to throw rocks at the gulls.

When we got home I saw that Dad was home. How I wanted to ask questions, but I knew well that he didn't want to be bothered with questions! Something seemed to come into my questioning mind when he said, "Now the boys are here. Let's eat early so I'll get ready and you boys help me."

"Now is my chance to ask," I thought. So I asked him, "Get ready? For what?"

His reply came the way I thought it would. "You don't need to know that. You boys will do as I say. Help me." Then, "Now let's eat before it's too late." Well, that was his answer. It was not new to me; it wasn't the first time.

After supper, he went out to get the boxes of Nagotak's supplies and belongings while we got the other things ready. When he came back we had everything just about ready.

Ben, Debby, and Marian came to say goodbye to us. It was, or it seemed, different, because we hoped that we would be seeing each other in the near future if things turned out as we were wishing they would.

With the evening chill the sun-softened snow froze to crusty hard and nearly ice. The yowling and howling of the harnessed dogs filled up the still, spring air. Even though we had a hope, just the same I felt lonely right after they left. I didn't care to join the night fun and mischief-making gang, my friends. I went in and got ready to go to bed. It was one of the moments that are always memorable to me—moments followed by emptiness and silence in our little home.

When the children were asleep, in our usual personal talking I asked Mom what Dad had said about our going to the camp. From the sound of what she told me, the future looked very pleasant and bright. Everything about our summer camp ideas was approved by everybody. At that instant, I got busier than ever in my already full-of-wild-ideas mind. She told me Nagotak was going to let us use his outboard motor. Kakianak was to bring it on his return trip. That would be night after tomorrow. Oh, how could I wait that long?

Now I thought of the next day. "If the weather is good for hunting, it will be all right, because the time will pass faster while I'm having fun. But if not good weather, it'll be terrible, because I will have to go to school. The time always drags there, even on the days we don't go hunting." I hadn't been attending school. "Who cares about the sissy stuff?" I always had said whenever Dad and Mom urged me to go.

The next morning I woke up to the whistling and howling sound of a tough north wind. I glanced at the clock and pulled up my blanket to cover my face, because the daylight shined brightly through the thin cloth window shade. I did that hoping I'd go back to sleep and over-sleep so I'd be late for school. Once I woke up, I couldn't go back to sleep, even though I tried my best. I tried to think of my classmates, Francis, Herbert, Virginia, and a special, Mildred. "Oh, I

340

haven't been in class with them for long. It would be nice to see them again . . . better yet, it's Friday. We will have only two hours of morning classes, and the rest of it will be recreational activities; and in the afternoon just one hour of English reading and a little spelling test." The rest of the hour would be our own free-will reading, or even games or a movie or slide pictures of ourselves taken by Mr. Riley.

I made up my mind. "I'll go to school." I got up and washed, then prepared breakfast.

Douglas got up and washed up after me. I was to take him to school, but he went to the other room and came home earlier than I did. We went together at 9 o'clock.

At the door Mr. and Mrs. Riley greeted us. Douglas went to Mrs. Riley's class and I was greeted warmly by her husband. I walked out of the cloak room and down the rows of desks to my own without looking around much. I dropped on my seat, then checked on my desk—and was pleased with the looks of it. When I had left, it had been a mess—scraps of old papers, wadded papers, unstraightened piles of books, and numbers of out-of-place personal items, like a sling shot, string, rustry screws, and bolts. Now it was all neatly taken care of. Wondering, I swept my glance around at my classmates. None of them paid any attention.

Then I looked behind me at my special classmate, Mildred Kangalik, and met her eyes. I turned around quickly before any of my boy friends could catch us doing that, but I felt her tap me on my shoulder. Then I turned around. She gave me a slip. I read it and scribbled a reply note and dropped it on her desk. Our brief classes didn't last too long, then we were all lost in the fun—singing, playing games until Mr. Riley's desk bell rang. Then automatically the desks got occupied, every occupant sitting and awaiting our teacher's words like squads of soldiers at attention. Everyone paid attention at that moment, because it was the last five minutes of the final hour of morning classes.

The teacher gave us a five-minute lecture, then dismissed us for the noon lunch hour. At the exact time, row by row, the pupils marched in one door into the cloak room, out the other, then out the exit.

We walked home, talking about how we did at school and what we would do after school. How my friends talked about the fun they were going to have, doing things such as going somewhere where they'd do some mischief! I wished I could join them, but I couldn't. I seemed to have to help around with the home work, and have no time for fun. They made fun of me, when they asked me what I had to do after school. They even called me names, making me feel hurt and out of place.

I wished the day would hurry, because the next morning Kakianak would be back from Southwest Cape, or else the day would be good for hunting, so I could enjoy myself.

But no matter what we did to each other, we were always good friends. So I liked the afternoon classes. First the spelling test; then English, which lasted less than an hour. The rest of it was just recreation. Our teacher surprised us with a movie he had made of us earlier that spring, showing when we had our classes out of doors and the lunch in the school. Some children held their faces when they saw themselves in the picture. I was embarrassed when I saw myself. I looked awfully ugly.

After that the teacher called me to his desk and asked me to stay after the class for a few minutes' talk with him. I stayed as he had told me to do. At his desk he talked to me about my leaving for the camp. He said that he wanted me to continue my school somehow. He didn't want me to drop it off completely; after all, I had gotten along well with it, he said. I didn't say anything.

"Be sure to let me know lots of time before you go, so I will pack some books, papers, pencils, and other things you'll need to keep up your school," he said.

I thought that was a good idea, so I told him I would like that.

"I'm packing books not only for you. I shall pack some for your cousins, and some for Douglas," said he. "And you will be a teacher for him, while Debby, Marian, and you work together."

I was thrilled at the idea. I told him I would be happy to do our schooling that way. After some more talk he

342

excused me. Then I went home, as if I was walking the whole way on the air.

That evening, even though I was so excited, I felt like going to bed early, after the hard afternoon of work, like refilling the water supply and fixing some meat for drying.

In the morning Kakianak woke us up when he came in early. He had already taken care of the dogs and his things.

I asked him, "Why didn't you wake me up to help you with the dogs?"

"Oh, I saw that you had worked pretty hard, so I wanted you to sleep good and late, as I'd expected you to do," he said.

I was much surprised at his being pleased and at the compliment. He didn't do that very much. Everything was taken care of; even breakfast was ready waiting for us.

After we had eaten and before he went to bed, he told me that he had brought the outboard motor from Southwest Cape. The best part was when he asked me if I wanted to go ahead in taking it apart to clean it. Exactly what I wanted to do! He also told me not to let any of my friends in where I worked. I did so. First I gathered some old rags, then took the motor to the upper room.

I stopped for a moment to think of what day it was. "Oh, it's Saturday," I thought. Soon I was very busy with wrenches and screwdrivers, putting screws into one bag and nuts into another bag. Then, with the parts of the motor laid out carefully, I started cleaning. While I was having the most fun, Ada called me down to get some snow for water.

I tried to reason—"I can't. I'm too busy."

"You have to get some snow right away for dinner," she replied stubbornly.

Well, no choice. I wiped my grease-stained hands on a rag and went down.

I stood holding buckets in each hand, hoping she would send Ann for snow instead; but she was busy with something else. In a nice, apologetic tone, she said, "It won't take you too long. Just hurry up." I did so. I ran all the way.

She was right. It didn't take too much of my time. Next moment I was at my pleasant work again. I got stuck on a part I didn't know what to do with. I was helpless, and I put it aside until Dad could help me. But I thought he might tease me again. He would say, "Why, you, a young man who goes to school, ask for help from me, an old man who has never been in school? Ah, you are not as good as me yet. You need more school, young man."

"But I will not mind that," I thought, "because the motor is not ours. Worse yet, if I break it I will spoil our plans to go to Southwest Cape." So I would rather take his tease. Just then Ada called me again.

"Now what is it?" I asked.

"The dinner is ready. We are going to eat and we are waiting for you," she said.

"Oh, I am too busy, and I'm not hungry," I said.

"You must come down anyway, or else I'll give you more work to do for me," she said.

Well, I lost again, so I went down. They were waiting for me. Kakianak had just woke up. He asked me how I was getting along with the motor. I told him I was about half-way through. "But I'm stuck on one thing," I told him. When I told him what the part was I'd become stuck on, he told me that he also didn't know how to clean it. He said Kenneth might know about it, and he would look him up to help with it.

When the dinner was over I went up to get back to my work while Kakianak went out to look for Kenneth. I had just about everything cleaned up when Kenneth and Kakianak showed up.

It didn't take Kenneth too long to fix that part. Kakianak had left us alone to our work, because he had other things to take care of. When there were two of us working on it, we got it done faster. While we worked on it Kenneth asked me, "Why don't you ask your Dad to let us go duck hunting or fishing to try out the motor?"

"Oh, that's what I'll do!" I replied. But that day was not the day for that, because the wind was from the wrong direction and too strong.

"Anyway, we might do that as soon as the weather becomes good for that," I told him. When we were through, every screw, nut, and part was in place. I asked Kenneth to have

344

some tea with me. "And why don't we ask him while we have some tea?" I said.

"Sure, you may do that while I'm around, and it's the best chance for us to do it, too," he agreed. We wiped our greasy hands on some rags.

I had been scratching my nose when it itched, and I hadn't noticed it until Kenneth looked at me in the dim light and giggled. I tried to guess what was so funny about me, but he only said, "Oh, you will find out for yourself."

Then we went down. When we entered the room everyone of the family laughed at me. I didn't know what was wrong with me. Ann handed me a mirror. Then I joined in the amusement. I had smeared some grease and carbon under my nose, so that it looked like a funny moustache. I washed up, and then tea was on.

Kenneth was across from me. He signaled me at the right moment to bring up what we were up to. So I said, "Hey, Dad. Since we have the motor all cleaned up, why don't we go out on a fishing trip?"

He looked up at Kenneth, then me, and replied, "I have a better idea than that. Why not make a trip to Savoonga?"

Kenneth and I were most pleased. Kenneth even offered to buy the gasoline for that.

In the next few days I found myself getting the things ready for the trip to Savoonga. I had told David Akoak about it at Sunday School, so he was very handy when he was needed—but sometimes too handy. Kenneth bought the gasoline and oil, so we were mixing them, and I bought some shotgun shells and some cartridges for my rifle.

Everything was ready, but the weather was holding us back. All the time we were busy storing our winter meat supply and putting away things to take to Southwest Cape.

While Dad and I were doing that together, I thought how much time and work was necessary to get ready for going to camp, and our trip to Savoonga was going to be much trouble, and would take lots of our time and be an added expense. I called to Dad, "Why the trouble of going to Savoonga, and why lose the time we need very badly? I can't think it's that important."

345

He looked at me for a moment, then replied, "It's important. We haven't seen your cousins, Pearl Awigiyak and Emily Saka, for a long time. And besides, I want to have a good operating test for the outboard motor."

He, of course, was right, but it was still quite a lot of lost time. I looked at him, and he had the same expression as mine must have been. Then he began, "Oh, you'll enjoy it. You can shoot ducks. Perhaps in some other ways also you'll like it." He paused, then went on. "Think of David Akoak. This might be the last time he is to enjoy a trip in our own boat."

I agreed with him when he mentioned David. I thought how hard he had worked helping us while we were building the boat. Oh, well, I had to enjoy it. I made up my mind and carried on with the task.

All the while I'd been attending school regularly, and somehow had been enjoying it. I hadn't been in school for a few weeks very regularly. Now for several days the west wind kept the ice pack into the shore, cutting out hunting. I had to write a sort of diary of my hunting days for my teacher. He said if I didn't keep up writing it, he wouldn't let me go out hunting. So I had to do it even though I didn't like it a bit, because it was very hard for me to do it. Whenever I told him I'd rather do anything else than writing diaries for him, he would say, "That's the only way you can earn your hunting permission. Besides, you are writing good stories." I even told him it was too hard for me to do it. He still said, "Oh, no. You are able to do it. I know you are learning to write too."

I thought of giving up, but hunting was something that I wouldn't give up, almost for anything. Whether I like it or not, I wrote funny, short diaries that consisted of four or five unrelated lines darkened or worn out from frequent erasing. Anyway, he gave me undeserved compliments on the diaries, and showed his appreciation.

For short periods after school I often did some catching up on certain things with the special help of my teacher, which made the other pupils think that my teacher had favoritism for me. That was not really so. His special help

346

was for anybody who wanted it. He told me so, and he said so to the class. But the boys were boys. They would rather go out to have some fun after school. I would rather do that, too, but I had to catch up, because I needed it. Every time we had a private discussion I would bring up our camping. He always talked about it with me.

At home I tried as much as I could to play with Douglas and Martin, but I always had something else to do. More and more my parents told me I was old enough to share family responsibilities, such as our daily chores, which were equally shared among us.

One day the wind had shifted to the south and the same evening it was dying down, when Kakianak came over to me while I was with David Akoak at their home, and called me so we could turn in soon to get up early in the morning, expecting a nice, calm day tomorrow. He didn't have to ask me a second time, because it would be a long-waited day if our hope came true. I said, "Good night" to David and he told me to come and call him early in the morning if the weather was good, and I told him to do the same to me.

The always pleasant moment of the day was the family gathering around supper. We did that when I got home, then bed time. It had been a hard day full of work with daily tasks, so I didn't have much trouble dozing off. I was worn out.

Next thing I knew my father was calling me. I jumped into my clothes. Then I ran out to wake up David. I didn't have to wake him up. He was up already, and was about to come to wake us up. We were all excited.

When I came back to our house, I started to take things out to the front yard, but my Mom called me for breakfast. I had forgotten all about it and it seemed to take much of our time when that time was needed. Actually it often took only a few minutes. Within the hour we were carrying our motors, rifles, gasoline, and other needed bundles down to our boat. Kenneth and Ben Nagotak, Kakianak, a Weather Bureau person, David Akoak, and I were going.

It was a nice spring morning, calm and bright, and the sky was blue. The Siberian mountains looked pretty in the morning horizon sky.

347

In the next half-hour we were afloat. I worked on the motor with all thumbs for fingers. Whenever I had to be careful and hurry, I could feel the eyes looking at me from the shore, and those in the boat making me very conscious. The motor was merciful. It caught at the first pull on the starting, and then I adjusted it to normal running speed and looked up to wave at the folks on the beach. Then Kenneth and I exchanged glances and grins in satisfaction and pleasure that our work was paying off. Everyone looked happy in the boat, but David Akoak was the most pleased.

Before we had started, Kakianak had given his orders: "Absolutely no bird shooting until I say so," he had said. So shotguns and .22 caliber rifles were put away in their cases until they would be needed. He didn't mean his orders were for everyone in the boat; the bowman could shoot as he pleased, even birds. We didn't feel bad about it, because every boat captain has the right to give orders for the good of everyone. Anyway, orders or no orders, it was a most enjoyable time for us. The motor hummed steady and it seemed like just another boat ride.

We kept close watch out for any black specks on the water that would mean some game, but it happened there wasn't much except for the ducks that flew in flocks. The situation went on that way for a long time—several hours. At the proper time David and I filled up the motor and once in a while I made the necessary readjustments. Kenneth scanned the distant water through his glasses, but he didn't make any signals of having spotted anything.

I became aware of a dark blue line that showed clearly to the north of us on the smooth water. That could mean a north wind brewing up. If so, it was bound to spoil the trip. It was too unpleasant, so I took my thought away from it. But I really couldn't help thinking of it. I started to talk to David to avert the thought of ill fate, or what could be ill fate. While we were talking, Kenneth caught my eyes, making signs after he had observed the water to the right of us dead ahead, which was the way we were headed. From his signs, I could make out he had sighted ice. That could make the things worse for sure.

Then the excitement began. Kakianak signaled me to cut off the motor. I did. The water was no longer glassy and smooth. It had turned blue and slightly ripply, and a biting sharp breeze could be felt from the north. I could see the narrow white line next to the shore, sparkling white against the dark brown shoreline, and the deep blue water, which was getting deeper and darker in blue. The bite of the breeze seemed sharper when the motor was cut off.

The purpose of our stopping was an unpleasant talk, but all the facts had to be faced. Kakianak asked Kenneth about the ice condition and then said, "No, we can't go through it, and we can't go toward the shore right now. The best place we can head to is back and try to make the best time toward Gambell we can. Now start the motor so we don't lose too much time."

I started the motor, then looked back for Kakianak to signal me for speed. He signaled for full speed. I made the adjustment, then sat facing David so we could talk away the time. It was hard to do. We pushed aside the subject and talked about every pleasant thing we could find in our minds, but the sharp wind kept bringing up the subject—the wind that was getting sharper and more penetrating all the time. The little ripples were getting fatter and higher. It was getting harder and harder to refill the motor tank.

I began to worry a little as I watched Gambell hill going up and down, up and down as the boat tossed, sometimes climbing one wave and falling, "Smack," on the next one, sending a spray out both port and starboard. What worried me was if the wind became a gale before we could make it to Gambell, there would be no place to land, and attempting to do so would probably wreck our new boat and spoil all our plans and pleasant dreams of going back to camp, which now seemed a little more likely to come true than ever before.

All these thoughts had shot into my mind. Another worry I had was that I was tending the motor, and if I let it stop, the boat would be hard to keep in control, or the spray might hit the spark plugs and kill it. All these would be my fault and my Dad would be like a wounded lion. A change of weather could worry a person in several ways.

Actually these were just unnecessary, useless worries. But to cut out one of those worries I looked for a piece of canvas to shield the motor from the spray, and found one. I was very glad that Kenneth and I had done the best we could do to put the motor in good operating order, and it hummed steadily. But every little change of its humming startled me.

The rocking of the boat lulled me, and a drowse dulled out my startled feeling a little bit. David and I avoided talking about what was happening with the wind, but we chatted about the future and whenever we brought up the subject, one of us would say something about another skin boat trip that had been better than this one.

Remarkably, with the wind partly from behind us and partly from our side, and the waves pushing us onward, the Gambell mountain was coming up to meet us faster than I thought. But with that, worries were getting harder to brush out of my mind, which made me look at Kenneth and Kakianak. Kenneth had a worried look, as if he felt as I did. But Kakianak's looks were not a bit changed. The usual half-grin and half-frown look on his face was there. That meant that there was not too much to worry about. I could be sure, because I believed he knew the situation much better than I did. He knew when to worry and when not to. I was sort of the opposite of that, and that was why they said I was funny. I would worry about things that were not things to be worried about. But at other times when something happened to cause a person fear and worry, I would stay calm and didn't mind almost anything.

In a fairly short time we were near the point of the mountain [a promontory, offshore from which the sea is quite turbulent] and for the first time Kakianak looked kind of restless, while I began to be relieved of my fears, since we were near home. And when I glanced at Kenneth he showed a complete expression of worry. He and Kakianak were exchanging a message by signal language that I couldn't understand.

Just as I was to look away, Kakianak signaled me to come to him. I did, and he told me, "The water ahead is pretty rough. Fill up the motor and see that everything is going on all right with it. Understand?"

350

I did as he said. With the help of David I refueled it and double-checked it and settled down once more, curled up the best I could to keep warm after I had wrung out my thin, soaked canvas work gloves that I was wearing. They looked like they were baseball gloves—they were too big.

Once more I kept a close watch on the motor. I could nearly worship it. It was running smoothly so I had some security that it would be dependable. I settled down, but I kept listening for any change in the steady hum of the motor and watched for any signals Kakianak or Kenneth would make.

Then we approached the point. The waves became sharper at the peak and greater in height, but closer together and somewhat irregular. The boat went up at the bow on one wave and then came down, crashing onto the next one dangerously. On each smacking, it sent spray out both sides and some water splashed into the boat.

I grabbed for the piece of canvas that we used to shield the motor from spray and put it to work to protect it. The crashing of the boat became so violent that the gasoline cans began to clang on one another, and the cans, paddles, and other things made a racket. Kakianak seemed to have a hard time controlling the boat. Finally I had to hang on to something to keep myself from jumping up and down on my seat. Kakianak signaled me to cut down the motor. I was beginning to get worried, but was also enjoying the fun. I didn't worry too much, since I wasn't aware of the danger.

When I cut down the motor, the ride got a little smoother, but Kakianak told me not to cut it too low. At the right speed, he evidently retained a good control of the boat and it didn't come down so hard, either.

I still had to have a close watch on the motor. However, tending the motor wasn't the only thing that kept me busy. I had to keep pumping the water that kept coming up deeper every minute. At the same time I was trying to keep away from the spray, especially to keep it out of my eyes.

I didn't know for how long and for how much distance that kept up. When at last we got onto the smoother water, everybody had a relieved look, changing from that tensed look. I felt that way, too. Maybe for the fiftieth time I wrung out my gloves and shook like a dog to dry, and pumped out the last few gallons of water from the bottom of the boat.

Around the next point the village would come into view. The motor coughed a few times. I rushed to it and opened the needle valve, because I was sure it had coughed from lack of gas. But it didn't respond. It died out. "It ran dry," I thought.

But when I opened the tank plug it was more than half full. "Hummm." That meant trouble. I had to take the carburetor apart to clean it and get it going again. But I had to work fast.

As I pulled off my gloves, I glanced around and saw gaping mouths and goggle-eyed faces. But not a word from any one of the gaping mouths. No time to look around. I had to get the motor going quick. I fished out a monkey wrench from the battered up old tool box and worked at the carburetor, doing my best to work fast, but my fingers were soaked and stiff from cold. I got it loose and unscrewed it.

Now to get at the little strainer. It was clogged with water and dirt. I blew it clear, ran some of the fuel to make sure it was free of dirt and water. Someone was hollering something at me. No time to listen; I had to work fast. Now putting it back together, I looked up for the first time to see how close we were from the rocky shore. We were being blown in quite close. Another two hundred yards and we would be smashed to pieces on the shore rocks.

Still I heard some hollering. I didn't pay any attention at all. Now I tightened the nut into place, adjusted it to starting position, opened the fuel valves wide, at last wound the starting cord around the groove on the flywheel, and put on all my strength in jerking. It caught. After I adjusted it to running position, I looked up. It must have been only a hundred yards from the shore. Now I looked around to see who had something to holler at me while I was so busy. Kenneth! He was right behind me with a serious look on his face.

I asked him, "What were you trying to tell me?" He looked at the motor and then at me. Then he gave me a big wide grin, and went back to his seat on the bow without saying a word. He was just scolding. That didn't help anything that way, not a tiny bit. He was in a panic.

Then I looked at my Dad. He had a slight grin and nodded a bit in approval of what I had done. I felt kind of proud. He signaled me to come to him. I did. He told me we had to go through another rough place once more, because we had to beach at the south shore. Since the north wind was blowing, the surf would be high at the north shore. He said I must repeat what I had done in the rough water we passed—the same close watch on the motor and check on the fuel. "But," he concluded, "don't listen to Kenneth. He is in a panic."

The village came into view. The water was fairly calm, but I could see the rough place at the point we were to round. I turned up the motor some, because I was getting impatient, and looked at Dad to see what he thought about that. Well, it was all right. Then I found out we were making better speed than I thought, with some wind and waves behind us to push us.

The boat was set on her course to Gambell, and the motor was humming a different pitch as if in response to the seas, which pushed us on and on as each one came and went. The north wind was rough, and whitecaps appeared on every sea; once one of the white caps hit us and sent a spray of water in the boat and drenched everybody within, including the motor, which coughed a few times but didn't stop. Trusty little thing! It never failed us. What was the rough sea and wind to be worried about? I had one security—that was Kakianak. Whenever worry forced its way into my head I would steal a glance at him and study his expression. He didn't look worried at all. Neither did he mind the seas or the wind; his look told me there was nothing to worry about.

Now it was a different story, with the others in the boat. David Akoak was too young to mind anything. Whatever the situation, he was one to take it with a giggle. Whenever I looked his way he'd give me a smile in a kind of stupid way. Kenneth worried big; hanging on to the tough leather rope lacing of the boat, he looked as if he was scared to death trying to figure out what to do in the unfavorable weather. The other person on board was a Weather Bureau person, who was enjoying a day off by going out in a skin boat, which must have been quite a little adventure to him. He was trying to be comfortable fighting the cold and sprays.

David and I began a conversation of some sort, beginning with complaining about the weather and our disappointment. For example, we had been bored because there were no birds to shoot at or any other game. At last we planned a dirty trick for some excitement. Our motor had been cut low to reduce the spray and the rocking of the little craft. To us that wasn't anything very pleasant. We had been keeping the tank filled, but now we planned we would let it run out and when we started it again I would put on more speed. We were both mad because we hadn't made the trip to Savoonga.

As planned, the motor died out and we pretended to gas it up before it ran out. Kenneth scolded us, but in defending us Kakianak said that it couldn't be helped, and told him to make some tea to warm us up. I was surprised when Kakianak told me to put on more speed when I started the motor; he had looked at the sky and water and then whispered to me that the wind was going to blow harder and we must make it before it got too rough at the base of the mountain. I knew why he whispered instead of telling me aloud—it was because of Kenneth. If Kenneth heard him say anything about the weather getting worse, it would panic him.

Working with numb fingers, I got the motor going and heaved the throttle lever open full and advanced the magneto lever forward as far as it could go. The boat went up on the seas, lifting its bow while the motor groaned, and then dropped with a bang and splash on the other side, sending spray out both port and starboard. Whee! This was fun and exciting! But it was no fun for Kenneth. He scolded sternly, flailing his arms to cut down the motor. He was a funny sight indeed. I couldn't help turning away from him so he wouldn't see my amusement, but something made me respond to him. I heard him above the motor, hollering at the top of his lungs, "Coffee. The coffee."

Oh, oh. I caught the motor and cut it down. Then he

354

scolded and complained over the spilled coffee he had been making. Poor fellow; I felt sorry for him. Soon the aroma of coffee reached our noses and cups were passed from bow to stern. Welcomed things they were.

Sure enough, as Kakianak predicted, the wind got higher and more whitecaps appeared, and I got the motor on full and kept it at that speed, only slowing it down when we had to fill it, which was a nauseous task. I had to stand up and lift heavy five-gallon cans to pour gas through the funnel, and try to avoid loss of precious gas by spilling when I missed the funnel, or by over-filling the tank. Then I would sit down and accelerate it again.

The Weather Bureau man, poor fellow, got seasick and threw up over the side. I didn't like the sight, because it gave me a sick feeling in my stomach. Fortunately, I had gotten used to rough water riding during the spring hunting with the Kogoyaks.

David and I fell into some talk again, forgetting the weather and everything else until Kakianak drew my attention by rapping on the gunwales to signal me. He called me to him and gave me some instructions for running the motor. He said, "The front of the mountain is rather rough. We have to put up the curtain and cut the motor low, but not too low. Fill it up just before we get on the rough water and don't let it stop at all. Otherwise we'll be in trouble. The waves may drive us into the rocks and wreck the boat. Be careful."

I nodded and carried on. First we gassed it up, then put up the canvas curtain, being careful to tie up every string to the posts securely. Then we were all set for rough water.

At certain points of the mountain where the current and wind meet with force, it stirs up the water until it's like boiling water. We soon reached such a place. I thought the mountain was still at quite a distance, yet it was out of sight, covered by thick fog. We had made better speed than I thought, with the wind and seas behind to push us.

The rough water caught me by surprise and a wave hit me from behind and buried me under, then lifted me, drenching and dripping wet. The motor was nearly stopped again, but I quickly caught a piece of rag from under my belt and wiped the drip of water from the spark plugs, and that took care of it. Then I grabbed a tarp to cover it and glanced at my father to see if he might scold or be displeased. He didn't mind. He still had that half-grin, half-serious look, which was a sure sign of "all-is-well."

The boat rocked as if it would tip over and spill us into the blue, rough water any minute. That kept on for about two hundred yards, while we were washed with a salty shower. Finally we passed it. The straight water ahead was a welcome sight. I saw the men look relieved, and I felt free to accelerate the motor once more. Then Kakianak told me we would have to go through rough, stirred-up water once more at the point of Gambell beach, since we had to beach at the south shore.

There was broken ice all along the north beach, pushed in by the north wind. We had to follow the edge of it and then go through it to reach the free water at the south beach. That was somewhat lucky for us, because the ice kept the water smooth. Yet there was one disadvantage in having broken ice. Going through it, the motor propeller hit upon a chunk of it which sheared off the pin, so I had to replace the pin while the rest of the crew paddled. Then we started again, only to hit another piece of ice. We finally got through the ice, and the south shore was good and smooth. Then we landed, which could be the worst part of the trip. It was all right for the others in the boat, but to David and me it meant disappointment. We would be ridiculed by some tough boys who were our schoolmates; the ridiculing and teasing would be about the unmade trip. But to our great pleasure there were no people around when we landed.

Having taken care of the boat and other things, when we were sitting around the platter over the meal, Kakianak and I had what I might call table talk. Noticing that the loss of time and fuel bothered me, he began to talk to me about it. It was clear to him that I didn't like the way this trip had turned out. We didn't gain anything at all. We just lost our much-needed fuel and time. I was sure we could have made it if we only hadn't turned back—my mind went over some of these thoughts.

But I was foolish to think that way, because I hadn't realized another reason why we couldn't make it. My father, having more, far more, experience than I had had, knew and was worried about the ice.

He wasn't stern or displeased when he began the conversation. He started with saying how at first I expected to bring home something every time I went out hunting. He said that I had to learn it was the same thing this time. It wasn't only because of the bad weather we had had to turn back. It was the ice that was driven to the shore by the wind. We couldn't have gone through it to the village. We might have had a better chance if we had been on the inside or the shore side of the ice floe, but Kakianak was very doubtful of our getting there that way, either, saying that we would lose more time if we got caught by the weather at Savoonga.

Then I asked, "What about the gas we lost? What about that trip to Savoonga? Are we going to forget it?"

"The time and weather will take care of that," he said. "What I mean is, if the good weather comes around before the *North Star* comes, we won't let it pass by; we shall try another trip."

The next few days Kenneth and I got together for ivory carving. That was one way we replaced the gas we lost. We got twice as much or more money as we had spent in gas.

Kenneth agreed with my father about going to Savoonga. He wanted to take advantage of the boat while we had it around, because we were to take it away to Southwest Cape as soon as we could get our groceries and ammunition.

The north wind blew itself out and it was calm enough once more. Somehow Kakianak was certain that the weather was to be pleasant, so he was willing to have Ann and Louise Mala with us, who were eager to ride in our nice new skin boat and have the fun of the trip, too. At first I didn't like them along very well. Sissy gals. Later, though, I was glad they came along. I was proud to tell them the names of places and other things they asked. And the best part was that they fixed our coffee.

The trip went well. David and I had a competitive game of who would be the better rifleman in shooting sea birds.

Soon we were there at Savoonga, with relatives making us at home and friends showing us around. The most thrilling part was going to the village store, where I saw things that interested me. I always thought we didn't have a penny under our name, but to my astonishment Kakianak pulled out a roll of green bills and bought me a pair of gloves and some smaller ones for Martin and Douglas, and socks for all of us, some bullets for my rifle to use on the way back, and more gas. I asked him why did he buy them there instead of at Gambell? He said they had better prices there, and that it was too bad we didn't have enough cans for more gas.

We stayed in Savoonga only a few hours that time, and soon were turning back to Gambell. I was a little sorry to be leaving so soon. I liked walking with friends in the swampy places, looking for wild flowers and crossing the stream. It was fun to wade across the fast water. But we were on our way again soon, while people waved to us from the beach.

We had started from Savoonga in the evening, and now it was daytime, and the sun was shining brightly, and it was quite warm. David and I resumed our game and at the same time I tended to the motor. But we were not as active as we had been on the trip coming down. Before I knew it I had fallen asleep, probably tired from so much running around in the village. Then somebody shook me and I unwillingly got up. The motor was dead.

I wanted to know why it went out—ran out of fuel, somebody told me. I gassed it up and looked around. The girls were all curled up and making queer, low noises of their snoring. Kenneth was up and had a grin over his face. I thought he was just amused at my sleepy looks, but it was something else, as I soon found out. As soon as I got the motor going I made myself as comfortable as I could, covering myself with tarps and whatever else was to be had, and then went to sleep. Again I woke up after some time. Hey! that old Kenneth—that's a dirty trick! I shook David as I exclaimed that Kenneth had got our rifles and was shooting birds with them. "Give me my rifle," I demanded.

"Do you mean your empty gun?" he said, with a joking laugh and handed me the gun.

358

I looked to Kakianak for defense, but he looked amused.

David asked why he did that.

"That's what the sleepyheads get," Kenneth said.

David looked at Kakianak and he just nodded, agreeing with Kenneth. We were not supposed to sleep in the boat. That was a lesson.

Actually, it doesn't matter whose rifle the bowman uses, since whatever game we get is always divided among the crew. However, it was a good thing I kept my shells in my pocket. Anyway, that was why he was grinning when the motor stopped.

Everything went well the rest of the way and we were soon at Gambell. Now everybody was evidently satisfied, and I was glad the trip was over so we wouldn't have to worry any more about it, and wouldn't spend any more time and money on it. Now we would pay more attention to our going to Southwest Cape.

# 17. Back to Southwest Cape

Soon we began to keep our ears open for the news from the *North Star,* and began packing our things away, both those to take with us and those to leave behind. At the same time we were gathering every bit of needed things we could get from the store, and from relatives and friends. All hands in the family were needed on such a task, but whenever I could I would steal away and look up my buddies and have a good time with them—and end up being scolded by Dad and Mother for wasting time and being absent while they needed my help. I deserved being scolded, because it was certain I was needed, but at the same time I felt hurt and deprived of my rights and the enjoyment of being with friends.

By and by the much expected and waited-for news reached us. We were informed of it by a neighbor calling at our door—one who couldn't keep such good news quiet—"*North Star* is at Savoonga." I went out and everybody I met had the same news. I went to the store to find out where I was to work.

Upon entering the store I found it crowded with men and noisy with cheery talk. The boat captains were gathered there and other men who were to be boat crew and shoremen. Mr. Naciknak was one of the captains, and when he saw me he asked me, "Did somebody get you?"

I didn't understand what he meant by that, but I said, "No."

Then he said, "How would you like to be a crewman in our boat for lightering?"

Who wouldn't want to be! I said, "If I may I would like it better than anything else."

He looked pleased and said, "That's very good. If some others ask you, tell them you are my crew."

I said, "Okay," and then ran home to tell my folks proudly of what I'd be when the *North Star* arrived. It was the first time I'd be a crewman on lightering and so I was excited about it. I met some boys on the way and discharged my news to them and ran on. At home I rolled in and told them my news and asked if Mom and Dad approved of it. They did, and were pleased because that job was better paying than the other jobs.

Later other boat captains dropped in to ask Dad and me if we were available, but Dad had his own captain, who was Mr. Kazighia, and I had mine now.

Everything went well until I came to remember that Peter, Mr. Naciknak's son, was a tough boy. "I wonder if he will be a bully and push me around at any opportunity while I'm there?" I thought, "Oh, well, I will have to face him and try to make the best of it."

In the late afternoon I helped my new captain with the whaleboat, which we had to move from the south to the north shore. All of the crew was there: Naciknak himself, and his sons, George and Peter, besides Melvin Tuntuk, their cousin, and myself. There were others who came to help with the boat, since it was a big, heavy boat to move. There were other people moving boats to the beach; some were helped by the school tractor. I didn't have any trouble with Peter all the time we were moving the boat. He was interested in me in a nice way and I did hope and pray he would be that way all through the work.

Mr. Kogoyak, who really was my captain, was to work on another job instead of with his boat, because his sons, Louis, Otto, and Noah were assigned to other jobs. Therefore he was short on crewmen. I was so sorry about that, because the Kogoyaks were very nice to me, and I knew them as well as my family.

Although we had so much to do, the time seemed to pass by slowly. It wasn't easy going to sleep when I went to bed. Like any other time, when I was to do something for the first time I was too excited to go to sleep, and keeping still was hard. I turned and tossed and watched the clock. Sometimes I thought the old thing was stuck at certain hours, but it was ticking away, yet seemingly getting nowhere.

Once or twice my father scolded me to keep still and go to sleep. I would try keeping very still and wait for sleep to fall on me for a few minutes, but I was just too wide awake. Then I would roll over just once more to look at the clock or try to think of something to do. There wasn't anything to do except to keep on and on, trying to keep still.

It was a blessed thing when I heard the primus stove; Dad had started to boil coffee. I finally had fallen asleep until then. It was time to be up and getting breakfast. I saw to it that my rain coats and rubber boots were handy.

I found people running around the village, but everyone seemed to have nothing to tell me. I hurried to the store, where the news will be. Sure enough, Mr. Naciknak was there and he told me to be around where he could find me, but didn't tell me anything about the arrival of the *North Star*. I went in to find someone asking Kapugan the question I had in mind. Kapugan told him the ship was at Savoonga lightering and was due here on the afternoon. He also told him to see for himself the message posted in front at the school.

That was what I wanted to hear, and I ran on up to the school. I found the slip of paper tacked on the front of the school, where our school teacher posted his written announcements whenever he had something to announce. I read the news and carried it back to the house as fast as my legs could carry me.

Storming into the house, I spilled the news, expecting excitement, but found Mom and Dad calm like they always were, and so was Ann. She never seemed interested in anything at all. And with Douglas and Martin the picture would be completely different. They were like wild animals who would be stampeded in the slightest presence of excitement, or even like explosives that you can touch off with a spark of liveliness. That was the way I liked them, because when I have exciting news to tell I want people to feel the way I do. The three of us would make a racket until baby Lucy was scared to death and wailing, and then Mom had quite a job of settling us down.

Even then it was no time for me to sit around twiddling my thumbs. I had to be hustle-bustling around with my share of daily family chores. Now what was there to do to pass the time until the ship came? I reminded myself to get the water supply replenished. It wasn't much to do, so it was done in no time. I voluntarily watered and fed the dogs. Then I found other things to do, whether they were necessary or not. All along I kept watching for a ship to appear in front of the mountain. How I wished I'd run off to be with the gang, but I knew that wouldn't be good, knowing Naciknak would have a hard time to find me and have to take somebody else in my place if I weren't around when the ship came. That would endanger my being reliable, something I was striving to be. So I stayed put around the house.

I gathered myself together and sat on the grass in front of our house. Sitting there, I began to be drowsy. Then I lay flat on my stomach. The sun shining felt nice and warm on my back. Sounds lost their distinctness: the dogs barking, children chattering and laughing merrily, somebody chopping wood, and a low rustling of the breeze among the grass. All had a lulling effect on my drowse. I was occupied watching bugs and flies before me. "Wonderful, beautiful world. In every way. If you look close enough. If you are still enough to hear and observe its wonders and beauties"—these were my thoughts.

I heard my name called by a very familiar voice, my mother's. Rising, I shivered a little in spite of the warm sunshine and blinked. "Oh why do people have to ruin my peace?" I thought.

"Come on, what are you waiting for?" the voice came again. Mom was strict about being on time for meals.

"The ship!" With that thought I jumped up and scanned the water where the ship was expected to show up. I thanked Mother for waking me up. I don't know how long I'd been sleeping in the sun, but I hadn't slept much the night before.

Walking lazily, I asked Mom, "What's to eat?"

"Come in and find out," Mom called back. Then she stared in my face, showing surprise in her eyes.

"What's the matter? Are you sick?" she wanted to know.

"No, but I'm hungry. Why?" I said.

"You don't look well. Your eyes are red and puffy and you are pale. Do you feel all right?" she asked, still with her eyes fixed on mine.

"Right. I'm dying. From starvation. Give me food before I die," I replied jokingly.

"I said, are you sick?" she said, with fire in her tongue.

"Okay. I slept out there and you woke me up so I'm just sleepy, not sick," I assured her. Douglas and Martin giggled mockingly until I gave them a face, meaning "This is no fun."

Glancing at the clock, I could see it was nearly 2 o'clock. No wonder I was hungry. Just as we were through with the meal, David came in with a bang and crash, and discharged his news, "*North Star* is arriving," almost at a shout. I jumped into my hip boots and grabbed my rain gear and followed David, sort of chasing him.

I knew where to run. The Naciknak's. I found him just coming out of their house. Naciknak gave me a compliment for being prompt. I asked for something to carry to the north shore. He handed me a coil of rope and I asked if there was anything else. He said there was more and gave me something. At that I rushed off to the north shore. All the crew followed.

When we launched the heavy boat, the *North Star* was dropping her anchor. I was amazed at how fast the people could launch their boats. In just five minutes all of them were in the water, and I counted fifteen white boats. I thought it won't take long to get the work done.

Soon all fifteen boats were lined up along the ship's side, waiting to be loaded, and the ship looked huge to me. It was an old wooden freighter, but she was a beauty to me. Right at once I wished I could be a crew member in her. Over the rail leaned the ship's mate, who called out his greeting. He was well known to the village people, who had seen him for many years. With him was the ship's nurse, who had been in the village caring for the whole village of Savoonga all by herself. We were all glad to see her, and exchanged greetings with her.

The work had begun already, and things seemed to go very quickly. The crew lowered a pile of boards of cargo into the first boat. On and on to the next boat, and then it was our turn—as quick as that. At the next instant I heard the man behind the rail shout, "Heads up!" I caught sight of a pile board full of boxes overhead and jerked a bit, jumping out of the way. How dangerous it looked, and I was clumsy, not knowing exactly what to do and how to handle things, being new to this kind of work. It was a new experience, interesting and exciting to me, and I was sure I liked it, although I worried a bit that the cable or boom of the donkey might snap and kill us all, wrecking the little whaleboat, which looked dwarfed when side by side with the *North Star*.

My biggest worry was that Peter, the bully, might make fun of my being clumsy and awkward in the work. After we were loaded to the full, the motor was started and around the ship we went toward the shore. Some boats already were nosed up onto the gravel beach and unloading. It was an interesting sight. The people running up and down the beach making piles of boxes here and there were something that reminded me of the school story book about ants and their hills, a swarm of them.

As soon as the boat's bow hit the beach, somebody threw the bow line to the waiting men, and it was caught and held tight. Hand to hand the load went from the boat to the shore so fast, with people laughing and talking and the surf rocking the boat, all of which rather confused me and made my worry deeper. Very soon the boat was empty. The bow line was pulled in and the boat was turned around with a big oar at the stern and the motor started. I sat down on a seat to rest my already sore back. At the same time with a corner of my eye I caught sight of Peter Naciknak.

"Oh dear," I thought, and I stayed put.

He called me and I said, "Huh?" shyly, to be sure, turning my head.

Then he asked me, "Is this the first time you ever worked on a boat?"

I told him it was—calmly and normally, not sternly, in a cross or smirking way.

"So I see that it is all new to you," he said.

"Yes, it is the very first time, and I don't seem to know exactly what to do or how to do things, and things happen and go on so swiftly I can't keep up with the rest of you boys," I told him.

Then he began to tell me about this and that, what to expect and how to do things. "As for being quick, you'll get used to the speed. We all do."

I was surely surprised and relieved about his behavior and manner. He didn't seem to be the same person. This was his real self, and I was glad. "Next time, keep close to me and I will help you the best I can," he offered.

I told him, "I will indeed be very glad to do that."

As we went around the stern of the *North Star* he told me, "Keep your eyes wide open and stay alert all the time."

We took our place at the end of a line of whaleboats alongside the ship, and Melvin and I hung on to the line at the side of the boat, still sitting on the seat next to Peter. He told me more about the job we were to do. He said what we were handling now was the best and easiest cargo to handle. The harder cargo would be the barrels of oil and gasoline. The lumber would be all right, but hard to place in the boat. And the worst and dirtiest would be the coal. I was already familiar with that work on the beach before. "So it won't be very different working with the different kinds of cargo in the boat from on the beach, eh?" I asked.

"Yes, it's all the same thing," he said.

As we got our load of cargo, I stuck around with Peter and he instructed me by means of our own signal language. That wasn't as hard as I thought after I was told about this and that, and had someone telling me how to do things. Now everything was within my liking.

On our way back to the shore we—Peter and I—lay on large crates, and talked some more. He told me that I did better this time and I felt more relaxed and knew my way around a little better.

Looking at his watch, he told me after one more trip to the ship we would have an hour for supper. I thought even that time went quickly. He told me to bring a thermos bottle of hot tea or coffee because we were to work until midnight. I said I would, and he said he would do the same, so that we would have refreshment between now and meal time.

On the next trip the whaleboat was pulled up and others had pulled theirs already on the shore, except for a few more still out at the ship. We waited for them to help pull up their boats. Then each boat was unloaded quicker than ever and pulled up on shore, and we all went home.

Dinner tasted just as usual, except Kakianak had brought some goodies from the store—just plain pilot bread, apples, oranges, a few crackerjacks and candy bars, but they were something special to us, really after dinner treats. Going without anything like such things for nearly a year made them taste very good.

The hour was nearly up even before I had had a minute to sit down to rest. I had to go right away. Mother had my thermos bottle ready, as well as Dad's, and she had buttered a few pilot breads and had me stick a couple of candy bars in my pocket.

The sun was low when I got to the north shore and none of my crew was there. There were some men flat on their backs, waiting for others. I was very glad to have a few minutes to ease off before my crew would come. After putting away my thermos bottle, I dropped onto the gravel on my stomach at the side of our boat. A while later the crew came and we were on again. The water was deep blue now, and a light south wind could be felt.

Work was resumed and I was having fun, since I was used to it now. It wasn't so hard after all, and I wondered why the older men kept saying, "Easy, take it easy; not so hard." I thought my way was the way to do the job, not knowing I was overdoing it, forgetting how long the work was to be. I was to find out soon—still my foolishness was getting the best of me.

Before the sun sank, the sky darkened, and the wind got stronger. We had to use our rain gear to protect us from spray, since now the waves were larger.

The next time we took our place alongside the ship, Peter said that it was 9 o'clock, which meant our coffee time. We poured cups for others, then had ours. It certainly refreshed me a great deal. As we were drinking our coffee, the men exclaimed, "Oh, no!" or something like that. I turned around to see what was wrong and caught sight of a sling full of sacks of coal being lowered into a whaleboat. I knew what that meant—a tough, dirty job.

Handling our first load of the black stuff went all right with me. A sack weighing a hundred pounds wasn't too hard to throw around, but our second trip seemed different. Each sack felt like it had lead in it rather than coal. To make the things worse, it began to rain and the wind was blowing in squalls. It blew the coal dust into our nose, eyes, and mouths and it stuck to our wet faces, darkening us so that we looked as funny as could be. When the funny face was on me, I didn't want to be laughed at.

At midnight a man from the ship announced quitting time for the day—a welcome thing to hear. Every boat headed for shore, unloaded, and I was really glad we didn't have to take another boatful of dirty coal. On the way to the shore the water was gray, with white caps on every wave. Each wave lifted the bow of the whaleboat, and held it clear out of the water. The bow would be in the midair for a few seconds and then violently come down with a splash, sometimes partly going under the next wave. Spray poured in and we had to fight salt water out of our eyes. This would have been fun and thrilling if I hadn't been so worn out. At least I was too tired to mind anything, and I was cold. Even though I had my raincoat and a pair of hip boots on, I was soaked through.

It wasn't very dark, even though it was midnight. We could clearly make out the white whaleboats being pulled up out of the surf by the tractor, and the quick-moving men on the beach. The surf was high, so with a few other boats we had to wait for our turn to the beach. The boats were pulled in two at a time, one by the tractor with the help of one man besides the crew, and the other by a group of men on the shore. I wished the tractor would pull in our boat for us. It didn't really make much difference which way, and, in fact, the men were doing better than the tractor, but I thought it was greater fun letting the machines do the job.

All the while our motor was running very low with the

bow toward the wind and strong current, so we hardly moved, and were even still at times. With this arrangement or calculation, our captain had our boat right where he wanted to bring it ashore when our turn came. At a fixed time the men on the beach signaled us to come in when the surf was not so high. The motor was turned up, and then cut off as soon as the bow hit the gravel and pulled out of its hole before it touched the bottom. At the same time the crew at the bow threw in the line, which was caught by the shoremen. They gave it a tug, with the crew jumping out on the gravel to help. Still others, boys, placed pieces of lumber down on the gravel for the keel of the boat to run over. Quick as that the boat was high on the beach.

While our captain saw to things, we ran to help others with boats. Soon all the boats were in, and was I glad! At the same time I realized how tired I was and began to feel my head aching, muscles getting sore, nose and throat tighten, and a sniffle in my nose. I knew what that meant—I was catching cold. Ugh!

I dragged myself home as the wind whipped rain against me. Some boys ran past me and I wondered if they ever got tired like I did. Women stopped running to walk with me and make fun of my dirty face. I wasn't a bit amused, but I didn't get mad at them. I felt too awful to do either. I just complained about the weather a bit and dragged myself home. Kakianak caught up with me and asked me if I was going to the store. I said, "No, I'm going home."

"Then do you have anything in your mind I could get for tonight?" he asked.

I replied, "Well, just get what you want and I'll like that."

I wasn't interested in anything except rest and sleep. I was trying to hide my feelings, partly because of my own pride, but also to please Dad, since he always wanted me to be tough. I strived to be.

At home Mother was up. I pulled off my wet raingear and when I came in she had the bedding spread and some hot water ready. She took one look at me and said, "You poor thing. Wash up," pouring hot water into the basin.

I said, "Don't go feeling sorry for me; and I don't want

to wash. Remember, I'm tough." I felt more pride once I was in a warm room out of the wind and rain.

Then she looked a bit stern and said, "All right; you are not going back to work with that dirty face."

I said, "We are quitting for the day."

"Poor tough boy—you won't get into bed until you wash."

I said no more and washed. The warm water felt so good. She asked me if she could fix me something hot as I dried myself with a towel.

I said, "No, I'll wait for Dad."

"Where is he?" she wanted to know.

"He went to the store for things," I told her.

"You've caught cold," she said, noticing my hoarse voice. "I'll put your feet in the hot water," she added as she filled the basin.

"She thinks I'm a sissy, but . . ." I thought. I put my feet in. That, too, felt good. I very well knew I was not as tough as I said I was. That was mostly done because Kakianak was a hard little man. So I thought if he noticed I got a cold, he wouldn't be too rough or call me names, like "sissy" or "old woman."

Of course Kakianak was not being cruel or wicked. He had a good reason for treating me that way; he wanted me to develop in physical strength and harden up, so I could meet with ease the hardships I would have to face in the future as a man. That was the same with everybody, sometimes even with the girls.

Kakianak came in with an armful of things. He caught sight of me right away and asked, "What's the matter? Caught cold?"

I told him I had. Then he said that we must rest soon, because he had caught cold, too.

Mother woke us up in the morning and Dad was up, too. I felt terrible with a cold. Kakianak said that I didn't have to go to work if I was sick. I told him I would be all right. I thought that I would feel better later that morning.

Just as we were through with breakfast, Naciknak came in and told us that the rain had stopped and the wind had subsided, so the lightering would be resumed at 8 o'clock.

I told him I would be at the north shore before that time.

I rolled up my rain coat and went out. Sure enough, it wasn't raining, and the wind was low from the south, but the fog had set it.

As I thought, I felt much better after breakfast. I walked to the north shore. Some of the captains were there. They gave me a compliment, saying that Naciknak talked a lot about me and said he was lucky to have me for a crewman. Compliments always make me feel funny and embarrassed, so I tried to dodge them by saying that I was lucky to have Naciknak for a captain, and I did mean what I said. He and others were very nice to work with.

At the north shore I stopped short and gazed at the group of whaleboats. I couldn't tell which one was my captain's. The boats looked alike. I wished that I had waited for one of the crew. Then I decided to ask one of the men, but then changed my mind. If I asked, they would tease me for sure.

As I stood there trying to think of what to do, somebody walked up behind me. When I turned around, I was glad. He was one of the crew of our boat. Then he asked if I was waiting for somebody. I asked which one was our boat.

"There it is," he said, as he pointed to the boat right in front of me, laughing, and I laughed with him, not minding being teased by him.

We untied the canvas covering. We were rolling it up when the rest of the crew arrived. Then the beach was lively once more. The boats were soon in the water and so were we.

The water was smoother and the boats were already alongside the ship while they were lowering away sling after sling of coal into the whaleboats. The men were merrily chattering while working, in spite of knowing in the back of their minds that they all disliked handling the coal.

The beach was alive with shoremen hurrying here and there. Bunches of boxes and piles of sacks of flour and sugar were being uncovered and loaded onto the sledge drawn by the tractor, while the girls and women giggled as they watched or worked. The children seemed to be in everybody's way having their fun. It was an occasion that the people looked forward to every year. It was a time of being merry, like a holiday, and the people make a celebration of it rather than just a time of work, like they do of just about everything.

I learned something else in this operation, something more than just how the operation is performed. A few trips back and forth to the ship and shore loaded with cargos of coal made a clown out of me. Again my face was smeared all over with black coal dust. People began to make fun of me again, but this time instead of biting back, I just hopped on and laughed and went along with the fun, and I wasn't the only laughingstock. Everyone was one, and the man on the bow, for example, would turn around making a face every time so that he looked funnier than he really was. Even our captain was amused and got his share of the fun. He said he had the best crew in the whole village.

On the beach I had more fun amusing the children now that I didn't mind being a clown, and I made faces at them. So every time we beached, they came running to hold the bow line while we unloaded and had a cartoon show.

By the time we had our coffee from the thermos bottles, the water was nearly glassy. Only ripples could be seen, and the fog had lifted. The coal was all ashore. The next cargo was barrels of oil and gasoline. Peter told me it was going to be much heavier to handle than coal, but cleaner. It would be good to change from the dirty cargo.

The cargo of barrels began. Four barrels to a boat. We had ours. I got hold of the slings with the other men and placed them at proper places in the boat, as I was told to do. While the other men guided one end of the barrel to the bottom, I guided the end to me on the seats. They explained that we did this—so they would be easier to tip up to attach a line to them at the beach.

Naciknak called me to him, "Come over here; let the older men handle that. It is too heavy and dangerous for you."

I was turning about to say that I was man enough to do that, but bit back my words. He was the captain and his orders had to be obeyed by the crewmen if they wanted to be good members. My father had often told me that.

I went to the stern as told to do. Then he gave me a short

375

lecture explaining that my safety was his responsibility. And so I understood what he meant. He was not belittling or underestimating me at all. Just doing his duty.

Then he assigned me to cleaning the boat and keeping the anchor for him. I was surprised at how hard handling the anchor was. As we approached the beach I had to drop it overboard at his signal and pay out the line. After nosing onto the gravel he watched the surf. When it was high, the boat had to be out at a distance away from the breaking surf, so the boat wouldn't ship water and we wouldn't be drenched with spray. In order to be out some distance, the men hanging onto the boat line on the beach had to pay out the bow line, while I pulled in the cable or anchor line. Then when the low surf came, I payed out the line while the men on shore pulled us in by the bow line. Then the lines attached to barrels would be thrown to the waiting men. One man heaved the barrels overboard and they were pulled up onto the beach, where the tractor took over and hauled them away.

Then we would go back for some more. I had to pull in the anchor, coiling the line carefully so it wouldn't kink or get caught on something when payed out. I got wet from the dripping rope. On the trip back to the ship I did washing (to get the salt off), throwing bucketfuls of water into the boat, and while waiting alongside the ship, I pumped the water out with a homemade wooden pump, which is slow and tedious and tiresome.

Before noon all the cargo was ashore, so farewells were exchanged and the *North Star* weighed anchor. With three blasts of her whistle she sailed away.

After the boats were taken care of, I went to the store and asked for some sort of job. They were short of men to work at loading and unloading the tractor sledge. I applied for that right away, and was told to be at the store at 1 o'clock.

I was pleased and ran home for lunch and to break the news that I'd got a job. I found Kakianak had a job at the store, too, piling boxes, and so had my sister and my mother—they were to work somewhere for a day.

After lunch I ran to the store and was told to wait for the

other workers. The driver was to find us there at the store when he was ready. There were two other boys and one adult, making four of us besides the driver.

We rode on the sled to the north shore. I was looking at the driver up ahead, wistfully, wishing that I could get a try at driving the tractor. It would be a whale of a lot of fun, for sure. I itched to riddle the driver, who was our teacher, with questions. But no soap for me. I couldn't ask him anything; the machine made a loud noise and we were too busy.

While we made our way over to the north shore, other children ran after us trying to hitch a ride. It was too bad that we had to keep them off, as we were required to do so for their safety. If only I had been on my own I would have let them on, thinking a sledge-load of these chattering, giggling kids would be lots of fun to have.

We passed people walking by with boxes strapped to their backs. That included women and children. It was the job I had used to do every year. It was hard, but the pay was small—about three cents for a twenty-five pound box taken from north shore to the store, four cents for a fifty-pound sack of flour, eight cents for a hundred pounds. I caught sight of my mother and sister doing that among the women, with my two brothers running along behind. Poor Mother, she had a box strapped to her back as well as my little sister on her shoulders.

The driver stopped with the sledge right alongside a pile of cargo. A man came up and told us to load the heavy and large boxes—so as to save the lighter and smaller ones for the women. We did so.

When we got through loading, our teacher took me to one side and said, "When I stop the tractor, call the people carrying things to come to the sled and have a ride. And when I stop again outside the village, have them get off. Do you understand?"

I replied, "Yes, sir!"

I saw that he was as sorry as I was for the people making beasts of burden of themselves. He had done that before. It was great act of kindness toward the people, but to the store . . . I didn't know.

As he said, he stopped and I waved to them to come. Very happily they did so. Then just outside the village he stopped again to let off our passengers. We proceeded to the store and unloaded. We kept that up, stopping for dinner at 6 o'clock. We were to work until midnight, then the other shift of men were to work with another driver.

My Mother quit at dinner time, but my sister kept up until the light stuff was all gone, and by midnight only part of the coal and barrels remained.

It had been calm and no rain. Now a new wind was beginning to blow from the north, a good wind for us.

At midnight I signed out and went home. Now I was very much worn out again, and my cold was worse than ever. At home I didn't care what anybody called me, or thought. I just washed carelessly, had a bite to eat and drink, and then I dropped on a mat to sleep.

In the morning when somebody woke me up it was late, everybody was up and had had breakfast. So they let me have my coffee in bed—this time no one minded my doing that. I wondered what was going on. Later my mother told me that she and my father thought I must have overworked, and were worried that I might be sick. So that was that. I felt numb and my muscles were sore, but I would be all right when I limbered up. It always happened that way after hard work of several days.

Kakianak brought in the news that the drums would be hauled in before noon and the workers would be paid in the evening or next morning. It was the most pleasant part of the occasion.

The north wind was blowing hard. Kakianak said it would blow for three days and would be calm on the fourth, then we would leave for our camp. That was exciting, indeed.

He asked how I felt. I told him I was all right. Then he said, "There are no more jobs in the store, so you better take it easy today. You have been working hard enough."

I thought, "Is he going to soften up on me now? Did he see that I'm strong enough and really tough?" But I thought wrong, as I was to find out later.

During the day I didn't do much. I went to the store and

378

watched the storemen open boxes. It was fun to watch them as they opened box after box of fine, new things. Like a window shopper, I thought of buying this and that, until I had a long list in my mind. Then when they unpacked new shotguns and rifles, I dropped everything out of my mind like hot bricks, and drooled over those things. How beautiful they looked! Then they put them on racks.

When finally they had things lined up, they announced, "It's pay time." I ran out the door and home to tell my father what I had seen and that it was pay time. When I got home I asked him if I could spend my pay on buying a rifle and a shotgun.

He looked sorry, but amused. Then he said, "That's too bad; you can't"

I was surprised and undoubtedly disappointed, and asked, "Why? I earned the money, didn't I?"

He said, "You earned the money, that's right. But those things cost too much."

"Then will you give me some of your pay?" I begged.

He replied, "I would, but still wouldn't do either, because it wouldn't be enough for even one of them."

Well, I discarded the idea and maybe cursed the world for my disappointment.

Kakianak comforted me, saying that I still had my .22 and my .28 gauge shotgun, and they both shot straight and true. That was true, of course, but they were very old.

Anyway, it was pay time and my sister and Mother were to do their shopping first, so they went to the store. Kakianak and I were to do the rest of the shopping the next day. We stayed in the house to mind the children. I was caring for Lucy, and I always found time to give her my affection. Everything would go fine unless she cried. Then I wouldn't know what to do—just let her wail or make her stop, and I wouldn't know how.

Ada and Ann came in after some time with armloads of their brand-new things—pots, pans, cloth for new snowshirts, and goodies for the children.

Next day my father and I went shopping. I had something to be proud of. The storekeeper showed us the amount of our pay. Mine was the same amount as my father's! I had got a man's rate of pay! (Later I found out that was Kazighia's doing. He worked it out that I got paid at that rate, knowing we were going to need money for groceries for camp.)

We started buying things. My father made sure we got enough ammunition, as it was the most needed thing in a camp. I asked for five boxes of 50 .22 caliber shells, but my father said it wasn't enough. I said then a carton of ten boxes. He said, "Make it two, if you like shooting." That was plenty for me. Then he got several boxes of shotgun shells and about twenty for his rifle. I thought we really were going to do some shooting. The rest of the things we got were two sacks of flour, a sack of sugar, gun powder, shots, and primers for our shotgun, a barrel of gasoline, some motor oil, kerosene, and fruits and clothing for the children. And I hadn't forgotten to buy some small things for the old folks, like cigars for Aiyaksaq, some things for his wife, and so on.

So I thought we had been pretty well paid. In fact, we had to use wheelbarrows to take our things home.

The next couple of days we were busy packing. During our packing Aiyaksaq came over with some boxes of rifle shells. I won't forget that. He had one for the 25-35, and two for the .22 caliber. He said, as he handed me the one for the big rifle, "This is for you to get me a young mukluk skin to use for harnesses," and as he handed me the others, "and these are for getting squirrels so you can bring some for my wife."

I thanked him and told him I would bring some if I was lucky enough to shoot them. I was pleased.

Other people came in with gifts of some needed things. Also David Akoak—he had a box for me that he told me not to open until I was at Southwest Cape.

The packing was done and all ready to be taken down to the beach when it was calm enough to go—in either night or day, my father said.

The next day after we had packed up it turned out to be very clear and calm. Lake Troutman was like a huge mirror. Just the day for a skin boat trip!

# Part Three

# Self and Society

Here we have a life story; or, at least, a portion of that stream of events we call a "life." Can something of value be accomplished now by taking it apart, looking at discrete pieces, using it as a series of data that have other contributions beyond the sheer telling of what it was like to be an Eskimo boy growing up on St. Lawrence Island during the middle years of the twentieth century? In my view it can, and my purpose in this section is briefly to translate these data into some of the concepts in a behavioral science framework, in so doing by no means, obviously, exhausting the range of interpretive possibilities.

One of the central processes studied in "culture and personality" research or psychological anthropology is the manner in which those phenomena we call values, beliefs, orientations, norms, role expectations, and so forth, are built into and accepted by individual members of a human group. This is the familiar process of "socialization" (some would prefer "enculturation," but in my view that is word quibbling). However, simply to put a word to the process does not dissolve away its problematic character; there is nothing straightforward and simple about the manner in which particular kinds of personalities are forged out of a particular sociocultural background. On the contrary, given the complexity of variables entering into the structuring of a human personality, it becomes an issue for detailed empirical investigation of the way such structuring comes about. And one of the important features is that it extends over time; it is not, *mirabile dictu,* created at one stroke. It is a process, a dialectic that evolves and unfolds, an emergent aspect of the daily encounters of a person with the experiences that come his way throughout life, although the early years are especially critical. Allport's comment on personality suggests the kind of concept I am referring to: "personality is less a finished product than a transitive process" ( 1955, p. 19).

If, then, "socialization" is a process that necessarily occurs over time and in a context of public social events, we can turn to a life history and use the concrete details presented in it for illustrating some of the dimensions of that process. Through the eyes of a person who lived them, can we not see the many ways in which "culture" or "society" interacts with an evolving human being, presenting daily dilemmas not only of conflict, decision, and threat but also of pleasure, achievement, and success? With behavioral detail, can we not close that synapse between "person" and "group" and in so doing convey a sense of the creative dimensions of what we call "socialization"?

Life histories are notoriously difficult to analyze. One reason is their length—an overabundance of data. Paradoxically, there is usually also an insufficiency of other types of observations that might be critical in resolving a given theoretical issue. Given these caveats, however, to the extent that Nathan's life history provides the materials for such a purpose, my comments in this section are directed at illustrating one paradigm in which life history materials may be used more fully in studies of human behavior, one way in which they can help throw light into the "black box" of socialization, help to answer the question of how, in fact— i.e., in terms of psychodynamic processes—does it come about that a person becomes the kind of adult he turns out to be at a given point in time?*

Of course no society ever directly interacts with a person. "Society" is a high order abstraction, a shorthand way of talking about patterned behavioral relations among a group of people over time. Other concepts than "society" are better honed to the task of analyzing the interface between a person and the social aspects of his environment. An intervening, mediating kind of concept is needed, and this "broker" function is served for the most part by the familiar concept of role.

"Role" is the most immediate expression of the connection of the "society" with the person; it is the operative aspect, so to speak, of such higher-order conceptions as "institution" or "social structure." The closer one gets to actual behavioral experience the more apparent it is that large segments and

---

* An earlier sketch of such a paradigm using some of the same life history data can be found in Hughes (1963).

wide reaches of a person's actions are channeled by culturally designated tasks and privileges appropriate to persons in particular social categories—categories either voluntarily assumed or ascribed on the basis of biological and behavioral criteria. In an analogic sense, then, the concept of role may be seen as the linking device, the primary transducer between the inner psychological world of the person and the outer universe of group structures (a transducer in physics being a device actuated by power from one system and supplying power to a second system). In such a way, through roles, the psychobiological energy of persons is channeled into the social arena; and, in reciprocal fashion, roles are the channels by which much of the impact of the sociocultural environment is made on the evolving life of the person.

Behavior programmed by role expectations, then, provides a range of psychodynamic outcomes (affection, dependence, threat, aggression-release, identification, conflict, a sense of mastery), for it selectively exposes persons to particular types of experiences; and persons who are completely "role-less" are nowhere to be found in human social reality, although the degree of clarity and consensus regarding behavioral expressions of any given role may well vary through time and circumstances. Spiro (1961) and Yinger (1965), among others, have discussed roles in this manner, as outlining behavioral arenas in which much of the "psychodynamic work" of the society and, conversely, much of the "social work" of the personality are accomplished. In short, through a psychodynamically sensitive and socially relevant use of the concept of "role," the modern behavioral science analogue of the Cartesian dilemma—how to link person and society—is resolved.

Spiro has put the nub of the problem succinctly. Discussing interrelations of personality, a cultural system, and the social system, he has raised the central question which here will be explored with data from Nathan Kakianak's life story:

How do human societies get their members to behave in conformity with cultural norms? Or, alternatively, how do they induce their members to perform culturally prescribed roles?

It is at this juncture in the analysis that the concept of personality becomes salient for the understanding of human social systems, for it is in the concept of *role* that personality and social systems intersect. If personality is viewed as an organized system of motivational tendencies, then it may be said to consist, among other things, of needs and drives. Since modes of drive-reduction and need-satisfaction in man must be learned one of the functions of personality is the promotion of physical survival, interpersonal adjustment, and intrapersonal integration by organizing behavior for the reduction of its drives and the satisfaction of its needs. If some of these needs can then be satisfied by means of culturally prescribed behavior—if, that is, social roles are capable of satisfying personality needs—these needs may serve to motivate the performance of the roles. But if social systems can function only if their constituent roles are performed, then, in motivating the performance of roles, personality not only serves its own functions but it becomes a crucial variable in the functioning of social systems as well. (1961, p. 100)

One could sketch in the total web of culturally structured roles for social behavior which converged upon Nathan Kakianak in the years covered by the life history. So extensive an analysis is not possible here, however, and my focus will be on three specific roles taken from three major classes of roles or institutional areas: the role of apprentice hunter; the role of schoolboy; and the role of son (to a father, rather than to a mother, for example). These particular roles are chosen because they represent aspects of the sociocultural environment which structure major areas of the life space, not only for the subject of this life history but for many others in the community as well. In fact, those three roles were invariant points of reference with which all young boys at that time had to deal and come to terms, assimilating the specific demands, requirements, and obstacles of those roles into their personalities with whatever rationalizations, defenses, and interpretations they found necessary.

There are other reasons for concentrating on these particular roles out of the total repertory of roles in the society. For one thing, each of them is a key role in a highly significant institutional area. The role of son exemplifies one of the central social relationships in the kinship system. The role of apprentice hunter, of course, is rooted in the primary subsistence activity of the traditional economic system (and typically, as in this case, is closely related to the role of son, although analytically separable). And, finally, the role of schoolboy reflects recognition of this society's need to adapt to the world of new institutional demands coming from the mainland.

Furthermore, each of these three roles is relatively sharply defined; behavioral boundaries are clear and the scope of each firmly outlined in a context of cultural specifications. Explicit ethical and normative edicts structure the role of "son," for example, providing a series of "do's" and "don'ts" applicable to various situations (which Nathan himself often comments on in the life story). And with the role of hunter, there are again relatively clear and comprehensive rules outlining the patterns of behavior expected of the would-be incumbent of the role, whether these expectations be of a sheer technological nature or more concerned with interpersonal conduct in such a context (e.g., the sharing of animal flesh if there has been only one successful hunter out on the ice that day).

The role of schoolboy is sharply structured in a different way. While the ostensible aim of the role is rather diffuse—to become "educated" through acquiring certain symbolic skills—the patterns of behavior implicated by performance of this role are clear and unequivocal. The person must attend school, must clearly set apart of each day, and most days of most weeks during the year, to the tasks of role performance. Such requirements are clearly in structural conflict with those of apprentice hunter, a conflict that Nathan manages partially to resolve at the personality level with the aid of a clever suggestion by his sympathetic teacher.

These three roles, then, representing only some of the roles composing the structure of this society, have been chosen because of their saliency for the group as a whole as well as for Nathan's personality. In such a light, they can well serve as points of entry into exploring something of the growth of Nathan's socially structured sense of self during the first fifteen years of his life.

The role of hunter in St. Lawrence Island Eskimo society may be taken as the most important aspects of the complex of technological activities traditionally demanded of the adult male. Without doubt it was the most dramatic and critical feature of the composite role of "general provider," a task orientation that included a wide range of skills: bird netting, fishing, fox trapping, and collecting, in addition to the several different techniques for hunting maritime mammals (seals, walruses, whales, sea lions, polar bears). Dog teaming and dog care were also traditional required skills. More recently other abilities were also required, such as as those of maintaining the outboard motor, constructing or repairing a boat or house, and using firearms and other weapons of the hunt. And also functionally tied in with the hunter's role (through providing money for equipment) and directly expressive of the role of "provider" has been wage work or other cash-earning activity, such as ivory carving, trapping, or helping unload supply vessels.

All these activities, however, were simple differentially emphasized facets of the array of technological activities which were built upon the capabilities of a single mature male. None was, in itself, the core of a specialized, full-time occupational role, except in rare instances (such as ivory carver in more recent times for those men unable or disinclined to hunt). Thus, in the following discussion it is primarily the hunter's role that will be referred to in representing this complex, although occasional examples from other technological areas will also be given.

The role of hunter also demanded qualities other than those of sheer technical or craft proficiency, as can be inferred from the life history. Involved first of all was a perspicacious turn of mind, a trained attentiveness to small details of land form, winds, ocean currents, clouds, and ice and the implications of such small details under changing circumstances. It needed a hardened body trained to endure long periods of punishing effort and lack of water, food, or rest. It demanded, perhaps above all, a high level of tolerance for frustration, the will and determination to push one's body beyond the point of fatigue and disappointment, the ego strength to control the impulse to retreat from cold and discouragement and stay with the appointed task. The role also demanded sustained courage in facing danger and physical challenge to life under the frequently treacherous ice conditions or threat of animal reprisal. In the normal course of psychosocial maturing, such courage would soon be masked by a calculatedly indifferent or fatalistic attitude which belied its depth and pervasiveness in the personality of the skilled and accomplished hunter.

Nathan's first inkling of what is involved in the role of hunter comes from his early life, and especially from observations of his father's activities. Often he seeks Kakianak and the other men of the small settlement preparing their weapons and gear, going out onto the sea, and returning home tired and cold, often without meat. He does not need to be told the importance of what his father does, for even as a young child he sees the direct connection between his father's activity and his own well-being, and that of the rest of the family. What Kakianak does therefore at least subliminally makes sense to Nathan in terms of the most basic gratifications—having food in the stomach, heat and light in the house, and skins for warm clothing; and the whole realm of experiences represented by his father's principal activities thus soon becomes directly linked with that of Nathan's own basic needs. This is especially emphasized in times of scarcity—and these are frequent in his life. As expressed in one graphic passage (p. 29), anxiety and fear of disaster are constant background features of life, the stressful implications of which are not lost on even a young child: "Not much hunting and lots of bad weather. Not much game, and during the long winter storms we ran out of fuel (seal oil), food, and almost everything. . . . What sad days we spent—no playing in or out-of-doors, because of darkness indoors and storm outdoors, and a wild one, too."

In such a context the child can also grasp the relationship between personal effort and social reward and approval. Nathan begins early to participate in the rejoicing and admiration for the hunter which follows a successful pursuit and kill; and, perhaps only dimly sketched at first, he forms an image of the prestige value and personal satisfaction of the role of skilled hunter. Something of this feeling becomes crystallized when he makes his first kill of an animal or catches his first birds; in accordance with tradition, he gives such first kills to the oldest member of his family, and the praise he gets both for his generosity and his accomplishment on such occasions marks important milestones in his psycho-social development.

He often sees how pleased the activities of his father make his mother and (perhaps reflecting one aspect of the competition between these two males who have strong ties to the same woman) wants to have the opportunity to do the same and receive admiration and praise from his mother. In one particular passage (p. 137) he comments on this feature as well as on how proud it makes him to be the focus of attention from his peers for his competence and skill:

> Once again it was a happy moment for our family. It made me happy to see Mom's happy face when she saw the birds and the happy voices coming from my brothers.
> In the morning Mom passed out my catch to the old folks, and my friends came over to see me. I had lots to tell about my hunt, and my friends were all pleased to hear my story. And I felt proud. We played with the bird catching pole and net, taking turns. One of us threw tin cans and one of us caught them with the pole and net. I proudly showed my friends how it is done.

Indeed, in the area of subsistence in Eskimo society, "achieve-ment needs" and an aggressive, enterprising disposition are given free rein, although they are muted in other spheres (e.g., in many contexts of interpersonal relations).

The incident of Nathan's picking up the rifle and shooting the seal when he can hardly lift the weapon (in Chapter 1) is illustrative of his eagerness to become fully involved in such prestige-giving activity. Even on those occasions when Kakianak has not taken young Nathan with him on the hunt, Nathan is preoccupied with the wish to be a companion to his father in the danger and excitement. Though unhappy about being left behind, at one point he takes consolation from being able to watch what happens through a telescope—"There was not a bit of my hard feelings left; just watching them was being with them" (p. 82). Often later he cajoles his father to take him along hunting, to let him have a chance to demonstrate skill and earn praise, and he repeatedly recalls his pride and sense of accomplishment after a successful hunting performance.

Over the ten or so years recounted in this autobiography, Nathan is inducted slowly and gradually into the set of technical skills required for success as a hunter, such as how to care for the equipment, or how to interpret weather signs and ice conditions accurately (as in Chapters 6, 9, or 10), and he also painstakingly learns many other features of the role through repeated trials and explicit verbal instructions. Included in such training, for example, are the assorted skills required of the dog team traveler; as Nathan notes in one passage when he and his father were traveling to their camp, Kakianak "pointed out the way we were to take and told me the names of the places" (p. 72). Or in regard to another aspect of the role, bird snaring: "He told me to watch him closely. Of course I did, because this type of bird hunting was very new to me, and I wanted to know how it was done" (p. 128). And when he at last is asked to join a boat crew as a regular member, he feels that he has become a man, a fully contributing member of his society. Rested and warmed at home after the first day of hunting with his boat companions, he recalls his pride in achievement and acceptance (p. 255): "Around the wooden eating platter I was proud and self-satisfied to tell the good hunting story with my Dad to the happy family. Mom was pleased with me for becoming a real help in providing for the family."

Not the least important aspect of preparation for this role is the strengthening of body and character required. In frequent passages his father admonishes him to get enough sleep and build up his endurance. In several episodes he is cautioned against impatience and urged to adopt an attitude of acceptance when he gets nothing for his efforts or when weather and natural conditions make it impossible to hunt.

Nathan does not easily acquire such stoicism in the face of pain and hurt. When he falls and injures his leg on rocks, cries, and is teased by his companions, he notes with a self-chastisement, "I felt ashamed and sort of mad and stopped crying" (p. 52); later (in Chapter 10) he recalls a particularly cold and frustrating hunting experience in which he receives more instruction and admonition from his father and another hunter to bear up under the trying conditions of the hunt, and with this he takes another critical step in mastering the role. This is the incident in which the older hunter deliberately chides him to make him angry and afterward tells Nathan that the reason for the teasing was to jar him out of his lethargy and discouragement and give him the energy (albeit aggressive energy) to make it back to the shore.

In another revealing passage related to the goal and image of "toughness" Nathan recalls his attempt to hide his sickness and fatigue after working to unload the ship (p. 372): "I was trying to hide my feelings, partly because of my own pride, but also to please Dad, since he always wanted me to be tough. I strived to be." But he goes on disarmingly to say, "I very well knew I was not as tough as I said I was."

In the same place he makes a similarly revealing statement of the difference between his inner feelings and their outward expression. When he comes home from helping unload the ship, tired and feeling sick, his mother notices his condition and attempts to soothe his feelings. His reaction is one of bravado: "Don't go feeling sorry for me; and I don't want to wash. Remember, I'm tough." In an aside to the reader, however, he confesses, "I felt more pride once I was in a warm room out of the wind and rain." After his mother fixes him some water to wash his feet and Nathan, somewhat reluctantly, accepts this soothing comfort, he remembers thinking to himself that there is a reason for such training—to harden his body for the rigors of later life:

"She thinks I'm a sissy, but . . . ," I thought. I put my feet in. That, too, felt good. I very well knew I was not as tough as I said I was. That was mostly done because Kakianak was a hard little man. So I thought if he noticed I got a cold, he wouldn't be too rough or call me names, like "sissy" or "old woman."

Of course Kakianak was not being cruel or wicked. He had a good reason for treating me that way; he wanted me to develop in physical strength and harden up, so I could meet with ease the hardships I would have to face in the future as a man. That was the same with everybody, sometimes even with the girls.

The hunting situation is a public arena for the exposure of ineptness as well as the demonstration of competence, and sometimes Nathan is overhasty in taking aim and misses his target. Given one of the central dimensions in his self-image (a strong ambivalence about himself, his appearance, and his capabilities), those moments of publicly demonstrated incompetence are perhaps felt even more keenly than they would be by someone else. He cannot simply shrug them off. On the contrary, such errors act as barbs to greater concentration and motivation to master the skills required. Judging from performances recounted later in the life story, they seem to have worked in that regard, culminating in his being accepted as one of them by other hunters out on the ice. He recounts this in a particularly graphic image (p. 196):

Dad had fixed the meat to the toboggan while I was having my sport, and had fixed a rope to my seal and ducks. He told me to draw my own seal. Oh! I felt proud as a person could be, with my rifle across my back and an ice tester in hand and drawing a seal. When I looked around I was surprised to see every hunter heading toward the shore. Soon we joined the rest, and there was a long line of hunters drawing their catch home.

We joined after the last hunter. Men were surprised to see me hunting. Everyone said good things to me, praising me for good hunting. I felt proud. The hunter next to us stepped aside and told my father to get in ahead. He said, "You have a young hunter to take care of. Get ahead." So we did.

So keen does Nathan become a hunter that he does not automatically follow his father's orders about necessary preparations and precautions for hunting, or refrain from acting on impulse. Sometimes when his father is away from the village he searches out other adult hunters to accompany out on the ice. The conflicts in his own mind which such initiatives bring about are searchingly portrayed in the life story itself. For example, after the first such expedition he arrives home with some freshly killed meat, only to find his father very upset about his disobeying the rules (Chapter 11). Nathan, though proud of his hunting performance, feels extremely guilty and remorseful—"I felt about to cry." But Kakianak is persuaded by Nathan's older companion that the matter can be set right and Kakianak, by a further statement of conditions, gives Nathan more subsequent independence of action but with equally greater responsibility, and appears to move Nathan further along the progression toward full manhood. In a sense, the incident represents an important *rite de passage* in the hunting role for Nathan. Kakianak admonishes: "From now on, don't go hunting or anything without letting us know about it before you go or do anything. We will let you go when we feel it's all right for you to do it." Nathan's response is one of feeling a resolution to the conflict has been achieved between demands of the two roles bearing down upon him in this instance, young hunter and dutiful son: "Now I felt real good. And they were very pleased with the meat that I'd brought home."

It is in the apprentice hunter role that Nathan has most succinctly and forcefully impressed upon him the need for obedience to direction and first begins to acquire something of a balanced and reasoned attitude toward authority, although training in this dimension of interpersonal relations and personality organization is, of course, not confined to this single role context. Insofar as his father and other adult males inducting him into the role of hunter present him with many demands (and not requests) for behavior of a particular kind, they are acting *prima facie* in a highly authoritarian manner toward him. His reaction—perhaps to some extent a reasoned, retrospective appraisal—is one in which he understands and accepts the arguments his father and others in authority present in support of their demands. At one point in an extended passage he expresses reasons for their strict training (p. 296):

I thought my parents were very wicked and cruel when they treated me roughly. But it was what I needed. All for my own good. They were trying to harden me for the future, so that I could take the hard life with ease. By now I had learned to take rough treatment, and I was not too sorry for myself anymore. But it was not easy at first. Gradually I started to be grateful for their teaching. They were sure wise, while I never thought of what I'd need in the time to come.

Such arguments are usually couched in terms dictated by the task itself, or by the need to prepare one's body or mind for the rigors of the task; it is significant that authoritarian demands are not made solely upon the basis of any inherent inequality between the two parties to the interaction. Rather, the child is assumed to be a miniature adult, one whose rational powers are latent and await only proper tutelage and grooming to mature. In this light, therefore, it is appropriate not simply to give a firm sense of direction for the behavior but also to present the observable reasons for the demand. Many passages illustrate this note of making experience, rather than the human agent, bear the brunt of the authoritarian imperative. Such an approach seems to instill a pragmatic and relativistic perception of many areas of experience and a lower threshold for adaptability of behavior, which is so prominent a feature of Eskimo life. The hunting role-structured situations thus become primary occasions for developing techniques of flexibility in reality-testing and a generalized approach to life that will emphasize observation and the drawing of reasoned conclusions from experience. This is not to say that there are no fantasy-based or religious conceptions and practices in connection with hunting; indeed, in Eskimo religion supernaturally based premises, beliefs, and actions were extremely important. But they existed over and above the obvious, tangible action that would kill the animal and did not interfere with techniques of survival based on a clear understanding of physical forces in the environment.

As Nathan matures, his father leaves more and more of the import of his remarks to such demonstration by experience— as when after a successful day's hunt Nathan prefers to remain outside the house playing with his friends instead of getting sleep to prepare his body for the hunt, and becomes the butt of chiding remarks from his companions the next day when he falls asleep while out in the boat hunting (Chapter 13). Or, when against his parents' advice he works too hard and long in ship lightering and again recognizes, in his tired and aching muscles, the worth of their advice (Chapter 5). Although from a different context, Nathan's first experience with smoking in defiance of his father's injunctions (Chapter 7) also illustrates the point that one of Kakianak's more effective devices was to let Nathan learn directly from the punishing effects of experience and not to take up on his own shoulders alone (and through only verbal exhortation) the winning of conformity to certain patterns of social behavior.

It may be also suggested (as many have done) that the role of hunter is a peculiarly critical one in Eskimo society, providing as it does an opportunity for the winning of approval at the same time as it allows a sanctioned and legitimate behavioral expression for much displaced hostility and aggression; for the role of hunter is essentially that of a trained killer of other animals. Eskimo society is one in which the direct expression of violence against members of the in-group is sharply curbed in the normal course of interpersonal behavior. (In the past there were clear instances of fighting and hostility, especially between members of different clans; but even they were kept within some institutional boundaries to prevent an extension of the quarrel.) The extent to which personality controls over violence against others are developed at an early age can be seen in Nathan's guilt over using a board to hit the boy who had been throwing gravel at him: "I felt very wicked because of what I had done" (p. 110); and the immediate actions of other people to mend this breech in proper conduct are illustrated by the other boy's mother trying to make them friends again by employing a most uncharacteristic type of threat to prevent future incidents—that she would tie them together and beat them if they ever fought again. It is uncharacteristic in that corporal punishment is only very rarely used as a technique for inducing conformity; Nathan notes in one passage, and his experience is common, "I never received a single spank from either of my parents" (p. 140).

One may well wonder at the relatively few statements of interpersonal hostility. There is, of course, reference to teasing, and gossip is an important covert outlet for aggressive impulses. But the document is largely lacking in instances of overt violence or direct interpersonal aggression. Even Nathan's antagonisms toward, and conflicts with, his father take on a disguised form, such as in the incidents of Nathan's somewhat taunting pride in beating his father in the race between his ice skates and the dog team (Chapter 9), or his scattered references demeaning his father's ability in some activity (such as the Fourth of July races). Most likely this means that such feelings as exist are at a repressed level, rather than the total absence of such feelings.

But when attention is turned outwards toward the animal world, opportunities for projection and displacement of aggression are manifold, and, in the act of taking the life of another, of exacting to the full the implications of the aggressive impulse, an environmental resource is turned to constructive psychodynamic purposes. For Eskimo society, the fact that the animals hunted are primarily the maritime mammals—seals and walrus—is also of some considerable importance; for seals in particular are a disturbingly human-like species and the possibilities of discerning a kinship between man and animal are many. The latter fact undoubtedly lies behind a number of Eskimo religious symbolizations and activities (in which, for example, seals are believed to have souls like men and like men are invited into the house as honored guests, in this case guests who have given their flesh for the nourishment of men).[*]

In fact, the close kinship between animals and men in Eskimo cosmology is further illustrated in Nathan's story when he is greatly disturbed at the killing of the birds (Chapter 6) and thinks of himself and his family as they would feel were they the victims rather than the predators. Again, his father uses the episode to instruct Nathan in how to think about

[*] See Lantis (1947) for a full discussion of traditional Alaskan Eskimo ceremonialism at this relates to treatment of animals.

what a hunter has to do and to give him a framework of sentiments with which he can dispassionately look upon the activity to make it as little threatening as possible.

The dream that Nathan has of the seal attacking him (pp. 187-88) is undoubtedly prompted by some of these conflicts over killing, the ultimate act of aggression, and his own guilt at being involved in it. Different interpretations can be offered, of course. Perhaps in orthodox psychoanalytic terms, for example, the dream might be viewed as an expression of Nathan's unease at the onset of adolescent sexuality, of his being seized by castration anxieties when facing the problem of an emerging sexual identity. There is, after all, the image of his being attacked by a fearsome, sharp-toothed ("fangs") monster; of his holding an impotent rifle, one which at first does not work and later is ineffective in actually killing the animal and putting it out of its misery; and, finally, of the animal begging to be killed and Nathan's raising his rifle to strike the monster. Such an image suggests oral-sadistic overtones and a perception of the female genitalia as a castrating instrument—the "vagina dentata" figure found in mythology and clinical literature (see Fenichel, 1945).

In this same framework another feature that could be noted is the parenthetical identifying of the seal with his father. The possibility of repressed latent homosexual urges might enter into such an interpretation, but another line of analysis could also be implied. In a comment possibly symptomatic of the depth of repression of the hostility dimension in his relations with Kakianak, Nathan recounts an intriguing conversation between the two of them immediately following the hunting incident on the day after he has dreamed of the seal. Kakianak has said, "but I still don't trust that rifle. It's nothing but a lead spitter." To which Nathan responds to the reader, tying in his father's remark with words of the frightening animal that had been attacking him in the dream, "All my dreams came back to me botheringly ("Don't ever trust that gun; it's no good"), but I warded off these thoughts and took up the sport." Is he saying, for example, "Don't ever trust your sexual prowess"—and thereby raising the possibility of unresolved Oedipal conflict? It may also be indicative of a general atmosphere of antagonism and competition between the two of them, since it was after this incident of the dream and the hunt on the subsequent day that Nathan challenged his father to a race between the dog team and the ice skates and took great pleasure in winning the race and thereby putting his father down.

One liability to interpretations couched in these terms is the paucity of other data dealing with the area of Nathan's psychosexual development. That such data were not reported extensively in the autobiography is clear; the reasons for their relative sparseness are not so clear. Repression? Or relatively successful progression through the stages of psychosexual development? The dream may indeed be expressive of psychosexual identity and competence problems, but more data are required to establish that particular type of interpretation.

There is an alternative approach to interpretation which, in the fullness of the empirical circumstances, has much to recommend it. The incident may be viewed as a relatively undistorted dream, one rooted in a realistic fear of the dangers of the forthcoming hunt, with the dream serving to protect the sleep of the dreamer and symbols being straightforward, undisguised representations of the central actors in the drama of killing and death which is to take place on the morrow. In such a case, the basis for Nathan's guilt over the anticipated killing is projected onto the seal, in the actions of which it takes the form of hostility and aggression directed toward Nathan himself. With the seal thus attacking him and threatening his life, Nathan can consequently feel justified in trying to kill the animal. The relatively faithful portrayal in the dream of the main elements of the drama which is to ensue suggests that in this late childhood dream there is a fairly direct transposition into the dreamworld of the anxiety-arousing aspects of reality (Cf. Freud, 1949, pp. 113-21; pp. 133 ff).

That Nathan was under a good deal of tension and was excited about the forthcoming hunt is clear in his recital of events of the preceding day which led to his being allowed to go with his father: the dilatoriness in school, the daydreaming and preoccupation, the rebuke by the teacher which led to the discussion after class and ultimately the agreement about his hunting on a school day, and finally his activity that evening at home, when he buckled down with alacrity to his schoolwork, cleaned and recleaned his rifle and prepared his equipment and clothing, and was too restless to sleep soundly. Another item possibly contributing to the content and theme of the dream in this connection was the explicit statement by his father that he did not believe Nathan's account of having the teacher's permission and that he, Kakianak, would have to verify it in the morning. This note of distrust might have been projected as hostility onto the figure of the seal (the father) in the dream itself.

Contributions of these early role experiences as a hunter to Nathan's evolving sense of self-identity, then, are several and can be restated briefly. First, there is laid down a clear sense of direction so far as future activities are concerned. Behavioral alternatives are nonexistent for Nathan; the "occupational" structure is a mono-valued one, and so far as Nathan can perceive, he knows what he will be doing for the rest of his life. Moreover, the nature and character of this future pattern of behavior is clearly and forcefully illustrated in the person of Kakianak, whose relations with Nathan are of a complex nature. Nathan is thus instructed in (and inducted into) the role of hunter in the context of a warm and affectionate human relationship, and the array of sanctions and motivations for learning the basic demands of the role is more than is strictly required in technological and universalistic terms. Such psychodynamic redundancy, however, serves an important end in undergirding the motivational base to accomplish the demands of the role well in order to please the chief object of identification in general and not just in specific terms.

Nathan also achieves some balance and perspective in his approach to the world with respect to the autonomy versus conformity issue. Through immersion in the technical tasks involved in hunting, he is taught the foolishness of an unwarranted and uninformed initiative, while at the same time learning the appropriateness of self-reliance and ego-assertion in other circumstances. He develops some sense of the proper

400

play of autonomy within prescribed structure and of himself in response to authority and authoritarian demands. Moreover, the hunting role is an arena in which techniques for coping with delay of gratification and with frustration of goal—both coping strategies with wide general import in the psychological life—are constantly involved and experienced in their use an important feature of the role. The other side of the same issue, however, is also evident in the role experience—the extent to which hunting allows a sanctioned release of hostility and a meaningful and tangible focus for displacing aggressive impulses and diffuse anxieties.

In engaging in this activity, Nathan begins to acquire some understanding of the range and depth of his competence and self-confidence, of his abilities to bend the environment to his gratification—both in the physical sense of providing food and other resources and also in the social sense, of being the focus for approval, encouragement, and acceptance as a person of worth. He discovers an important resource for facilitation of pleasurable interpersonal relations, in having exciting events to speak of and tense incidents to describe—and he enjoys being the center of attention as he gathers with his schoolmates or sits around the eating platter with his family and tells of his hunting prowess.

Thus he begins, in broad terms, to become aware of some of the basic dimensions of his world and to feel a degree of familiarity with the techniques by which specific problems arising within those bounds are to be solved. At the same time, however, disturbingly in the background and existing as a parallel diversion is an image of another set of behavioral parameters, a diversion represented by the school. In the early years of his life, it was only a tangential set of concerns, one that was seen more as a "figure" in the "ground" which was basic Eskimo subsistence institutions. But as his life evolved toward the middle years of youth, the new world itself began to loom larger and present more of a challenge to the established order of things. It is therefore appropriate to look more closely at Nathan's perceptions and incorporation of aspects of that new world and the extent to which his image of self—of what he is and what he is capable of doing with reference to the world—became augmented and enriched in the schoolboy role experience.

## Role and the Self: Schoolboy

In the life story Nathan is highly insecure and lacks self-confidence in the presence of other people whom he does not know well. This character trait is graphically expressed very early in his life story, when he discusses his initial trip to Gambell village and recounts his anxiety about meeting many strangers. But it especially appears when he goes to school for the first time. Confronted with so many unfamiliar persons with wishes and wants perhaps different from his own, persons who can hurt or take things away from him, he sees the entire situation in threatening terms. He does not feel he has the ability to control events and cope with any threats directed his way. How will such other people react to him? Will they accept him on friendly terms? Will they ridicule and tease him? Will they laugh at him?

Assuming that Nathan had a typical Eskimo infancy—warm and succorant—it is by no means clear where the roots of his interpersonal insecurities of this nature lie. But perhaps an important clue can be found in the demographic characteristics of his early life; for up to that point his whole world had been the small hunting and trapping camp and he had, indeed, seen very few other human beings. Certainly later in life, after he has grown to know most of the people in his immediate environment, he is more comfortable in their presence and his insecurities take a different form. But in the beginning the school experience represents a focus for an entirely new dimension to interpersonal relations, which up to now have moved within the bounds of the familiar, the predictable, the warm and friendly. His anxieties center not only on the schoolteachers, a white man and his wife, whom Nathan does refer to as "strange," but also his classmates, none of whom he has known, and he reacts with a not unfamiliar (but perhaps exaggerated) "school phobia." So disturbed and uneasy does Nathan become at his initial school experience, in fact, that at one point he makes a firm effort to refuse to go altogether, an act effectively countered by his parents' somewhat grisly threat to crucify on the school door an old woman of whom Nathan was very fond.

Throughout the document he fears being ridiculed for his appearance or inept performance, and the behavioral setting of the school is one replete with possibilities for such ridicule, for the very basis of the institution is that of public performance and invidious evaluation of that performance. The school situation is thus a powerful arena for disparagement of self-image as much as enhancement of image; and Nathan frequently comments on his disquietude over shabby clothing or the poverty of his Christmas presents. In fact, a recurrent theme in the life story is that of worry over being poor and not having the resources to satisfy objective need and, especially, social demands. Thus, in regard to the Christmas program, Nathan expresses his keen pleasure at its coming— and at the presents he will receive—but then stops short when he remembers that he has no decent clothing (p. 62): "But at the same time I was almost just as unhappy. How was I going to get the presents for my friends and relatives? What would I wear on the day? I had no good clothing." His subsequent joy at receiving a new suit of clothes from Akoak to wear at the school's Christmas program is undisguised and taken not only as a private pleasure but also as an instrument with which he can put down in public those of his classmates who have teased him over his appearance.

But after a while this initially unfamiliar situation becomes both familiar and on the whole reassuring to Nathan. Apparently of an intellectual turn of mind, he finds an "ecological niche" of a psychosocial character which is to his liking and his talents. Indeed, his writing, whether stories of his hunting experiences or a diary of his activities, is begun at the teacher's suggestion and serves as good experience for his subsequent autobiographical writing. He does well in school; so well, in fact, that apparently he becomes one of the teacher's favorites, which thereby once again raises in him the fear of ostracism and ridicule from his classmates for having thus been singled out of the crowd and made the center of attention. Except with a small group of friends, he is not poised in withstanding the public eye, although he has a great striving for any attainment which attracts attention. This can also be seen in the recounting of his participation in the school and mission Christmas programs; he is extremely anxious over the forthcoming performances and wishes to do well to please his parents and relatives—and, no doubt, to please himself as well, for he has a keen desire to succeed in this activity as much as in schooling itself or the more traditional role of young hunter.

His schooling is frequently interrupted by his family's need to move back and forth to camp, as well as by extended periods of hunting. Such interruptions place an additional burden upon Nathan, for he falls behind his classmates in their schoolwork and advancement and is called upon to exert effort to stay with them. So his formal schooling in these early years is a thing of shreds and patches, but apparently enough base was laid in language and conceptual skills that he could develop further on his own. His initiative in this respect is illustrated by the several occasions (and no doubt there were many others) when he took work home in return for some special dispensation from his teacher, such as being allowed to go out hunting.

An important facet of his assuming and practicing the role of schoolboy was the support he received from his parents and other adults in his primary social group. Although abstractly the two institutional worlds represented by the roles of hunter and schoolboy were in conflict, in the immediate circumstance such conflict was ameliorated by the strong encouragement and reasoned discussion of the activity which Nathan got from his father. Kakianak frequently said—and Nathan accepted it—that an important feature of his preparation for the life to come was to learn basic formal educational skills as well as those of the hunter. In fact, in one passage (p. 40) he reviews in the same stream of association several of these aspects of schooling—his desire for education, the support and encouragement from his parents, and at the same time his timidity and anxiety about going to school:

Another thing I wanted to have was to learn how to read and write. But I had to have some school to learn these things, and there was no school of any kind in our camp. We would have to get our schooling in the village, and I wasn't sure I wanted to be in the village. I was used to camp life. I didn't want to be with so many strange people, even my own age. Besides I didn't know what the school was like. I didn't know if I would like it in school. But if I wanted to learn, I must have some schooling.

And my parents wanted me to learn, too, because they knew themselves it's real hard if we don't learn these three: reading, writing, and speaking English. Our parents said we (the children in the camp) must have some school somehow. And the school teachers wanted us to have some, too. They sent us old books and some school material, but without a teacher they were useless. To us the books were nothing much more than to look at the pictures in them; and the pencils and papers were nothing but to draw pictures with. But some of our parents had been in school a little bit. It was too bad, but they had lost what little they had learned, because they didn't have much time for reading and writing or they weren't too interested in that. But they gave us what they had learned—such as how to say and write the numbers and alphabet. And they did something for me by that—at least they got me started and increased my interest in learning.

It was clear to Kakianak and others of his generation (and it had been for thirty years) that the world of the white man had much to offer to the Eskimos in pursuit of their own way of life; and, further, that formal schooling was the most important way of getting the skills necessary to use the emerging set of environmental resources to the fullest. Thus, although Kakianak himself had no schooling, he saw the necessity for it and strongly encouraged Nathan to do well in it.

This clear difference between Nathan and Kakianak in the extent of their preparation for dealing with the outside world, however, did raise some threatening issues and incidents between Nathan and his father. For example, in the incident in which Nathan is called upon to use his English language skills as an interpreter, the normal guidance relationship is reversed and Nathan is put on the spot as the intermediary— again a position that makes him uncomfortable. Although he does not clearly reveal his feelings with regard to this aspect of the incident, it is probable that he enjoyed for the moment the reversal of the authoritarian roles which in other situations characterized his relationship with his father.

After the initial period of becoming adjusted to the role of schoolboy, and aside from periods when the work seems to become routine and no longer exciting to him, Nathan's chief problem is that of reconciling the conflict that exists between the demands of the schoolboy role and that of the hunter. To him, each world of tasks is highly valued socially, and each has become an important source of gratification and contribution to his self-esteem and his sense of dealing effectively with the world: "At the close of school for the day I asked our teacher to let me take my books with me for home work, but that was not the real reason why I asked. It was that I wanted to show them off to my folks" (p. 174). "The good part of it was that we were more respectable by our fellow schoolmates, and we got the praise of our parents" (p. 281). His parents' approval of his school achievements, as much as for his hunting prowess, is clearly evident throughout, and he wants to give up neither one. He does not want to stop going to school—a choice made by his cousin Ben— nor does he wish to give up hunting, which by this time has become important to him in providing a sense of release of many energies, as well as opportunities for the growth of a sense of self-confidence. So he eagerly agrees to the teacher's suggestion for bridging the structural inconsistencies which bear down upon him, that suggestion being that he write stories of his hunting experiences and thereby satisfy both sets of institutional demands. The plan succeeds for a time in resolving the conflict, although on other occasions Nathan just gives up school entirely and goes out to hunt, rationalizing his actions by recalling that, as much as schooling, hunting was also to be a part of his future life: "That was my biggest mistake, but it didn't seem so at that time, because it was more necessary for me to have more hunting experience than school. In fact, everybody needs knowledge of hunting, since it is our chief source of living. Just like a student getting into higher grades, I was taking more of the position in being a boat crew member: they thought of me as more dependable in the way that they acted toward me" (p. 310).

Working this plan out with his teacher and then for a time keeping it as a secret arrangement between the two of them also serves some of his dependency needs, insofar as the teacher seems to represent a father-surrogate training him in the new world of role responsibilities represented by schooling. In fact, the language and images Nathan used to describe the teacher are strikingly similar to those he uses in referring to his own father, a combination of firmness, gentleness, and reasoned approach to solving problems.

It is in the school situation also that for the first time Nathan becomes exposed to sustained contacts with girls outside his immediate family and other kinsmen. Indeed, the incident (p. 332) in which one such young girl somewhat forces her attentions upon him by cleaning his desk and being inquisitive about the notes he is writing—and his consequent embarrassment over the attention—may be interpreted as one of the few expressions here of an adolescent sexual interest.

Thus in more general terms the school experience has another latent effect in Nathan's social maturation: it provides an interpersonal arena in which he can develop some understanding of, and techniques for, relating to other boys and girls of his age group who are not within the system of kin-prescribed relatives that was largely instrumental in structuring his social relationships in the early years. In St. Lawrence society, even up to the time of Nathan's childhood, the primary social world in which a person moved was that of his patrilineal kinsmen and his mother's immediate family. Beyond these relatives—the "in-group" in a cogent phenomenal and social sense—the world was made up of "outsiders," not outsiders in the sense of being unknown in manner or relation to a person, but outsiders in the interpersonal dimension of not being immediately available as sources of support and assistance. The society was still strongly segmented into clan units, and kinship-based social boundaries were among the first things a child learned as he grew into social awareness. Even visits to other places, such as the trips to Savoonga described in Chapters 3 and 14, are structured within the network of mutual aid and unquestioning hospitality which was one aspect of the clan system.

In one passage (p. 60) he comments on some of these (and other) interpersonal implications of his school experience: "I was happy in school, but every day like always I wasn't too happy when the older boys were bullying around with us, and when it was a hard time in spelling and math. Even though I missed my brothers, I had fun with the other boys and girls my age—without the bother from the little ones to take care of. Almost every day there was a group of us in my home. I invited a few for lunch quite often."

For Nathan, therefore, coming as he did from an isolated camp populated only by his kinsmen, the schooling experience represented one of the first and most persistent challenges to him in requiring that he develop ways of relating to other children not connected to him by either consanguineal or affinal ties. His most common mode of relation is that of withdrawal or hesitant social contact; he exhibits none of the adventuresome, socially aggressive, and self-assured manner that apparently some of his classmates do, and he is both delighted and perhaps overly surprised whenever one of them does offer friendship and acceptance.

He slowly and gradually perceives something of the character of the new order of social relationships which is emerging in village life, an order of relationships based on more general criteria than those of clan membership and operating in terms of another set of prescriptions. The school is an important formative device for transmitting such new criteria; for in the classroom, clan affiliation no longer matters so far as the teacher is concerned (indeed, it is unlikely that he ever clearly knew very much about the clans of the village). In the classroom it is performance with respect to the new demands of the social environment that matters. And, as often comes out in the life story, Nathan's very success in meeting the new role demands sometimes creates further problems for him with respect to his nonclan peers in the playground situation and outside the defining bounds of the school. He does not like to stand out from the group and be an obvious center of attention. Indeed, his device of writing notes to the teacher serves not only as a way of developing a special relationship with this commanding adult figure but

408

also of doing so in a way that will not bring taunts and threats from his classmates. But with each demonstrated success in the classroom, he adds to his self-confidence and trust in his own capacities that to some extent goes beyond the classroom.

Thus exploration of his capacities is encouraged and his dimensions of self become greatly enlarged through the role-structured experiences provided his evolving personality in the school. He discovers another source of esteem, another arena for expressing his talents and capabilities, and perhaps most critically, other modes of dealing with and controlling some increasingly important aspects of the environment, the symbolic aspects. And, through the experiences structured in the role of schoolboy, he begins explicitly to include as an element of his self-image the capacity to move with some degree of ease and assurance in either the Eskimo world of the hunter or the white man's world of the schoolbook, of arithmetic and spelling. At one point, for example, when he is sitting in school doing his arithmetic, he imagines himself as the storekeeper. His assessment of himself and his poten-tial—his inventory of capacities in relation to experience—becomes further differentiated, modified, and to some extent integrated (for he is able to compromise some of the salient elements of the structural conflict between the two principal roles that are contending for his future).

Further, the role of schoolboy provides another spawning ground and outlet for autonomy needs. Indeed, a wide range of new possibilities is opened to him. He is strongly en-couraged to proceed on his own initiative, to demonstrate curiosity and exploration in the realm of books and learning, and to accept learning also as a challenge to be mastered through his own resources, inventiveness, and industry. He takes great pride, for example, in being given the responsibil-ity for not only his own instruction but that of his sister and cousins when the family returns to their camp for a period of several months during the school year (p. 342). The principal curbs placed on his independence come from the requirements for social order imposed in the classroom and the teaching process, but he seems to accept these willingly enough and without discernible rebellion. Indeed, he appears to have a healthy balance between dependency and independency so far as his relations with the teacher are concerned.

Thus, the role of schoolboy, conceived as a channeling of environmental pressures, gradually provides relatively few conflicts and threats and at the same time gives Nathan a firm platform to stand on in his further growth and development in areas of competence, mastery, self-esteem, and a positive self-image with respect to an increasingly important dimension of his environment.

## ROLE AND THE SELF: SON

Beginning when it does in the developmental process, socialization to the role of son has lifelong implications, for it carries much of the initial burden of giving socially acceptable structure to the impulse life of the child. One of the central issues involved as an outcome of this particular aspect of socialization, but of course not the only issue, is the child's coming to terms with the basic psychological hurdle of complying with other people's demands and directives and acting upon those directives as an aspect of self. The particular form of such confrontation varies among societies, but sufficient research has been done in regard to this issue of autonomy versus interdependence to underscore its being one of the nuclear problems in the human psychosocial career. Typically the earliest context in which it emerges as a problem for the young child is the family; and, because normally the child has little significant contact with persons beyond the family, the specific interpersonal relations and experiences he has in that setting, for example as a son to a father, may well provide episodes of critical learning, the setting of models for behavior, and the development of attitudes toward authority figures in general which color many subsequent kinds of interpersonal behavior.

For Eskimo children the problem of acquiring a healthy stance toward authoritarian demands, of developing a flexible formula for assertion of autonomy versus amenability as a mode of interpersonal adjustment, is initially perhaps more

410

difficult than in some societies, for infancy and childhood experience is characterized by an extreme leniency, permissiveness, and encouragement and tolerance of the child's expression of impulse (see Honigmann and Honigmann 1953, and Briggs 1970 for comparative statements from different Eskimo groups). A psychodynamic base is laid in which the child is made to feel highly secure in regard to his place in the world, to feel that other people exist principally to serve him and gratify his every demand, to feel that the world is constructed in such a way that he has but to indicate displeasure and he will be obeyed. Indeed, the young child's sense of omnipotence is indulged as much as possible; he is made to feel that he is "the greatest," is "Number One."

The techniques used to accomplish these ends are those of much succorant behavior not only by the infant's mother but also by all other adults (and older siblings, as illustrated in the life story) in the immediate vicinity; of breast feeding upon demand; of extremely lenient toilet training procedures, in which the child is largely allowed his own pace of self-restriction on bladder and bowel movements (and this applied even when the baby is being carried close to the mother's body); of extremely permissive and lenient social training and punishment procedures, in which the child is directed away from some behavior annoying to adults or dangerous to the child. Further, the pace of weaning is protracted and gradual; the child is never forcibly taken from the breast, nor is any traumatic device or irritating substance used to dissuade him from nursing. He simply loses interest as he grows older and becomes more concerned with other types of food, but when he wants it he is still able to have the fondling and other close bodily contact with his mother that had accompanied the nursing experience.

Training in sexual matters and attitudes toward the genitalia is similarly straightforward and not enshrouded with sentiments that might contribute to a negative or punitive self-image. Indeed, sometimes mothers will fondle a boy's penis to soothe him when he is crying or upset. And given the highly crowded, very public conditions of Eskimo houses, in which all bodily activities—including defecation, urination, and copulation—occur as processes natural to man's functions, the child has many opportunities to learn about matters relating to sexual functioning.

So the background is apparently laid in early experience for a bouyantly self-confident, highly self-assured, optimistic, and independent personality as the child enters early childhood. What happens then, when he begins to confront the frustrations of both the physical world and the social demands for the structuring of behavior which come from his parents? And, more particularly in the present case, what were the early experiences of Nathan like—how well did they conform to this generalized picture of Eskimo child rearing?

First of all, there are no substantive data concerning the specific ways by which Nathan was brought into the world of childhood, but it is most unlikely that his early experience was markedly different from the modal picture just sketched. Indeed, some twenty years after his childhood, children were still being inducted into the world in much the same fashion (see Hughes, 1960). The picture was that of great child-centeredness, of gradual tutelage in and enforcement of demands, with many efforts being made to reinforce the child's sense of power to control the human environment. Further indirect data for an inference of this nature about Nathan's early career can be seen in the quality of references to his early family life, his fondness for his brothers and sisters, his homesickness when separated from them, his affection for his mother, and combination of respect and love for his father.

So Nathan had the problem of transition which all other young Eskimo children had—of learning to live with a constraining authority as he emerged from infancy and grew into childhood, with frustration and denial of impulse after an early experience of almost complete indulgence, with a sustained and varied confrontation with the social manifestations of the reality principle. So far as evidence from the life history goes, Nathan seems to have come through that transition—the Oedipal transition in a psychoanalytic framework—with a healthy balance of sentiments toward his father, although competitive claims for his mother's attention obviously exist between him and his father. In the life story itself certainly there is no lack of solicitous concern by his mother for Nathan, and this is reciprocated well into childhood. In regard to another aspect of this particular period of transition in a person's life, Nathan gives occasional but trivial evidence of rebelling against the authority that Kakianak imposes, of rejecting him as a proper object on which to model his own behavior, but on the whole this is no syndrome of rebellion. On the contrary, there emerges from the life story the inference that Nathan's sentiments toward his father are predominantly those of admiration, respect, love, and protectiveness. After infancy and childhood a man and his son are culturally inhibited from free and open expression of emotion toward each other—of either a positive or negative nature—and Nathan acts shy or, in his words, "bashful" toward Kakianak. He reveals such "bashfulness" toward his father on several occasions, and the depth of his affection is gauged inferentially by his actions, his disguised comments, and his controlled but anxious demeanor as he awaits his father's return from a trip or some other activity. Telling instances of this feeling are cited in Chapters 4 and 15, when Nathan describes Kakianak's experiences in the Territorial Guard unit, or when Nathan and his mother mutedly express their fear for Kakianak's life as they anxiously look for his sled through the blowing snow when he returns to Gambell during the blizzard.

That Kakianak is an important object of emulation for Nathan, a person whom he wants to please and from whom he wants praise, is illustrated early and often. One example is Nathan's hope that Kakianak will return to Gambell from camp in time to see him perform in the Christmas school play (p. 64). There is also evidence that the superego function has begun to take hold—Nathan's uneasiness in disobeying his parents' directives, and his indecisive behavior until he does return home (p. 140). Further, cogent illustrations of the pivotal role which Kakianak plays in his life are the incidents in which Nathan has successfully managed to keep the boat motor running in the rough seas and turns to his father for recognition. Kakianak nods his approval and Nathan notes, "I felt kind of proud"—and competent. And in the same incident perhaps the depth of his positive sentiments toward his father and sense of reliance on him are summed up in his recollection of the crisis when the boat is in danger of being swamped by the high waves and Nathan is trying to keep the motor running (p. 353). Nathan says: "Was the rough sea and wind to be worried about? I had one security— that was Kakianak. Whenever worry forced its way into my head I would steal a glance at him and study his expression. He didn't look worried at all. Neither did he mind the seas or the wind; his look told me there was nothing to worry about."

In this span of ten years from Nathan's life, there are numerous clear instances of Nathan's progressive identification with his father and toward his incorporating as a central strand in his image of self, his ego-ideal, numerous action patterns and attitudes copied from his father. These deal not only with specific behavioral techniques but also with such diffuse and critical issues as gender identity. The hunting instances have already been cited; but other data from the role behavior of the son are also relevant. There are the several instances in which Kakianak is leaving the village to take a trip to the camp, for example, or is to be away from the family for some other reason, and he explicitly leaves Nathan in charge of the family's welfare. Sometimes this is against Nathan's wishes to accompany his father, and at those times, Kakianak reminds Nathan that he is the "man of the family now," and Nathan consoles himself with that thought. He also begins to acquire and practice habit patterns around the house with exemplify his taking the role of his father, as when he begins on his own to do the chores of getting water or ice, or feeding the dogs. His own statements are particularly apt in this connection. When, for example, Kakianak leaves the family behind at the refugee camp and returns to Gambell to serve in the ATG, he says to Nathan, "Be a man. Take care of Mom and the children." Nathan, in response to this injunction, notes to the reader, "That gave me something to think of and made me shake off my fear. For the first time he told me to be a man" (p. 86). So much does Nathan identify with his father in this instance that he wants to wear Kakianak's insignia and arm bands and march around with his rifle on his shoulder. In a later place Nathan notes, "While Dad was away I took over the work a family man had to do" (p. 222). And at one point Nathan tries to talk Kakianak into letting him accompany him on a fox trapping trip to the camp and again is told that he has now grown to an age of responsibility for caring for the family in Kakianak's absence (p. 236):

Finally I collected myself and blurted out some words: "The school is out until next month. I wish I could go with you to see my cousins."

His serious look on his face turned into tender kindness. He said, "I've been thinking about that myself. But then I came to think of your mother and family. They are very helpless without you. Remember, you are the man of the family when I'm away. Besides, our dogs are not very good. They can't take two of us that far. Just think of how much your mother needs you here. There will be a time when you'll have your own dogs and go any place you want to." I felt disappointed, all right, but the way he talked of me as a man of the family made me feel better.

During the severe sickness when Kakianak was away at camp and both Nathan and his mother attempted to keep the household together, Nathan, chagrined at his mother's working while he was lying in bed, scolds himself for not acting like "a man" (p. 299): "I am a man, and Mother is a woman, and she takes her sickness better than I do. Why let a woman take care of me, while I am supposed to care for her?" His behavior as an apprentice "man of the house" is further shown when Kakianak almost dies in the blizzard, and Nathan and his mother work together to get supplies and keep the younger children of the family safe. Nathan himself is torn between the feelings of childhood and those of nascent adulthood when his mother directs him to wait behind as the dog sled approaches the house through the blinding snow while she sees whether Kakianak is alive or frozen to death. Nathan feels it is his responsibility to help his mother and be brave in accepting whatever his father's fate might be, but he also is ready to break down with the grief of a child if his father has died on the return home.

Nathan often assumes responsibility for the care of his younger brothers and sister and clearly recognizes that he is responsible for what they do and therefore must give them direction and impose restraints. In an anticipatory manner, he often explicitly acts toward them as he infers his father would act, both in terms of laying down authoritarian restrictions and in giving love and support.

In other subsistence areas than hunting Nathan also has many opportunities to learn from and emulate his father; in fact, there is almost constant companionship between father and son, giving many occasions for inferential and observational learning. The father's main activities are not isolated and compartmentalized outside the child's perceptual awareness. The activities of family life and the round of life in general comprise a phenomenally meaningful whole, as, for example, fox trapping, when at an early age Nathan has his own traps (p. 28) and then helps his father in the cleaning and preparing of skins for sale. Ivory carving is another joint activity in which father and son often engage, an important subsistence pursuit, one that provides Nathan with the chance to learn a valued skill as well as to receive social praise and commendation, and one that gives Kakianak the occasion for instruction not only in certain skilled arts but also in more generalized modes of behavior which will be important later in life, such as care, thoroughness, and persistence in the job, and not being content with sloppiness or shortcuts.

Again, in this role, as in that of young hunter, much of the effect of instruction in proper ways of behavior is sought through demonstration by experience rather than by exhortation only; the attention of the child is turned outward to the phenomenon in question and to a reasoned inspection of it, rather than toward abstract verbal injunctions. At one point, for example, with reference to his questions about a forthcoming activity, Nathan comments on his father's reticence to answer the incessantly curious questions in the following way: "As he always did, he let me learn it by my own self" i.e., by engaging in the activity directly and in that way learning the consequences of one action as against another. There is, in fact, a widespread and strong emphasis in this role on developing a clear reality orientation in as many empirical contexts as possible and upon directing the child's attention outward to phenomena and to the effectiveness of his functional relationship with them, rather than leaving the matter phrased in absolute or moralistic standards. Thus in large measure any sense of the deficiency or failure is behaviorally and situationally based, defined by the relative efficacy of the child's relationship to forces in his environment, and is not an inherent quality residing in the child's personality, transcendent from circumstances or performances. Chiding comments are never made except with reference to some action or functional consequences for the child, and their import is couched in terms of their implications for the child's relationship to reality, to his adaptive and manipulative potential as a consequence of failure to obey or correct a fault. Some illustrations of this general point have been cited before but they may be drawn again to the reader's attention. Nathan, for example, is told not to overexert himself when working on lightering the ship—or else he will have sore muscles and get sick—which he does; he is told to go to bed and get sleep to prepare for the next day's hunt, or else he will be tired, fall asleep in the boat, and be teased by his companions, which he is; he is told that he might hurt himself on his homemade skis (but he is not expressly forbidden to use them), and he does.

A more general statement about principles and values in the socialization regime in this (and other) Eskimo groups would warrant being inferred from these data. One of the consistent themes seen in diverse contexts in Kakianak's approach to the shaping of Nathan for life in his society seems to be what might be called the principle of an emergent egalitarianism in interpersonal relations. By this is meant, first of all, a recognition of the inherent, although latent, equality of persons and the gradual unfolding and releasing of more and more areas of responsibility and reward as the child himself demonstrates competence in behavior. It is not that the child is accorded instant equality with the parents, for the parent is still the principal source of instruction, punishment, affection, and well-being. But, after the indulgence of infancy, the child is seen as a person who is to be brought along into full adult status and activity as quickly as capacities and opportunities allow, with the whole seen as a continuum of action and events.*

It may well be that in such a philosophy of the relations between parents and children there is more than a chance relationship with one of the central features of the religious belief system of the Eskimos. It will be recalled that the central, defining aspect of each person's being—the most important of the several souls or soul-aspects which he is accorded in traditional belief—is that of the name-soul. The name, possessing a spiritual life and status of its own, is immortal and only temporarily is it incarnated in the body of a given person. Thus the child, whose body serves as such a repository, is in the reality of Eskimo belief not an infant, unformed in capacities and by nature inherently irresponsible. On the contrary, the child's body merely serves for the time being as the vehicle by which the immortal soul (one of the members of the clan) expresses its existence at this given moment in time. In one dimension of belief, therefore, the training of the child is conceived to be a process of drawing out many of the abilities already possessed by the personality indwelling in the body, a sharpening and polishing of inherent capacities, and not simply the shaping anew of a being that possesses no talents, interests, or predilections.

Such a conception itself finds many behavioral expressions that are related to the notion of egalitarianism. One of the earliest may well be in refraining from physical punishment as a socialization technique; in fact, it is said that to strike one's child is to strike a dearly beloved relative, and the very thought is repugnant. Such a conception would also be congruent with the extreme permissiveness and leniency displayed throughout the child-rearing techniques; insofar as the soul of the departed relative has only recently taken

* See comparable data from a Canadian Eskimo group in the intimate account by Jean Briggs, *Never in Anger* (1970, pp. 109-12).

418

entrance into the body of the newborn infant, to deprive the infant or frustrate him in any of his desires is to express lack of hospitality and acceptance of the relative himself—a possible consequence of which is the departure of the soul back to the nether world and the physical death of the infant. In a society with high mortality rates a consequence of that nature is greatly feared.

But other expressions of this basic theme appear as the infant grows into the child and into the young adult. It is expressed throughout in the incorporation of the child as much as possible into the activities in which the father spends his time. Such incorporation can be seen in Nathan's story in several contexts. The instruction by demonstration theme discussed above in connection with the role of the hunter is one example. Kakianak assumes a rational function on the part of Nathan; he assumes that, by suggesting that Nathan look at the evidence, he will exercise the ratiocinative capabilities which he has and draw proper conclusions. Kakianak's frequent comment, "Look around you and see what is to be done," is perhaps a succinct expression of the strategy.

Second, in several areas of decision-making: allowing Nathan to go out hunting with other men, asking him where he wishes to spend the night on the visit to Savoonga, asking him how he wants to spend his money in the store and giving considerable leeway in that respect, involving him in the making of the boat, asking him with which captain he would like to hunt—in all these areas, and more, the child is the incipient adult who is conceived as proceeding through a series of stages that in large part actualize capacities which are already present and which merely want practice and occasion to be perfected. Closely allied with this theme is the notion of privacy and personal possession. Nathan has the right of disposition not only (of much at least) of his earnings but also of other articles such as toys; and at one point he refers to the other side of the picture—Kakianak's refusing to show Nathan the checks that he has received for work on the Weather Bureau establishment on the grounds that it was none of his business.

419

Throughout the life story there is the theme of a future orientation that is closely related to this view of the course of growing up: not only the training for the future occupational role of hunter, or a provider in other respects, but also more generally the training for the responsibilities of family-hood. Nathan, caught up in the enthusiasm of future possibilities, thinks longingly of the day when the family can return to their camp, and works with gusto on building the family's boat and saving money to purchase a motor and the other necessary equipment. And it is the vision of the future goal which holds many other such diverse activities together in a meaningful motivational framework: "I was proud to be of some help to my Dad, because he said I'd be the captain of the boat some day" (p. 273). And in another passage he notes his father saying, "Sometime in the future when you finish your school you and I will take the whole family down there and we will stay there all we want to" (p. 236). To which Nathan says to his reader, "Well, that was really something that he hadn't mentioned before. It gave me something to think of" (p. 237). Such a consistent theme in the early upbringing of a child (after the hiatus between infancy and childhood proper) is perhaps a good example of what Benedict meant in her article of some years ago, "Continuities and Discontinuities in Cultural Conditioning" (1953)— the relatively smooth flowing of one period of life into another, the progression from one step to another, with values and behavior patterns learned at one stage in life being basically congruent with and reinforcing of values and behavioral demands subsequently encountered.

Nathan's experiences as son in a family group thus appear to serve in many ways as a proving ground for learning values and relational patterns appropriate to life in the environing Eskimo social world as a whole, in that he confronts and has to contend with the foremost issue of social reality: accommodation of wide areas of his own behavior to the wishes and directives of others. The orientations toward social action he receives, especially those from his father, equip him with some of the requisite behavioral values that will make him more effective and competent in relating to others and winning social approval from them. For in his early family experience, he is given the chance to learn modes of social behavior in a context of warm and accepting human relations, which give the learning task added motivational impetus. It is here, in the family seen as a small society, that many aspects of interpersonal relationships later to be exemplified in other contexts first emerge, such as being helpful and cooperative, taking informed initiative and responsibility, being selfless and sharing with others, and, perhaps above all, somehow repressing much of the disruptive effect aroused by frustrations of his own desires and finding ways to discharge hostilities arising from competition with a powerful, disciplining male figure. In the present instance, indeed, it may be suggested that much of the interpersonal reserve and politeness emphasized as the proper mode of behavior between a father and an adult son may well have developed culturally as a preventive against any open expression of the hostility and aggression felt by a son for the father, the principal person who is given the task of conducting the boy out of the world of infantile and early childhood omnipotence into an acquaintance with the frustrating, demeaning, and punishing effects of reality.

One can put this point another way, bringing to bear the main implication of Parsons's sociologically oriented discussion of what happens during the Oedipal transition (1964). In his early family experience, Nathan has a chance to develop a conception of, and cathect as a positive object in its own right, the idea of a social system, of a network of personal relations toward which he feels strong bonds of loyalty and affection. Indeed, he frequently speaks of the family in just these terms. This is, then, the genesis of a commitment to group, the laying down of a set of sentiments and values centering on a complex image of social relationships and not just a person or physical object. Parsons cites this as one of the critical issues in the Oedipal period, the advancement to what he calls "higher order" types of cathexis as a necessary step in the development of the fully socialized person in any society. That it comes at the time of the Oedipal transition is understandable in view of the fact that it is at this time in his life that the child begins to broaden his social horizons beyond the strong and exclusive dyadic relationship with the mother that has prevailed up to this point. Now the father enters as a significant figure in his own right, providing the model for the boy child's identification with a personal life style; but also as the embodiment of the very principle of other persons' calls for the time, attention, and conforming behavior of the child.

In Nathan's specific case it was not, of course, a single father figure who served the role of disciplinarian and mentor. One of the chief influences in his life was his father's older brother, Akoak, and it was upon the latter that Nathan centered (and from whom he learned) many of the sentiments and expectations appropriate to Kakianak himself. The closeness of the bond that developed during the time Nathan lived with Akoak's family is best gauged by Nathan's grief when Akoak is taken to a mainland hospital and subsequently dies there. But, perhaps illustrating Parsons's point about a pattern of social relationships being an object of cathexis in its own right, Nathan is able to transfer or rather extend his feelings about participation in a family life back to the family into which he was born when he returns to living with them. Such transferability of feelings, going beyond ties to particular persons, may well be one of the important psychodynamic outcomes of an extended family network, where designated individuals in a kinship network can function interchangeably in relation to others in that network. Such, at least, is illustrated with these data from one of the putatively simpler societies of the world, where the specific nature of the kinship system provides a buttress against disruption of cultural continuity through the death of particular persons, in this case highly probable, at critical periods in the life cycle.

# Postlude

A human life has many sides. To him who lives it, it is a poignant chain of experiences, memories, and hopes unlike those of anyone else, unduplicable, a creation unto itself in the sweep of time and circumstance. An outsider can never, therefore, expect to "know" another human life as the person himself has known it—in all its richness, scope, and immediacy. At best, he can only vicariously (and selectively) apprehend its experiences and the web of purposes which over time comes to inform it.

But even that is difficult, for only rarely is entrance allowed into the private world of meaning and feeling which lies behind the protective walls of the social personality. Given man's ingenious capacities (conscious and unconscious) for defending himself from insult and invidious observation—including the effective device of simply not talking about himself—the laying bare of the essential structure and life forces of the self is rendered formidable from the outset. If, in addition, there is the hurdle of penetrating a cultural world different from one's own, a world in which almost every act, gesture, utterance, and conception may be shaped by contrasting assumptions about nature and man, then the goal of knowing another human being is further confounded.

If the subject of concern is one's contemporary, another difficulty presents itself, for the more insightful the analysis of past events and the more comprehensive the scope of investigation of the person's actions and potentials for action, the more time has elapsed since the data were gathered and the more likely it is that the person himself has grown and evolved further in the context of time and circumstance. Indeed, as Allport (1955), Murray (1953), Maslow (1954, 1962), Erickson (1959), and others have stressed, personalities are more pertinently to be characterized by an idiom of becoming and evolving than one of structure and trait.

So it is in the present case. Even though the emergence and early development of a central sense of self can be seen in the preceding pages, this person—this personality—did not cease becoming. He has, in fact, continued to evolve, modifying and being modified by the events and circumstances that have come his way. He has faced new and often traumatic experiences—an extended period of hospitalization for severe tuberculosis, and the subsequent deaths of his mother, two brothers, his cousin David, and one of the sisters who are mentionèd so frequently in the life story. He has had more schooling and has assimilated new areas of skill and knowledge. He has taken new values for the life career. Much that would have happened to any young Eskimo male of his generation from the island has happened to him—marriage, a family, a life on the island in which he creatively attempts to combine the most rewarding elements from both the Eskimo cultural world and that of the industrialized world across the water.

But that is another story, one perhaps remaining to be told. What I have attempted here is a presentation and brief analysis of the formative elements and settings that provided the basic structure and network of purposes lying behind the Nathan Kakianak of today.

# References Cited

Allport, Gordon W., 1955. *Becoming: Basic Considerations for a Psychology of Personality.* New Haven: Yale University Press.

Benedict, Ruth, 1953. "Continuities and Discontinuities in Cultural Conditioning." In *Personality in Nature, Society, and Culture,* edited by Clyde Kluckhohn and Henry A. Murray. Rev. ed. New York: Alfred A. Knopf.

Block, Jack, 1971. *Lives through Time.* Berkeley: Bancroft Books.

Bowlby, John, 1953. *Child Care and the Growth of Love.* Baltimore: Pelican Books.

Briggs, Jean L., 1970. *Never in Anger: Portrait of an Eskimo Family.* Cambridge: Harvard University Press.

Chassan, J. B., 1960. "Statistical Inference and the Single Case in Clinical Design." *Psychiatry,* Vol. 23, pp. 173-84.

————, 1962. "Probability Processes in Psychoanalytic Psychiatry." In *Theories of the Mind,* edited by Jordan M. Scher. New York: Free Press of Glencoe.

Erickson, Erik H., 1959. "Identity and the Life Cycle." In *Psychological Issues,* edited by George S. Klein. New York: International Universities Press, Inc.

Fenichel, Otto, 1945. *The Psychoanalytic Theory of Neurosis.* New York: W. W. Norton and Co., Inc.

Freud, Sigmund, 1949. *A General Introduction to Psychoanalysis.* Trans. by Joan Riviere. New York: Perma Giants.

Honigmann, Irma, and Honigmann, John J., 1953. "Child

Rearing Patterns among the Great Whale River Eskimos." In *Anthropological Papers of The University of Alaska,* Vol. 2, No. 1.

Hughes, Charles C., 1958. "An Eskimo Deviant from the 'Eskimo' Type of Social Organization," *American Anthropologist,* Vol. 60, No. 6, pp. 1140-47.

————, 1960. *An Eskimo Village in the Modern World.* Ithaca: Cornell University Press.

————, 1965. "The Life History in Cross-Cultural Psychiatric Research." In *Approaches to Cross-Cultural Psychiatry,* edited by Jane M. Murphy and A. H. Leighton. Ithaca: Cornell University Press.

————, 1968. "Structure, Field, and Process in Siberian Eskimo Political Behavior." In *Local Level Politics,* edited by Marc J. Swartz. Chicago: Aldine.

————, in press. "The St. Lawrence Island Eskimos." In *Handbook of North American Indians.* Washington: Smithsonian Institution.

Kluckhohn, Clyde, 1945. *The Use of Personal Documents in History, Anthropology, and Sociology,* by Louis Gottschalk, Clyde Kluckhohn, and Robert Angell. Bulletin 53, Social Science Research Council, New York.

Langness, L. L., 1965. *The Life History in Anthropological Science.* New York: Holt, Rinehart and Winston.

Lantis, Margaret, 1947. *Alaskan Eskimo Ceremonialism.* Monographs of the American Ethnological Society, Vol. 11.

————, 1953. "Nunivak Eskimo Personality as Revealed in the Mythology." In *Anthropological Papers of the University of Alaska,* Vol. 2, No. 1, pp. 109-74.

————, 1959. "Alaskan Eskimo Cultural Values." *Polar Notes,* No. 1, pp. 35-48.

Mandelbaum, David G., 1973. "The Study of Life History: Gandhi." *Current Anthropology,* Vol. 14, No. 3, pp. 177-206.

Maslow, Abraham H., 1962. *Toward a Psychology of Being.* Princeton: D. Van Nostrand Co.

————, 1954. *Motivation and Personality.* New York: Harper and Bros.

428

Muir, John, 1917. *The Cruise of the Corwin.* Boston: Houghton Mifflin.

Murray, Henry A., 1953. "Introduction to Volume I." In *Clinical Studies of Personality,* edited by Arthur Burton and Robert E. Harris. New York: Harper and Bros.

Parsons, Talcott, 1964. "Social Structure and the Development of Personality." Chapter 4 in his *Social Structure and Personality.* New York: Free Press of Glencoe.

Sapir, Edward, 1951. *Selected Writings of Edward Sapir in Language, Society and Personality,* edited by David G. Mandelbaum. Berkeley: University of California Press.

Spiro, Melford E., 1961. "Social Systems, Personality, and Functional Analysis." In *Studying Personality Cross-Culturally,* edited by Bert Kaplan. Evanston, Ill.: Row, Peterson and Co.

White, Robert W., 1952. *Lives in Progress: A Study of the Natural Growth of Personality.* New York: Dryden Press.

————, 1959. "Motivation Reconsidered: The Concept of Competence." *Psychological Review,* Vol. 66, No. 5, September, pp. 297-333.

————, 1960. "Competence and the Psychosexual Stages of Development." In *Nebraska Symposium on Motivation, 1960.* Lincoln: University of Nebraska Press.

————, 1963a. *Ego and Reality in Psychoanalytic Theory: A Proposal Regarding Independent Ego Energies. Psychological Issues,* Vol. 3, No. 3, Monograph 11. New York: International Universities Press, Inc.

————, 1963b. *The Study of Lives: Essays on Personality in Honor of Henry A. Murray.* New York: Atherton Press.

————, 1965. "The Experience of Efficacy in Schizophrenia." *Psychiatry,* Vol. 28, No. 3, August, pp. 199-211.

Wrong, Dennis N., 1961. "The Oversocialized Conception of Man in Modern Sociology." *American Sociological Review,* Vol. 26, pp. 183-93.

Yinger, J. Milton, 1965. *Toward a Field Theory of Behavior: Personality and Social Structure.* New York: McGraw Hill Co.